Where it's always the
Year of The Traveller

AIR CHINA
www.air-china.co.uk

THE
YANGZI RIVER
AND
THE THREE GORGES

This world tendency toward democracy is like the Yangzi River, which makes crooks and turns, sometimes to the north and sometimes to the south, but in the end flows eastward and nothing can stop it. Just so the life of mankind has flowed from theocracy to autocracy and from autocracy now on to democracy, and there is no way to stem the current.

Sun Yat-sen, *San Min Zu Yi: Three Principles of the People*

THE
YANGZI RIVER
AND
THE THREE GORGES

JUDY BONAVIA, RICHARD HAYMAN,
KEVIN BISHOP, PADDY BOOZ,
MAY HOLDSWORTH

PRINCIPAL PHOTOGRAPHER
WONG HOW MAN

Airphoto International Ltd., 903 Seaview Commercial Building,
21–24 Connaught Road West, Sheung Wan, Hong Kong
Tel: (852) 2856-3896; Fax: (852) 2565-8004; E-mail: sales@odysseypublications.com
www.odysseypublications.com

Distribution in the United States of America by
W.W. Norton & Company, Inc.,
500 Fifth Avenue, New York, NY 10110, USA
Tel. 800-233-4830; fax. 800-458-6515
www.wwnorton.com

Distribution in the United Kingdom and Europe by
Cordee Books and Maps,
3a De Montfort Street, Leicester, UK, LE1 7HD
Tel. 0116-254-3579; fax. 0116-247-1176
www.cordee.co.uk

Library of Congress Catalog Card Number has been requested.
ISBN: 962-217-733-6

Grateful acknowledgment is made to the following authors and publishers:
John Murray (Publishers) Ltd for Forgotten Kingdom by Peter Goullart © 1957 Peter Goullart; Alfred A Knopf, Inc and Brook Hersey for A Single Pebble by John Hersey © 1989, 1984, 1956 First Vintage Books; Houghton Mifflin Co, Aitken, Stone & Wylie Ltd and Michael Russell Ltd for Sailing Through China by Paul Theroux © 1984, 1983; Penguin UK and Random House Inc for Riding the Iron Rooster by Paul Theroux © 1988 Cape Cod Scriveners Company; Jonathan Cape Ltd for Birdless Summer by Han Suyin © 1968; Foreign Language Press, Beijing for Mao, Swimming in the Yangzi; In Lijiang: Rock's Kingdom © 1987 Bruce Chatwin; Macmillan Publishing Company for Riding the Dragon's Back by Richard Bangs & Christian Kallen © 1989

Maps: Mark Stroud, Moon Street Cartography
Photography credits: see page 568

Production by Twin Age Ltd, Hong Kong
Printed in Hong Kong

Cover: Tiger Leaping Gorge, Yunnan Province (see page 163 for full caption)
Backcover: Wu Dou Bridge, Wu Gorge (see page 253 for full caption)
Page 1: Tiger Leaping Gorge in northwestern Yunnan Province
Pages 2–3: The road to Deqen in northwestern Yunnan Province, where the Yangzi is known as the Jinsha Jiang—the River of Golden Sand
Page 4: For centuries boatmen would risk their lives to negotiate the rapids of the Three Gorges
Page 6: Misty light paints an ethereal picture of the Three Gorges, rendering the waters placid and benign, which belies their true nature
Opposite: Crossing the Dadu River, a tributary of the Yangzi in Sichuan Province

CONTENTS

SPECIAL TOPICS

LITERARY EXCERPTS

MAPS AND DIAGRAMS

Preface

I warmly recommend this fine and comprehensive guidebook to visitors who have an interest—whether for business or for pleasure—in the Yangzi River Basin. The Yangzi, some 6,380 kilometres in length, is Asia's longest river and forms a link between the more advanced eastern seaboard and the resource-rich areas of western China. It is China's principal inland waterway and one of the world's busiest rivers. From its source in the mountains of Tibet, the river flows through a dozen provinces and autonomous regions containing almost 50 per cent of China's population.

Historically, culturally, socially and politically—with a recorded history of more than 5,000 years—the Yangzi Basin is one of the most developed parts of China. It is the granary of China and about half of China's agricultural output is grown there, including 70 per cent of the rice crop. The Yangzi Delta region, with historic cities such as Suzhou, Hangzhou and Nanjing, has played a major role in China's history, economy and culture over the last 2,000 years. Indeed, during the Song dynasty, in the 13th century, Hangzhou's population of more than one million made it not only China's but also the world's largest city. While the huge metropolis of modern-day Shanghai is well on the way to re-establishing itself as one of Asia's—and the world's—most important international centres.

Today, the Yangzi region accounts for about one-half of China's GDP and 40 per cent of the country's urban population live in the region's 241 cities—75 of these cities have a population of between one and five million inhabitants! And a vigorous economic belt connecting towns and cities is emerging with four main nodes: Shanghai, Nanjing, Wuhan and Chongqing. Profound changes are also under way both in the infrastructure (some of it gigantic, such as the Three Gorges Dam project) as well as in the local bureaucracies and their administrative policies and practices. Production factor costs, including technology, are still at a very considerable discount to established areas on the east coast.

The Yangzi Council, registered in Shanghai, is a not-for-profit and non-government organization that draws on the experience of Hong Kong businessmen as well as the Shanghai government and enterprises to assist authorities in the Yangzi region to improve the climate and conditions for foreign investment and trade. Our extensive network of contacts is at the disposal of foreign investors who need to satisfy themselves that they are covering all the right bases as they explore business opportunities in the region.

The only way to appreciate fully the natural beauty and the business opportunities of this area is to visit it and I hope that this book will encourage you to do so!

Vincent H.S. Lo
President
The Shanghai-Hong Kong Council for Promotion and Development of Yangzi

Introduction

大江永流

The Great River Flows Forever

'The color of the moon is eternal, but the river flow has sound.' This classic Chinese expression on a pavilion at Leshan in Sichuan Province expresses the living and changing nature of the Yangzi River, China's greatest moving feature, ever flowing with life.

The Yangzi Valley is a vast terrain of many different regions from the Tibetan highlands to the dramatic Three Gorges, from broad and fecund middle reaches to the rich delta lands around the booming commercial city of Shanghai. The Yangzi is central to the history, present economy and future of China. It has been likened to a great golden dragon, a symbol for the Middle Kingdom, a source of life in its bounty and a bearer of miseries in times of flood and famine.

The river gods of old are still said to reside in its murky waters, even as modernization and industry hold center stage. Small craft fall victim to the rapids, their hapless boatmen becoming 'water ghosts'. The launching of each new ship still witnesses the traditional sacrifice of a chicken at the bow with popping firecrackers to propitiate the river spirits—just in case!

This is the river so great, its flow is the third largest in the world and its course is so long—6,380 kilometers. Until a few decades ago no one had traversed its full length to know where the great waters came from. To contemporary Chinese, it is usually called Chang Jiang—the Long River or Eternal River. It is also commonly referred to as Da Jiang—the Great River. Each section also has its own name, as if the river is too long to hold a single appellative. The name commonly used internationally is the Yangzi meaning 'Son of the Sea'. This is actually the old name for the tidal waters near the East China Sea, below the old city of Yangzhou, where the river delta begins and the ocean waters mingle with the brown earthy river. The old Wade-Giles transliteration system spelled the name Yang-tze K'iang, which endures even in a Monty Python song. An alternative phonetic used the spelling Yang-tse. In this edition we continue to use the current pinyin romanization, Yangzi.

The middle reaches of the river are locally called Xi Jiang, or the 'West River', referring to the Jiangxi Province region upstream and west of Nanjing. The Three Gorges section is sometimes called the Xia Jiang, or 'Gorges River'. In Sichuan

A view of the Jinsha Jiang (River of Golden Sand) near the town of Xiaruo in northwestern Yunnan Province

One of the last sailing sanpans on the Yangzi River, taken in the Wu Gorge in 1997

Province the river is called the Chuan Jiang, after the province's name meaning 'Four Streams'—tributaries that swell the main river to its major scale. Above the Sichuan Basin and beyond the head of navigation the river is called the Jin Sha Jiang, or 'River of Golden Sands', as it tumbles from the Tibetan Plateau in great rapids, scouring the mountains and carrying gold dust. Above this, on the broad 'roof of the world', the river is known as the Tongtian, or 'Way to Heaven'. At its source, where the river is little more than rivulets that wander the Tibetan tundra dripping from glaciers in the Tungla Mountains, it is known as the Tuotuo, which means 'murmuring' in Tibetan.

Like its many names, the Yangzi exists in many dimensions, its physical and human qualities looming in a daily presence and also extending into the past and future.

There is the river of nature, cutting through mountain ranges, with lakes and wetlands that are breeding grounds to large numbers of migratory birds, fish stocks that feed the nation and unique yet endangered species, especially the symbol of the river, the large Yangzi sturgeon. The waters that give life also take it, with ravaging floods and persistent diseases that have taken great tolls.

There is the river of people, with a great population receiving daily sustenance from its waters and industries. Many famous lives lived along the river banks have been instrumental to culture and fate of the nation. Today the Yangzi Valley is home to some 500 million people, a society in remarkable transformation from a subsistence rural economy into a region becoming a leader in industrial and global integration.

There is the river of literature, music and painting, as much of China's cultural heritage has been created in its cradle, with classical gardens and magnificent scenery inspiring many an artist and philosopher. The lower Yangzi is the home of much of China's more delicate and subtle creativity, a reflection of its warm and gentle lands and waters.

There is the river of contemplation, with the deep religious traditions of Daoism, Buddhism, Confucianism and the more recent fervor of the missionaries of Christianity and Islam. Ancient pagodas, temples and mountain retreats are contrasted with newly built churches and mosques. An ancient saying goes, ' The River flows East; the Way of the Buddha comes from the West.' The same may be said of the new religions that make for the variety of spiritual-seeking to be found along the Yangzi today.

There is the river of history, along whose banks early humans developed, nations arose, revolutions unfolded, myriad battles were fought and the political future of China was often determined. The term *guo jiang*, 'to cross the river', meant that when a force could assert itself on the other side of the Yangzi, this would lead to unification of the extended territory of China and to a period of stability and peace. The last time this occurred was in 1948 when the Red Army crossed the Yangzi near Nanjing to win the final battles of the civil war and establish the People's Republic.

There is the river of time, as slow motion geology and the persistence of its waters have created deep gorges, great lakes, washed over plains and provided the setting for the rise of a great civilization. The dramatic man-made changes in the river now underway are directing the future in ways that command the attention of the world community.

Then there is the river of one's personal experience. If you have never visited the Yangzi, it is a goal of travel and inner fulfillment. Whether you are in a major city on business, on a cruise through the Three Gorges, visiting friends or relatives in a quiet domestic setting, studying the rich culture or religious traditions of China, climbing a holy mountain amidst wondrous scenery, or an intrepid visitor to the Tibetan highlands, there is always more to see and do and learn than one life can contain.

My own journey began with my ancestors. Early and still unnamed mariner cousins perhaps visited as sailors aboard clippers ships or naval gunboats. My grandfather was a US military advisor to the Chinese Army throughout World War II, flying from India over the 'Hump' of the mountains of the upper Yangzi to be stationed in Chongqing. His tales and mementos of those difficult times inspired me to return on my own when China opened to the world. In 1980, I took a train from Hong Kong to Wuhan. I booked passage on one of the old 'East is Red' passenger river liners to the old and drab city of Chongqing, sharing the dormitory with cheerful peasants and soldiers. The Gorges were then in a natural state with small villages and towns, with the ship making a dramatic ascent of the rapids amidst mountain quietude, now lost in the roar of development.

I returned to the Yangzi working as lecturer and host aboard the State guest ship *Kun Lun*, charted by Lindblad Travel as the first vessel fitted for foreign visitors. Life was charming and full of first revelations in those years when China was largely closed to the outside world and not yet commercialized. Little did we think then that the opening and reform of China would lead to the current transformation of the nation and people's living standard and style.

On a quiet day in 1984, I once launched my folding kayak off the *Kun Lun* out onto the broad river near Zhenjiang. Just as I was relaxing contemplating the fresh breeze and lapping waves, a marine police boat came steaming up alongside and arrested me for unauthorized navigation. I was flying a United Nations flag as a token of peace, but nevertheless I was arrested, interrogated and released to the recognizance of the angry political commissar aboard the *Kun Lun*, who had been roused from his afternoon nap. I was lectured in angry Hubienese at length about how no foreign vessels were allowed on the Yangzi since the last British gunboats was chased off in 1949. The imperialism of history was still a fresh memory and how dare I offend China by going for a paddle? I confessed my ignorance and guilt and was confined to the ship thereafter.

Foreign vessels are still not allowed up the Yangzi past the ocean terminals near Shanghai, but now all people are welcome to visit. I have since sailed on many Chinese ships the length of the navigable river and hiked the Three Gorges and Tiger Leaping Gorge, and have traveled upland to near the source in Tibet. There is always more to see and discover, as if the Great River really does come from heaven.

A journey on the Yangzi is full of contrasts: ancient walled towns and grandiose broadcast towers; delicate bamboo and silk handicrafts and belching factories; backbreaking menial laborers and blaring limousines sharing a common traffic jam; market peddlers hawking and businessmen barking on cellular phones; ancient temples smoky with burnt offerings for the dead and flashing neon nightlife. Socialist feudalism is giving way to the Age of Karaoke Comm-Fucianism.

The river valley is home to some 500 million people and produces a bounty of foods, goods and services—from herbal medicine in Tibet to computer chips in Shanghai. This 'land of fish and rice' feeds the nation and exports myriad products, including its indigenous contributions of tea, silk and porcelain. The Yangzi Valley is the focus of major national investment like the giant Boshan steel complex near Shanghai, new highways and dam projects.

The river is also bearing the brunt of increasing pollution, ship traffic, agricultural run off and heavy silt from the extensive deforestation of eastern Tibet. Many native species are under threat from extinction—pandas, large river sturgeon, pink river dolphins, alligators and giant salamanders. An ever-growing stream of waste, debris and toxins makes some stretches of the river look like an open sewer. The government environmental regulations are often ignored as the population grows and prosperity overrides protection. A comprehensive biodiversity survey of the Three Gorges has never been made. Much of what has been lost to the construction of the Three Gorges Dam will never be known.

The first dam across the Yangzi, the Gezhouba at Yichang, and the immense new Three Gorges Dam, have forever changed this magnificent region and its ecology all the way to the sea. This new dam is an environmental sacrifice for the much needed benefits of electrical power, flood control and navigation. The improvement of navigation to Chongqing and the booming Sichuan Basin is a major boost to the economy of the region's 130 million residents. This dam project is fraught with serious engineering, social and financial challenges. It may never realize its benefits but may, instead, prove to be an unprecedented danger.

By the year 2006, the Three Gorges Reservoir will reach 600 kilometers long to the new embankments of the great city of Chongqing. The canyons of the Gorges will be inundated, with new housing built for approximately 1,500,000 residents. Among these are the indigenous Gorge inhabitants, the Tujia people, or 'People of the Earth', descendants of the Ba Kingdom, who have lost their ancestral lands and the tombs of their ancestors. Salvage archaeology has yielded a wealth of artifacts. Some are now on display in a new museum in the city of Wanxian with a major museum planned for Chongqing.

The construction of new roads, towns and agricultural terraces has been dramatic, making a new era in the region. Much of the natural beauty is impinged by massive new concrete wonders. Today, one can cruise this 'sea in the mountains' with a sense of loss. But one must credit the visible gains in the improvement of human conveniences and the living standards of the people.

Future generations will look back at the end of the 20th century when the 'Great Wall across the Yangzi' was built and remember the natural and cultural heritage of the river. They will, one hopes, judge this project as a monumental benefit to the people of China, and not as a disaster of the era of state planning. There are eight new dams planned for the upper Yangzi and two already under construction near the Great Bend.

Will the Great River, like Chinese civilization, long flowing and surviving many troubles, still sustain a wealth of life, and endure?

Capt. Richard P. Hayman, New York, 2004

Barbarian at the gate!
Captain Richard Hayman in the Pudong District of Shanghai

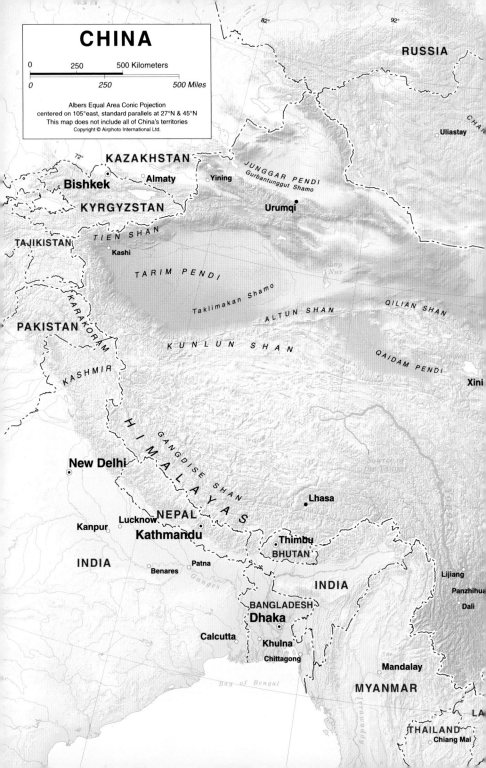

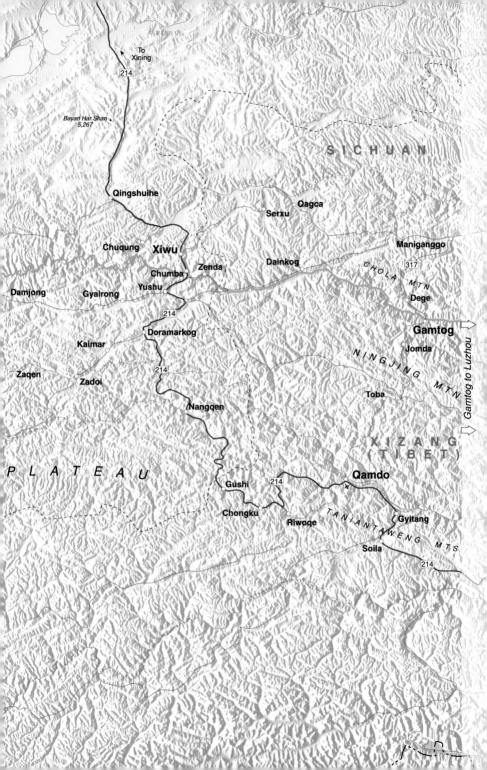

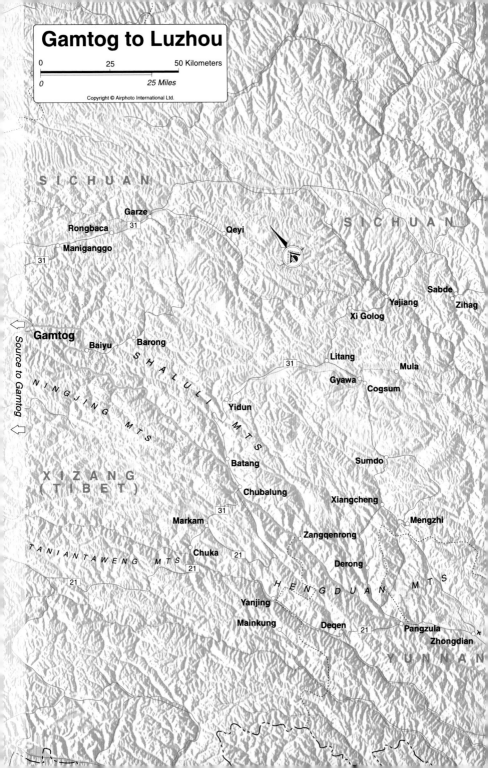

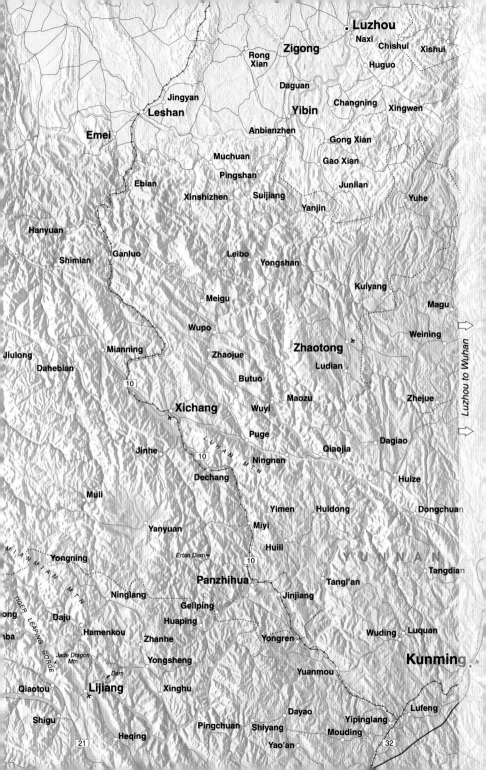

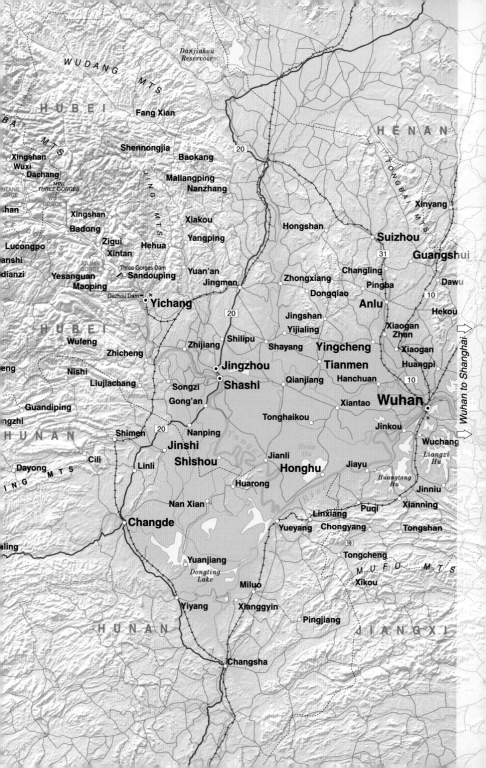

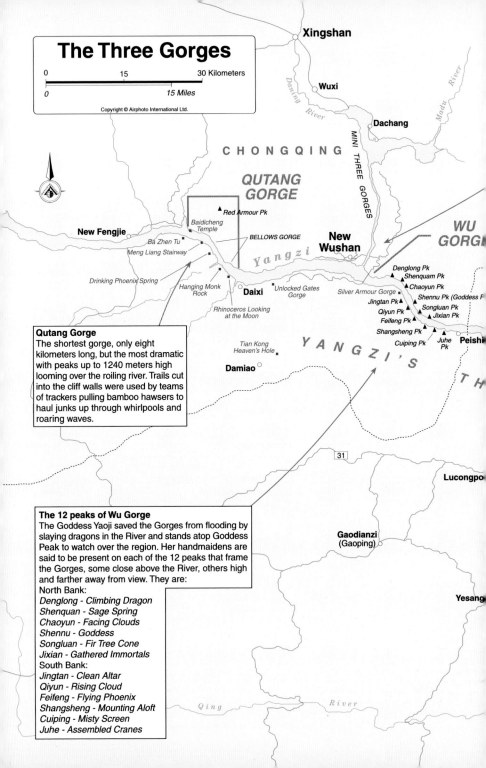

The Three Gorges

0   15   30 Kilometers

0   15 Miles

Copyright © Airphoto International Ltd.

Xingshan

Wuxi

Dachang

C H O N G Q I N G

QUTANG GORGE

MINI THREE GORGES

New Fengjie

▲ Red Armour Pk

Baidicheng Temple

BELLOWS GORGE

Ba Zhen Tu

Meng Liang Stairway

Yangzi

New Wushan

WU GORGE

Drinking Phoenix Spring

Hanging Monk Rock

Daixi

Unlocked Gates Gorge

Rhinoceros Looking at the Moon

Silver Armour Gorge

Denglong Pk ▲
▲ Shenquam Pk
▲ Chaoyun Pk
Jingtan Pk ▲   Shennu Pk (Goddess P
Qiyun Pk ▲   ▲ Songluan Pk
Feifeng Pk ▲   ▲ Jixian Pk
Shangsheng Pk ▲
Cuiping Pk ▲   Juhe Pk ▲   Peishi

Qutang Gorge
The shortest gorge, only eight kilometers long, but the most dramatic with peaks up to 1240 meters high looming over the roiling river. Trails cut into the cliff walls were used by teams of trackers pulling bamboo hawsers to haul junks up through whirlpools and roaring waves.

Tian Kong Heaven's Hole

Damiao ○

Y A N G Z I ' S

T H

31

Lucongpo

The 12 peaks of Wu Gorge
The Goddess Yaoji saved the Gorges from flooding by slaying dragons in the River and stands atop Goddess Peak to watch over the region. Her handmaidens are said to be present on each of the 12 peaks that frame the Gorges, some close above the River, others high and farther away from view. They are:
North Bank:
Denglong - Climbing Dragon
Shenquan - Sage Spring
Chaoyun - Facing Clouds
Shennu - Goddess
Songluan - Fir Tree Cone
Jixian - Gathered Immortals
South Bank:
Jingtan - Clean Altar
Qiyun - Rising Cloud
Feifeng - Flying Phoenix
Shangsheng - Mounting Aloft
Cuiping - Misty Screen
Juhe - Assembled Cranes

Gaodianzi (Gaoping) ○

Yesang

Qing   River

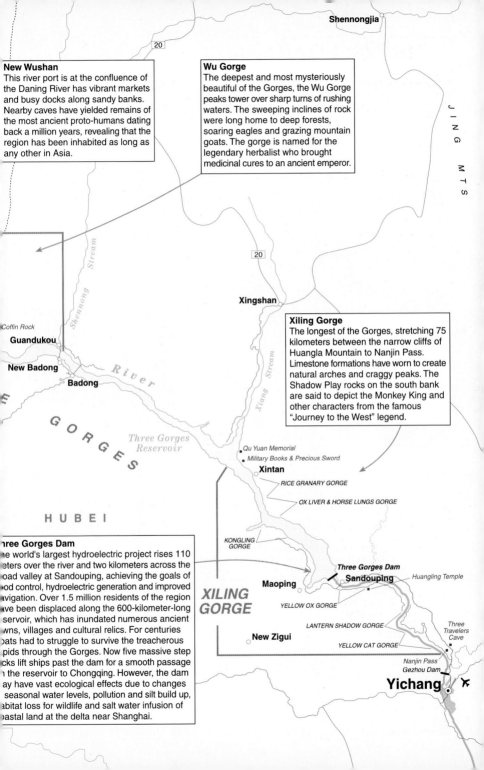

Shennongjia

20

New Wushan
This river port is at the confluence of
the Daning River has vibrant markets
and busy docks along sandy banks.
Nearby caves have yielded remains of
the most ancient proto-humans dating
back a million years, revealing that the
region has been inhabited as long as
any other in Asia.

Wu Gorge
The deepest and most mysteriously
beautiful of the Gorges, the Wu Gorge
peaks tower over sharp turns of rushing
waters. The sweeping inclines of rock
were long home to deep forests,
soaring eagles and grazing mountain
goats. The gorge is named for the
legendary herbalist who brought
medicinal cures to an ancient emperor.

J I N G M T S

20

Xingshan

Xiling Gorge
The longest of the Gorges, stretching 75
kilometers between the narrow cliffs of
Huangla Mountain to Nanjin Pass.
Limestone formations have worn to create
natural arches and craggy peaks. The
Shadow Play rocks on the south bank
are said to depict the Monkey King and
other characters from the famous
"Journey to the West" legend.

Shennong Stream

Coffin Rock
Guandukou

New Badong
Badong

River

G O R G E S

*Three Gorges
Reservoir*

Xiang Stream

· Qu Yuan Memorial
· Military Books & Precious Sword
Xintan

RICE GRANARY GORGE

OX LIVER & HORSE LUNGS GORGE

H U B E I

KONGLING
GORGE

hree Gorges Dam
he world's largest hydroelectric project rises 110
eters over the river and two kilometers across the
oad valley at Sandouping, achieving the goals of
od control, hydroelectric generation and improved
avigation. Over 1.5 million residents of the region
ave been displaced along the 600-kilometer-long
servoir, which has inundated numerous ancient
wns, villages and cultural relics. For centuries
ats had to struggle to survive the treacherous
pids through the Gorges. Now five massive step
cks lift ships past the dam for a smooth passage
the reservoir to Chongqing. However, the dam
ay have vast ecological effects due to changes
seasonal water levels, pollution and silt build up,
abitat loss for wildlife and salt water infusion of
oastal land at the delta near Shanghai.

*XILING
GORGE*

Maoping

Three Gorges Dam
Sandouping   Huangling Temple

YELLOW OX GORGE

LANTERN SHADOW GORGE

New Zigui   YELLOW CAT GORGE

*Three
Travelers
Cave*

Nanjin Pass
Gezhou Dam

Yichang ✈

The Physical Characteristics of The Yangzi River

The River from a Geologists' Perspective
by Raynor Shaw

FACTS AND FIGURES

The 6,380-kilometre-long Yangzi River drains an area of approximately 1.8 million square kilometres, or almost 20 per cent of the country, contains 36 per cent of the water resources of China, and supports about 30 per cent of the country's 1.2 billion population. There are approximately 100 million hectares of fertile agricultural land in the Yangzi Basin (about 60 per cent of the area), particularly in the Sichuan Basin and in the Middle and Lower Yangzi valleys, representing about 11 per cent of the total land area of China. About 40 per cent of the national economic and industrial output is concentrated in the Yangzi Basin.

In addition to being a main artery for inland navigation and an avenue for trade for 2,000 years the river has, until recently, divided the country into north and south, thus providing both a lifeline and a barrier to economic development. The first bridge across the Yangzi was built at Nanjing, and opened in 1968. Placed in the context of the Mississippi River (5,970 kilometres long), in 1989 there were only six bridges across the Yangzi (at Nanjing, Wuhan, Yidu (near Yichang), Chongqing, Yibin and Dukou) compared to 28 bridges across the Mississippi between Baton Rouge and Minnesota. However, by September 2003 there were 25 bridges across the Yangzi, either built or under construction, including four at Wuhan and six (of a total of 11 planned) at Chongqing.

The river is navigable for about half its length—the 3,060 kilometres from Yibin to Shanghai. Chongqing, 2,735 kilometres from the sea, is an important port that, prior to construction of the Three Gorges Dam, could receive vessels up to 3,000 tons only during the wet season (dry season water levels prohibited the passage of large vessels). When the dam is completed the water level at Chongqing will be raised by 45 metres, allowing year round navigation. Vessels of up to 3,000 tons currently ply to Yichang, and 10,000 ton tankers berth at Wuhan, 1,100 kilometres from the sea. These will proceed to Chongqing in the future, reducing transportation costs to the growing economy of southwest China.

Upper Yangzi River near Lijiang in Yunnan Province, just below Tiger Leaping Gorge. The only access to this valley is via the narrow path cut into the cliff face on the right.

THE FOUR GREAT STEPS OF CHINA

Continental China is highest in the west, near the Himalayas and the Tibetan Plateau, and lower in the east. Overall, four major topographical units are recognised: the Tibetan (Qinghai-Xizang) Plateau in the southwest; the central area of mountain ranges, plateaus, plains and basins; the continental margin of hills, coastal plains and islands; and the offshore shelf. Chinese geographers liken this topographical profile, down which the Yangzi flows, to Four Great Steps.

The Yangzi River originates in the Tanggula (Tanglha) Mountains on the first Great Step of the Tibetan Plateau, which has an average elevation of about 4,000 metres asl (above sea level). Several of the large rivers of the region, the Bramaputra, Salween, Mekong, Yangzi, and Yellow rivers have their sources on the Tibetan Plateau. The second Great Step is located between the eastern margin of the Tibetan Plateau to the northeast-southwest trending line of the Da Hinggan-Taihang-Wushan Mountains, a belt of ridges and valleys on the eastern margin of the Sichuan Basin. Average elevation of the ranges declines from about 1,000 metres asl in the west to 700 metres asl in the east, with individual peaks reaching over 2,000 metres asl. Eastwards to the coast is the third Step, a belt that comprises the largest plains in China, including the Middle and Lower Yangzi plains that are dotted with hills generally below 500 metres high. The fourth and final Step is the offshore continental shelf, which is generally less than 200 metres deep.

The key to the topography of China, and also to the climate and to the characteristics of the river system of the country, was the uplift of the massive Tibetan Plateau. With an area of about 2.5 million square kilometres and an average elevation of about 4,000 metres asl, this plateau created the monsoon system, which dominates the climate in China, a system that features significant changes in wind direction as well as seasonality of rainfall between summer and winter. In addition, the plateau creates a pronounced climatic continentality (isolation from the ameliorating influences of the ocean).

Prior to the rise of the Himalayan Mountain range and the Tibetan Plateau, the Chinese monsoon system did not exist. About 200 million years ago, the Tethys Sea covered the site of what is now China, with a connection to the present day Mediterranean Sea. Sediments steadily accumulated in the Tethys Sea until the northward migration of the Indian Plate began to buckle these sediments against the Asian Plate. Thus began the slow rise of the Himalayas and the Tibetan Plateau during the Himalayan Orogeny (mountain-building period between about 10 to 20 million years ago). By the Late Pliocene geological period (about 3.4 to 1.6 million years ago) the plateau had risen to about 1,000 metres asl, and a weak high pressure system had developed over the present site of Lhasa (at about 30 degrees north). At the end of the Tertiary Period (1.64 million years ago) the plateau was violently uplifted to about 3,000 metres asl, which resulted in the strengthening of the incipient high pressure system that was pushed north to the southern rim of the Tarim Basin at about 40 degrees north. During the Late Pleistocene to Early Holocene (0.8 to 0.01 million years ago) the area experienced a renewed more violent and massive final uplift to about 4,000 metres asl. At this stage the monsoon system was established in its current form, with the Siberian-Mongolian high pressure system located at about 55 degrees north, and the vast deserts of northwestern China fully developed.

THE COURSE OF THE YANGZI

The Yangzi River is remarkable in that, on the basis of the geological structure of China, it should not be a 'Long River' at all. Normally, rivers take the easiest course across a landmass. They flow downhill from their source to the sea, they carve their courses along bands of softer rock, they exploit weak and more easily erodible geological features such as faults or joints, and, importantly, they normally flow around any isolated mountains. However, throughout the world there are examples of rivers that, seemingly illogically, cut across geological structures or mountainous areas. If it were not for the intervention of several remarkable geological circumstances, the Yangzi River would not be following a course across China from west to east, but would flow out to sea via the Mekong or Red rivers, or be ponded in the Sichuan Basin. However, the river has overcome potential geological barriers in at least two localities to establish a propitious course across the width of China. The key to understanding the peculiarities exhibited by the course of the Yangzi River lies in interpreting the geological history of the region, and in tracing the development of the mountains and basins and their associated drainage patterns.

Initially flowing northeastwards from its source in the Tanggula Mountains, the Yangzi River swings around to follow an eastward course across the Tibetan Plateau, before gradually turning southwards to adopt a north-west to south-east alignment that follows the geological 'grain' of the folded rocks. These folds form a sweeping arc of subparallel mountain ranges, separated by deep, narrow gorges. This intractable terrain has formed a natural border between Myanmar (Burma) and China, an obstacle that has effectively prevented communication and mutual invasion between the two countries. Constrained within these steep-sided gorges, 600 to 1,200 metres deep, are the parallel courses of (from west to east) the Salween, the Mekong and the Yangzi rivers. These rivers are fast flowing and unnavigable, tightly confined between the heavily forested valley sides. In one area the courses of the three rivers are less than 100 kilometres apart.

About 1,600 kilometres from the source, or a quarter of the way into its 6,380-kilometre-long course, the first peculiarity of the Yangzi River occurs. At latitude 27 degrees north, near the small town of Shigu in northwestern Yunnan Province, the river undertakes the first of several extraordinary changes of direction. Viewed on a map, the logical continuation of the Yangzi beyond Shigu would be to the southeast through Vietnam, connecting it to the Mekong River. However, the river encounters Cloud Mountain (Yun Ling) and turns abruptly from a south-southeastward to a north-northeastwards course, at what is termed the First Bend of the Yangzi River.

The river then enters the impressive Tiger Leaping Gorge, a massive cleft through the Jade Dragon Snow Range, that is 3,000 metres deep and constrains the river to only 30 metres wide. After flowing north-northeast for about 120 kilometres, the river undertakes a second pronounced change of direction and turns abruptly southwards at the Second Bend of the Yangzi River, thus creating a great sweeping curve that is known as the Great Bend. The eastern limb of the Great Bend is directly aligned with the Red River that flows southwards via Hanoi and Haiphong to reach the sea in the Gulf of Tonkin. However, instead of continuing in this direction, the Yangzi makes a third major turn, this time to the east-northeast. Another sudden change of direction occurs where the Yangzi meets the Yalong River, turning southwards again, before finally swinging to the northeast.

The reasons for these pronounced changes of direction can be found in the geological history of the region. Approximately 225 million years ago India was part of a large continent known as Pangaea, located to the south of the Asian continent and separated from it by the Tethys Sea. Then, about 200 million years ago, Pangaea broke apart and India began a remarkable northward journey. By about 80 million years ago India was approximately 6,500 kilometres to the south, but moving northwards at almost nine metres a century. India finally collided with Asia between 50 and 40 million years ago, an event that slowed the progress of India to almost a half and generated immense earth pressures that caused the rocks in the collision zone to fold, to fault, and to be pushed up. This impact created ridges of fold mountains rising to ten kilometres high, and a grid pattern of faults separating blocks of terrain that were squeezed and rotated. Displacement along these broadly northeasterly and northwesterly aligned faults is a lateral, not a vertical, movement. Thus, terrain blocks on opposite sides of the fault shift horizontally in relation to each other, disrupting the course of the Yangzi River and producing the abrupt changes of direction described.

Careful inspection of a map will reveal that, in this section of the river, several large left (north) bank tributaries enter the Yangzi River, each following courses that broadly conform to the regional southeasterly flow direction. However, no large tributaries enter from the south. This phenomenon is interpreted to be the result of a process termed river capture whereby, following progressive disruption of the Yangzi's course by lateral displacement along the faults, the River successively abstracted the headwaters of first the Mekong River, then the Red River, then the

Yalong River. This process increased the discharge of the Yangzi River, increasing its erosive ability and consolidating its dominance. Major rivers on the right (south) bank are truncated remnants of once more continuous rivers, which continue to flow southwards, but with considerably reduced catchments.

After the Great Bend the Yangzi River follows a zigzag course, within a series of deep gorges that are alternately transverse to and parallel to the geological structure, until it reaches the Sichuan Basin at an elbow bend near the town of Xinshizen. The Sichuan Basin is an impressive feature that is surrounded on all sides by high mountains. Logically, the Yangzi River should have been expected to flow into the Sichuan Basin, create a large lake there and remain as a basin of internal drainage. However, this clearly was not the case. Remarkably, the river follows an eastward course, cutting a series of gorges through the upstanding barrier of the northeastward-trending Wushan Mountain Range (see satellite images on pages 52–5). The existence of the Three Gorges is the third peculiarity of the Yangzi River.

Geologists believe that the Wushan Mountains were formed by folding during the great earth movements of the Yanshanian Orogeny, which occurred between about 130 to 190 million years ago. The gorges have developed over the succeeding period. Three possible mechanisms have been advanced to explain the discordant course of the Yangzi River. The first mechanism is termed 'river capture', which postulates that two rivers initially developed on opposite sides of the mountain range, flowing in different directions. Over time, as they both cut down their valleys, the headwaters of the more powerful eastern stream eroded back across the summit and captured the headwaters of the weaker western river. Eventually the flow of the western river was totally reversed and became the headwaters of the new, larger, Yangzi River. The second mechanism is termed 'antecedence', which postulates that the river course was well-established on the landscape before the fold mountain range came into existence. Uplands can rise relatively rapidly and divert or disrupt an existing drainage system, or they may rise relatively slowly so that the rate of river vertical downcutting corresponds with the rate of vertical uplift of the mountains. Thus the river cut down through the gradually rising folds. The third mechanism is termed 'superimposition', which postulates that a river system is established on a sequence of horizontally bedded rocks that were deposited on, or covered, the older sequence of folded rocks. Over time, the river incised a channel down into the folded rocks below and regional erosion removed the surrounding cover rocks. Ultimately the river system was discordantly superimposed upon and therefore traversed the range of fold mountains. Although interpretations differ, there is general agreement with the conclusion reached in 1936 by the geographer G B Barbour that the Yangzi River is a superimposed river, having originally established a course on a higher surface.

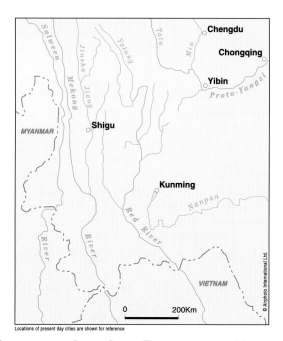

THE COURSE OF THE JINSHA JIANG, TRIBUTARY TO THE MEKONG RIVER, ABOUT 20 MILLION YEARS AGO

THE COURSE OF THE JINSHA JIANG, TRIBUTARY TO THE RED RIVER, ABOUT 7 MILLION YEARS AGO

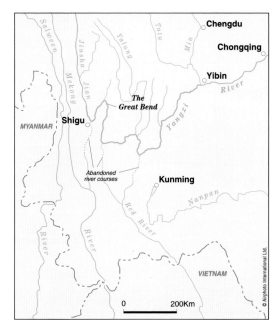

THE COURSE OF THE PRESENT DAY JINSHA JIANG (YANGZI RIVER)

NATURAL HAZARDS ALONG THE YANGZI RIVER

The Yangzi River is remarkable in many ways. Life giving, the river is an important source of water for drinking and irrigation, a national waterway, a transport lifeline, and an internal trade route. Life threatening, the river presented many dangers prior to the construction of the Three Gorges Dam. These included the challenges of navigation through the rapids of the awe inspiring Three Gorges, and the annual floods that caused extensive damage, both to crops and to property, and resulted in considerable loss of life. It is said that prior to 1800 about 33 per cent of all boats and 25 per cent of all goods passing through the Yangzi Gorges were destroyed. Outside the river channel is the danger of landslides from the steep valley sides, and lurking below the ground surface is the potential threat of damaging earthquakes.

RAPIDS

The major hazards to navigation through the gorges were the shoals and rapids that occurred along the pre-Three Gorges Dam channel. During the Nationalist period the river inspector for the Chinese Maritime Customs, one G R G Worcester, recorded 72 rapids in the 560 kilometres of channel between Yichang and Chongqing. The majority of these were in the first 240 kilometres above Yichang. In particular, the Xiling Gorge was noted for its dangerous rapids and shoals. Many of the obstacles were removed by dredging and blasting.

River Capture

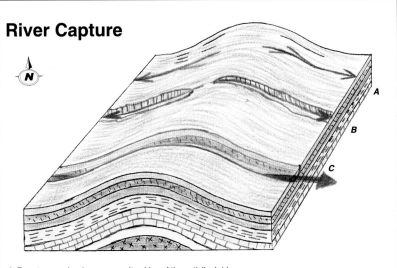

A: Two streams develop on opposite sides of the anticlinal ridge.
B: The eastern stream is more vigorous and cuts back into the ridge.
C: The eastern stream captures the headwaters of the opposing stream and reverses its flow.

© Airphoto International Ltd.

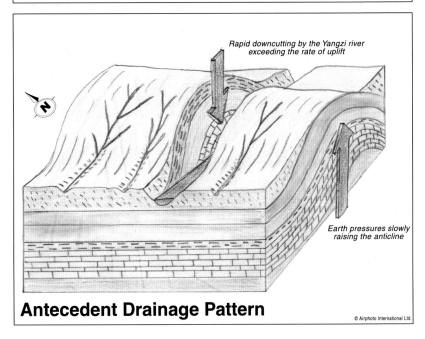

Rapid downcutting by the Yangzi river
exceeding the rate of uplift

Earth pressures slowly
raising the anticline

Antecedent Drainage Pattern

© Airphoto International Ltd.

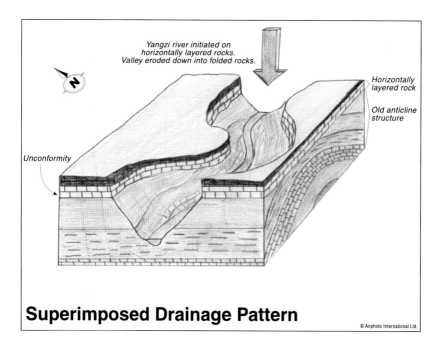

Superimposed Drainage Pattern

© Airphoto International Ltd.

FLOODS

The Yangzi River is located in the subtropical monsoon climatic zone of central China, which is characterized by a pronounced summer wet season, and a dry season from December to February. Consequently, the maximum flow in the river occurs in summer, earlier or later, depending on the strength of the monsoon pattern. On average, the river discharges 980,000 million cubic metres of water each year, which is about 17 times greater than the discharge of the Yellow River, and the fourth largest river discharge in the world. Almost 70 per cent of this total flows through the channel during the six months from May to October.

Water in the Yangzi River is mostly derived from tributaries entering in the upper (46 per cent) and middle (47 per cent) reaches. Ten of the 700 major tributaries to the Yangzi have flows greater than 1,000 cubic metres a second. In fact the flows of the Min Jiang, Jialing Jiang, Yuan Jiang, Xiang Jiang, Han Jiang, Gan Jiang, Ou Jiang and Nanxiang tributaries all surpass that of the Yellow River. Notably, the Min Jiang, with a drainage basin only 20 per cent that of the Yellow River, has an annual flow twice that of the Yellow River.

Throughout history, devastating annual summer floods have been a constant feature of the lower reaches of the Yangzi River. One of the major reasons for the

COMPARATIVE DIMENSIONS AND DISCHARGES OF SEVERAL MAJOR RIVERS

River	Outlet	Total length (kms)	Drainage area (sq kms)	Annual water discharge (million m³)	Annual sediment discharge (mill'n tons)
Nile	Mediterranean Sea	6,695	2,960,000	30,000	122
Amazon	Atlantic Ocean	6,437	6,150,000	6,300,000	400
Yangzi	East China Sea	6,380	1,807,200	979,350	490
Missouri-Mississippi	Gulf of Mexico	6,264	3,270,000	580,000	584
Ob	Gulf of Ob	5,411	2,500,000	385,000	16
Ganges-Bramaputra	Bay of Bengal	5,403	1,480,000	971,000	2,400
Yellow	Bohai Gulf	4,672	752,445	57,450	1,600
Zaire	Atlantic Ocean	4,667	3,820,000	1,250,000	71
Yenisei	Arctic Ocean	4,506	2,580,000	560,000	13
Heilong	Tartar Strait	4,416	1,850,000	325,000	52
Lena	Arctic Ocean	4,400	2,500,000	514,000	12
MacKenzie-Peace	Beaufort Sea	4,241	1,810,000	306,000	100
Mekong	South China Sea	4,200	795,125	501,485	187
Niger	Gulf of Guinea	4,180	1,210,000	192,000	40
Salween	Gulf of Martaban	3,200	280,000	47,310	33
Indus	Arabian Sea	3,180	968,655	121,430	480
Pearl	South China Sea	2,197	452,620	349,200	69
Irrawaddy	Bay of Bengal	2,150	429,940	441,560	330
Red River	Gulf of Haiphong	800	120,000	123,000	143

Note: The figures quoted vary markedly between different publications.

construction of the Three Gorges Dam was to prevent these floods. The flood season begins in March/April and lasts for about six to eight months. Early season floods usually occur in the Dongting Lake drainage system, with later flood waves from the main stream of the Yangzi west of Yichang, and later from the Han Jiang River. Typically, 20 per cent to 30 per cent of the flood waters originate from the Dongting Lake drainage system, about 60 per cent derives from the main river west of Yichang, and seven to nine per cent from the Han Jiang. In years when the high waters combined, the floods were prolonged and severe.

Pre-dam river levels fluctuated on average by about 20 metres, with rises up to 50 metres or more in the narrow gorges. For example, at Old Zigui (in the Xiling Gorge) the level varied seasonally by 21 metres, but during the flood of 1871 a rise of 84 metres was recorded. Winter water depths were about two metres at Wuhan, rising to 15 metres deep in the flood season. Rates of rise were also impressive. The maximum daily rate of rise was ten metres, recorded at Wanxian (at the entrance to the Qutang Gorge).

Alternatively, discharge volumes can be compared. The average flow of the Yangzi River is about 30,000 cubic metres per second, but at Yichang in 1954, during the worst flood for a century, a flow of 76,000 cubic metres per second (over twice the mean flow) was measured. Discharge at Wuhan was measured at 100,000 cubic metres per second during the 1931 flood, and 83,000 cubic metres per second during the 1954 flood.

Over 1,000 major floods have been recorded since 206 BC, with five serious floods this century in 1931, 1935, 1949, 1954, and 1998. The most devastating was in July 1931 when a series of seven cyclonic storms crossed the area in rapid succession, generating six flood surges that passed down the river destroying 23 dams and associated dykes, inundating 88,000 square kilometres of land, killing an estimated 140,000 people, leaving 40 million people homeless and devastating the economy. A water level of 16.3 metres was recorded at Wuhan, rising about two metres above the bund. Wuhan and Nanjing remained underwater for weeks. Water levels rose higher during the 1954 flood. In the 1998 flood, about 7,000 people died.

Faced with natural hazards of this magnitude, the construction of protective dykes began about 1,500 years ago. Because they broke so frequently however, the flimsy earth structures were disparagingly known as the 'Tofu (bean curd) Dykes'. Fortunately, flood control measures have improved over the years, with a concerted effort being made after 1949 to repair, strengthen and raise dilapidated dykes along the main river and major tributaries, to straighten several large river bends, and to dredge the more than 1,200 large and small natural lakes along the middle and lower reaches that can store, and thus regulate, flood waters. Works also include the large Jing Jiang and Han Jiang flood diversion projects, and the construction of over 500 medium and large reservoirs for irrigation and power generation, and about 40,000 small reservoirs, which have contributed to a 350 per cent increase in the area of irrigated agricultural land. Two large artificial flood control basins have been constructed at Sashi and near Xiantao on the Han River. The Sashi Basin, with an area of approximately 900 square kilometers and a capacity of about 7,000 million cubic metres, was constructed in 1954 by an army of 300,000 workers in a mere 75 days. The dry basin is cultivated in the winter months, but prepared for flood control in the summer.

Notable among the large natural lakes are Poyang, Dongting, Chao and Tai lakes. Poyang Lake can store 33 per cent of the flood water in Jiangxi Province, receiving water from the Gan Jiang, Xiu Shui, Fu He, Xin Jiang and Po Jiang. Similarly, Dongting Lake stores water from the Yangzi River during flood surges, and regulates discharges from the Xiang Jiang, Zi Shui, Yuan Jiang and Li Shui in Hunan Province. For example, it is estimated that at the peak of the major flood on the 30 July 1954, Dongting Lake reduced the flood waters of the Yangzi by 40 per cent.

However, siltation of the lakes is a constant problem. The annual average silt inflow to Dongting Lake is calculated to be 168 million cubic metres, of which 84 per cent derives from the Yangzi River. Silt outflow at Yueyang is only about 40 million cubic metres, thus the lake receives an annual input of about 128 million cubic metres, causing the lake bed to rise by about five millimetres a year, with a consequential reduction in flood water capacity. Thus, the lake requires constant dredging to remain effective.

LANDSLIDES AND ROCKFALLS

Landslides and rockfalls are ubiquitous geological processes in steep terrain, presenting serious hazards to infrastructure and human activities. They are common phenomena in the more mountainous sections of the Yangzi valley above Yichang. Historically, landslides have created many problems. For example, the Xintan landslide in Zigui County blocked the Yangzi River on two major occasions in 1030 and 1542, obstructing navigation for 21 and 82 years respectively. On 12 June 1985 the Xintan landslide reactivated, completely destroying the 1,000-year-old town of Xintan and resulting in large economic losses. A two-million-cubic-metre mass of sliding rock entered the river, creating a devastating 35-metre-high wave surge and temporarily blocking the navigation channel. The Jipazi landslide in Yungang County failed on 17 July 1982, blocking the navigation channel and costing 100 million yuan in channel dredging and landslide control works.

During the period 1985 to 1990, an engineering geological survey in the projected reservoir area of the Three Gorges Dam identified over 400 landslides and rockfalls. A total of 35 of these were classified as large scale. Of these, 24 are located west of Fengjie in the broad valley of the Sichuan Basin and 11 are located to the east of Fengjie in the broad valley sections of the Yangzi Gorges region, outside the Three Gorges proper. The majority (31 examples) are bedrock landslides, occurring in bedded (layered) sedimentary rocks. Of these, 30 are in sandstones and shales, and only one example is in carbonate rocks (limestone). Only four occur in superficial deposits (loose, weathered rock debris). None occur in the igneous (granite) or metamorphic (schists) rocks.

By way of illustration, the Gaojiazui landslide, near Guling Town, consists of a mass of rock 18 million cubic metres in volume above an inclined sliding plane. Other notable large landslides are located at Baota near Yunyang Town (100 million cubic metres), Baihuanping near Fengjie (129 million cubic metres), Liujiawuchang near Wushan (18 million cubic metres), and New Badong (15 million cubic metres).

Large scale rockfalls are concentrated in the steeper sections of the Three Gorges, originating from the vertical rock walls. Very few rockfalls occur in the broad valley areas. Most of the rockfalls are developed in carbonate rocks (limestone).

EARTHQUAKES

Geological and seismological (earthquake) research in the valley of the Three Gorges Project was carried out to assess the crustal stability of the region. The study concluded that the seismic potential in the region was of medium to strong magnitude, but that at the dam site it is weak. Earthquakes with a magnitude of greater than 4 were only recorded at a distance of 50 kilometres from the dam site, and earthquakes with a magnitude of greater than 6 were only recorded at a distance of 200 kilometres away.

The survey further concluded that the probability of Reservoir Induced Earthquakes (RIE), that is adjustments of the earth's crust in response to loading by the water in the reservoir, was low in the granite rocks surrounding the dam site. It was concluded, however, that there is a higher probability in the four reservoir sections underlain by weathered limestone rocks, namely Niuganmafei Gorge and the Jiuwanxi, between Nanmuyan and Peishi, between Daxiaodong and Daninghe, the outlet of the Wu Gorge, and the branches of the Longchuanhe and Wujiang.

An important component of the study was the establishment of a seismic monitoring network, set up specifically to record the pattern of seismic activity immediately prior to and post reservoir filling. Interestingly, between 1 June 2003 (when dam filling to 135 metres asl began) and the middle of September 2003, about 2,000 small earthquakes of magnitude two or less were detected by the monitoring network.

CHARACTERISTICS OF THE FOUR RIVER SECTIONS

Rivers develop distinctive concave long profiles (hydraulic profiles or thalwegs), characterized by steeper gradients in the upper reaches and flatter gradients in the lower reaches. Overall, the 6,380-kilometre-long Yangzi River falls from about 6,300 metres asl at its source in the Tanggula Mountains of the Tibetan Plateau to sea level (or zero metres) at Woosung (the Yangzi sea level or survey datum), near Shanghai. Thus, the average gradient of the channel is about one metre per kilometre over the entire course.

In the upper reaches between Tanggula and Chongqing (at 186 metres asl), the river falls a total of 6,114 metres in 3,645 kilometres, an average gradient of 1.7 metres per kilometre. Over the 1,190 kilometres from Chongqing to Yichang (at 40 metres asl) the river has an average gradient of about eight metres per kilometre, although over the 192 kilometre length of the Three Gorges section the average gradient is only 0.25 metres per kilometre. The lower plains, extending from Yichang to Shanghai, have an average gradient of about 0.03 metres per kilometre over the 1,545 kilometre distance.

Topographically, the course of the Yangzi River falls into four distinct sections, the torrential upper mountain reaches, the Sichuan Basin (including the Three Gorges), the middle basin, and the coastal delta region.

THE TORRENTIAL UPPER MOUNTAIN REACHES

Determining the source of the world's major rivers is a quest that has occupied great minds and intrepid explorers throughout history. The Yangzi River is no exception. Before the Ming dynasty (1268–1644) Chinese scholars believed that the source of the river was the Min Jiang in Sichuan Province. By the 16th century, Chinese geographers held that the Jinsha Jiang was the source river, but the upper reaches were never systematically explored.

During the 1970s Chinese geographers turned their attention to the Tanggula Mountain Range, which extends for more than 500 kilometres across the Tibetan Plateau. These mountains include 22 summits that exceed 6,000 metres in height and nurture over 100 glaciers. Isolated and largely uninhabited, the region is located at high altitude and experiences a severe climate, but has a pristine ecology little affected by human activity. Three major tributaries were considered to be possible sources, either the Qumar River in the north, the Tuotuo River in the southwest, or the Dam Qu in the southeast.

In 1976 a team of Chinese geographers explored the headwaters of the Tuotuo River and declared this stream to be the source of the Yangzi River. The Tuotuo River is fed by meltwater from the Jianggendiru Glacier on the southwestern slopes of Mount Geladandong (meaning Sharp Hill in Tibetan), which is 6,621 metres high and snow capped all year. The Jianggendiru Glacier has two branches, the north branch currently being 10.1 kilometres long and 1.3 kilometres wide, and the south branch 12.5 kilometres long and 1.6 kilometres wide. The two glaciers were once joined, but have now retreated into their separate valleys, receding a distance of 600 metres in the last 30 years. Milky-grey meltwater, coloured by a large load of glacial rock flour (finely ground rock fragments), issues from the snouts of the glaciers at 5,500 metres above sea level and flows northwards until, at 130 kilometres from its source, it is deflected eastwards by the Ulanula Mountains. The Dam Qu

(previous pages) At over 5,000 metres sheep graze near the tongue of one of the glaciers whose meltwaters feed the upper Tuotuo River in western Qinghai Province on the border with Tibet. For several years this river was considered to be the source of the Yangzi

joins the Tuotuo from the southeast at a point 60 kilometres below the Tuotuo River Bridge, the first bridge across the Yangzi River on the Qinghai-Tibet Highway, where the river is 250 metres wide.

In 1985 another expedition explored the Dam Qu (meaning river of the marshes in Tibetan) and, determining that it was 60 kilometres longer than the Tuotuo with a discharge five times larger, declared this to be the true source of the Yangzi River. The expedition traced the river to a spring that issues from a vast marshland near the foot of the eastern Tanggula Mountains, the highest marshland on earth at about 4,800 metres above sea level. Located about 20 metres below the crest of a saddle known as Jari Hill, the spring feeds a stream that is here called the Guangzhougou. Over the crest of the saddle the Jaqu stream rises, which flows southwards to join the Mekong (Lancang) River.

The combined Tuotuo and Dam Qu rivers form the Tongtian River (River to Heaven), a very broad, braided stream that flows in a 400-kilometre-wide valley between the Tanggula Massif and the Kunlun Mountains. About 100 kilometres downstream from the confluence, the Qumar River enters from the northeast. A further 300 kilometres downstream, the Tongtian River leaves the wide open valley at 4,000 metres above sea level and, turning to the south-southeast, enters narrow and deep gorges. Upon meeting the western edge of Sichuan Province, the Tongtian is renamed the Jinsha Jiang, which forms the border between Tibet and Sichuan Province for a distance of almost 700 kilometres. Reaching the lowlands at Xinshizhen near Yibin on the western edge of the Sichuan Basin, the Jinsha becomes the Chang Jiang, or Long River in Chinese.

From Qidukou to the Sichuan Basin the Jinsha is tightly constrained by the fold mountain ranges that sweep in a great arc around the northeastern corner of India, ridges pushed up during the Himalayan Mountain building period (about 10 to 20 million years ago). In this section the Great Bend occurs (see above), where the Yangzi escapes the topographical constraint and drastically changes course from southeast to northeast, flowing into China rather than out to sea through Vietnam.

THE SICHUAN BASIN (INCLUDING THE THREE GORGES)

The 260,000-square-kilometre Sichuan Basin, or Red Basin, is one of the largest basins in China, formed during the Indo-Sinian Orogeny at the end of the Cretaceous Period (about 65 million years ago). Fold mountains enclose the topographical depression on all sides. Defining the western boundary are the 3,000- to 4,000-metre-high Longmen, Qionglai, Daliang and Emei mountains, marginal mountains of the Tibetan Plateau. In the north are the Micang and Daba mountains, while the Wushan Mountains occur to the east, and the Yunnan-Guizhou Plateau rises to the south.

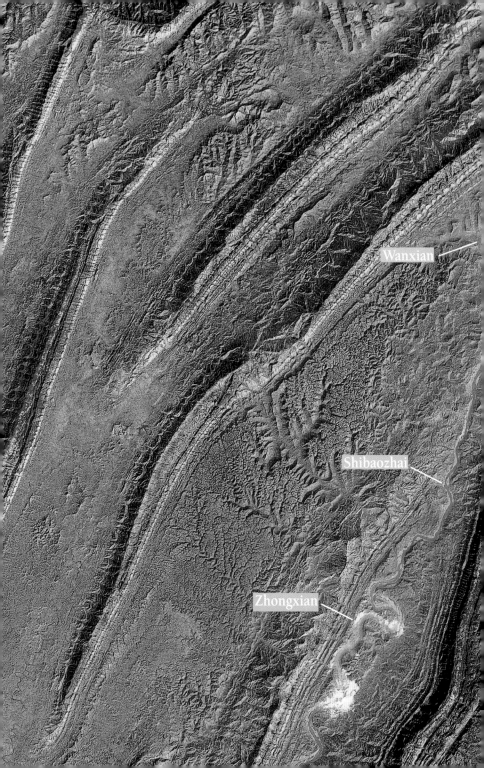

Yunyang

GEOPIC™ 1975 satellite image of the Yangzi River on the eastern margin of the Sichuan Basin. In this section, before entering the Three Gorges, the river flows concordantly with the geological structure, following a wide depression in softer, more easily eroded rocks between upstanding ridges. This false colour image emphasizes the rock materials, clearly revealing the layered and folded sedimentary rocks (limestones and sandstones), which dip to the northwest (top left of image). The more resistant rocks form a series of prominent, curved ridges. In the southeast the rocks have a more complex structure. This belt of rocks extends northeastwards beyond the image and, where it is traversed by the Yangzi, forms the Three Gorges (see satellite image on following pages).

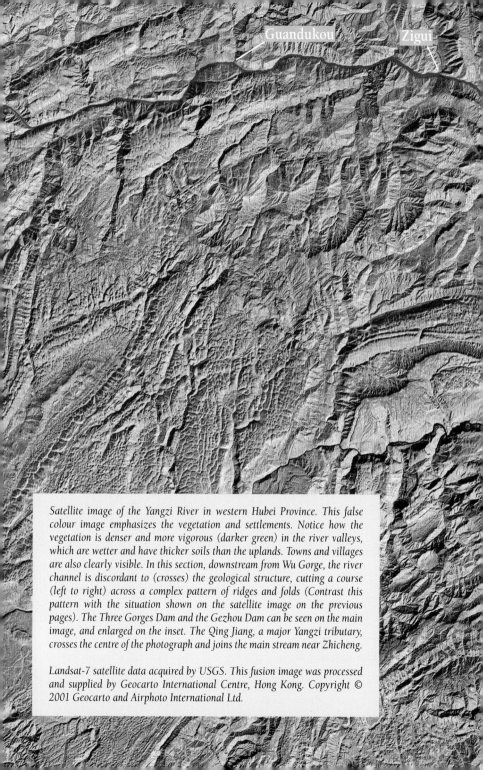

Guandukou

Zigui

Satellite image of the Yangzi River in western Hubei Province. This false colour image emphasizes the vegetation and settlements. Notice how the vegetation is denser and more vigorous (darker green) in the river valleys, which are wetter and have thicker soils than the uplands. Towns and villages are also clearly visible. In this section, downstream from Wu Gorge, the river channel is discordant to (crosses) the geological structure, cutting a course (left to right) across a complex pattern of ridges and folds (Contrast this pattern with the situation shown on the satellite image on the previous pages). The Three Gorges Dam and the Gezhou Dam can be seen on the main image, and enlarged on the inset. The Qing Jiang, a major Yangzi tributary, crosses the centre of the photograph and joins the main stream near Zhicheng.

Landsat-7 satellite data acquired by USGS. This fusion image was processed and supplied by Geocarto International Centre, Hong Kong. Copyright © 2001 Geocarto and Airphoto International Ltd.

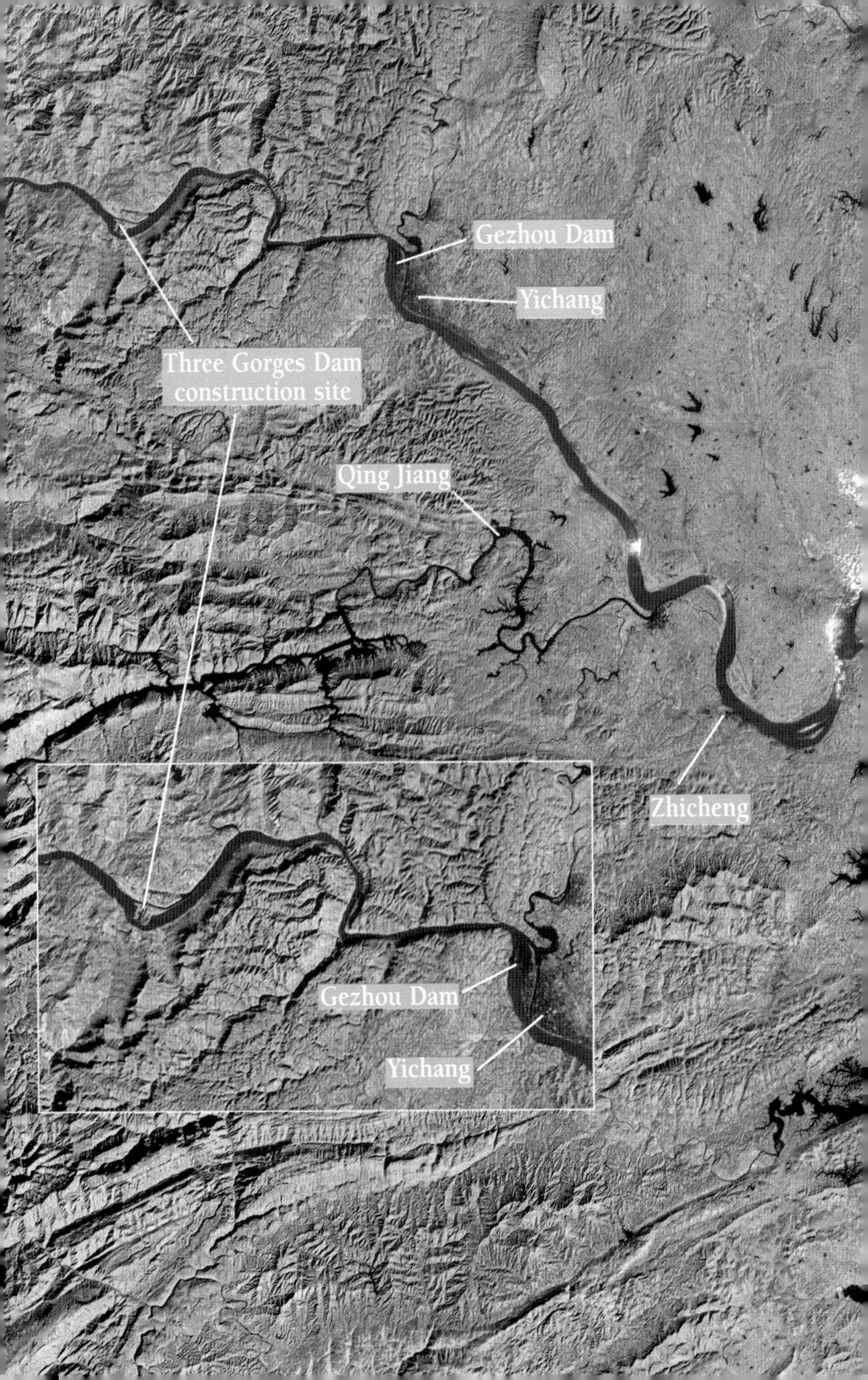

Three Gorges Dam
construction site

Gezhou Dam

Yichang

Qing Jiang

Zhicheng

Gezhou Dam

Yichang

Geologically, the basin is underlain by nearly horizontal, Jurassic and Cretaceous age (144 to 65 million years ago), red sandstones and purple shales laid down on folded limestones containing coal seams. From the Late Cretaceous (about 99 million years ago) to the Middle Pliocene (about 3.4 to 1.6 million years ago) the basin was an arm of the sea and saline water is still extracted from deep wells (see text on Zigong on page 244). Mineral resources of the region consist of coal (both anthracite and bituminous coal), salt, oil, natural gas and iron ore. Today, the Sichuan Basin is a fertile depression, with an average elevation of about 700 metres asl, supporting a population of about 100 million people.

The floor of the basin slopes gently from about 900 metres asl in the north to around 450 metres asl in the south. The Yangzi River flows against the high ground to the south of the basin, occupying a narrow valley that is only about 300 metres wide at Chongqing and extends from Yibin, the head of navigation, in the west to Baidicheng, Fengjie County in the east. Summer and winter water levels vary up to 21 metres in this section. More than 50 tributaries with a length of over 100 kilometres enter the Yangzi in the Sichuan Basin, increasing the discharge before the river enters the Three Gorges. Six of these rivers, the Jialing Jiang (at Chongqing), Min Jiang, Tuo Jiang, the Qu Jiang, Fu Jiang, and Wu Jiang, exceed 500 kilometres in length. These rivers, which are fast flowing and unnavigable except for small river craft, have cut deeply into the soft red sandstones to create deep valleys that have made travel across the basin difficult. However, valley erosion has exposed the harder limestones and the coal seams in many areas, which were mined locally along adits (inclined tunnels).

The famous Three Gorges of the Yangzi extend through the Wushan Mountains, between Chongqing Municipality and Hubei provinces, for a distance of 192 kilometres from Baidicheng in Fengjie County, Chongqing Municipality, to the Nanjin Pass at Yichang in Hubei Province (see satellite image on pages 54–5). In descending order downstream are the Qutang, Wu and Xiling gorges. Surrounded by towering mountains and enclosed by precipitous cliffs, each gorge has its own distinctive and characteristic scenery, features that are largely determined by variations in the geology. Most of the popular names given to sections of the gorges, or features within the gorges, are geological phenomena.

Careful observers will note that in many cases the bedded (layered) sedimentary rocks exposed along the river cliffs are steeply dipping, indicating folding or tilting from their originally horizontal attitude. Steeply inclined bedding is clearly visible, for example, in the Wu Gorge. The exposed rocks also vary in their colour, the thickness of the beds (or bands), and the spacing of joints within the beds. Joint patterns and block detachment also create other features, such as blind arches where closely jointed rocks have collapsed to expose an unjointed (massive) slab of rock framed on the sides and top by a rock canopy.

A 'ramp' or wedge-shaped slope commonly occurs at the foot of the cliffs, or at higher levels where a shelf or platform exists. This feature, which may or may not be vegetated, is termed a scree slope. Screes are accumulations of loose rock debris comprising blocks that have weathered from the vertical rock faces and fallen to the base of the cliff to form a distinctive, linear deposit. Where the cliffs plunge directly into the river, screes will be present below the waters. Their surface gradient varies depending upon the size of the rock fragments, which determines their characteristic equilibrium slope (or angle of rest). The size of the rock fragments depends upon the rock type and the joint pattern and joint spacing in the rocks. Well-developed scree slopes can be observed, for example, on the south bank of the river at Kuimen (at the entrance to the Qutang Gorge), and along much of the Qutang Gorge.

THE QUTANG GORGE

The shortest and most spectacular of the three gorges, Qutang Gorge extends for eight kilometres from Baidicheng in the west to Daxizhen in the east. Enclosed by peaks that rise to over 1,000 metres above the river, the gorge is noted for its precipitous walls and overhanging precipices. Consequently, sailing through the gorge is commonly likened to passing along an underground cave.

Qutang Gorge is eroded through the anticline (originally flat-lying rocks folded into an arch) of the Qiyue Mountains, forming vertical cliffs of Mesozoic (deposited between 248 to 65 million years ago) limestone and sandstones, associated with metamorphic (rocks altered by the heat and pressure of folding) gneisses and schists, and intruded by granite. Prior to the Three Gorges Dam, the gorge would channel flows of up to 60,000 cubic metres per second during the wet season. In this section, the river could rise by ten to 20 metres in one day, and 50 metre annual variations were recorded.

Qutang Gorge begins at Kuimen (*men* meaning gate), also known as the Kui Gorge or Qutang Pass, where the river is only 100 metres wide. Prior to 1954, when it was blasted away, a huge rock at the entrance to the gorge was responsible for wrecking innumerable boats over the years. Standing sentinel on the north bank is Red Armour Rock, a magnificent peak stained by ferric oxide (iron) weathered out of the rocks. In contrast, White Salt Mountain (Mount Baiyan) on the south bank results from dissolved calcium carbonate precipitating on the surface.

THE WU GORGE

Upon emerging from the Qutang Gorge and reaching the confluence with the Daning River, a north bank tributary, the Yangzi River enters the secluded beauty of the Wu Gorge (or Great Gorge). Extending from the mouth of the Daning River to Gundukou in the east, the 45-kilometre-long Wu Gorge is the longest of the Three Gorges.

Wu Gorge is eroded through the anticline (originally flat-lying rocks folded into an arch) of the northeast to southwest aligned Wushan Mountain range. Following a zig-zag course, the river approaches blind walls before turning abruptly to flow relentlessly onwards through deep and beautiful clefts between strangely-shaped peaks. The most spectacular are the famous Twelve Peaks of the Wushan Mountains, which include Goddess Peak (Shennu Feng) and the 2,400-metre-high Rising Cloud Peak. Two distinct sections of the gorge are distinguished. Golden Helmet and Silver Armour Gorge is named after the distinctive yellow-brown limestone peak that rises like a golden helmet, and the closely-bedded, folded, scaly, greyish white rock that looks like armour.

THE XILING GORGE

After flowing past the town of Zigui, located in the broad valley of Xiang Xi (Xiang Stream), a north bank tributary, the Yangzi enters the Xiling Gorge, which extends for 66 kilometres to the Nanjin Pass near Yichang. The Xiling Gorge comprises two distinct sections, west and east, separated by the 31-kilometre-wide Miaonan Valley.

Historically, the Xiling Gorge achieved notoriety for its feared torrential rapids and dangerous shoals that took a great toll in vessels and lives. Since 1949, over 100 of these obstructions to navigation were cleared by dredging and blasting, and numerous signal stations erected. Especially notorious were the Xintan, Xietan and Kongling shoals, along with the Qingtan and Yaochahe shoals. The Xintan Shoal consisted of rock debris from two big landslides that occurred during the Eastern Han (25–220 AD) and Eastern Jin (317–220) periods. The Kongling Shoal, near Miaohe, was a 200-metre-long rock that has since been removed.

Most of the Xiling Gorge is eroded through soluble limestone. Consequently, 174 limestone caves have been recorded between Nantuo and the Nanjin Pass. These caves occur in five distinct elevation groups, which correspond to different levels of the river, and the associated water table, as it cut down over time. Caves developed at between 40 to 55 metres asl, 80 to 90 metres asl, 120 to 140 metres asl, 240 metres asl, and 280 to 290 metres asl. The 80 to 90 metre level had only sparse cave development, but the caves at the 120 to 140 metre level are characterized by large entrances and rich sinter (precipitated calcium carbonate) deposits.

THE MIDDLE BASIN

The region between Yichang and the Yangzi Delta is also known as the East China (or Jiang Han) Plain, an area that is characterized by low-lying topography with scattered hills that rise abruptly from the surrounding plains. These plains are the remnants of former basins, underlain by limestones, micaceous sandstones, quartzites and conglomerates, which are being filled with sediments eroded from upstream, notably the red sandstones of the Sichuan Basin. Economic minerals include high-grade iron ores, coking coal, cement, and oil.

In this region the Yangzi is a placid, mature river with a gradient of only 0.03 metres per kilometre. During the winter, water depths at Wuhan are as little as two metres and the river traveller sees only high brown mud banks. Large areas of the Middle Basin were prone to devastating floods. During the summer the river could rise by 15 metres, transforming the landscape. Consequently, there are several thousand kilometers of dykes and culverts in the region. Much of the site of the city of Sashi is from one to three metres below river level. There are also more than 1,200 large and small lakes scattered over the plain, including Poyang, Dongting, Chao and Tai lakes, and intricate networks of tributaries. Colloquially termed 'the land of fish and rice', it is a fertile agricultural district that produces 70 per cent of the country's rice and is among the most densely populated areas of China, supporting 30 per cent of the country's population. Over 4,000 square kilometers of agricultural land have been reclaimed around the shallow margins of Dongting and Poyang lakes.

Topographically, the East China Plain can be subdivided into the Upper, Middle and Lower Yangzi plains. The Upper Plains extend from Yichang downstream to near the town of Huangshi, about 120 kilometres below Wuhan, where the Yangzi River cuts a channel only 800 metres wide between spurs of the Dabei Mountains to the north and Wanfu Mountains to the south. The largest tributaries enter the Yangzi in this section. From the north the Han River enters at Hankou ('mouth of the Han'), which along with the towns of Hanyang and Wuchang make up the metropolis of Wuhan. The Yuan Jiang and the Xiang Jiang enter from the south via Dongting Lake.

The Middle Plains extend from Huangshi downstream to near the river port of Anqing. Here the river is again constricted where it crosses the Dabai Mountians. This plain is drained by the Gan River, which feeds into Poyang Lake. The Lower Yangzi Plain ends downstream near Ma'anshan, midway between Wuhu and Nanjing. Below Ma'anshan the landscape assumes a more deltaic character, being generally flatter and wetter.

THE YANGZI RIVER DELTA

The Yangzi is tidal upstream as far as Ma'anshan. This point defines the start of the Yangzi Delta region. Where the Yangzi River reaches the sea some of the sediments it carries are deposited to form the Yangzi Delta, a flat, featureless plain dotted with hundreds of lakes, the largest being Tai Lake. Several thousand years ago, the mouth of the Yangzi River was further inland and further to the north but it has steadily migrated eastwards and southwards to its present position, depositing five

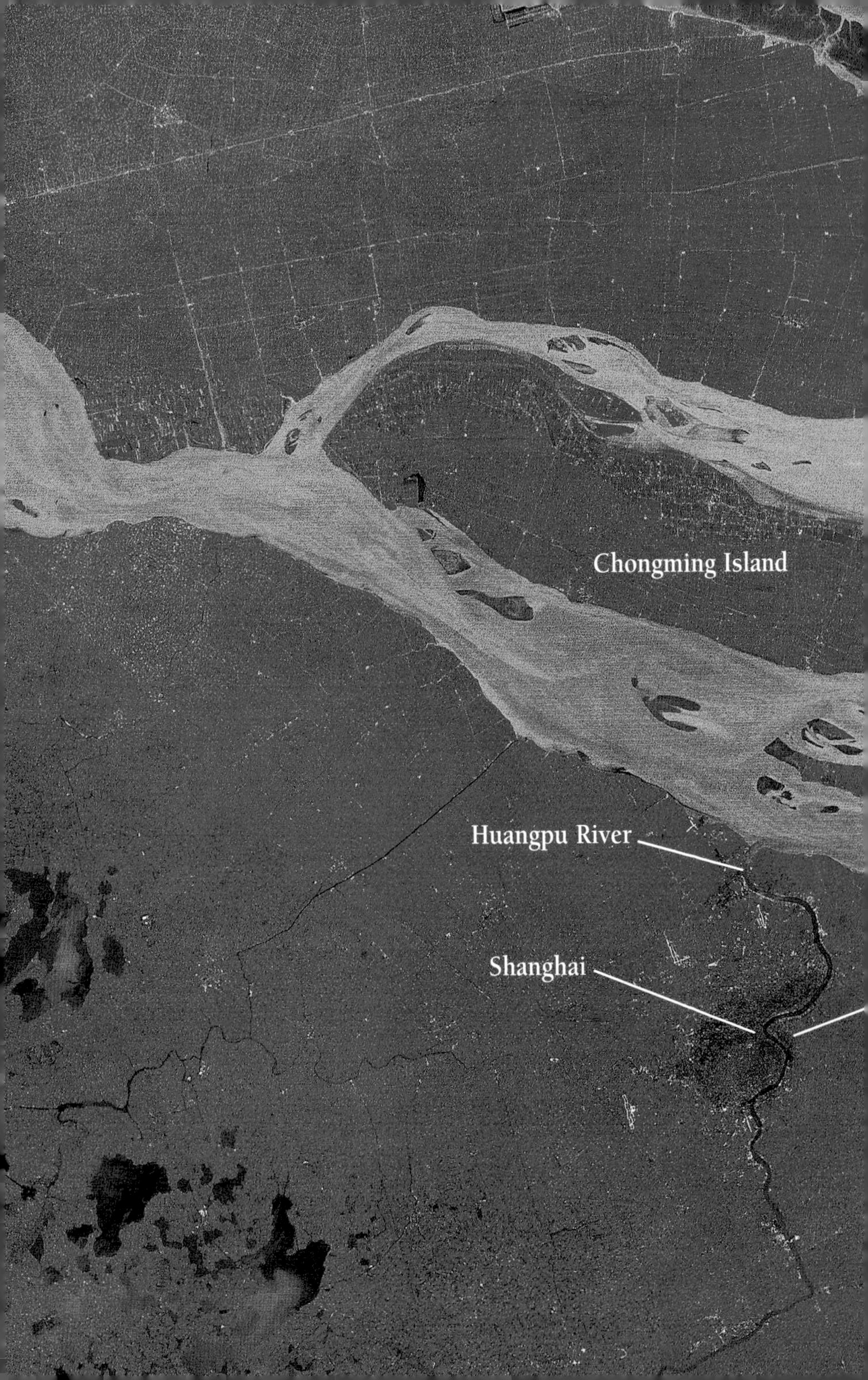

Chongming Island

Huangpu River

Shanghai

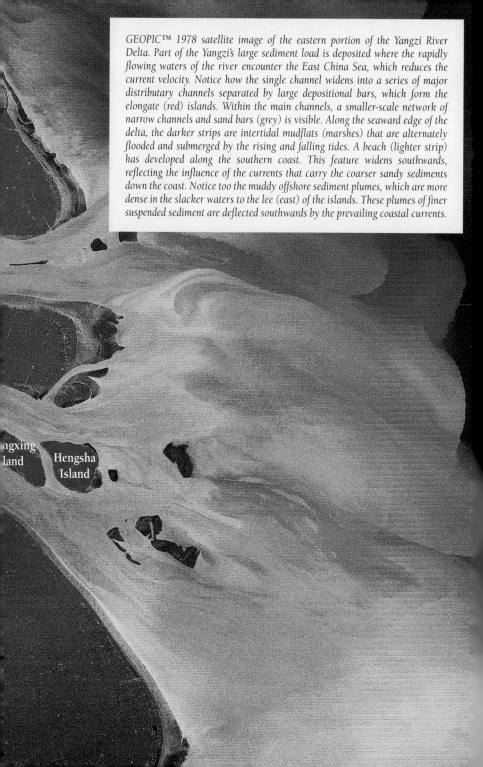

GEOPIC™ 1978 satellite image of the eastern portion of the Yangzi River Delta. Part of the Yangzi's large sediment load is deposited where the rapidly flowing waters of the river encounter the East China Sea, which reduces the current velocity. Notice how the single channel widens into a series of major distributary channels separated by large depositional bars, which form the elongate (red) islands. Within the main channels, a smaller-scale network of narrow channels and sand bars (grey) is visible. Along the seaward edge of the delta, the darker strips are intertidal mudflats (marshes) that are alternately flooded and submerged by the rising and falling tides. A beach (lighter strip) has developed along the southern coast. This feature widens southwards, reflecting the influence of the currents that carry the coarser sandy sediments down the coast. Notice too the muddy offshore sediment plumes, which are more dense in the slacker waters to the lee (east) of the islands. These plumes of finer suspended sediment are deflected southwards by the prevailing coastal currents.

ngxing
land

Hengsha
Island

large sand bodies during the past 7,000 years. These have merged into the northern river plain or form extensive offshore sand ridges. The present delta extends southwards to the edges of Hangzhou Bay, where it is demarcated by rolling uplands.

In the modern estuary the river separates into two distributary channels, one to the north and one to the south of the massive, elongate sand bank of Chongming Island (see satellite image on pages 60–1). About 1,000 years ago, Chongming Island consisted of two smaller sand islands, Dongsha and Xisha. Progressive erosion and shifting of the sand banks during the last 500 years has resulted in the build up of the present island with an area of 1,083 square kilometres. Today, two lesser islands, Changxing and Hengsha islands, occur to the southeast. Within the estuary channels, sand shoals and sand bars occur. The Yangzi River has a tidal range of 2.6 metres at the mouth.

Each year about 490 million tons of sediment pass through the river mouth, which is 3.5 times less than the sediment load of the Yellow River. These sediments are predominantly silt sized (0.002 to 0.06 millimetres diameter), but include a significant fraction of fine sand (0.06 to 0.2 millimetres diameter). However, because the Yangzi River has a greater water discharge than the Yellow River, a larger proportion of its sediment load reaches the sea. Consequently, the delta is steadily advancing seawards. The sediment plumes are generally deflected southwards by the coastal currents that flow along the inner continental shelf, which is about 500 kilometres wide in this area.

The world sea level fell during the last Ice Age, reaching a maximum depression of about minus 120 metres between 20,000 to 18,000 years ago, exposing the continental shelf for about 15,000 years. Research has shown that during the Holocene Period (the last 10,000 years) offshore deltaic sediments have accumulated in an elongate lobe that extends for about 80 kilometres to the southeast. The Holocene deposits range from less than ten metres to more than 60 metres thick, indicating an average rate of deposition of between one to six millimetres a year over the period. Measurements on the Shanghai tidal flat indicated a vertical accumulation rate of about 120 millimetres a year, and a progradation (forward or eastwards building) rate of about 60 metres a year.

However, in common with all river deltas, the plain is subsiding. This results from two processes: depression of the earth's crust resulting from the weight of the sediments and compaction of the loose sediments under their own weight. Average subsidence rates over the 10,000 years of the Holocene period are about 1.1 millimetres a year for the land sediments and 3.7 millimetres a year for the offshore sediments.

Shanghai has been built on a raised part of the river delta. Although the site is economically advantageous, being strategically located as an important river trade and maritime port, the site poses several potential problems. Hard bedrock to provide firm foundations for building is at considerable depth, being buried below hundreds of metres of soft sediments. The low-lying topography present a flooding hazard. Storm waves and typhoon incursions already cause frequent floods. Hence the Bund has recently been raised and strengthened. Ground subsidence, accelerated by ground water pumping and a consequent lowering of the water table, is increasing the dangers. In addition, with a tidal range of 1.9 metres at Shanghai, the city is particularly vulnerable to the effects of global warming and sea level rise. Measurements published in 1991 suggest that the eustatic (global) sea level rise in the East China Sea is about one millimetre a year. Ground water pumping, in addition to accelerating ground subsidence, increases the risk of salt water intrusion, that is the replacement of the fresh groundwater with saline water. Critics of the Three Gorges Dam contend that the reduced water flow in the area will further encourage salt water intrusion and will also markedly reduce the sediment supply to the delta, disturbing the current equilibrium between deposition and erosion, leading to major environmental changes.

Raynor Shaw studied geography and geology at London and Edinburgh universities, specializing in geomorphology. He lectured in geomorphology at McMaster University in Canada and has worked in West Africa and Venezuela prospecting for alluvial diamonds and gold. Since 1983 he has been living in Hong Kong, making geological maps and publishing reports about the geomorphology, weathering and Quaternary sediments.

Heights Above Sea Level—The Woosung Datum

Most national topographical surveys adopt Mean Sea Level (MSL) as the datum for levelling. All surveyed heights are referred to this datum. MSL is the mean height of the surface of the sea, at a convenient, stable location on the coast, calculated by means of hourly readings from tide gauges over a period of at least five years. Regional height datum points are then demarcated across the country as part of the primary geodetic (triangulation) network.

In China, the national height datum is the Yellow Sea Datum (or Yellow Sea Mean Sea Level), calculated at the tide gauge station in Qingdao City, Shandong Province. This datum was re-established in 1985.

The Yangzi sea level, or survey datum, is located at Woosung, near Shanghai. Between 1871 and 1900, Woosung Zero was located at a site that is now occupied by the Dong Hai Shipyard. However, in 1920 a permanent monument for Woosung Zero was set at She Shan, Songjiang County. Woosung Datum (or Woosung Zero) is 1.63 metres below Yellow Sea Datum (1985).

Note: All heights quoted in this guide are in metres above Mean Sea Level.

STAGE I

THE UPPER REACHES: THE SOURCE TO YIBIN

THE SOURCE

The melting glaciers and snowfields of the rugged Tanggula Mountains in Qinghai Province form the headwaters of the Yangzi. But exactly which of its two main tributaries, the Tuotuo He or the Dam Qu, is the true source still remains a point of conjecture.

In 1976, following a major scientific expedition organized by the Changjiang Valley Planning Office, it was announced that the Yangzi's source was that of the Tuotuo He (Murmuring River in Tibetan): the Jianggendiru Glacier on Mount Geladandong, at 6,621-metres, the highest peak of the Tanggula Mountain Range situated on the Tibetan (Qinghai-Xizang) Plateau. Further survey work was again carried out by a Chinese government research team in 1978, but no evidence to the contrary was presented.

However, after two years of exploring the Yangzi headwaters, Hong Kong born explorer How Man Wong successfully discovered a new source of the river in 1985. Further analysis of figures by the Chinese research teams had revealed some important data on the other major tributary. It appeared that the Dam Qu (Marsh River), although similar in length to the Tuotuo He, had almost five times the flow volume. It was this information that encouraged How Man Wong to mount the first expedition to locate the source of the Dam Qu, and possibly the source of the Great River itself.

Towards the end of his exploration, How Man Wong arrived at the town of Yushu (3,700 metres), capital of the Yushu Tibetan Autonomous Region in southern Qinghai Province. The Yangzi River, at this point called the Tongtian He (River to Heaven), runs several kilometres to the east of the town and already by this stage is

Near the source of the Yangzi River at over 3,000 metres, high on the Tibetan plateau

flat and wide and slow flowing. The expedition continued west to the small town of Zadoi on the upper Lancang River, which becomes the Mekong, another of Asia's great rivers. The source of the Dam Qu lay to the west, several days away by horseback in a marshland some 4,500 metres high. The rest of the story is told in How Man's own words from his book, *Exploring the Yangtze, China's Longest River*, published in 1989:

For four days we rode up mountains, through plush green valleys, in rain, hail and, at times, snow. The fast-approaching winter took what little air we had left out of us. Along the way, I spoke with many nomads who had roamed the area in search of pastures for their herds. Soon, a geography of the area became apparent, which contradicted what I had previously read about the source of the Dam Qu. Everyone spoke with certainty that the Dam Qu did not originate from Xiariabashan, but began in a high marshland only four days west of Zadoi. Xiariabashan was still farther west, about seven days away.

On the fourth day, we arrived at a high mountain marshland basin called Kaxigong. Around it were many undulating hills and the snowcapped peaks of the Tanggula Range rose in the distance to the south. We were told that the river meandering through the basin formed by these hills was one of the headwaters of the Dam Qu, and the source was near the top of a saddle-shaped hill to the northeast of the basin. We set up camp among other nomad tents. If indeed the nomads were right, we had made a very important discovery—a newer and longer source of the Yangtze. Our new discovery added approximately 60 kilometres to the length speculated by the Chinese team. This meant the Dam Qu was a much more important source than Tuotuohe.

I spoke at great length with some of the most experienced nomads of Kaxigong, trying to pinpoint exactly where we were on the map. The basin falls at 32.7°N, 94.6°E and at 4,500 metres, as far as we could ascertain. They pointed out that the actual source was approximately five kilometres further, at a watershed on a hill called Jari. To the other side of this saddle-shaped hill, all water drained toward the Jaqu, a tributary of the upper Lancang River system. The stream, which originated from an underground marshland spring 20 metres from the top of Jari Hill, was called Guangzhugou by the nomads. This, the Tibetans said, was the source of the Dam Qu.

With the help of the local nomads, I began drawing sketch maps of the region, trying to identify hills, rivers and valleys by their Tibetan names, to help future explorers relocate the site. We explored some of the tributaries to verify that the Guangzhugou was indeed the longest tributary. Another important source, Shaja, originating from a hill called Wolak ten kilometres to the southeast of Kaxigong, was also explored.

On September 3, with our Tibetan guide Bumai and Jeff, I followed the Dam Qu toward Jari Hill on horseback. The sky was greyish-black. It had been half hailing and half snowing since we left camp. As the altitude rose, the temperature dropped. We rode for 90 minutes through marshes; all the while, many thoughts flooded my mind. We were approaching the Yangtze water at its purest; the water was becoming more and more sacred with every step. I took great care not

(previous pages) Glacial peaks of the Tanggula Range form a backdrop to horses of the Tibetan Jiri nomads grazing at an altitude of over 4,500 metres, near the headwaters of the Tuotuo River

to disturb the water, as I felt a connection to the 300 million people living downriver, all of whom would be familiar with the famous proverb: 'When drinking water, think of the source.' I finally arrived at a hole oozing water from the ground.

I dismounted in front of the spring. Without saying a word, I fell to my knees. Using my two hands, I scooped up some water to my mouth. Jeff kept our video machine rolling. He wanted to record that moment of satisfaction on my face. There was one thing he could not have captured: the water was freezing; but it warmed my heart.

Explorer How Man Wong drinks from a spring called Guangzhugou by Tibetan nomads—the source of the Dam Qu tributary and the source of the Yangzi River

In January 1986, How Man Wong published a preliminary report on the discovery of the new source of the Yangzi, and later the same year the Chinese press also reported that the Dam Qu should be considered the official source of the River. The source of this greatest of China's rivers had long been a geographical conundrum. The area is largely in permafrost, moraine-covered and windswept; an inhospitable and discouraging environment for explorers. A treatise written in the Warring States period (480–221 BC) by geographer Yu Gong stated the source to be in the Mingshan Mountains of Sichuan Province. By the 16th century, explorers had named Jinsha River in Qinghai as the head stream. In the first half of the 18th century, an official Qing government expedition found its way to the Qinghai–Tibetan Plateau; their reports were an impetus for further explorations.

From the bitter cold and treeless alps of Upper Qinghai, around the source of the Yangzi, the snow that gradually melts in the summer sun trickles down the beds of ancient glaciers, and finally reaches the pastures where man and beast can survive. The snowmelt forms small streams which sing through the tilted plateaus and nourish the grassroots and the hardy little flowers and plants that the local Tibetan people use as medicine for a variety of ills.

The streams flow more swiftly down the lower Qinghai mountains, which give an impression of Central Europe. On successive steps of mountain and plateau, the people of the Yushu Tibetan Autonomous District cultivate barley and shelter the herds in winter, sending them up to the high pastures only in spring. Their diet consists of meat, milk (fresh and fermented), and barley-meal, which is the staple. Sometimes they add sugar brought from distant parts of China. And in the remaining forest belts they cut timber for the construction of new towns.

The ubiquitous yak is the most useful beast, but sheep are reared for meat and wool and there are some goats. The tough, shaggy little ponies of the mountains are used as a means of transport, and mares' milk is a treasured delicacy and cure-all.

Animal husbandry is the main occupation of these Tibetans and they continue to lead a semi-nomadic life, living in thick black yak-hair tents lined with bags of precious barley, and surrounded by their grazing flocks. For several days each spring the people gather together to sing, dance, hold horse races and tugs of war, before again returning to their lives of isolation.

TONGTIAN HE

Among the many rivulets in this region, the Tuotuo He winds its way towards the Qinghai–Tibet Highway and eastwards for a further 60 kilometres, where it is joined by the Dam Qu and later the Qumar. At this point it becomes the broad upper reaches of the Tongtian He (River). This plateau abounds in wildlife: Tibetan antelopes, Mongolian gazelles, snow leopards, otters, martens, lynxes and deer, as well as dozens of species of birds. Carp throng the cold waters of the lakes. Nature reserves are being established to protect the beautiful and threatened snow leopard and the primeval forests in which the wild ass and the snow cock still roam.

The 813-kilometre Tongtian He, descending sharply, flows through the Yushu Tibetan Autonomous Region of Qinghai, where the flat lands are cultivated for highland barley or *qingke*—the Tibetan staple diet—and hill slopes provide grazing for the yak, sheep and white-lipped deer owned by Tibetan herdsmen whose dwellings are black, yak-wool tents.

Small villages, decorated with Buddhist prayer flags, take the place of tent encampments. Despite their poverty, the women dress gaily in black and a rainbow of decorative colours, plaiting their hair, and wearing it in braids, sometimes interwoven with red cord. To commemorate special religious festivals, pilgrimages are made to monasteries (often many days' riding away) for they are social as well as religious occasions.

Jinsha Jiang

Below the Yushu region the river, navigable here only for short distances by skin coracle boats, becomes known as the Jinsha Jiang (River of Golden Sand) and flows southwards, forming the border between Tibet and Sichuan on a 2,308-kilometre journey sweeping down into Yunnan Province and looping back up into Sichuan. On this southward sweep the Yangzi runs parallel to the upper reaches of the Mekong and Salween Rivers (both of which also rise in the high plateau of Tibet) and the eastern branch of the Irrawaddy. At Shigu (Stone Drum) in Yunnan, the river curves sharply north, actually flowing parallel to itself, separated by only 24 kilometres. Here the river is wide in summer, but in winter, when the water level is low, the currents form sandbars that become the breeding grounds for many varieties of water birds. Further on the river again plunges south and east and eventually flows northwards towards Chongqing.

This southern region of the river was, for centuries, an area few Westerners ever penetrated. In the second half of the 19th century, the British and French sought to establish back-door trade routes from their colonial possessions in Burma, Laos and Vietnam, through Yunnan and up to the navigable stretches of the Yangzi in Sichuan. Secret missions were sent into southwest China, as the British were anxious to study the feasibility of a railway link between Burma and Chongqing. It was these intrepid travellers (such as Isabella Bird and others, some of whom never lived

(following pages) As the Jinsha Jiang (River of Golden Sand) the Yangzi first defines the border between Tibet and Sichuan, and then between Sichuan and Yunnan

An entrenched, tight meander bend of the Jinsha Jiang north of Benzilan. The Jinsha is characterised by a generally straight to sinuous course in this region, confined between parallel mountain ridges. This unusually tight bend probably reflects

the presence of a hard rock band, or fault, that has created the prominent spur and deflected the channel. Here the Jinsha forms the boundary between Yunnan Province (this bank) and Sichuan Province (opposite bank).

to tell their tale) who recorded their encounters with the many tribal minority peoples inhabiting this area.

Western missionaries were a second source of information on customs and attitudes. But the first Westerner to explore and photograph the area extensively was an American, Joseph F Rock, leader of the National Geographic Society's Yunnan Province Expedition. His amazing black and white photographs, taken in the 1920s and developed by himself under the most difficult conditions, are outstanding even today.

Among the sloping forests of pine and spruce are alpine meadows of moss, blue gentians and white edelweiss bordered by hemlock and flowering rhododendron bushes. In the narrow valley floors live tribes of the Tibeto-Burmese ethnic group— the Lisu, Naxi, Moso, Pumi, Lolo (also known as the Yi), Nu, Lahu, Xifan and Jing peoples. They have inhabited western Sichuan and northeast Yunnan since earliest times, cultivating barley, wheat, vegetables and indigo and keeping sheep or pigs. For the most part these people are Tibetan Buddhists, but some, like the Naxi, are animists whose priests, or *dongbas*, practice exorcism in the pre-Buddhist tradition of the Bon sect of Tibet; others are simply shamanistic. They are brave hunters and warriors, who fought among themselves and against the Han Chinese for centuries. Until 1949, Buddhist kingdoms, such as the tiny kingdom of Muli, were ruled by reincarnated monk kings.

The Black Yi of Daliang Shan were landowners of simple means who kept their fellow tribesmen, the White Yi, as slaves enforced by violence. For centuries the Black Yi would raid the lowlands and capture Han children to raise as slaves. The Yi—in their striking long thick black capes—were a constant headache to the Chinese administration, as they kidnapped officials and fomented rebellions. Their exploits were recorded as early as the first century BC by the great Chinese historian Sima Qian (c. 145–85 BC). Kublai Khan (1215–94), in an attempt to bring Burma under his sway, lost half his 500,000-man army to disease, exhaustion and tribal harassment in these mountains. Slavery and lawlessness was proscribed in 1956 when the Red Army moved into the area. The slaves were liberated and given their own lands. Some of the Black Yi resisted and were suppressed. To this day the Yi are known as energetic and occasionally violent people. Around their mountain homesteads they have practiced slash and burn agriculture, which combined with the ravages of the lumber industry have left vast tracts of Sichuan and Yunnan deforested, arid and eroded. The government has now initiated programs and assistance to encourage reforestation and settled agriculture of fruit-growing and goat herding.

The Yi are the largest of the minority peoples of the region numbering over 5.5 million and still growing. Their practice of *wa wa hun* or child marriage, combined with the requirement of all males to set up their own homesteads at marriage, has led to wide expansion of their territory into once virgin mountain forests.

Though the great Three Gorges of the Yangzi near Yichang are the most famous, there are even more spectacular gorges in the vicinity of Lijiang, where mountains rise more than 5,700 meters and canyons plunge 3,900 meters, through which the water flows deeply, turbulently and treacherously. Access in this region is still in many places only by mountain pathways and cliff-hugging tracks. Single-rope bridges slung high above the water's surface are not uncommon; the rider is conveyed in a sling attached to a pulley which must be well greased with yak butter to avoid any build-up of friction (see photograph on page 9).

The area is rich in mineral resources and timber. The 1,085-kilometre Chengdu–Kunming railway, which was constructed in the 1970s, has brought profound changes to this remote region. This railway was cut through steep valleys with many tunnels in a remarkable feat of engineering. It is one of the most spectacular train rides in the world.

A map of China published in 1748 clearly shows the Yangzi River (Yang tse Kiang)

Yunnan Province

Yunnan is the sixth largest of China's 28 provinces, similar in size to California or Sweden. It contains great variety, with towering, ice mountains adjoining Tibet and Burma in the northwest and lush jungles bordering Laos and Vietnam in the south. Half of all China's animal and plant species can be found somewhere in Yunnan, and its nearly 40 million people include members of 25 different ethnic groups—a third of its total population.

Geologically, Yunnan is an offshoot of Tibet, whose soaring tableland spreads eastwards, creating a plateau of red earth over a mile high (about 2,000 metres). Yunnan's southern latitude, astride the Tropic of Cancer, combined with its high altitude, gives it a gentle climate. Winters are mild and sunny; summers bring cool monsoon rains.

In western Yunnan mighty ranges fan south from Tibet's border, channelling some of Asia's greatest rivers through immense deep canyons. The Salween, the Mekong and the Yangzi race side by side far below the snowcapped peaks, barely 80 kilometres apart. Movements in the earth's unstable crust continue to thrust the mountains upwards and subject Yunnan to periodic earthquakes.

Fertile lake basins lie in geological faults on the plateau, where movement has caused the earth's crust to pull apart and form extensive down-dropped areas. These form the agricultural, political and cultural heart of the province. Kunming's Lake Dianchi and the surrounding plain is the largest such area. The red soil produces rice in abundance, along with year-round vegetable crops, and teas that are considered to be among the best in China.

Botanical gardens in Kunming display an amazing array of plant life. Many valuable herbs, staples of Chinese medicine, originate in the mountains. Botanists come to see the camellias and rhododendrons, the province's special pride, since all species of these splendid shrubs trace their ancestry to Yunnan. Wild animals and birds also exist in great variety, though population pressure and destruction of habitat threaten them. Sadly, many rare animals are being hunted to extinction for their fur or for those parts that are valued in medicine.

Yunnan has a very long history. Mankind first appeared at least a million—or perhaps as much as three million—years ago. For many years Peking Man, discovered in 1921, was the oldest known example of prehistoric man in China—until geologists began planning the Kunming-Chengdu railway in 1965 and saw Yunnan's fossils. An old cowherd from the village of Yuanmou, northwest of Kunming,

Xiao Putuo Dao Temple, Erhai Lake, Yunnan Province

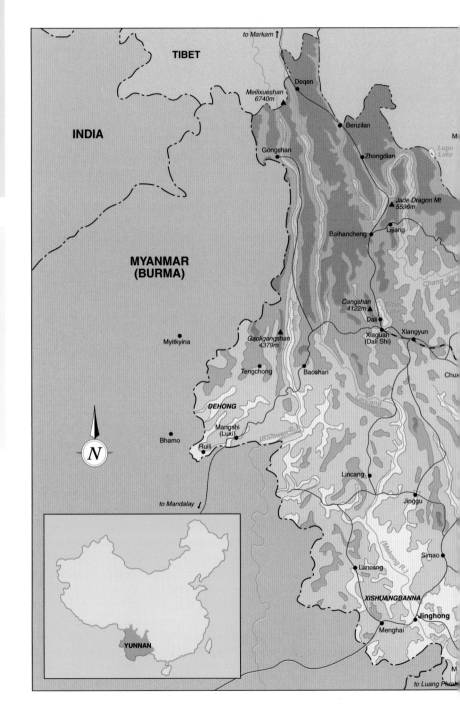

to Markam ↑

TIBET

Meilixueshan
6740m

Deqen

INDIA

Benzilan

Gongshan

Zhongdian

Lugu
Lake

**MYANMAR
(BURMA)**

Jade Dragon Mt
5596m

Baihancheng

Lijiang

Chang Jiang

Cangshan
4122m

Myitkyina

Dali

Gaoligongshan
4379m

Xiaguan
(Dali Shi)

Xiangyun

Tengchong

Baoshan

Chux

DEHONG

Mangshi
(Luxi)

Bhamo

Salween R.

Lincang

Ruili

to Mandalay ↓

Lincang

Jinggu

N

Lancang

Mekong R.

Simao

XISHUANGBANNA

Jinghong

Menghai

YUNNAN

to Luang Phrab

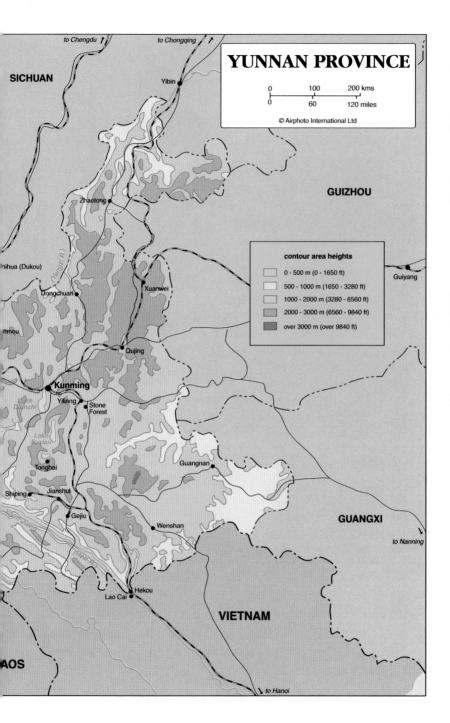

YUNNAN PROVINCE

0	100	200 kms
0	60	120 miles

© Airphoto International Ltd

SICHUAN

to Chengdu

to Chongqing

Yibin

GUIZHOU

Zhaotong

contour area heights

☐ 0 - 500 m (0 - 1650 ft)
☐ 500 - 1000 m (1650 - 3280 ft)
☐ 1000 - 2000 m (3280 - 6560 ft)
▨ 2000 - 3000 m (6560 - 9840 ft)
▮ over 3000 m (over 9840 ft)

Guiyang

hihua (Dukou)

Dongchuan

(Yangzi R.)

Xuanwei

nmou

Qujing

Kunming

Yiliang

Stone Forest

Lake Dianchi

Lake Fuxian

Tonghai

Guangnan

GUANGXI

Shiping

Jianshui

Gejiu

Wenshan

to Nanning

Hekou

Lao Cai

VIETNAM

AOS

to Hanoi

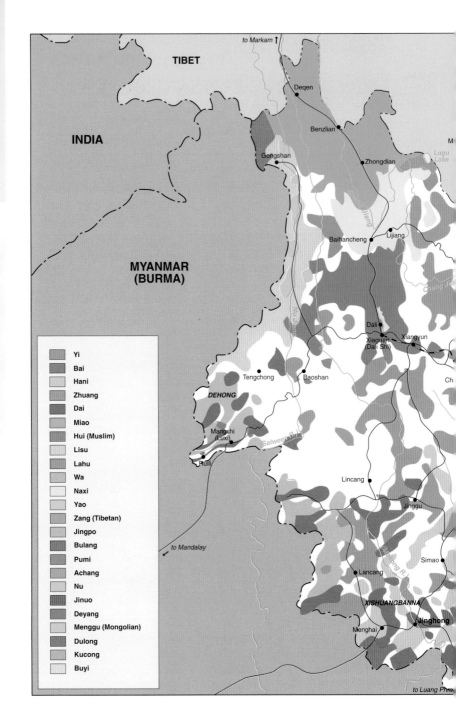

TIBET

to Markam ↑

Deqen

Benzlian

INDIA

Gongshan

Zhongdian

Lugu
Lake

M

Baihancheng

Lijiang

MYANMAR
(BURMA)

Chang Ji

Dali

Xiaguan
(Dali Shi)

Xiangyun

Ch

Tengchong

Baoshan

DEHONG

Mangshi
(Luxi)

Salween R.

Ruili

Lincang

Naxi

to Mandalay

Jinggu

Simao

Lancang

to Luang Phra

XISHUANGBANNA

Menghai

Jinghong

Yi
Bai
Hani
Zhuang
Dai
Miao
Hui (Muslim)
Lisu
Lahu
Wa
Naxi
Yao
Zang (Tibetan)
Jingpo
Bulang
Pumi
Achang
Nu
Jinuo
Deyang
Menggu (Mongolian)
Dulong
Kucong
Buyi

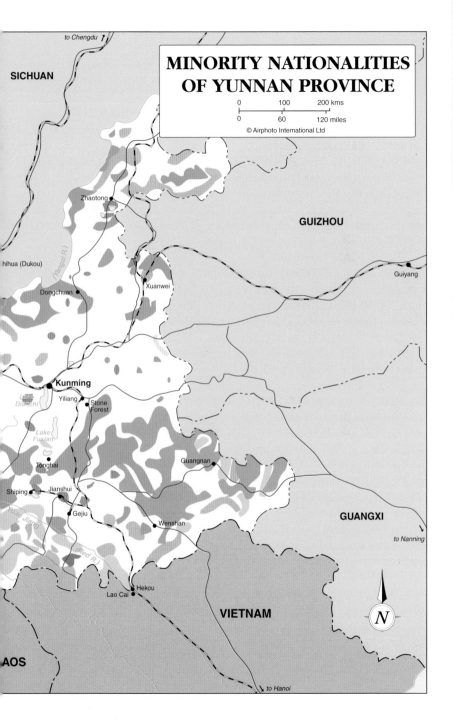

MINORITY NATIONALITIES
OF YUNNAN PROVINCE

0	100	200 kms
0	60	120 miles

© Airphoto International Ltd

SICHUAN

GUIZHOU

to Chengdu

Zhaotong

hihua (Dukou)

(Yangzi R.)

Guiyang

Dongchuan

Xuanwei

Kunming

Lake Dianchi

Yiliang

Stone Forest

Lake Fuxian

Tonghai

Guangnan

Shiping

Jianshui

Yuan Jiang

Gejiu

(Red R.)

Wenshan

GUANGXI

to Nanning

Hekou

Lao Cai

VIETNAM

LAOS

to Hanoi

N

mentioned that villagers had been grinding up 'dragon bones' as medicine for years. The surveyors, recognizing the common name for fossils, found a deep gully near Yuanmou whose cliff-like walls contained quantities of ancient mammal fossils. Among them, a young geologist discovered two human front teeth. The Forest of Earthen Hills (Zhima Lin) in Banguo, outside Yuanmou, is now famous for its abundance of animal and plant fossils.

Palaeontologists from China's Academy of Sciences named this ancient man *Homo erectus yuanmouensis*, or Yuanmou Man. The formation of the teeth convinced them that he was Peking Man's ancestor, China's oldest known humanoid. Later excavations in 1973 indicated that Yuanmou Man knew the use of fire, and shared a lakeside plain with primitive forms of elephant and an early ancestor of the horse, extinct species that helped to date him.

In 1988 further palaeontological evidence came to light when scientists from the Yunnan Provincial Museum unearthed the fossil skull of *Ramapithecus hudiensis* at Hudieliangzi, also near Yuanmou. This great discovery filled in the human fossil record of the Pliocene epoch and provided evidence that a complete process of evolution from early hominid to man has taken place in China. This find advanced significantly the story begun by the discovery of Yuanmou Man.

Vast expanses of time passed with no record to show how Yunnan became populated or how its people lived. For the first thousand years of China's recorded history, it was known only as a savage region inhabited by non-Chinese tribes, beyond the reach of Chinese civilization. In 1955 a sophisticated Bronze-Age culture was discovered when 48 untouched tombs, dating from 1200 BC, were found at the southern end of Lake Dianchi (see pages 92–3). These ancient people, living in a kingdom named Dian, described their daily life in great detail, using bronze figurines to depict miniature scenes on the lids of their huge treasury vessels. The people of Dian were slave-owners and head-hunters; they took part in an animal cult featuring bulls, reminiscent of their close contemporaries in King Minos's Crete; the Dian folk also practised advanced methods of agriculture and were fine artists as well.

The first recorded Chinese invasion was in 339 BC, when a prince of the Yangzi River valley sent his general over the mountains to conquer the 'southwest barbarians'. The campaign lasted ten years, during which his return route to China was cut by the prince's rivals. When the general found himself isolated, he set himself up as the King of Dian in a capital near present-day Kunming. For two centuries his descendants ruled the kingdom, completely cut off from China, and intermarried with the Dian people.

The great Han dynasty ruled China from 206 BC to AD 220 and struck up an important silk trade with Europe. Citizens of the Roman Empire quickly developed a taste for silk togas. One branch of the transcontinental trade, known as the

Southwest Silk Road, ran through Yunnan to India. The Han emperor, wishing to control the entire trade route, launched the second Chinese invasion of Yunnan. The King of Dian welcomed the invaders, hoping his new allies would help him to subdue neighbouring tribes. He thereupon received an imperial seal recognizing Dian as a tributary state. But the Chinese army could not get past Yunnan's formidable western mountains and eventually withdrew. Dian's tribal chiefs ruled in the name of the emperor and when the Han dynasty finally collapsed, Yunnan continued on its own course as before. In time, the Dian kingdom weakened and tribes from the south seized power. In the eighth century, six princes ruled the southwest. One of them is said to have travelled north to China, which was enjoying a golden age under the Tang dynasty (618–907). When asked where he came from, the prince replied that his home was south of Sichuan's rainy weather—at which the emperor dubbed the land Yunnan, meaning 'South of the Clouds'. (This tale is disputed by some historians, who claim that the Han emperor chose the name many centuries earlier.)

In 732, the most ambitious prince treacherously invited the other five to a banquet. When they were suitably drunk, he set fire to the wooden banquet hall, killing them all. The triumphant prince seized their lands and named himself Nanzhao, Prince of the South. For five centuries, the Nanzhao Kingdom and its successor, the Kingdom of Dali, remained strong and independent, on a par with China and Tibet, its warring neighbours. Its capital was Dali, on Erhai Lake in western Yunnan.

The kingdom came to an end in 1253 at the hands of Kublai Khan, the famous Mongol, grandson of Genghis Khan. Kublai's efforts in the southwest were part of a great strategy by the Mongols to subdue the Song dynasty, first taking Yunnan, then pressing the attack from both the north and west. When the Dali Kingdom fell to the Mongol invaders, most of the population fled west and south, leaving an empty land. Kublai Khan's successes were in part due to the help of tough Muslim mercenaries from Persia and Central Asia; he sent these fierce troops to Yunnan, partly to keep them out of mischief, far from the northern capital, but also to repopulate the southwest. The Muslim settlers also served as the emperor's watchdogs against any movements for independence.

Yunnan became a land of foreigners, Muslim and Mongol. It was the last area of China to hold out when the indigenous Ming dynasty overthrew the Mongols in 1368, thus inviting another invasion. The Ming forces drove out or killed all foreign groups brought in by the cosmopolitan Mongols. Only some of the Muslims were allowed to stay. One such Muslim from Yunnan, Zheng He, rose to become the new emperor's admiral, and a great explorer of the world (see page 97). Ming viceroys in Yunnan built an extensive canal system, added a massive city wall to Yunnanfu (Kunming) and constructed Chinese-style temples.

For centuries, the Ming dynasty, and the Qing (Manchu) dynasty that followed it, ruled Yunnan as a colony rather than as a true province of China. It served China as a kind of Siberia, a place of exile for criminals, dissidents, and officials who fell out of favour with the emperor. The actual number of progressive thinkers and intellectuals banished there was relatively small but they brought with them the language, architecture and customs of north China. One lasting sign of their influence is the style of roofs in many central Yunnanese towns, reminiscent of the imperial splendour in Beijing.

In the 18th century, the Qing emperor used Yunnan as a springboard for launching successful military expeditions against the Burmese. Thereafter, 'tribute elephants' carrying jade from Upper Burma and rubies from Mandalay plodded along the old Burma Road to Yunnanfu. There the tribute was transferred to pack horses and sent north to Beijing. Yunnan was still treated as a semi-barbaric colony, only fit for exiles, but along its borders big changes were taking place. Burma soon fell under the influence of the ever-growing British Empire, and the French established themselves in Tonkin, their first step into Indochina. Both European empires eyed Yunnan's rich tin and copper mines covetously.

In 1855, a dispute between Muslim and Chinese miners escalated into a full-scale Muslim rebellion against Chinese rule. It raged on for almost 20 years. Muslims ransacked Kunming's old temples, burned its monasteries, destroyed Buddhist monuments (except for two pagodas), and levelled most public buildings and large private homes. They set up their own capital in Dali. The European powers were quick to take advantage of the chaos in Yunnan. Britain supplied arms to the Muslims through Burma, while France sent arms to the emperor.

Chinese troops finally crushed the rebellion with great cruelty in 1873, slaughtering Muslim men, women and children in Dali and sweeping on to massacre thousands more in smaller towns. Plague broke out, killing many of the survivors. Yunnan was nearly depopulated for the second time in its turbulent history. France and Britain both wangled concessions from the failing Qing dynasty—the French to build a railway into Yunnan from their new colonial capital in Hanoi, and the British to open trade. In 1911 China became a republic and Yunnan fell into the hands of local warlords.

Japan's invasion of China in 1937 heralded World War II and inflicted immense damage. The upheaval there included the evacuation of factories, universities and government agencies when the Japanese occupied China's east coast. Industries were set up and money poured in. The Burma Road and flights from India funnelled supplies into Yunnan, destined for Allied war bases all over West China. Strategically placed Kunming became a major American base, host to General Chenault's Flying Tigers and General Stilwell's land troops.

Colonel Robert L Scott, Jr, first commander of the 23rd Fighter Group, China Air Task Force, with armourers on the wing of his P-40 prior to his last combat mission, January 1, 1943, Kunming

The war convinced Yunnan's population that its best interests lay with China. In 1949, there was very little resistance to Chairman Mao's liberation forces. Since then, Yunnan has enjoyed more prosperity than at any time in its history, though remote mountain areas remain among the poorest in all China. Its mines and natural resources have been developed, and modern transportation has overcome its old curse of remoteness and inaccessibility. In the last decade Yunnan has changed rapidly, developing links with Southeast Asia and becoming a major entrepôt and tourist destination of southwest China.

Its natural beauty, healthy climate, and the friendliness of its people have combined to make it one of China's most attractive areas, and a trip through Yunnan is unlike any other in China for the geographic and cultural variety.

KUNMING

Kunming, the capital of Yunnan Province, retains only a degree of its former charm; rapid modernization and development have left much of the city centre resembling most other major cities in China. This transformation was triggered by the hosting of the International Horticultural Expo in 1999. Nevertheless, Kunming remains an interesting place to visit, especially with its proximity to Lake Dian and the beautiful scenery of the Western Hills. Known as the 'Spring City', it has a very mild climate—an average temperature of 9°C in winter and 23°C in summer—and can comfortably be visited at any time of year.

Kunming has a total population of more than 4.5 million, of which just over 12 per cent are made up of 26 ethnic minority nationalities. Of its ethnic groups, those with more than 4,000 members are the Yi, Hui, Bai, Miao, Lisu, Zhuang, Dai, Hani, and Naxi.

During the 1980s and early 1990s, Kunming was the traditional jumping off point for travellers to the upper Yangzi valley. It took almost a full day's drive just to reach Dali; from there it was north to Lijiang and few ventured beyond into the Tibetan counties of Yunnan, which was illegal until just a few years ago.

Now airports at Lijiang and Zhongdian have made easily accessible some of the most spectacular mountain and gorge terrain in the world. For many travelers, however, Kunming still remains an entry point and travel hub for southwest China, with its well-connected roads, railway and impressive international airport, which has regional air routes to Bankok, Chiangmai, Hanoi, Kuala Lumpur, Osaka, Seoul, Singapore, Tokyo, Vientiane, Yangon (Rangoon), Hong Kong and Macau, with more than 40 domestic routes. An even more ambitious airport facility is scheduled to open in 2007.

A recently built, decorative arch constructed in a traditional style frames the modern skyline of tall buildings in Kunming

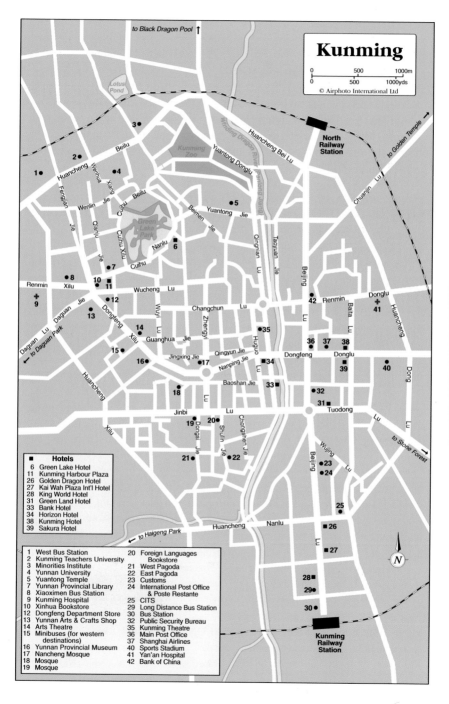

Kunming

© Airphoto International Ltd

to Black Dragon Pool ↑

Lotus Pond

to Golden Temple →

North Railway Station

Beilu

Kunming Zoo

Winding Dragon River (Panlong Jiang)

Huancheng Bei Lu

Chuanjin Lu

Huancheng

Wenhua

Fengjiu

Xiang

Wenlin Jie

Cuihu Beilu

Yuantong Donglu

Yuantong Jie

Qinglian Lu

Taoyuan Jie

Beijing

Beimen Jie

Renmin

Xilu

Green Lake Park

Nanlu

Cuihu

Cuihu Xilu

Olanju

Jie

Daguan Lu

to Daguan Park

Wucheng Lu

Wuyi

Changchun Lu

Dongfeng Lu

Zhengyi

Lu

Renmin

Donglu

Batta Lu

Huancheng

Xilu

Xilu

Guanghua Jie

Jingxing Jie

Qingyun Jie

Nanping Jie

Hugo Lu

Dongfeng

Donglu

Huancheng

Jinbi Lu

Baoshan Jie

Tuodong

Lu

Jinbi Lu

Dongsi Jie

Shulin Jie

Chongshen Jie

Lu

Beijing Lu

Wujing Lu

Dong Lu

to Stone Forest →

to Haigeng Park →

Huancheng Nanlu

Lu

Kunming Railway Station

N

Hotels

6	Green Lake Hotel
11	Kunming Harbour Plaza
26	Golden Dragon Hotel
27	Kai Wah Plaza Int'l Hotel
28	King World Hotel
31	Green Land Hotel
33	Bank Hotel
34	Horizon Hotel
38	Kunming Hotel
39	Sakura Hotel

1	West Bus Station	20	Foreign Languages Bookstore
2	Kunming Teachers University	21	West Pagoda
3	Minorities Institute	22	East Pagoda
4	Yunnan University	23	Customs
5	Yuantong Temple	24	International Post Office & Poste Restante
8	Yunnan Provincial Library	25	CITS
8	Xiaoximen Bus Station	29	Long Distance Bus Station
9	Kunming Hospital	30	Bus Station
10	Xinhua Bookstore	32	Public Security Bureau
12	Dongfeng Department Store	35	Kunming Theatre
13	Yunnan Arts & Crafts Shop	36	Main Post Office
14	Arts Theatre	37	Shanghai Airlines
15	Minibuses (for western destinations)	40	Sports Stadium
16	Yunnan Provincial Museum	41	Yan'an Hospital
17	Nancheng Mosque	42	Bank of China
18	Mosque		
19	Mosque		

SIGHTS IN KUNMING

YUNNAN PROVINCIAL MUSEUM

Some tourists skip museums on principle, but in this case they really should make an exception. Kunming's museum, housed in a monumental Russian-style building, holds some truly superb cultural treasures. One collection consists of textiles, costumes, handicrafts and artefacts of Yunnan's many ethnic minority groups, though the outstanding, priceless assemblage consists of bronzes going back 3,000 years (see pages 92–3).

YUANTONG TEMPLE (YUANTONGSI), PARK AND ZOO

The well-restored, 1,200-year-old Buddhist temple lies in the north part of the city at the foot of Yuantong Hill. Its elaborate entrance is on Yuantong Jie and the impressive gateway dates from the Ming dynasty.

The temple was founded in the eighth century, when Yunnan was an independent kingdom adjacent to Tang dynasty China. The whole complex was greatly enlarged in 1320 after the conquest of southwest China (1253) by the Mongol Kublai Khan. For centuries it remained the largest Buddhist monastery in Kunming. Today, Yuantong Temple consists of a Great Hall of the Buddha, the Octagonal Pavilion and garden-like walkways around a pond. In 1990 a Thai-style temple was built behind the main hall to accommodate the large number of Thai tourists in Yunnan, and a small Tibetan chapel on the east side rounds out the complex's Buddhist ecumenism.

Legend says the temple and monastery were first built to control a malicious dragon who lived in a small pond behind the present buildings. Two huge pillars inside the Great Hall are adorned with carved dragons, reminders of their ancient ancestor.

Yuantong Park's main entrance lies at the end of Qingnian Lu by the bus terminal. The park, spreading over the slopes of Yuantong Hill, is famous for its flowers and trees. Four main gardens exhibit exquisite blossoms at different times of the year. In summer, many varieties of Yunnan's celebrated rhododendrons are on display. Autumn brings a riot of variegated chrysanthemums. Throughout Kunming's pleasant winter there comes a succession of magnolia, cassia, flowering plum and camellia. The best display of all occurs in late February and March when avenues of Japanese and Oriental cherry create a fairyland of delicate colour.

Kunming's zoo forms the western part of Yuantong Park. Many of Yunnan's indigenous species are found here, including the handsome, red, raccoon-like lesser panda— as well as the giant panda from Sichuan Province. All Chinese zoos are a bit sad.

EAST AND WEST TEMPLE PAGODAS (DONGSI TA, XISI TA)

South of Jinbi Lu stand two ancient pagodas, the oldest surviving structures in Kunming. As historical and architectural monuments they are invaluable though they may seem insignificant or run-down at first glance. Both pagodas were constructed in the first half of the ninth century, by a famous artisan named Weichi Chingde, and display marvellous skill in engineering.

The 13-tiered pagoda rising 40.5 metres above Shulin Jie is known by three different names: East Temple Pagoda, Golden Chicken Pagoda (Jinji Ta, the popular name, designating four golden roosters on its summit) and Changle Temple Pagoda (the scholarly name, denoting a temple that once surrounded the site). The dilapidated, wild chickens are still there, made of copper rather than gold. The solid base, eight metres tall, is abutted on the right by a lovely series of semi-circular stairs. An important Qing-dynasty stele at the base describes the history of the two pagodas and their many renovations.

The West Temple Pagoda, also with 13 tiers, is slightly shorter, squatter, and better preserved than its twin, though it lacks the ancient grandeur of East Temple Pagoda. It stands 35.5 metres tall.

GREEN LAKE PARK (CUIHU GONGYUAN)

This lively, attractive park lies in the northwestern quarter of the city. Originally a marsh on the outskirts of Kunming, it was transformed into a park in the late 17th century under Emperor Kangxi; his servants drained the swamp, put in the lake, built the main pavilion and installed the causeways and arbours.

In the early morning the park hums with traditional Chinese life: elderly gentlemen practising martial arts or airing their pet birds, children exercising, old women gossiping. The park is a gathering place for singers who have revived long-dormant folk songs and operas. The open-air performances can be enjoyed at any time of day, but most frequently on weekends. Green Lake Park is especially colourful on festival days, such as Mid-Autumn Festival or Chinese New Year.

MOSQUES (QINGZHENSI)

At least five mosques serve Kunming's 40,000-strong Muslim population. The two main ones welcome visitors who behave in a modest and circumspect manner. The oldest and leading mosque of the city is located adjacent to the Central Department Store at 51 Zhengyi Lu. The original Nancheng Ancient Mosque was some 400 years old and noted for its murals depicting the holy Islamic sites of Mecca and Medina. Sadly, this was torn down in 1997 to make way for a larger, more modern and altogether unattractive alternative.

A larger mosque is situated down a white-washed alley that leaves the main road at 90 Shuncheng Jie, in the centre of the Muslim quarter. Shops and halal restaurants specializing in beef and lamb dishes cater to Muslims in the neighbourhood. The well-preserved mosque is an interesting mixture of Chinese and Arabian styles.

THE BRONZES OF YUNNAN

Bronze art seems to arise almost spontaneously in China. As more discoveries are made and the location of sites increases, the possibility of independent development increases as well.

The discovery in Yunnan of magnificent bronze artwork from the dawn of history excited archaeologists around the world. Farmers ploughing near Lake Dian unearthed some mystifying bronze vessels in the early 1950s and notified the provincial museum in Kunming. In 1955, archaeologists struck a treasure trove of 48 Bronze-Age tombs at Stone Village Hill (Shizhaishan), 40 kilometres south of Kunming.

Bronze is an alloy of copper and tin which is stronger than iron if made in correct proportions—eight parts copper to one part tin. Bronze was the first metal ever used by humans. It first came into use in northern China during the Shang dynasty, around 1800 BC. Yunnan's bronze culture dates from about 1200 BC, near the end of the Shang dynasty, though most of the bronze artifacts from the 48 tombs date from the Warring States period (475–221 BC) and the Western Han dynasty (206 BC–AD 24).

The Dian people in Yunnan mastered many advanced techniques in creating their bronzes, including gold plating and silver inlay decorations. Skill and sophistication of workmanship equalled and surpassed that of the Han. And whereas Han bronze culture seemed to undergo a change in favour of porcelain, the Dian bronzes took on new confidence and variety. Free from the constraints of orthodoxy, the Dian artists could create more freely and respond to the calling of their aesthetic choice. One can even say that 'art for art's sake' was being created in Southwest China at that time.

The tombs at Shizhaishan yielded thousands of bronze objects—sewing boxes, figurines, headrests, mirrors, weapons, farm implements, belt buckles and more. Animals, hunting and fighting, took a predominant place among the statuettes and decorations. Archaeologists found 34 recognizable species along with many mythological beasts. Subsequent digs in western Yunnan produced a little bronze house with six kinds of domesticated animals—cow, goat, chicken, dog, pig, horse—pointing to an advanced agricultural society.

Even more revealing were elaborate, three-dimensional scenes cast on the lids of huge cowrie containers and on drums, showing the daily life of a vigorous, productive, slave-owning people. To archaeologists, this was a unique moment in the history of bronzeware. Only in Yunnan did Bronze-Age artisans realistically record the intimate and unmistakable details of their social activity. There were ferocious miniature battles and lively domestic scenes showing the work of women. The rhythms and rituals of agriculture and religion came to life, along with grisly depictions of head-hunting and human sacrifice. The bronze figurines laughed, wept, got drunk. One scene showed pompously dressed chieftains, surrounded by slaves, offering tribute to the King of Dian. Who were these people?

The first historical reference to the Kingdom of Dian appears in the second century BC. Sima Qian (145–85 BC), China's greatest classical historian, mentions that the King of Dian, in the savage southern border region beyond China, allied himself with the emperor of the Han dynasty in order to subdue neighbouring tribes. In recognition of Dian's new tributary status, a seal was presented to the King of Dian. Other references to Dian appeared here and there in ancient Chinese literature but there was no hard evidence to confirm the kingdom's existence until 1956. That year, tomb Number 6 at Shizhaishan yielded up the seal itself. Four clear characters on its bronze face—Dian Wang Zhi Yin (Seal of the King of Dian)—bound this remote, remarkable tribe to the vast empire of China.

Dian originally referred only to the mysterious, non-Chinese tribe. Later the name came to mean the territorial kingdom as well. The Lake of Dian (Dianchi) outside Kunming has kept its ancestral name for three millennia and the word Dian remains synonymous with Yunnan.

On the basis of available material, archaeologists divide Yunnanese bronze age culture into four categories, according to geography. Dianchi culture, Erhai culture (in the area around Dali and Erhai Lake), Northwest Yunnan culture and Yuanjiang culture (or Red River culture, in southern Yunnan). The most important Dianchi culture is concentrated around Lake Dianchi outside Kunming, but extends to Qujing in the northeast, to the Red River in the south, Luling County in the east and Lufeng County in the west.

A major element in the bronze culture of Yunnan is the bull, symbol of property and wealth. The depictions of the beast are powerful and realistic, where even the veins on the head and neck stand out. The tiger, too, appears again and again as a creature of strength and awe, holding forth the aspiration of invincibility.

Ancestor worship is clearly presented in the bronze work of Dian. In some cases there is presented a beautiful house-shrine with a snake-staircase that leads to a roof. It is designed to reach ever upward and to lead the eye that way. A figure with hair braided upward mirrors the stairway. The visual story seems to say: The Dian people can reach to Heaven to communicate with their ancestors by means of the snake ladder; the spirit of the snake stands as an intermediary between the world of men and the celestial world.

SIGHTS NEAR KUNMING
WESTERN HILL (XISHAN)

The name Western Hill refers to a range of four mountains stretching over 40 kilometres along the western shore of Lake Dian. It offers the best scenery and some of the finest temples in the entire region. Its highest temple, Dragon Gate, is nearly 2,500 metres high.

Western Hill affords four major attractions. On the lower and middle slopes are two important Buddhist temples. On the steep, higher reaches are a Daoist temple, grottoes and a superb view across the lake and the whole Yunnan plain from the Dragon Gate itself.

From the bus stop at the mountain's base, a walk of 2.5 kilometres along the road brings you to **Huating Temple** (Huating Si), the largest Buddhist complex in Kunming. Two wrathful deities, known as Heng (with mouth closed) and Ha (mouth open), stand at the temple entrance. Coloured with lacquer, they are considered to be among the best representations of these celestial guardians in all China. Inside the entrance hall are even larger statues of the Kings of the Four Directions, dressed in the splendid armour of Chinese warriors a thousand years ago, before Mongol and Manchu invasions introduced alien martial regalia.

Earliest references to Huating go back to the 11th century. An important monastery in the 14th century, it continued to grow and reached its present dimensions only in 1920. Today, there are 40 monks in residence and renovated quarters can accommodate pilgrims and visitors.

The main temple contains a trinity of gilded lacquer Buddhas seated on lotus thrones. Their huge size, blue hair, and sumptuous setting make an impressive sight. The side walls are covered with a phantasmagoria of folk characters—these are the same 500 luohan (holy men, spiritual adepts and disciples of the Buddha) as the ones in the Bamboo Temple—made deliberately comical to contrast with the calm solemnity of the great Buddhas. One, on stilt-like legs, grabs for the moon; another has eyebrows reaching to his knees.

Behind the three Buddhas, facing the back of the hall, is a shrine to Guanyin, the Goddess of Mercy. Against an elaborate backdrop, a kind of mythological bestiary, she rides across the sea on a dragon's head to meet the Dragon King, who waits for her on the left.

Leaving Huating, follow the main road up the mountain for two kilometres to **Taihua Temple** (Taihua Si), which many people feel is aesthetically superior to the larger complex below. Nestled in a deep forest, Taihua's site is one of its charms. Age-old camellia and magnolia trees give shade in a meticulously cultivated garden. The top level at the back offers a stunning view over temple roofs to the lake far below. A visit to this Buddhist retreat in the late afternoon or the cool of the

*This guardian deity stands over nine metres tall and guards
the entrance to Huating temple, Western Hill*

Pairs of cranes decorate a temple roof

evening, when the crowds have gone, can transport you to another century, far removed from modern China.

At the entrance, a handsome stone archway is covered with fine carvings: Buddhist symbols, flowers and creatures, including an animated cockatoo. In the Four Guardians entrance hall beyond, an image of Guanyin replaces the usual fat, merry Buddha, as Taihua is dedicated to the Goddess of Mercy.

The main temple building bears the name Hall of the Precious Hero, in honour of a statue near the back representing Zishi, a Daoist hero-god. His prominent place in a temple of a different religion is explained by his local popularity and the eclectic nature of Buddhism in China. Behind the temple's trinity of Buddhas and a high, finely worked wooden pavilion, stands an altar to Guanyin, facing the rear. Here Yunnan's favourite goddess fulfills her role as Deliverer of Sons, holding out an unmistakably male baby to newlyweds and barren couples. Beside her stand Zishi, the Daoist, and Wen Cheng (Sanskrit: Manjushri), God of Wisdom and Literature, clad in yellow. These two anticipate the shrines awaiting on the final stretch of the mountainside.

A two-kilometre (1.25-mile) walk brings you to the end of the paved road and the climax of Western Hill, **Sanqing Pavilion** (Sanqing Ge) and the **Dragon Gate** (Longmen). Halfway along, a short distance to the right, lies an old cemetery with many traditional tombs and gravestones. A late addition contains the ashes of Nie Er, the brilliant young musician who composed China's present national anthem. He was tragically drowned in Japan in 1936 at the age of 24.

As an alternative to the tourist tram or chairlift, at the end of the road, a long flight of steps ascends to the Pavilion of the Three Pure Ones (Sanqing Ge), a collection of almost vertical buildings stacked against the face of the mountain. Unfortunately, little is left in their interiors except for the central Sanqing pavilion, where three statues of Zishi present him as a black-faced heavenly potentate as well as the familiar warrior god. Sanqing was originally built in the early 14th century as a summer resort for a Mongol prince of the Yuan dynasty. Renovated 400 years later as a Daoist shrine, it now contains a large teahouse with a splendid view and gives a welcome pause before the final climb.

A stone path leads up past a series of caves and grottoes to the Air Corridor, a tunnel chipped out of living rock. At the far end, it opens out through a stone arch-way to a temple eyrie on the side of a sheer cliff. The characters longmen (dragon gate) are inscribed in red and gold upon the arch. The view from the terrace is excellent and worth the walk.

A shrine in the rock wall, called Attainment of Heaven Cave, holds the lively golden image of Kui Xing, patron god of scholars. He rides a dragon-fish while hero-ically brandishing a calligraphy brush and blithely balances a potted pomegranate

THE EUNUCH ADMIRAL

In the year 1381, a ten-year-old Muslim boy named Ma Ho played among the fishing boats of his village, Kunyang, and dreamt that Lake Dianchi was a boundless ocean. His father and grandfather had made the pilgrimage to Mecca and had told rousing tales of the seas beyond China. The distinguished family, descended from an early Mongol governor of Yunnan, remained loyal to the dynasty of Kublai Khan, and helped Yunnan put up resistance to the new Ming dynasty that had seized power in China.

That year, a Ming army stormed into Yunnanfu, as Kunming was then called, and encircled Lake Dianchi, sweeping up captives. Ma Ho was seized, along with other boys, castrated, and sent into the army as an orderly. By the age of 20, the bright lad had become a junior officer, skilled at war and diplomacy. His abilities won him influential friends who helped him move to Nanjing, then China's capital, during a turbulent period of wars and revolts. There he gained power and prestige as a court eunuch and the emperor gave him a new name—Cheng Ho or, as now spelled, Zheng He.

For 300 years, China had been extending its seaborne power, building up widespread commerce, importing spices, aromatics and raw materials from different parts of Asia. The arts of shipbuilding and navigation reached their height during the early Ming Dynasty. In 1405, the emperor appointed Zheng He as 'Commander-in-Chief of All Missions to the Western Seas', whereupon the eunuch admiral set sail on a mission of exploration and trade. He took 62 ships carrying 27,800 men—the largest naval fleet in the world at that time. It was the first of seven far-flung voyages that took him to the Indian Ocean, Persia, Arabia and the east coast of Africa.

On his fourth trip, Zheng He visited every major port of South and Southeast Asia and returned with envoys from some 30 states to forge diplomatic relations and pay homage to the emperor. The ambassadors resided for six years in the new capital of Beijing, after which Zheng He took them home again.

Thanks to Zheng He's genius, China held power over much of maritime Asia for half a century. However, China never established a trading empire, in contrast to the European nations who soon began exploring the earth's oceans, too. Instead, Zheng He's discoveries encouraged Chinese emigrants to settle in foreign countries, where their communities have flourished ever since.

Zheng He's atlases, logs and charts bequeathed a priceless record to the world and made maritime history. On his seventh and last voyage, between 1431 and 1433, Zheng He revisited all the distant places he had discovered 25 years earlier. He died in 1435, honoured throughout China but best beloved by the people of the southwest in the land of his birth, Yunnan.

plant, the symbol of long-lasting success, on the sole of his foot. Candidates for the all-important imperial examinations struggled up Western Hill to pray for his help. He is flanked by Wen Cheng, the God of Wisdom and Literature, and Guan Gong, the God of War and Justice. Symbols of bounty, happiness and longevity surround the trio. Cranes and peaches, representing long life, adorn the ceiling. Phoenixes and peacocks, chess-boards and horses, stand for power and intellectual pleasure. Coloured clouds represent happiness and prosperity. High above the cave, the stone head of a benign old man peers down from a niche. He is none other than Laozi (Lao-Tse), the founder of Daoism.

This particular gathering of gods, sages and emblems symbolized the ambitions of candidates aspiring to high office in the imperial bureaucracy or the army. Successful scholars have left grateful poems and inscriptions along the route above Sanqing. A few failed candidates leapt to their death in despair from the top of Dragon Gate.

It is possible to take a cable car from the tomb of Nie Er to Haigeng Park and from the northern entrance a bus to the railway station. An alternative route back to Kunming from the Western Hill follows a steep path straight down the mountain. It starts from the paved road close to Sanqing Ge and comes out at Dragon Gate Village (Longmen Cun) at the base. From here you can see a long, narrow causeway extending across Lake Dian. Go to its end and walk east on a clearly marked path by the water's edge to the resort village of Haigeng, where you can catch a bus back to Kunming, ten kilometres away.

DALI

Dali is the capital of the Dali Bai Autonomous Prefecture west of Kunming, a large region made up of 12 counties. It is the historic home of the Bai minority, one of Yunnan's most numerous and prosperous ethnic groups. The name Dali refers to several things: Dali City (Dali Shi), the administrative centre that includes Xiaguan, the main metropolis and Yunnan's second largest city; the old stone town, known formally as Dali Old City (Dali Gu Cheng); and the general surrounding region of towns, villages and Erhai Lake. The old town of weathered grey granite stands on a sloping site at about 1,900 metres above sea level—a long, narrow rice plain between the Azure Mountains (Cangshan) and the bright blue Ear Lake (Erhai). Deep black soils mantle the plain, which contrast with Yunnan's typical red clay. This natural configuration seems specially designed for a good, bountiful life. In late winter, when fields of brilliant yellow rapeseed shimmer and sway between snow-capped mountains and the sapphire lake, one can agree with the Bai that theirs is the most blessed spot on earth.

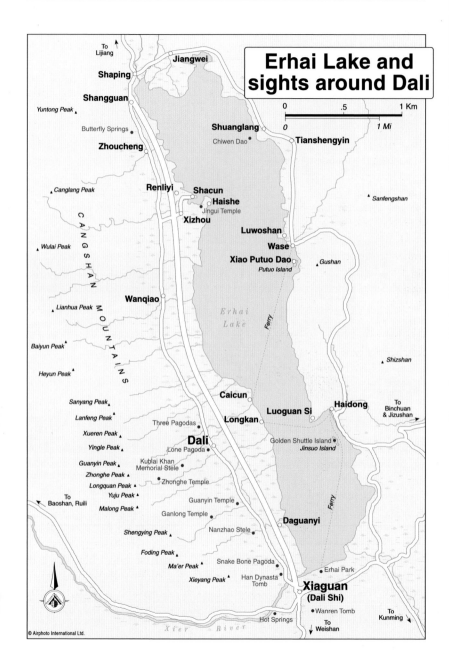

Erhai Lake and sights around Dali

To Lijiang

Jiangwei

Shaping

Shangguan

Yuntong Peak

Butterfly Springs

Zhoucheng

Shuanglang

Chiwen Dao

Tianshengyin

0   .5   1 Km

0   1 Mi

Canglang Peak

Renliyi

Shacun

Haishe

Jingui Temple

Xizhou

Sanfengshan

Wulai Peak

C A N G S H A N

Luwoshan

Wase

Xiao Putuo Dao

Putuo Island

Gushan

Lianhua Peak

Wanqiao

M O U N T A I N S

Erhai Lake

Ferry

Baiyun Peak

Heyun Peak

Shizshan

Sanyang Peak

Lanfeng Peak

Caicun

Luoguan Si

Haidong

To Binchuan & Jizushan

Xueren Peak

Three Pagodas

Longkan

Yingle Peak

Dali

Lone Pagoda

Golden Shuttle Island

Jinsuo Island

Guanyin Peak

Kublai Khan Memorial Stele

Zhonghe Peak

Zhonghe Temple

Longquan Peak

To Baoshan, Ruili

Yuju Peak

Malong Peak

Guanyin Temple

Ganlong Temple

Shengying Peak

Nanzhao Stele

Daguanyi

Foding Peak

Ma'er Peak

Snake Bone Pagoda

Xieyang Peak

Han Dynasty Tomb

Erhai Park

Xiaguan

(Dali Shi)

Ferry

Wanren Tomb

To Kunming

Hot Springs

To Weishan

Xier River

© Airphoto International Ltd.

Fishing boat and stone village, Erhai Lake

The elongate lake, named for its ear-like shape, lies in a geological fault between parallel mountain ranges, south of the great river trenches of eastern Tibet. Erhai Lake, 41 kilometres long and three to nine kilometres wide, is part of the Mekong River system. The small Xi'er River, fed by glaciers and snow water, enters the lake at its northern end through Dragon's Head Pass. It leaves the lake's southwest corner by a canal at Xiaguan, but soon tumbles boisterously through the Cangshan at Dragon's Tail Pass, a cleft so narrow that a boulder stuck between cliffs forms a natural bridge above it.

The Cangshan Range stands like a wall behind Dali's plain, with a long, looping skyline shaped by 19 peaks averaging about 4,000 metres. Unlike the craggy ranges piled up elsewhere in western Yunnan, the Cangshan alone is underlain by granite that, aeons ago, forced its way up through the soft limestone rocks of the area, metamorphosing them into hard marble. Today the great volumes of high quality marble add to Dali's prosperity.

The western plain, 56 kilometres long but only three or four kilometres wide, is watered by 18 perennial mountain streams, which farmers channel to every plot and terrace. The 19 peaks and 18 streams are the emblems of Dali. Towns and villages perch on the mountain's lower slopes or on the lake shore, leaving the entire plain for agriculture. Rice grows abundantly in summer and autumn; beans and wheat are secondary crops. In former times, Dali thrived on its winter opium crops, until the Chinese government suppressed the trade in the 1930s.

Herbal medicine on sale in a Dali market. The rare herbs to be found high in the mountains of Yunnan and Sichuan are much sought after for use in Chinese medicine.

The eastern shore of Erhai Lake is totally different. The low, barren, Red Rocky Mountains (Hongshi Shan) rise directly from the water, with small villages clinging to the foothills. Although receiving little rain, the sparse, red soil is good for peach and pear orchards. Fishing is the main occupation of this shore, for Erhai Lake contains more than 40 varieties of fish. Bai boat owners also transport building materials around the lake, and nowadays match the Bai farmers in prosperity.

Bai means 'white' but the origin of this name is not clear. It has nothing to do with skin colour or colour of dress—Bai women wear a variety of brightly coloured costumes. They call themselves Speakers of the White Language, a tongue distinct from Mandarin, or People of the White King, though the king's identity is lost in conflicting myths.

Dali, their ancestral home lies three kilometres from the lake shore, under the highest peak of the Cangshan, roughly in the middle of the plain. The city of Xiaguan, 15 kilometres south, occupies the southwest corner of the lake. Xiaguan began as a trade centre at the crossing of two major caravan routes, linking China with Burma, and eastern Tibet with the tea plantations of southern Yunnan. Xiaguan remains the more important commercial centre, whereas Dali has historically been a seat of cultural and political power.

Dali was the capital of an independent kingdom named Nanzhao during the eighth and ninth centuries, while the Tang dynasty reigned in China. At its height, Nanzhao conquered much of Burma, attacked parts of Laos and Thailand, and repeatedly invaded China's Sichuan region in a border war that helped to weaken the Tang dynasty. The royal family of Nanzhao came to an end in 902, when the Chief Minister murdered the infant heir to the throne and proceeded to wipe out all other members of the family as well, initiating decades of turmoil. In 937, a Bai official usurped the throne and renamed the realm the Kingdom of Dali. It prospered for three more centuries, until Kublai Khan conquered it in the autumn of 1253 and made it an outpost of China.

Under the Song dynasty (960–1279), China's army faced a grave crisis when it lost its steady supply of horses. Wars in the north deprived it of vast pastures and traditional horse-breeding grounds. The Kingdom of Dali provided the solution. Yunnan's breed of strong horses had been known for centuries to the Chinese, who prized the animals for their endurance. About the year 1130, Dali began delivering 1,500 horses a year to the Song government, in exchange for silk, silver and salt.

Fine horses are still traded in Dali. For over a thousand years, the Bai have staged a great annual fair on the open land outside Dali's west gate. The Third Month Fair (Sanyue Jie) of the lunar calendar takes place each year in April. This fair evolved from religious gatherings in which Buddhist monks, disciples and laymen met on the Dali Plain at the time of the third full moon to pray, fast, chant and preach. Fruits and flowers, incense and oil were the main devotional offerings and in time, with the growth of the annual worship festival and subsequent social interchange, trade naturally followed to fulfill the material needs of the faithful. Today, mountain tribes and buyers from many parts of China gather for five days of trading, horse-racing and traditional games. A city of tents and booths springs up, livestock of every sort can be found mooing, bleating and squealing in the animal market, but the fair's greatest drawing power nowadays comes from the rare herbs and medicines that Tibetans and others bring down from the remote mountains on Yunnan's borders. Ranking second to medicines are horses, ridden bareback or in full regalia around a small racetrack to show off their speed and prowess.

The Dali city wall and four gate towers at the cardinal points are still largely intact, although the eastern section is a grass covered earth embankment. They were originally built during the Ming dynasty (1368–1644). The southern gatehouse and southwestern section of the city wall have been reconstructed so that visitors can, for a small fee, walk along a part of the walls and gaze up at the snow-capped mountains above. The southern gate tower, known as the Tower of Five Glories, was one of the finest in all China, far outshining in splendour the present 1984 reconstruction.

The city walls surround a well-preserved old town consisting of interesting, two- to three-storey buildings standing along narrow streets that are mostly paved with flagstones and pedestrianized. Many of the buildings have been renovated and turned into tourist shops. Consequently, the compact city can be very conveniently explored on foot.

With all Dali's prosperity, its famous marble and rich agriculture, with its colourful and vigorous life, it is small wonder that the Bai people consider Dali the best spot in China and never want to leave it.

GETTING TO DALI

The Dali-Erhai Lake region lies exactly 400 kilometres west of Kunming; this route is part of the famous Burma Road, which acted as Free China's lifeline to the outside world during the early part of World War II. Today it remains the main east-west highway in Yunnan. The trip by express bus takes five hours and passes through Xiaguan, Yunnan's second largest city. With a population of over 500,000 Xiaguan, now known formally as Dali City (Dali Shi), spreads around the south-western tip of Erhai Lake and rises part way up the surrounding hills. In contrast to small, charming Dali, 15 kilometres to the north, it has a good deal of ugly indus-trial sprawl and little outstanding architecture. It is the main commercial and transportation centre of western Yunnan and all buses make a stop here.

Remarkable changes in Yunnan's transportation have come with the opening of an airport at Xiaguan, to the southeast of the city. Daily flights between Dali and Kunming take less than an hour. Alternatively it is possible to take the train to Xiaguan, a journey of about eight hours, where buses to Dali leave from the station square and take about an hour.

FOOD AND DRINK IN DALI

Because of Xiaguan's large Muslim population, many of the restaurants are halal, offering a good, simple fare of noodles, flat bread, mutton, beancurd and fried vegetables. A number of restaurants can be found in the northern part of the city and along Cangshan Xi Lu. Local specialities are *erkuai*, a noodle-like dish made from pressed rice, usually fried with green onions, and dog, euphemistically known in this part of Yunnan as *diyang*, or 'earth goat'. The earth goat can be missed, but one really should try the dairy products known as *rushan* and *rubing*, the former folded, brittle, fan-shaped cheese, sometimes referred to as fried milk, the latter a mild, soft, white goat's cheese, often fried with beans.

The eating scene in Dali has changed dramatically over recent years as local entrepreneurs have catered to the tastes of foreigners and many small restaurants have sprung up offering a wide range of international dishes.

SIGHTS IN THE DALI REGION

Dali Prefectural Museum (Dali Zhou Bowuguan) Sometimes referred to as the Xiaguan museum, it is an imposing institution with high roofs and yellow tiles and is well worth an hour's visit. Standing in Xiaguan's northeast sector near the approach to Erhai Park, it is somewhat difficult to find on foot. The entrance faces north. The museum presents in a series of rooms the material culture, art history, architecture and ethnic variety of Dali Prefecture's 12 counties.

MOSQUE (QINGZHENSI)

Xiaguan's main mosque stands at the end of Wenming Jie in the old part of town west of Renmin Lu. The streets here are small, on a human scale, and the houses rarely more than two storeys. Their handsome wooden exteriors are painted red-brown, or green, and retain the atmosphere of a hundred years ago.

The mosque itself, Xiaguan Qingzhensi, stands beyond a stone and marble entrance gate, beyond a courtyard. Enter respectfully and you will be greeted and welcomed by the residents—several families live within the compound and care for the site and the religious needs of the community. Most families in this part of town are Hui (Chinese Muslims)

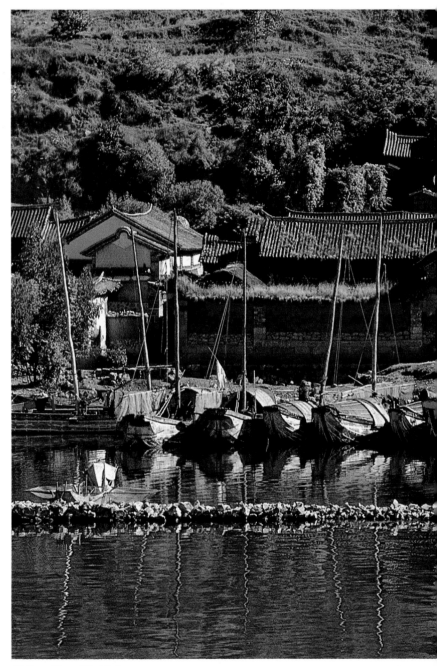

Fishing village, Erhai Lake

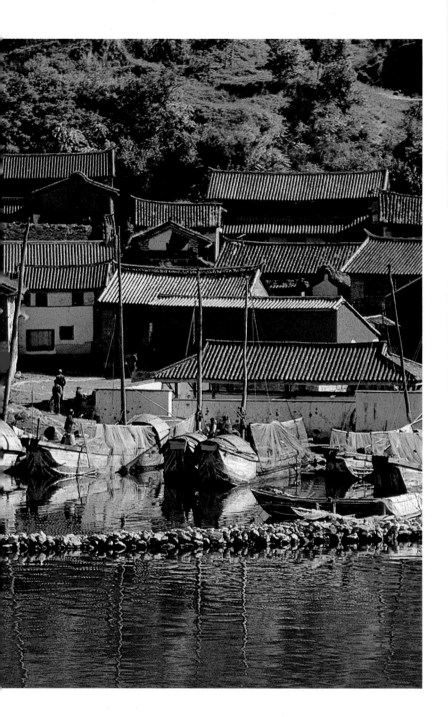

ERHAI PARK (ERHAI GONGYUAN)

Xiaguan's most attractive park stretches along Tuanshan Hill at the southern end of Erhai Lake. Royal deer belonging to the Nanzhao kings used to graze here 1,200 years ago, and on a clear day it is easy to see why the spot was chosen for a modern park. The view looks directly up the lake for miles. To the west, fading away majestically, all 19 peaks of the Cangshan range are visible.

The park is well-kept, dotted with pavilions, staircases and flower gardens, and it has a teahouse. A small but meticulously maintained botanical garden lies at the eastern base of the hill, reached by a long descending flight of stairs. Its outstanding collection of camellias, magnolias and azaleas gives an idea of the botanical riches that are native to the Cangshan Mountains. Sometimes fishing fleets of 20 or 30 boats are pulled up at the base of Tuanshan Hill, giving visitors a chance to stop and chat with the lake dwellers.

ERHAI LAKE

The great Erhai, blessing and bane of the Dali Plain, is a constant fixture in the consciousness of the Bai people. It is deep and full of fish. Predictable winds blow from the north in the morning and change direction at day's end, filling the sails of the wooden boats transporting quarry stones, fish, livestock, fodder or wood around the shores. But the lake has another face that is far less benign. Heavy rains can bring devastating floods. Today, dams and predictions from provincial weather stations help to avert disasters.

There are innumerable ways to enjoy the lake—walking along the shore or hiring boats to explore islands and inlets. It is said that the waters are infested with the schistosomiasis parasite (which causes an infestation of blood flukes in the body). It is therefore unsafe to swim.

Three main islands and several temples and villages along the lake's dry eastern shore are worth visiting. About an hour by boat from Xiaguan is **Golden Shuttle Island (Jinsuo Dao)**, with a small fishing community on the east side and a cave for exploring. On the shore, directly north of the island, is a rocky peninsula crowned by a pavilion and temple. Sacred Buddhist buildings, destroyed and rebuilt many times, have stood on this spot for nearly 1,500 years. **Luoyuan Temple** was badly damaged during the Cultural Revolution but has been put back together and has great charm. Visitors can have their fortunes told by an old priest who guides them in shaking and selecting a single bamboo stick from a bundle of 100. The numbered stick corresponds to a specific fortune.

Much farther up the lake sits a tiny, picturesque temple island, **Xiao Putuo Dao** (see picture on page 78), dating from the 15th century. It is devoted to Guanyin, the Goddess of Mercy. The outside walls have been restored with paintings of birds,

Fishing on Erhai Lake, photographed in 1985

animals and flowers and the fanciful roof with pointed eaves is especially attractive. On the shore nearby is the fishing village of Haiyin, whose boatmen are steeped in the lore of the lake. One of their specialities is night fishing for the huge 40-kilogram (88-pound) 'green fish'.

Near the northern end of Erhai is the village of Tianshengyin and the twin islets of Chiwen Dao and Yuji Dao, a beautiful grouping with old buildings and a pagoda. Sometimes it is possible to catch a boat from here across the lake to Shangguan, near Butterfly Spring, and then ride a bus home to Dali or Xiaguan.

THREE PAGODAS OF DALI (DALI SANTA)

Standing below Lanfeng Peak, slightly to the northwest of Dali Old Town, are three elegant pagodas, known as Chongsheng Santa, the Three Pagodas of Saintly Worship. The outstanding landmarks of the region, they were once part of the greatest temple complex on the Dali plain. The Chongsheng Temple itself has long since disappeared and now only the towers remain. Note: In recent times the Three Pagodas site has become extremely popular with tourists, the inevitable result being that it is over-run with stalls selling marble wares. Visitors should also note that the compound enclosing the three pagodas has been extensively renovated, and the entrance fee may be daunting, particularly as the pagodas are closed and cannot be climbed.

The tallest pagoda, named **Qianxunta**, measures nearly 70 metres and has 16 tiers. It is thought to have been constructed in about 850 by engineers who were prisoners brought from Chengdu when the Dali empire overran the area that is modern-day Sichuan. The two smaller pagodas, each with ten tiers and standing 42 metres high, were built 200 years later and have characteristics of architecture from the Chinese Southern Song (1127–1279).

Pagodas are ubiquitous structures throughout the Buddhist world. Their Sanskrit name is stupa, originally a mound or round dome or cylinder on a square base with a shaft emerging upward.

Stupas probably evolved in India from prehistoric times as burial mounds for local rulers and heroes. Legend says that in the fifth century BC Shakyamuni, the historical Buddha, asked to have his ashes interred in a stupa. Since that time stupas have become symbols of the Buddha, reminders of his earthly existence, cult objects and places of devotion. As Buddhism spread through Asia the shape of stupas adapted itself to local architecture, giving rise to the huge variety of styles. Generally speaking there are three types of stupas, or pagodas, in China.

The Storeyed style: This results from traditional Chinese storeyed architecture and is marked by panoramic views from large windows and outer railings at each level.

The Pavilion style: This is also known as the 'single-layered stupa', with one storey only.

Qianxunta, the finest pagoda on the Dali Plain, as it was in 1981

Dali

To Lijiang

Marble Factory

North Gate

Three Pagodas

To Town God Temple

Hospital

Pingdeng Lu

Garden

Yinchang Lu

Yu'er Lu

Garden Teahouse

Bus Stop

Muslim Restaurant

Yunnan Cafe

To Stadium

Bus Stop

Neeman's Tibetan Cafe

Post Office

Huguo Lu

Chez Mrley's

Salvador Dali's

Bank of China

Bicycle Hire

Sunny Garden Hotel

Jim's Cafe

Number Two Guesthouse

Department Store

Cafe de Jack

To Cangshan Mts

Minibuses to Xiaguan

Bank

Renmin Lu

To Erhai Lake

Catholic Church

Cinema

Dali Hotel

Bus Station

Bus Stop

Mosque

Yonghong Lu

Dali Museum

Handicrafts Shop

Jiefang Lu

Lone Pagoda

Bus Station

South Gate

To Xiaguan

Main Highway

Bo'ai Lu

Fuxing Lu

Xinmin Lu

Guangwu Lu

0   250   500m

0   500yds

© Airphoto International Ltd.

The Close-eaved (or *Miyi* style), or multi-eaved style: These pagodas are characterized by a spacious first storey, low subsequent storeys and all eaves spaced closely to one another. Windows are small or nonexistent and the interior space is cramped and dark. Close-eaved pagodas are an early style whose popularity rested on the extreme simplicity and gracefulness of form. They are best viewed from a distance where their lines can be seen in relief against a mountain or the far horizon.

The Chongsheng Santa are clearly of the third type, as are nearly all remaining pagodas on the Dali plain. They were built by the 'earth stacking method', whereby terraces of earth were constructed around the pagoda as it rose storey by storey. The immense outer structure of dirt, functioning as a scaffolding, was finally removed to reveal the finished masterpiece.

The pagodas were founded for two main reasons. First, they were holy structures that invoked the Buddha's protection against the frequent disasters of floods and earthquakes. A carved marble inscription in front of Qianxunta bears the four Chinese characters *yong zhen shan chuan*, Subdue Forever the Mountains and the Rivers. Secondly, the pagodas were reliquaries for the ashes and bones of saints and a storehouse for scriptures and precious objects. During reconstruction work in 1979 a priceless hoard of 400 objects—statues, paintings, sutras, jewels, unguents and medicines, copper mirrors, gold and silver ornaments, utensils and musical instruments—was discovered in the roof of Qianxunta pagoda. A small museum behind the pagodas recounts their history.

DALI CITY MUSEUM
Located in the south part of the old town of Dali, just off the main street, this well-kept, well-presented museum has few displays but contains some treasures.

The centrepiece on the ground floor is a large, horizontal, topographic map of Erhai Lake and the Dali region. It is useful as an aid in memorizing the area's geography—it has 48 numbered entries (in Chinese only) that identify major cultural sites. In this room also are neolithic potsherds and axe heads, Spring and Autumn period (770–476 BC) bronze swords, hoes and axes, Han dynasty (206 BC–220 AD) weapons and pottery and, from the site of Dazhatuo, a remarkable bronze stand and lamp on a strange pedestal. A central pole supports branch-like decorations that sprout coins like fruit (a money tree?) and below a dragon-reptile resembling a thecodont curves its long neck and fierce head.

From the Nanzhao and Dali Kingdoms (738–1253) are cowrie shells, roof tiles with decorations, a pagoda brick from Hongshengsi Temple with Brahmi script, bronze bodhisattvas from Sheli Pagoda and *dorjes* (ritual bronze thunderbolts) with finger ring holders. From Snake Bone Pagoda (see below) are more *dorjes* and miniature pagodas. Backing the displays is a reproduction of the Nanzhao Scroll and finally there sits a 10th-century stone Buddha with moustache and excellent eyebrows. Upstairs are a number of outstanding bronze mirrors. Those from the Song dynasty (960–1279) are particularly interesting, with images of sage, crane, acolyte, trigrams and tortoise. Large seals were once used by the Ming-dynasty garrison at Dali.

The main glass exhibition cases display six wooden sculptures: the Four Guardian Kings (*tianwang*) and the bodhisattvas Samantabhadra (Puxian) and Manjushri (Wenshu). These figures, each standing one metre, are first-rate pieces of religious art that date from the Yuan dynasty (1279–1368); they comprise some of the little wooden sculpture to survive from that era. These pieces were carved in Jianchuan County to the north of Dali and are typical of that regional style. Manjushri rides a lion, Samantabhadra an elephant. Both wear spectacular crown-headdresses and rest their feet on lotus-stirrups. All six statues were once gilded.

Other displays in the large upstairs room include cremation jars from the Yuan and Ming, stone rubbings related to the death ritual and dozens of ceramic tomb figurines, many of them lively, colourful and humourous. Court ladies carry games, goods, offerings, a whisk, and a *guzheng* (a Chinese zither). Cavaliers, bards, musicians and dancers proclaim the good life after death.

A row of zodiacal and mythical animals—a friendly dragon, a disgruntled tortoise, a chicken waiting to lay an egg, a bored dog—are whimsical and wonderful in their expressiveness. They date from the Ming dynasty (1368–1644).

Behind the main museum building, in a back courtyard, are exhibitions of Ming and Qing pottery, cut and polished marble and a 'forest of steles' (*beilin*) with many Yuan and Ming steles that are valuable for scholars.

DALI MARBLE FACTORY (DALISHI CHANG)

There are over 30 large marble factories throughout China but this is the most famous. Small wonder considering the Chinese word for marble is *dalishi* (Dali stone). Marble of the finest quality has been quarried here for 1,200 years and the great scars high up on the faces of Cangshan have only begun to eat into a supply that will last for millennia.

The factory, on the northern outskirts of Dali, was set up in 1956 and most of its employees have ancestors who were marble workers. Products are made from a choice of four kinds of marble: 'pure white', 'coloured flower', 'cloud grey' and 'handicraft marble'. It is fascinating to see giant slicing machines slowly cutting through five-ton blocks of marble, a process that takes two or three days. Each year, vast amounts of marble are prepared—most is sent to Guangzhou for export to Hong Kong, Japan and throughout Southeast Asia.

Marble carvings and statuary abound throughout the markets of Dali, though most of the wares are not to the taste of foreigners, being either too kitsch or too heavy. With time and a discerning eye, however, some really worthy marble objects can be found. Thinly sliced discs or fan-shaped pieces of marble, polished but uncarved, sometimes have a natural pattern resembling a classical Chinese mountain landscape.

NANZHAO STELE (NANZHAO DEHUA BEI) AND TAIHE RUINS

The Nanzhao Stele, also known by its formal name of Nanzhao Dehua Bei (Nanzhao Sinicization Stele), is an historically important stone tablet from the year 766. It records the offices of a bureaucracy under the Nanzhao Kingdom, describes the economic and political system and specifies the distribution of people within the realm. More important, it recounts Nanzhao's on-again, off-again alliances with the Tang dynasty.

The stele, a time-pocked black monolith three metres tall, stands in a pavilion halfway between Dali and Xiaguan on the rising slopes of the plain, above the main road. It is located between the Cangshan range's Shengying and Foding peaks.

This site was formerly within the city walls of Taihe, Nanzhao's first capital; remnants of its walls appear as long mounds on the hillsides. The Old Nanzhao Highway can still be seen nearby as a shallow furrow running away to the north.

The Nanzhao Stele was accidentally rediscovered, copied and studied by a Qing-dynasty scholar at the end of the 18th century. Were it not for him, the carved characters and the history they tell would have been lost. Much of the writing has indeed been obliterated, worn away by time and pilfered through the centuries by people seeking pieces of the stele to grind into powder for medicine.

SNAKE BONE PAGODA (SHEGUTA)

The dragon, one of China's most complex mythological symbols, has one manifestation whereby it rules over springs, lakes and water courses. Dragons were frequently blamed for the flooding of Erhai Lake and pagodas were erected for protection from the scaly monsters. Snake Bone Pagoda was built to commemorate a brave young man who died while vanquishing one of these 'dragons', which in fact turned out to be a large python, a perfect surrogate and scapegoat. The common people burned the devil snake and buried its bones under the pagoda.

Snake Bone Pagoda is similar in form to Qianxunta, stands over 30 metres tall and was built at the end of the ninth century. The pagoda was a part of the Fotu Temple complex (destroyed) and as such is formally known as Fotusita. It is located under Xieyang Peak, four kilometres northwest of Xiaguan.

BUTTERFLY SPRING (HUDIEQUAN)

This prosaic site in no way approaches its high reputation, and today, with its aggressive, overcrowded market and hordes of gawping tourists, one can say it is

Outside the south gate of Dali city wall

repulsive. But by hiking under the last of Cangshan's 19 peaks and exploring the northern end of Erhai Lake, a visit here can be turned to good advantage.

The legend of Butterfly Spring tells how this spot was a tryst for two young lovers of the Bai nationality. They were happy beyond words but, tragically, hidebound social rules, inflexible elders and persecution drove them to a double suicide. Ever since, they have re-emerged each spring as a pair of butterflies, accompanied by their mascot companion, a golden deer, which now appears as a small, yellow butterfly.

The spring, in a shady grove on the lower slopes of the Cangshan, was justifiably famous for centuries because of a breathtaking convergence every springtime of tens of thousands of butterflies at this spot. The phenomenon was documented many times. Alas, since the mass introduction of insecticides in 1958, the numbers have steadily diminished and the spectacle no longer occurs.

Butterfly Spring lies just off the main road, 35 kilometres north of Dali. The spring itself forms a clear pool and the hills above afford a fine view of the lake.

ZHOUCHENG AND XIZHOU VILLAGES

These two villages, containing some first-rate architecture, still carry on the unspoilt daily rhythm of life on the Dali plain. Zhoucheng Village lies near Butterfly Spring, 30 kilometres north of Dali on the main road. Its inhabitants are nearly pure Bai, with only 50 of its 1,500 households belonging to non-Bai people (Han, Naxi and Dai). Zhoucheng rests below Yunlong Peak and has achieved considerable wealth through its dynamic agriculture and diversified industries. In recent years the locals have set about producing confectionery, noodles, liquor, toys and tie-dyed cloth. There is a boom in house building as well. The solid construction, attention to detail, roofing and stone masonry are all impressive.

Two giant fig trees (*Ficus stipulata*) stand in the main market square, a place where young and old gather to buy and sell produce, meet with friends, swap stories and enjoy themselves. Every Bai village tries to maintain such trees for beauty, shade and blessing.

Xizhou Village has a more mixed population and cosmopolitan background. It grew and flourished in the Ming dynasty (1368–1644) along with the fortunes of Dali's renowned tea merchants. Each year enormous trains of pack animals would set out from Xiaguan loaded with bricks of tea for the thirsty markets of Tibet. This lucrative trade spawned a class of financiers and agents who in time gathered in Xizhou to build their gardens and pleasure-houses. Although sadly run-down, many of these eccentric structures remain, including a French *fin de siècle* mansion.

Xizhou is also famous for producing carved doors and staircases, which can be seen for sale on market days up and down the Dali plain. The village lies three kilometres east of the main north-south road; the turn-off is 20 kilometres north of

Dali, just before the bridge over Wanhua Stream. The journey takes about one hour by local minibus. Farther down a side road beyond Xizhou lies the protected port of Haishe in a serene lakeside setting of spits, promontories, islets and inlets. A hotel in Xizhou is a good place to stay for a few quiet days, away from the crowds of Xiaguan and Dali to the south.

OTHER SIGHTS

The Dali Plain, with a long and florid history, is dotted here and there with miscellaneous cultural sites and tumbledown ruins. Listed below are some less well-known places that can form part of a day trip from either Xiaguan or Dali.

Around Xiaguan are the Confucian Temple, Han dynasty Tomb, Wanren Tomb and Gantong Temple. Slightly to the northwest lies Jiangjun Temple, erected to honour General Li Mi, a Tang emissary who fought against the Dali Kingdom (936–1253).

Near Dali, beyond the town's southwest corner, is Lone Pagoda (Yita), a close-eaves style pagoda built during the tenth century. In any other country this magnificent cultural treasure would be honoured, but here the ground floor has been broken into and the interior used as a toilet.

Farther north, below Zhong He Peak on the grounds of the Dali Fair, stands the Kublai Khan Memorial Stele, a huge 4.4-metre inscribed tablet formed by two separate pieces of stone mounted on an enormous turtle. Two styles of calligraphy were used to inscribe more than 1100 characters that praise Kublai Khan's exploits and his conquest of Dali in 1253. The date of the inscription is 1304, and the stele is known formally as the Pacification of Yunnan Stele.

The small Goddess of Mercy Temple (Guanyintang) lies five kilometres south of Dali. It is built over a great rock which, legend says, was brought there by the goddess herself to block the path of an invading army. This temple has some excellent stone and wood carving.

The tomb of Du Wenxiu (1823–72) lies in the village of Xiadui, a few kilometres southeast of Dali. He was a Muslim from Baoshan District to the west who led a vast uprising between the years 1855 and his death. This is sometimes referred to as the Muslim Uprising, and Du Wenxiu was its leader.

At the far northern end of Erhai Lake, beyond Butterfly Spring, lies the village of Shaping, host to a lively, colourful market each Monday. There is a small hotel here. Boats from Caicun to Wase on the eastern shore leave each afternoon. Wase has a market every Saturday. Shuanglang, at the far northeast end of Erhai Lake, is a bucolic village with a Sunday market.

A number of lesser temples dot the eastern slopes of the Cangshan Range. Going north from the foothills above Dali, they are Zhonghe Temple, Wuwei Temple, Shengyuan Temple and Luocha Pavilion.

The lush countryside around Dali

The village of Zhoucheng, north of Dali, on the shore of Erhai Lake

SIGHTS BEYOND DALI
CHICKEN FOOT MOUNTAIN (JIZUSHAN)

Northeast of Dali in Binchuan County's Liandong district stands Jizushan, a high, sacred mountain that rises 3,220 metres. It has been an important pilgrimage site and monastic centre for both Buddhists and Daoists since the seventh century. The mountain gets its peculiar name from the configuration of the entire range, which is made up of three separate ridges in front and one in back, thus forming the shape of a giant chicken's foot. It can be reached by taking a bus from Xiaguan to Binchuan, a distance of 70 kilometres, and then carrying on another 24 kilometres to the Bai village of Shazhi at Jizushan's base.

The long walk up is amply rewarded by the view from the summit, although, if your time or energy is limited, there is now a cable car that can assist you over the top half of the trail. The mountain's isolation and splendid position between Erhai Lake and the upper reaches of the Yangzi River have frequently been praised by poets:

Sunrise in the East
Cangshan's nineteen peaks in the West
Snow to the North
Endless hills and clouds to the South

This holy mountain, once alive with over 360 temples and hermitages and 3,000 monks, was systematically attacked by Red Guards in the late 1960s, purportedly to end superstition, alchemy and madness. Every major site was damaged or destroyed and only now have some of the pieces been put back together. Even so it is impossible to hope or imagine that Jizushan will ever come close to recreating its formidable past when representatives from Buddhist countries all over Asia came here to live. Weather-beaten Tibetans arrived regularly after travelling the pilgrim road for months or years. On this mountain the diverse theologies of Theravada, Mahayana and Tantric Buddhism mingled freely in one place.

Sacred Wish (Zhusheng) was the central temple on the mountain. It honoured the monk Jiaye who came from India to spread Buddhism. Legend recounts how Jiaye established Buddhism on Jizushan by mastering magical forces and overcoming the wicked Chicken Foot King in titanic battles. Zhusheng Temple was renowned for its bronze statuary and two enormous brass cauldrons, each capable of holding enough rice to feed 1,000 people.

Mid-mountain Temple (Zhongshan Si) lies half way up and has a community of monks. This is a good place for tea and a rest on the ascent. Huashoumen (gate) and temple did largely survive the Cultural Revolution and mark the beginning of the steep climb to the top.

The walk up the mountain leads through remnants of famous walnut forests that once supplied Dali with house beams and wood for the coffins of the rich. The top of the mountain is called Heavenly Pillar Peak (Tianzhu Feng) and nearby on a precipice, known as Golden Summit (Jin Ding), is the crowning spire, Lenyan Pagoda. It is a square, close-eaves style pagoda with 13 storeys that rises 40 metres above the summit (altitude 3240 metres). It was probably first built in the 11th century and has remained the symbol of Jizushan despite all the devastation.

STONE TREASURE MOUNTAIN BUDDHIST CAVES (SHIBAOSHAN SHIKU)

China is rich in Buddhist cave centres. Most notable among these are Bezeklik and Kizil in Xinjiang, Dunhuang and Maijishan in Gansu Province, Yungang in Shanxi Province, Longmen in Henan Province and Dazu in Chongqing Municipality. The Stone Treasure Mountain caves, though less extensive than these, are Yunnan's finest, a complex of three main sites carved and constructed primarily in the ninth century. They are in a remote mountain region 130 kilometres north of Dali by road in Jianchuan County. Follow the main highway towards Lijiang as far as the village of Diannan, eight kilometres before Jianchuan. There is a complicated intersection here. As you turn left (west), be sure to stay on the road that angles back towards the southwest. Do not go in the direction of Yangling. Rather, follow the southwest road for 16 kilometres until you find a conspicuous stone marker next to the main road. This is the entrance to the cave complex by way of a dirt road. The main group of caves is carved into a cliff face at Stone Bell Mountain (Shizhong Shan) above Stone Bell Temple, some eight kilometres beyond this turn-off.

Apart from fine depictions of Buddhist deities and disciples, these caves are outstanding for their presentation of life under the Nanzhao Kingdom. The works are entirely carvings, with no frescoes. Statues of foreigners with aquiline noses, beards and high brows indicate distant contacts through trade and diplomacy. Habits, clothing and customs of the Nanzhao royal family are shown in vivid detail. Grotto Number One at Stone Bell Mountain holds nine imperial figures with one seated amidst the others; he wears a long, elaborate gown. This is King Yi Mouxun (reigned 779–808), under whose rule Nanzhao increasingly adopted Tang models for political institutions, and borrowed Chinese cultural and literary forms.

Another cave at Stone Bell Temple is known as the Ge Luofeng Grotto. Ge Luofeng was a Nanzhao king, 30 years before Yi Mouxun. During his reign Nanzhao forces dealt the Tang armies a series of crushing defeats. This grotto is carefully carved to give the impression of a resplendent hall, with three overlapping tiers.

Certainly the most extraordinary cave is the Grotto of Female Genitalia. Here artists have carried the praise and veneration of fertility to an amazing degree, with a graphic depiction of a 50-centimetre-high (20-inch) vulva. There are two lesser sites within the entire Stone Treasure Mountain complex. Lion Pass (Shizi Guan), across a small ravine from Stone Bell Temple, has three caves. Grotto Number Two at Lion Pass is historically significant for its carving of a Persian noble. Small caves and carvings near Shadeng Village are spread across a long stretch of mountainous land several kilometres south of Stone Bell Temple.

WEIBAO SHAN

Sixty-five kilometres south of Dali rises Yunnan's most famous Daoist mountain, Weibao Shan. It stands within the Weishan Yi and Moslem (Hui) Autonomous Region; Weishan is the county seat and point of departure for the mountain. The town is outstanding for its 100-year-old architecture, mosques and markets. Weibao Shan had more that 20 temples before the Cultural Revolution, but now there are only three, although reconstruction continues. It is possible to find peace, quiet and beautiful views on this mountain if you go at the right time (late autumn). If you want company, expect thousands to join you from the first to the fifteenth day of the second lunar month; this is the mountain's annual pilgrim festival.

LIJIANG

The once remote town of Lijiang is the centre of the Naxi people, a relatively small (250,000) minority group with a richly textured culture. Lijiang is divided by Lion Hill into two distinct parts. New Lijiang, only about 40 years old, is an uninspiring cement clone, like so many modern Chinese cities, while Old Lijiang known locally at Dayan, is an intimate mountain town of stone and tile, laced with swift canals.

The Old Town is the largest remaining ancient town in China left virtually unchanged, but for electricity and sanitary plumbing, for 750 years. It was founded in 1253 at the Old Stone Bridge when Kublai Khan and his 300,000 Mongol troops camped during their campaign against the Kingdom of Dali.

In 1999, the Old Town, known as Gu Cheng in Chinese, was placed on the United Nations World Heritage Site list. A new placard inscription, written by Jiang Zemin, at the entrance to the Old Town celebrates its international status. This is near the large water wheels and new sculptures and a giant video screen with advertising glowing over the nearby Minzhu Lu and Qi Xiong Jie shopping streets. International attention and the 1996 earthquake have made Lijiang so famous that it is now swamped with domestic visitors. Consequently, the lanes of the Old Town are now a maze of souvenir shops. It is nonetheless a wonderful urban environment, with no cars and graceful bridges over the streams that run along the lanes.

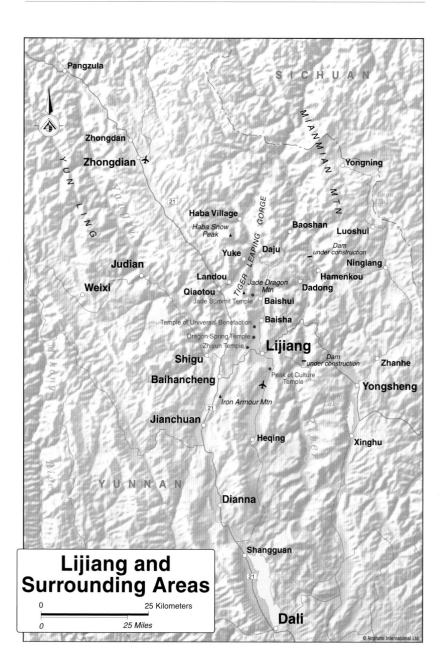

Lijiang and Surrounding Areas

0 —————————— 25 Kilometers

0 —————————— 25 Miles

© Airphoto International Ltd.

UPPER REACHES

YUNNAN PROVINCE

Corn and chilli peppers drying in the eaves of a Naxi home in Lijiang

The old food market on the north side of the Old Town has been relocated on the southern outskirts of town, with a new marble plaza. A 'new extension' of the Old Town is being built on the north side, with construction in traditional style.

In February 1996, Lijiang was devastated by a massive earthquake measuring over seven on the Richter scale. Five counties were severely affected—Jianshan, Huangshan, Lashi, Mingyin and Baisha—leaving more than 50,000 people needing rehabilitation. While help was being administered by Chinese and international relief agencies the disaster was compounded by a series of powerful aftershocks that continued to strike many months after the initial quake. A shock in July 1996 left the total number of lives claimed in five months at over 300, with a further 16,000 people injured. The damage has since been repaired, though much of the funding was used to build the New Town area, which is now broader than the Old Town. New Han immigrants have made the Naxi a minority in their own capital town.

Old Lijiang has long been a gathering place of rugged mountain people from various ethnic groups—Lisu, Pumi, Nuosu Yi, Tibetan—but the majority are Naxi. New Lijiang, populated largely by Han Chinese, is growing and encroaching on the old city. The origin of the Naxi, like many of China's minority groups, is not fully known. Most scholars agree, however, that there was a proto-ethnic tribe, the Qiang, who dwelt in the mountains of northwestern China (today's Qinghai, Gansu and Sichuan Provinces) several thousand years ago. Northern invaders drove them south where they splintered into individual tribes. The Naxi are one of these; they speak a Tibeto-Burman language of their own.

The Naxi themselves believe they came from a common ancestor named Tabu who helped them hatch from magic eggs. Their creation myth is depicted in booklets made of resilient, insect-proof paper dating back hundreds of years. Shaman-like priests, called *dongbas*, were the only people who could read and write the unique Naxi picture-script. Except for special ceremonies, *dongbas* have vanished as a functioning element in modern Naxi society, but efforts are under way to preserve their wisdom and lore.

One characteristic that strikes the visitor is the predominance of women in all types of work. Women seem to run the market and control the purse-strings.

Traditional tiled rooftops of Old Lijiang

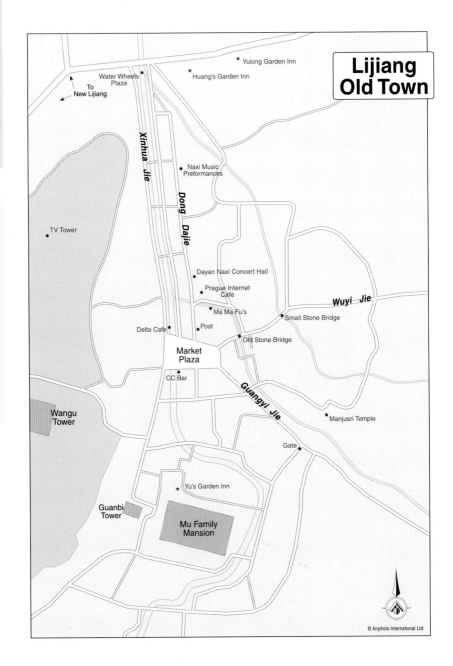

Lijiang
Old Town

Yulong Garden Inn
Huang's Garden Inn
Water Wheels Plaza
To New Lijiang
Xinhua Jie
Naxi Music Preformances
Dong Dajie
TV Tower
Dayan Naxi Concert Hall
Prague Internet Cafe
Ma Ma Fu's
Wuyi Jie
Small Stone Bridge
Delta Cafe
Post
Old Stone Bridge
Market Plaza
CC Bar
Guangyi Jie
Wangu Tower
Manjusri Temple
Gate
Yu's Garden Inn
Guanbi Tower
Mu Family Mansion

© Airphoto International Ltd.

Early morning in Old Lijiang before the shops open their doors

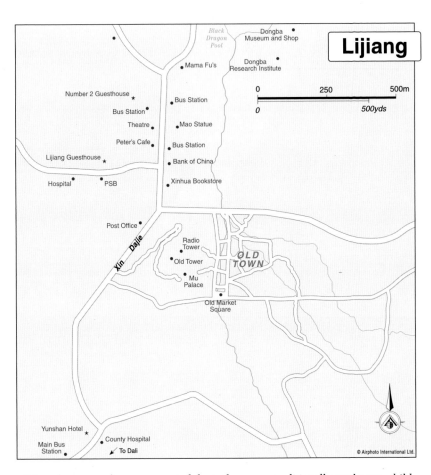

Although men are by no means indolent, they were traditionally gardeners, child-rearers and musicians. In recent years there has been a remarkable resurgence of traditional music, an ancient legacy the Naxi have kept alive since Kublai Khan's invasion in the 13th century. Twenty-two compositions remain from the original repertoire, with sweet, peaceful names such as 'Wind from the River', 'Summer has Come', 'Ten Gifts from God' and 'The Water Dragon is Singing'. At least four full orchestras of elderly men have formed in and around Lijiang. The old instruments are thrilling to see; a weathered transverse flute, a copper gong-frame, Chinese lutes, three-stringed 'banjos', enormous cymbals, a wooden fish-shaped drum. Every visitor should try to spend an evening listening to the marvellous, slow, lilting music.

Men have also always had time to indulge their passion for horses. Lijiang is still known by the nickname Land of Horses. Horses and mules are the focus of two animal fairs every April and September, reminders of grander days when Lijiang formed one end of Tibet's caravan route between India and China. The Naxi acted as middlemen, and at times a quarter of Lijiang's population was made up of Tibetan traders. The main modern road and its freight have bypassed Lijiang. Robbed of their old role, the practical Naxi now profit from their abundant forests which they harvest for timber-hungry China.

The Naxi people have had a long history of interaction with the Chinese and today, under the irresistible force of modernization, contacts are increasing and traditional ways of life are changing fast. Nevertheless, the Naxi still desire to hold onto their cultural roots and in the remote hinterland to the north many customs continue largely untouched by the outside world.

Getting to Lijiang

Lijiang lies 196 kilometres north of Dali. The trip takes half a day by bus and as little as three hours by private car. Several buses leave from Xiaguan's main bus station each morning; most stop in Dali and some originate from there.

Traversing the Dali Plain at sunrise, cutting through the early morning mist, with the mountains and lake all around, is a memorable experience. The road starts to climb at Upper Gate (Shangguan), the strategically important town that has always guarded Dali's northern approach. Peaceful Erhai Lake is soon out of sight. Jianchuan is the first large town along the way, 136 kilometres from Xiaguan. On a clear day the bright, jagged peaks of Lijiang's Jade Dragon Snow Range can be seen on the northern horizon, sharpening the traveller's anticipation. The important Buddhist cave site of Shibaoshan is southwest of Jianchuan. On the west side of the city is a small mountain called Jinhuashan. Half way up its slope the image of a Nanzhao general is carved on a cliff face, and nearby lies a sweet reclining Buddha whose rosy cheeks are created from two naturally formed red stones. Even farther west, on the banks of the Yongfeng River (Yongfenghe), stands the 18th-century Longbaota, a square, nine-tiered pagoda that rises 18 metres. Its outstanding feature is the construction of small external shrines at each storey, with 32 Buddha images in every shrine.

Jianchuan is a county seat, predominantly Bai in its ethnic make-up. It serves as a way-station for buses. The town has a lively street market that occasionally produces remarkable items: ancient agricultural calendars, crude handmade jewellery, and old coins.

The dividing line between the Bai and the Naxi is a high ridge called Iron Armour Mountain (Tiejiashan). The road starts winding up it 24 kilometres after

Jianchuan. Common lore, often borne out by observation, states that there is a preference for all things white south of Iron Armour Mountain, while to the north black is the favoured hue. For example, the Bai and Pumi minorities call themselves 'white', wear bright colours and keep white sheep and goats. Beyond the mountain, the Naxi, Tibetans, Yi, and others favour black. Women's costumes are mainly black or dark blue and domesticated animals are black. Most of their names derive from roots meaning 'black'.

The main north-south road in this part of Yunnan does not go directly to Lijiang; at Baihan Chang a road branches to the right. From here it is 45 kilometres to Lijiang, beginning with a long climb through azalea and rhododendron forests and including a wonderful straight section with an unobstructed view of the Jade Dragon Snow Range. The bus terminal is at the southwest edge of New Lijiang.

An airport has now been completed to the southeast, halfway between Lijiang and Heqing. After some teething problems regular flights to most major cities in China began leaving in early 1996. Flights to Kunming, of which there are several a day, take about 40 minutes.

FOOD AND DRINK IN LIJIANG

Naxi cuisine may seem indelicate; it depends on corn, wheat, beans and some rice, all of which conform to the short growing season, while the main meat is pork.

The national dish is called *baba*. There is a Naxi ditty praising the bounty of the three big local towns: Heqing for wine, Jianchuan for pretty girls, Lijiang for *baba*. *Baba* is a thick, fried wheat cake with many kinds of filling: meat, onions, jam, melted sugar, honey, pork fat. A variation is *nuomi baba*, a smallish, chewy pancake of glutinous rice stuffed with something sweet. Some *babas* are really quite good and perfect for taking on picnics.

The Naxi make palatable wine which they drink from childhood. Honey wine (*yinjiu*) is a smoky, nutty, honey-flavoured wine somewhat like sherry. Before the communist revolution of 1949, wine shops, run by women, abounded in towns, where men spent endless hours gossiping. *Yinjiu* is now bottled commercially, for local distribution, and can be bought at stalls throughout Lijiang.

SIGHTS IN THE LIJIANG REGION
BLACK DRAGON POOL (HEILONGTAN)

At the north end of town, directly under the steep slope of Elephant Hill, is Black Dragon Pool, the best known and most frequently visited park in Lijiang. Walkways lined with willow and chestnut trees surround the pool, which is really a small lake or pond. Lijiang's picture-postcard view incorporates a willow, Black Dragon Pool, Moon-Embracing Pavilion and the towering Jade Dragon Snow Mountain as a backdrop.

(opposite) Moon-embracing Pavilion at Black Dragon Pool in Lijiang, with Jade Dragon Snow Mountain (Yulongxue Shan) in the background; (following pages) traditional Naxi musicians in Lijiang

MARKETS AND WINESHOPS

*S*tarting in distant villages early in the morning, the streams of farmers began to emerge on Likiang [Lijiang] soon after ten o'clock, along five main roads. The streets were jammed with horses loaded with firewood; people bringing charcoal in baskets on their backs and others carrying vegetables, eggs and poultry. Pigs were either carried, tied up, on poles by two men, or led by women, who held the leash in one hand and gently prodded the animal with a switch in the other. Many other kinds of merchandise were carried either on the backs of the people themselves or on their animals. There was the noise of hooves on hard stone, loud talk, shouting and much laughter. In the market itself there was great tumult with all these crowds trying to pass each other and jockeying for the best positions on the square. On the previous night sturdy stalls had already been pulled out of the common pile, or dragged from surrounding shops and set in rows in the centre. Women and girls brought heavy bales of textiles and spread bolts of cloth on the stalls. Haberdashery, spices and vegetables were displayed in separate rows. Shortly after noon the market was in full swing and was a boiling cauldron of humanity and animals. At about three o'clock the market session reached its climax and then began to decline.

Main street was lined with dozens of 'exclusive bars' and thither thirsty villagers, men and women, turned their steps. After a tiring day in the market the numerous tea-shops in Chinese towns and villages are crowded with congenial parties of men and women relaxing over pots of tea. In this respect, the customs of Likiang were quite distinct. There were no tea-shops, and if anyone drank tea at all during the day it was brewed in miniature earthen jugs on the brazier concealed somewhere in the back room. Everyone, men, women and children, drank wine, white or sweet yintsieu. No self-respecting child above two years would go to sleep without a cup of yintsieu.

The 'exclusive bars' were neither bars nor were they exclusive. They were general stores where, in addition to salt, sugar, salted vegetables and haberdashery, wine was kept for sale, both to be taken away in customer's own jars or to be consumed on the premises. The shops were uniformly small in Likiang and, in addition to the counter facing the street, there was a longer counter at a right angle to it, leaving a narrow passage from the door ro the inner rooms of the shop. A couple of narrow benches were put before this counter and there the people sat drinking wine.

Anyone could have a drink at any shop, but some villagers acquired preferences for particular shops. These regular and faithful customers grew intimate with the lady owner, and always gave her the first option on whatever they were bringing to the market for sale. Similarly the lady favoured them with special discounts on whatever they wanted to buy from her. Actually such relations between the established clients and the shop owner were not so simple. The lady also acted as their broker, banker, postmaster and confidante. Baskets with purchases were left in her keeping whilst the customers went out for more shopping. Small loans were negotiated with her on the security of the next deliveries of whatever they usually brought to the market or against growing chickens or pigs. When clients could not pay for their drinks or purchase, credit transactions were permitted by the lady, who got her husband or son to record them in simple Chinese. Wallets with cash were sometimes deposited at the shop for safe-keeping by the farmers whose villages were not safe from robbers. As there was no postal service to remote villages, the wine-shop was a favourite accommodation address. Letters were duly forwarded to the recipients by safe hands. Confidential advice was sought by the clients from the lady on the problems of engagement and marriage, childbirth and funerals. And, of course, every lady wine-shop owner was a Bureau of Information par excellence. She knew the curricula vitae of everybody within a radius of a hundred miles, and I doubt whether there ever existed a secret in Likiang that was not known to her.

Madame Lee was an old woman, very erect, stately and handsome, with aquiline features and large lustrous eyes. She belonged to the cream of Likiang society and was much respected both in the town and in the villages. Everybody knew her and she knew everybody.

It was not easy to get a seat at Madame Lee's shop in the late afternoon. In an emergency she permitted me to sit behind the counter on a small stool, facing the other customers. Men and women came to have a drink or two before starting on their trek back to the village: but in accordance with nakhi customs, no woman sat down in company with a man. Women usually took their drinks standing in front of the shop and chatting meanwhile with Madame Lee. It was quite common for women to treat men to drinks; nobody tried to prevent her from paying the bill. As soon as his drink was finished, a man would go and somebody else would drop into his place. *It was wonderful to sit at the back of the shop in comparative gloom, and watch through the wide window the movement in the narrow street, as though seeing on a screen a colour film of surpassing beauty. Sooner or later everybody who had attended the market session had to pass through Main Street at least once or twice. Old friends could be seen and invited for a drink or new acquaintances made. Any stranger could be waved to and asked to share a pot of wine, without any ceremony or introduction, and I was sometimes stopped in street by total strangers and offered a cigarette or a drink. No such liberties were allowed for women, but now and then one of them, who knew me well, would slap me on the shoulder and say, 'Come and let us have a drink!' and she would have to take her drink standing up so as to avoid a local scandal.*

With the deep blue sky and brilliant sunshine, the street was a blaze of colour, and as we sat and sipped our wine from Madame Lee's porcelain cups, mountain youths, in the sheer joy of life, would dance through the streets playing flutes like the pipes of Pan. They looked wild woodland creatures in their sleeveless jerkins and short skin pants.

Occasionally something would happen to shock or amuse the town. Once, I remember, a stark-naked man appeared in the market and proceeded leisurely up Main Street. I was sitting at Madame Lee's. He went from shop to shop, asking for a drink or a cigarette. Women spat and turned away their faces but nothing was done to stop him. The truth was that the brazen Likiang women could hardly be shocked by anything, but they had to put on some show of modesty and embarrassment in order to avoid acid and biting gibes from the men. A policeman was never to be seen in the streets, and it was only at the end of the day, when somebody bothered to rout one out from the police station, that the demented man was led away. He was not jailed, for there were no laws or statutes in Likiang about indecency in public. Such matters were largely decided by public opinion. One could always go a few hundred yards towards the park and see dozens of naked Tibetans and Nakhi swimming in the river or lying on the grass in the sun in full view of the passers-by and in front of the houses. There was a lot of giggling and whispering amongst the passing women and girls, but there were no complaints. A line, however, had to be drawn against nakedness in the public market.

Peter Goullart, Forgotten Kingdom, 1957

The main entrance is guarded by four stone lions that originally protected the Temple of Mu Tian Wang, now destroyed. Passing through and going to the right, the first building is a library. It was brought to this site in 1982 from its original home at Fuguosi, where it was the second gate hall of that temple. Its reconstruction and repair were well handled by an old Naxi artisan. The building possesses intricately joined, beautifully painted eaves. Fuguosi, formerly 30 kilometres to the west, was the oldest and one of the most important Tibetan monasteries of Lijiang.

The second building, just beyond the library, houses the Dongba Cultural Research Institute (see below).

Further along is Dragon God Temple (Longshenci), now turned into an exhibition hall for seasonal horticultural shows and art displays. It is a 17th-century structure with attractive permanent gardens of forsythia, cherry and bonsai.

The most flamboyant structure within the park is **Five Phoenix Hall** (Wufenglou), built in the first years of the 17th century and moved to this spot from Fuguosi between 1976 and 1979. Together with the library, Wufenglou is all that remains from the temple complex of Fuguosi. This wooden building received the name Five Phoenix Hall from its exaggerated eaves; there are eight flaring roof points on each of the three storeys and an observer is always supposed to see at least five of these 'phoenixes' from any angle.

A new museum, located outside the back gate at the northwestern corner of the park, is filled with exotic and artistic gems. On display are clothes, head-dresses and

A re-enactment of the horse caravans that once passed through Lijiang

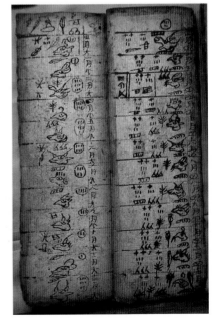

(top) Locals enjoying the afternoon sunshine in a typical Naxi square in a village near Lijiang. (bottom left) Corn with husks braided in preparation for hanging. (bottom right) An example of Dongba scripture on display at the Dongba Research Institute

swords of the *dongbas*, painted scrolls and *dongba* manuscripts, Tibetan prayer wheels and artifacts, and engraved stone tablets, along with charms, amulets and arcane shamanistic accoutrements. The displays are well organized, and include a large relief model of the local landscape, historical maps, photographs and archival publications. An enthusiastic English speaking guide is also on hand to explain aspects of the local culture.

Moon-Embracing Pavilion (Deyuelou) is the serene, beautifully proportioned structure that holds a place of honour next to Black Dragon Pool and the white marble Belt Bridge. The original three-storey pavilion dated from the late Ming dynasty (1368–1644) and survived without significant damage until 1950. In that year, it is told with some glee, a high official took his paramour to Moon-Embracing Pavilion, where together they ate cakes and drank wine until the moon rose. Then the couple spread oil about, ignited it and offered themselves up in a spectacular double suicide, destroying the pavilion in the process. The present pavilion is a reconstruction from 1962. Belt Bridge, originally named because it resembled a mandarin official's belt, was also rebuilt after 1949.

DONGBA CULTURAL RESEARCH INSTITUTE (DONGBA WENHUA YANJIUSHI)

Following the Chinese revolution of 1949, the folklore and history of the Naxi people might have been lost were it not for a few local scholars who started a small museum in 1954. The Yunnan Academy of Social Sciences incorporated it into a formal institute in 1981, the Dongba Cultural Research Institute. Its purpose is to study, document and preserve the ancient Naxi culture of the *dongbas*, religious shamans who played a pivotal role in traditional society. Only 30 or so *dongbas* are still alive, and a handful of these men are attached to the institute. Researchers are primarily engaged in the laborious work of translating thousands of *dongbajing* into Chinese. These small 'booklets', written in an archaic and peculiar script, are read aloud and taken down syllable by syllable; Naxi meaning and grammar are unscrambled and put into Chinese form and finally a proper translation is made. Awaiting scholars are the deeper investigations into the intriguing fields of *dongba* religion, mythology, origination and history.

About a thousand of these booklets were written over the centuries, covering subjects ranging from accounting, through history and mythology, to exorcism and magic. Some 20,000 copies are scattered around the world. The Dongba Institute has approximately 5,000; the rest are held in foreign university collections and a few are in private hands. The goal of the Institute is to preserve, record, and ultimately produce an encyclopaedia of Naxi culture.

A branch of the Yi minority lived under a hierarchical slave society that lasted until the late 1950s. Travellers entered the Great Cool Mountains of Sichuan at their own peril, risking enslavement or death. Today slavery has ended and life under the Chinese government improves steadily for the Yi People. Happily they have not entirely relinquished ethnic individuality, as these girls—wearing the deeply-dyed costume and ornaments—display to charming effect.

FIVE MAIN TEMPLES OF LIJIANG (LIJIANG WUDA MINGSI)

The 17th century was a great period of economic, political and cultural flowering in Lijiang. This renaissance is embodied in the life and works of Celestial King Mu, Mu Tian Wang, a ruler descended from the ancient lineage of Naxi chiefs. Mu Tian Wang came to power in 1598 at the age of 11 and within two decades had chalked up a string of accomplishments that would be added to as his reign continued: poet and author, and an exemplary administrator who supervised large public works and enriched the entire region, he was appointed guardian of China's frontiers and pacified rebels and brigand tribes. The Ming Empire lavished deeds and titles upon him, built arches and town gates in his honour, and held up this non-Chinese as a model for other border peoples to emulate.

For all these worldly achievements, Mu Tian Wang was a deeply religious man who championed Buddhism through printing and publishing Buddhist works and through the support of communities of monks. He had a direct hand in the construction of major temples around Lijiang and paid for the establishment of an important monastery on Chicken Foot Mountain (Jizushan) in the area east of Dali.

His contributions were for the propagation of the Karmapa school of Tibetan Buddhism. The practices of this school, dating from the mid-12th century, have always been closely bound up with the life of the common people, aiming not so much at theoretical knowledge as at its practical realization. Yoga and magic were frequently employed in Lijiang, on the wild border of Tibet, mixing with, and borrowing from, the dongba religion.

The main temples described below, patronized by Mu Tian Wang in the 17th century, are (or rather, were) all embodiments of the Karmapa school.

Jade Summit Temple (Yufengsi) lies 11 kilometres northwest of Lijiang high up on a mountainside in the midst of pine woods, commanding a magnificent view over the valley. The group of buildings with white and grey tiled roofs is connected by stone steps and paths on several terraced levels. The first large hall on the left is the main Buddha hall, now acting as a friendly teahouse. It has remnants of Tibetan-style murals. To the right is a small cluster of enclosed buildings with a shrine containing a strange assortment of faded pictures.

The one superior building, at the highest level of the temple complex, deserves slow savouring. Its courtyard is laid out in beautiful geometric pebbled designs, doors and windows are finely carved, and in the middle, close to the entrance, grows a remarkable centrepiece, an enormous and ancient camellia tree famous throughout Yunnan. Each year in late February or early March it unfailingly opens to display '20,000 blossoms'. Whether this number is actually correct becomes insignificant in the face of such a tour de force of nature. Everyone far and wide cherishes this tree so it is essential to avoid Yufengsi on overcrowded Sundays.

Temple of Universal Benefaction (Pujisi) sits above the village of Pujicun, five kilometres northwest of Lijiang. From the plain it takes half an hour to climb through a maze of steep goat trails to reach the temple. Don't give up; local herdsmen will point you in the right direction. Two huge trees, Chinese flowering crab apple (*haitang*), stand within the courtyard. Beyond them is the Buddha hall, formerly desecrated, but still containing murals, Buddha images and thankas, Tibetan painted scroll-banners presenting pictorial instruction on theology, astrology, and the lives of Buddhas, saints and deities. There are ruins above Pujisi that offer a fine view over the green and yellow fields far, far below.

Peak of Culture Temple (Wenfengsi) lies under the unmistakable landmark of Calligraphic Brush Mountain (Wenbishan) nine kilometres south of Lijiang. The mountain, steep and pointed, is the most conspicuous within the Huangshan Range. The road to Wenfengsi passes through Baihua, the richest village in the entire region. At the foot of the mountain it begins a long climb along a rugged dirt track. It is much nicer to leave the vehicle here and walk straight up to the temple through orchards and woods, silent save for the birds. This once-famous complex was ruined in the 1960s, then rebuilt, and is now looked after by two old monks. It is still a marvellous and holy place, hidden within a glade surrounded by giant, shady trees. There remain some gems of painting and carving: Tibetan mandalas and writing, the Eight Sacred Emblems of Buddhism, roof murals (still bright and beautiful) and six central square red columns with lotiform capitals.

Wenfengsi was a centre for occult and ascetic practices. Just above the temple at the edge of the forest is a sacred spring where initiates underwent an amazing training. A simple hole in the earth nearby became the home of an ascetic who would proceed to spend three years, three months and three days within, meditating, chanting, praying and doing battle with psychic demons. Local monks would think nothing of striking out on foot for a two- or three-year walk to the great pilgrimage sites of Tibet. If you want a good hike, it is a three-hour walk from the temple to the top of holy Wenbishan.

Zhiyunsi, the fourth main temple, has been converted into a school for the children of Lashiba, a town southwest of Lijiang. Nothing remains of **Fuguosi** (Kingdom of Blessing Temple), oldest of the five temples, except for one small house. Two important buildings were transported intact from the original site to Black Dragon Pool Park in Lijiang.

BAISHA VILLAGE AND GREAT PRECIOUS STOREHOUSE TEMPLE (DABAOJI GONG)
Baisha is the most important village on the plain north of Lijiang. It was the Naxi capital before Kublai Khan came south to claim this region as part of the Yuan

Empire (1279–1368), at which time Lijiang was made the centre. The name Baisha is the sinicized form of Boashi, which means 'dead Pumi', a reference to the victorious battle and slaughter of the Pumi tribe in ancient times.

Great Precious Storehouse Temple (Dabaoji Gong) is also known as Coloured Glaze Temple (Liulidian). It can be found near the village school, which is itself a converted temple. The complex was built and decorated over a period of more than 200 years, from 1385 to 1619, employing the eclectic artistic energies of Chinese Daoists, Tibetan and Naxi Buddhists and local *dongba* shamans. This rich fusion has resulted in a tremendously powerful art, heavy in spirit and awe-inspiring in its presentation of the mystical world. Dominated by black, silver, dark green, gold and red colours, the murals in the back hall, overlaid with centuries of brown soot, are doom-laden and bizarre. The scenes and figures, some still vivid in detail, are largely taken from Tibetan Buddhist iconography and include the Wheel of Life, judges of the underworld, the damned, titans and gods, Buddhas and bodhisattvas. There are trigrams, lotus flowers and even Sanskrit inscriptions on the ceiling. The deliberate damage done to the paintings is apparent and terrible, but the loss of the irreplaceable wooden statuary that filled the temple, of which there is no trace, is even more tragic.

A separate building called Pavilion of Great Calm (Dadingge) stands outside the front wall of the main temple. Although built later, in the Qing dynasty (1644–1911), it is considered part of the whole grouping, and though damaged has some exquisite, delicate paintings of flowers, birds and jewellery.

JADE DRAGON SNOW RANGE (YULONGXUESHAN)

The formidable Jade Dragon Mountains dominate the Lijiang Plain, defining its western edge with their towering mass that culminates in Shanzidou peak, at 5,596 metres. The mountains' western flanks drop steeply to the Upper Yangzi River (Jinsha Jiang), forming the impressive Tiger Leaping Gorge. Storms frequently rage around the cliffs, permanent snowfields and glaciers of the five primary summits. However, the alpine meadows on the lower slopes, where herders sing to their goats and cattle and collectors of wild medicinal herbs go happily about their business, are excellent hiking country. Such excursions are a natural extension of visits to the many temple sites around Lijiang. There is a new gate to the area with an entrance fee to finance more 'improvements'.

One of the new features is the Dongba Golf Resort with a clubhouse dominated by a large totem sculpture of Ding Ba Shi Luo, the shaman founder of the Naxi Dongba religion.

The road leading to the village of Nguluko, just north of Lijiang, where the pioneering American botanist, explorer and photographer, Joseph Rock, made his home

One of Joseph Rock's servants sits outside the American's old home in Nguluko, outside Lijiang,
during Bruce Chatwin's visit in 1985, after which Chatwin wrote his well-known article,
Rock's Kingdom *(see excerpt on pages 148–56)*

NGULUKO, THE HOME OF JOSEPH ROCK

Nguluko (Chinese: Xuesongcun, Snow Pine Village) is a small, typical Naxi village, whose lovely name in the local language means 'at the foot of the silver stone mountain'. It lies slightly north of Jade Lake Village (Yuhucun) and is unremarkable except for being touched by a remarkable man.

In 1922 an Austro-American botanist and explorer named Joseph Rock arrived in Lijiang and made this area his home, on and off, for the next 29 years. He was a contrary man of tremendous energy and terrible temper who lived like a foreign prince in the wilds of western China, always engaged in activities from plant collecting and surveying to photography and linguistics. His prodigious output of articles and books and contributions to several sciences is impressive. He will probably be best remembered for the introduction of innumerable plant species to the West and his rigorous works on Naxi ethnology, in particular for compiling the only dictionary of the Naxi language.

Nguluko, Rock's country home, was where he kept his retinue of a dozen Naxi servants perpetually busy, pressing plants for herbaria, summing up the discoveries and specimens of the last expedition or preparing for the next one. His house still stands, and is today owned by the family of Li Wenbiao, Rock's own muleteer. Here is the site of the accomplishments of a strange and splendid man. The house is a good example of Naxi domestic architecture; a wall and gateway that open onto a three-sided courtyard, the residence ahead, and the wood and animal shelters aside.

DRY SEA (GANHAI)

The Dry Sea is a section of the Lijiang plain 22 kilometres north of the city that receives less rain than other areas. The road runs straight through the middle of the valley, parallel to the mountains on the left. This is the road to Daju. Agriculture is replaced by the rock-strewn plain of Amendu, a curious name meaning 'Rocks Without Tails'. The road rises slowly but steadily until it crosses a gentle pass and breaks up into random tracks that crisscross one another in a dry 'sea' of short brown grass, sand and pebbles. Scattered, solitary pines break the monotony as the road skirts the base of the mountains, giving an exceptionally close view of the Jade Dragon massif.

BLACK WATER, WHITE WATER (HEIBAISHUI)

The road picks up again at the far edge of the Dry Sea and climbs into the mountains past vistas of long, forested valleys with no sign of human habitation. Water is finally reached after several kilometres at the swift river of White Water (Baishui), named for the white stones in the riverbed. The limestone, washed down from mountain peaks, sometimes contains recognizable coral, proof that this land was once covered by the ocean. Further up the mountain rushes Black Water (Heishui) in a bed of black rock. Tradition dictates that you drink only the white water.

At Bai Shui Creek, teams of horses with Yi trail leaders offer rides up the mountain. Cable car rides are also available to the Jade Dragon Mountain Glacier and Spruce Meadows and from Mao Niu Ping to a yak grazing meadow run by Tibetan families.

Roads and logging camps in the area have changed traditional patterns of tribal interaction and now Naxi meet and mingle with the indigenous Yi, who, with 30 branches and distribution over four provinces, are China's fourth largest minority.

Heishui is also a small Yi community high in the hills north of Lijiang, with a population of perhaps 250 people. The village is close to the pine forests that rise steeply up the Jade Dragon slopes, and the immediate area is composed of fields cleared by the locals for potatoes, corn, and their small flocks and herds. Terracing and fences protect the fields and plots from erosion and animals.

Women as well as men wear the black felt cloak. They live in the most primitive fashion; their houses made of pine boards, tied together with vines, are not much better than pigsties… When not occupied cultivating their land, they hold up lonely travellers and rob their Naxi and Chinese neighbours. Joseph Rock, 1935

IN LIJIANG: ROCK'S KINGDOM

*I*t is a cold, sunny Sunday in Yunnan. On the plain below Jade Dragon Mountain, the villagers of Baisha are letting off fire-crackers to celebrate the building of a house, and the village doctor is holding a feast in his upper room, in honour of his firstborn grandson.

The sun filters through the lattices, bounces off rafters hung with corn-cobs and lights up everyone's faces. Apart from us, almost all the guests are members of the Naxi (Nakhi) tribe.

The Naxi are the descendants of Tibetan nomads who, many centuries ago, exchanged their tents for houses and settled in the Lijiang Valley, to grow rice and buckwheat at an altitude of over 8,000 feet. Their religion was—and surreptitiously still is—a combination of Tibetan Lamaism, Chinese Daoism and a far, far older shamanistic belief: in the spirits of cloud and wind and pine.

The Doctor has seated us, with his four brothers, at the table of honour beside the east window.

Below, along the street, there are lines of weeping willows and a quick-water stream in which some pale brown ducks are playing. Led by the drake, they swim furiously against the current, whiz back down to the bridge and then begin all over again.

The panelled housefronts are painted the colour of ox blood. Their walls are of mud brick, flecked with chaff, and their tiled roofs stretch away, rising and sagging, in the direction of the old dynastic temple of the ancient kings of Mu.

None of the Doctor's brothers look the least bit alike. The most vigorous is a leathery, Mongol-eyed peasant, who keeps refilling my bowl of firewater. The second, with bristly grey hair and a face of smiling wrinkles, sits immobile as a meditating monk. The other two are a tiny man with a wandering gaze and a shadowy presence under a fur-lined hat.

Looking across to the ladies' table, we are amazed by the fullfleshed, dimpled beauty of the young girls and the quiet dignity of the older women. They are all in traditional costume, in the celestial colours—blue and white. Some, it is true, are wearing Mao caps, but most are in a curved blue bonnet, rather like a Flemish coif. Our Shanghai friend, Tsong-Zung, says we might well be guests at Bruegel's 'Peasant Wedding'. Apart from the bonnet, the women's costume consists of a blue bodice, a *pleated white apron and a stiff, quilted cape secured with crossbands. Every Naxi woman carries the cosmos on her back: the upper part of the cape is a band of indigo representing the night sky; the lower, a lobe of creamy silk or sheepskin that stands for the light of day. The two halves are separated by a row of seven disks that symbolize the stars—although the sun and moon, once worn on either shoulder, have now gone out of fashion.*

Girls come up from the kitchen with the sweet course: apples preserved in honey, melons in ginger, sour plums in alcohol. More girls then come with the Nine Dishes—the Nine Dragons, as they've been called since the Zhou (Chou) Dynasty: in this case, cubes of pork fat and winter sausage, water chestnuts, lotus root, carp, taros, bean tops, rice fritters, a fungus known as tree ears, and a heap of tripe and antique eggs that go, like sulphur bombs, straight to the gut.

From time to time, the Doctor himself appears at the head of the stairs, in a white clinician's mobcap and silver-grey cotton greatcoat. He surveys the company with the amused, slightly otherworldly air of a Daoist gentleman-scholar, and flicks his wispy beard from side to side. As soon as the meal is over, he appears again, hypodermic in hand, as if to remind us that healing, even on the 'Big Happy Day' is work without end.

The grandson's name is Deshou: 'De' for virtue, 'Shou' for longevity. On a sheet of red paper, now pinned to the porch, the old man has written the following:

> The grandfather grants his grandson the name 'Deshou'.
> De is high as the Big Dipper.
> Shou is like the southern mountain.
> De is valued by the world.
> Shou is respected by men.
> De is an oily rain.
> Shou the fertilized field.
> Long life and health to him, born 10.30am, 9th Moon, 14th Day.

The focus of all this adoration is swaddled in a length of gold-and-purple Tibetan brocade, and has the face of a man born wise. He is on show downstairs, in his mother's lap. The bedroom has white-papered walls to which are pasted scarlet cut-outs of characters representing happiness and of butterflies flying in pairs.

Apart from the Doctor's herbal and his English dictionary, the swaddling clothes are the family's only treasure to survive the Cultural Revolution, when Red Guards ransacked the house.

The Doctor takes the baby and cradles him in his arms.

'I have plenty,' he says, gesturing to the revellers in the courtyard. 'Six years ago I had nothing. But now I have plenty.' His wife comes from the kitchen and stands beside him. And with her deep blue bonnet, and smile of tender resignation, she reminds us of Martha or Mary in a Florentine altarpiece.

The Red Guards stripped him of everything, and he was forbidden to practise. 'It was she who saved me,' he says. 'Without her I could not have lived.'

Their son, the father of three weeks' standing, is a young man of 27 in a neat blue Chinese suit. He is a self-taught teacher of English, and now also a student of medicine.

Proudly, he shows us his wedding cup—a porcelain bowl painted with peacocks, on which the village calligrapher has added a couplet by the Tang poet Bai Juyi:

One only wishes that people will live forever
And be in couples even at a distance of 1,000 li.

The calligrapher—a courteous, hook-nosed old gentleman—is the Doctor's cousin and also one of the party. He has spent many years, as an ideological bygone, in jail. But now—in this new, relaxed, undoctrinaire China—he has retired to his tiny house by the stream: to practise the arts of seal cutting, brush-work and the culture of orchids. On Tuesday, when we called on him, he showed us a lilac autumn crocus with a label in Chinese reading 'Italian autumn narcissus'.

The Doctor, too, is a passionate plant collector, though of a rather different stamp. Behind his surgery is a garden with paths of pebblemosaic where a plum tree casts its shadow, like a sundial, on the whitewashed walls, and there are raised beds for growing medicinal herbs. Most of the herbs he has gathered himself, from the slopes of the Snow Range: heaven's hemp (for the bladder); orchid root (for migrane); Meconopsis horridula (for dysentery); and a lichen that will cure shrunken ovaries, or bronchitis if taken with bear's grease.

He owes much of his botanical knowlegde to his student days in

The doctor and his family during the meeting with Bruce Chatwin in 1985. His wife holds their firstborn grandson, Deshou, wrapped in Tibetan brocade, while the doctor clutches his faithful English dictionary. The doctor's son and his wife stand behind, together with the nursemaid.

Nanjing. But some he learned from the strange, solitary European—with red face, spectacles and a terrible temper—who taught him his first smattering of English; at whom, as his retinue passed up the village street, the boys would clamour: 'Le-Ke! Le-Ke!'—'Rock! Rock!'—and scamper out of reach.

Joseph F. Rock—'Dr. Lock' as the Naxi remember him—was the Austro-American botanist and explorer who lived in the Lijiang Valley, off and on from 1922 to 1949. He is our excuse for coming here. My interest in him goes back many years to a summer evening in the Arnold Arboretum in Boston, when I found that all the trees I liked best bore Rock's name on their labels.

'Tell me,' the Doctor asked on a previous visit, 'Why was Le-Ke so angry with us?'

'He wasn't angry with you,' I said. 'He was born angry.'

I should perhaps have added that the targets of his anger included the National Geographic magazine (for rewriting his prose), his Viennese nephew, Harvard University, women, the State Department, the Guomindang, Reds, red tape, missionaries, Holy Rollers, Chinese bandits and bankrupt Western civilization.

Rock was the son of an Austrian manservant who ended up as majordomo to a Polish nobleman, Count Potocki. His mother died when he was six. At 13, already under the spell of an imaginary Cathay, he taught himself Chinese characters. I like to think that, from the library of his father's employer, he read, and acted on, Count Potocki's novel of aristocrats in far-flung places: 'The Saragossa Manuscript'.

Tuberculosis not withstanding, young Rock ran away to sea: to Hamburg, to New York, to Honolulu—where, without training, he set himself up as the botanist of the Hawaiian Islands. He wrote three indispensable books on the flora, then went to Burma in search of a plant to cure leprosy. He 'discovered' Lijiang, thereafter to be the base for his travels along the Tibetan border: to the former kingdoms of Muli, Choni and Yungning, and to the mountain of Minya Konka, which, in a moment of rashness, he claimed to be the highest in the world. (He had miscalculated by about a mile.) Yet, though he introduced hundreds of new or rare plants to Western gardens and sent off thousands and thousands of herbarium specimens, he never wrote a paper on the botany of China.

Instead, he gave his life to recording the customs, ceremonies and the unique pictographic script of his Naxi friends. Lijiang was the only home he ever knew; and after he was booted out, he could still write, in a letter, 'I want to die among those beautiful mountains rather than in a bleak hospital bed all alone.'

This, then, was the meticulous autodidact, who would pack David Copperfield in his baggage to remind him of his wretched childhood; who travelled 'en prince' (at the expense of his American backers), ate off gold plate, played records of Caruso to mountain villagers and liked to glance back, across a hillside, at his cavalcade 'half a mile long'.

His book The Ancient Nakhi Kingdom of South-West China, with its eye-aching genealogies and dazzling asides, must be one of the most eccentric publications ever produced by the Harvard University Press.

Here is a stretch of his embattled prose: 'A short distance beyond, at a tiny temple, the trail ascends the red hills covered with oaks, pines, Pinus armandi, P. yunnanensis, Alnus, Castanopsis delavayi, rhododendrons, roses, berberis, etc., up over limestone mountains, through oak forest, to a pass with a few houses called Ch'ou-shui-ching (Stinking water well). At this place many hold-ups and murders were committed by the bandit hordes of Chang Chiehpa. He strung up his victims by the thumbs to the branches of high trees, and tied rocks to their feet; lighting a fire beneath he left them to their fate. It was always a dreaded pass for caravans. At the summit there are large groves of oaks (Quercus delavayi)…'

No wonder Ezra Pound adored it!

Pound appears to have got hold of Rock's Nakhi Kingdom in 1956, at a time when he was locked up as a lunatic in St. Elizabeth's Hospital in Washington; from it, he extrapolated the upland paradise that was to be, in effect, his lifeline.

Over the last week we have been walking the roads of Lijiang country and finding, to our delight, that the world Rock 'saved us for memory'— to say nothing of Ezra Pound's borrowings—is very far from dead.

At Rock's former lodgings in Lijiang town, we have seen his bookcase, his pigeonhole desk, his wide chair ('because he was so fat!') and the remains of his garden beside the Jade Stream.

At Nuluko (the name means 'the foot of the silver cliffs') his country house is almost as he left it, except that, instead of herbarium specimens, the porch is spread with drying turnip tops. The present occupant, Li Wenbiao, was one of Rock's muleteers; he showed us the master's camp bed and the washhouse where he would set up a canvas bath from Abercrombie & Fitch.

We have been to Tiger Leaping Gorge and seen the cliff line plummeting 11,000 feet into the Yangzi. We have watched the Naxi women coming down from the Snow Range, with their bundles of pine and artemisia; and one old woman with a bamboo winnowing basket on her back, and the sun's rays passing through it:

> Artemisia
> Arundinaria
> Winnowed in fate's tray….
> —'Canto CXII'

The wild pear trees are scarlet in the foothills, the larches like golden pagodas; the north slopes 'blue-green with juniper'. The last of the gentians are in flower, and flocks of black sheep brindle the plain.

> When the stag drinks at the salt spring
> and sheep come down with the gentian sprout….
> —'Canto CXII'

One evening, walking back to town across the fields, I came on a boy and girl reading aloud beside the embers of a fire. Their book was a traditional Chinese romance and, on its open page, there was a picture of Guanyin, Goddess of Mercy.

The Naxi are a passionate people, and even today, rather than submit to a hated marriage, young lovers may poison or drown themselves, or jump to their death from the mountain.

At the Naxi Institute in Lijiang, we were shown a pair of pine saplings, adorned like Christmas trees, commemorating two people who killed themselves for love. Rock wrote that such suicides become 'wind-spirits', reminding Pound of Dante's Paolo and Francesca, whose shades were 'so light on the wind,' and who, readers of the Inferno will remember, fell in love while reading a romance of chivalry.

At Shigu, where the Yangzi takes a hairpin bend, we have seen the Stone Drum:

> by the waters of Stone Drum,
> the two aces….
> —'Canto CI'

The drum is a cylinder of marble in a pavilion by the willows. The 'aces' refers to two Chinese generals—one lost in legend, the other of the Ming Dynasty, whose victory is recorded on the drum itself. Our friend Tzong-Zung raised his hand to the surface and rattled off the characters:

> Snowflakes the size of a hand
> Rain joining sunset to sunset
> The wind quick as arrows....
> Commands quick as lightning
> And the bandits loose their gall....
> Their black flag falls to the earth....
> They run for their lives....
> Heads heaped like grave mounds
> Blood like rain....
> The dikes choked with armour and rattan shields
> The trail of foxes and the trail of jackals
> Have vanished from the battlefield....

Rock wrote of a tradition that, should the Stone Drum split, a catastrophe will fall on the country. About fifteen years ago, some Red Guards did, indeed, split it. (It has since been stuck together.) We wondered if, secretly, the iconoclasts had seen the foxes and jackals in themselves. We have listened to a Naxi orchestra that in the bad years would practise in secret: on a stringless lute, a muffled drum and a flute tuned at a right angle to the mouthpiece.

In the hills above Rock's village is the Jade Summit Monastery, Yufengsi, where we have sat with the lama hearing him tell how he would sneak into the monastery at night, on pain of prison or worse, to save the 500-year-old camellia that stretches, trained on a trellis, around the temple court.

Of all the places we have seen, the monastery seems the loveliest. But this is what Rock had to say of it: 'It is the home of rats, whose excrements lie inches deep... dangerous to visit... books wrapped in dusty silks... the most forlorn and forsaken lamasery I know of.'

Also paying his respects to the lama was the Regional Commissioner for Monuments. I asked him about the horribly battered temple, dating from the Tang Dynasty, which we could see in the valley below. It is dedicated to the mountain god, Saddo, lord of the Snow Range, and protector from calamities.

The Commissioner answered, emphatically: 'The restoration will begin next month,' as if also to say that the world's oldest, subtlest, most intelligent civilization has now returned to the sources of its ancient wisdom.

In the village of Baisha, around the corner from the Doctor's house, there is another, smaller temple, its garden desolate, its cypresses fallen, its balustrades smeared with graffiti: 'Confess and we will be lenient!'

Here, under Daoist symbols of the Eternal Return, the Red Guards set up their so-called courts. Yet it occurred to us that these ill-tempered scrawls were not, after all, so distant from the spirit of the Daodejing (Tao-te-ching) of Laozi (Lao-tze):

> How did the great rivers and seas gain dominion over the hundred
>   lesser streams?
> By being lower than they.

The sun goes down behind the mountain, and we must, finally, say goodbye to the Doctor. He is anxious to give me from his pharmacy a plant with the windblown name of 'Saussurea gossipiphora', which only grows on the snow line. Soon, he hopes to leave his practice in the care of his son and be free to gather herbs in the mountains. He lifts his eyes to Jade Dragon Peak and, suddenly, in his silver greatcoat, becomes the living image of my favourite upland traveller, the poet Li Bo (as he appears in later pictures):

> You ask me why I live in the gray hills.
> I smile but do not answer, for my thoughts are elsewhere.
> Like peach petals carried by the stream, they have gone
> To other climates, to countries other than the world of men.

Bruce Chatwin was an eminent novelist and travel writer. His books include *The Songlines*, *In Patagonia*, *On the Black Hill* and *The Viceroy of Ouidah*. This article first appeared in the *New York Times Magazine* (16 March 1986), as '*In China: Rock's Kingdom*'. He died in 1989.

The roughcut timber, planks and clothing can still be found here, though influence from the 'big city' of Lijiang is evident. Smoky fires still form the centre of family life. Heishui is a good point of departure for high pastures, forests and ridges of the mountains.

BEYOND HEIBAISHUI

Downstream from the confluence of Heibaishui lies the small community of Jiazi, and further still downstream the fascinating town of Dadong, a traditional Naxi community. Twenty kilometres to the northeast of Dadong on the Yangzi lies Hongmenkou, the site where Kublai Khan's army made the treacherous river crossing on inflated skin boats in the 13th century to conquer the Dali Kingdom. Farther north still is the ancient walled town of Baoshan Gu Shi Cheng (Baoshan Ancient Stone City), one of the last of its kind in China.

BAOSHAN STONE CITY

Nearly 130 kilometres northeast of Lijiang lies the remarkable community of Baoshan Shi Gu Cheng (Baoshan Ancient Stone City), usually called Baoshan, but not to be confused with the much larger Baoshan, the main city of western Yunnan, southwest of Dali. This Baoshan has only 100 families. It occupies a dazzling site,

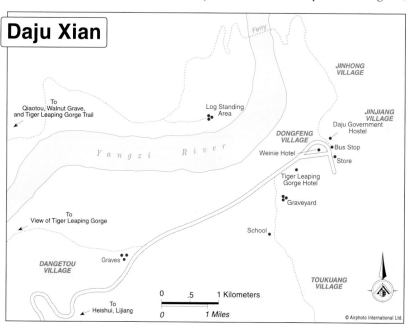

high on a ridge overlooking the Upper Yangzi River (Jin Sha Jiang), surrounded by tightly ascending terraced fields. Many of the houses are carved in the solid rock or have sections built of the red stone. Some even have tables, stools, beds and cupboards cut from the rocky ridge.

DAJU XIAN

Daju is a collection of isolated Naxi villages on an extensive plain near the northern end of Tiger Leaping Gorge beneath the Jade Dragon Snow Range. It is a region of stark beauty amidst nature's hugeness. Haba, second tallest mountain of the range and only one on the far side of the Yangzi, is across the water where the Tibetan counties of Yunnan begin. Daju is famous and necessary for the ferry crossing that leads to the Tiger Leaping Gorge trail.

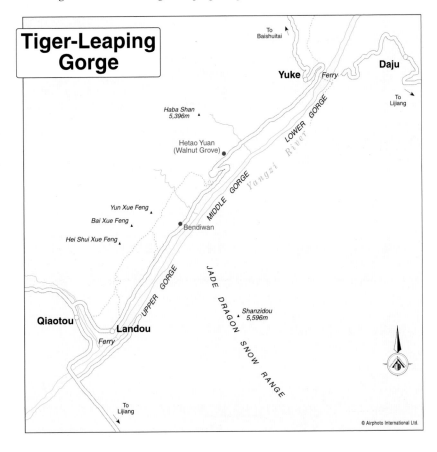

UPPER REACHES

YUNNAN PROVINCE

The Jinsha Jiang leaves the wide and open valley after the First Bend at Shigu and enters the narrow confines of Tiger Leaping Gorge. Jade Dragon Snow Mountain rises to the right.

TIGER LEAPING GORGE (HUTIAOXIA)

After the renowned Three Gorges (Sanxia) in Sichuan and Hubei, Hutiaoxia is the Yangzi's best known gorge. Wedged tightly between titanic cliffs, the river is so narrow here, so legend tells us, that a hunted tiger made his escape to the other side in a single bound. Yunnan's main northern road to Tibet crosses the Yangzi near the gorge at Lunan, 90 kilometres from Lijiang. From Qiaotou it is possible to see how such a geological phenomenon was created: two huge mountains leaning close to each other and a large volume of fast moving water between them cutting deeper and deeper into the bottom of the gorge along a geological fault line between the two massifs. In some places there is a drop of 3,000 metres to the water, a beautiful and vertiginous place to go for a walk.

STONE DRUM (SHIGU)

The village of Stone Drum stands at the First Great Bend of the Yangzi River (Changjiang Diyiwan), 70 kilometres west of Lijiang. (Although the river here is known as the Jinsha Jiang.) The route from Lijiang follows the main road to Dali for 45 kilometres, then branches west and winds downward towards the river through huge forests.

Tiger Leaping Gorge is famed for its tremendous drop, 210 metres within a 17-kilometre stretch. On both sides the Yulong Snow Range and the Harba Snow Mountain rise over 5,000 metres in altitude, making the gorge one of the deepest in the world.

Narrow paths are carved out of the mountainside along the gorges of the upper Yangzi. Here in Tiger Leaping Gorge a mule caravan proceeds cautiously along the precipitous cliff toward a tungsten mine 4,000 metres up the mountain. The path can just be seen running about two-thirds of the way up the cliff face in the photograph opposite.

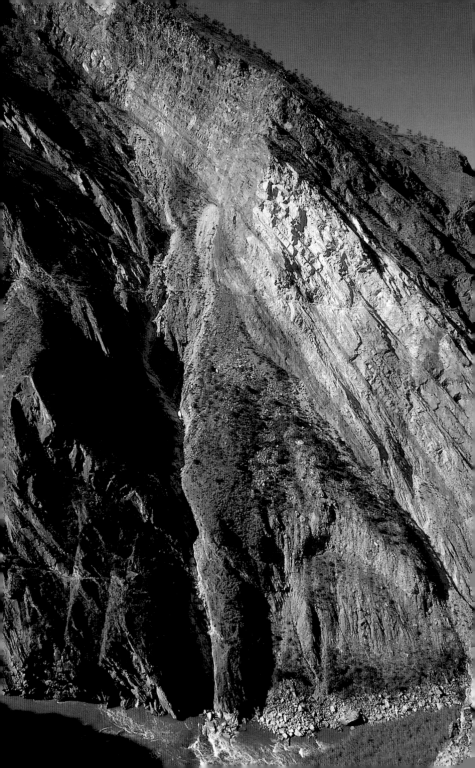

(above) Tiger Leaping Gorge on the upper Yangzi in Yunnan where the river is so narrow a tiger is said to have leapt across on the rocks. (opposite) The Gorge as it appeared in the mid-1980s, before the boom in tourism resulted in a road replacing the walking track seen in the photograph.

The Stone Drum Memorial in Shigu, inscribed with an account of the Chinese and Naxi victory over an invading Tibetan army in 1548, when the Yangzi is said to have flowed red with blood

The approach to Stone Drum offers a dramatic view of the Yangzi's near-180-degree turn, where the wide, swift waters perform a miraculous about-face. The river, first flowing south, turns northward to run parallel to itself for nearly 20 kilometres. Locals say if it were not for their village standing guard at the bend, China would lose the water of the Yangzi to Southeast Asia, like that of the adjacent Mekong and Salween Rivers.

Stone Drum derives its name from a large, cylindrical, marble tablet shaped like a drum, an engraved memorial that honours the Sino-Naxi victory over a Tibetan army in the summer of 1548. It was an awful slaughter on the banks of the river. A Tibetan force of 200,000 men was completely routed and

In April 1936, 18,000 troops of the Red Army crossed the Yangzi at the Great Bend at Shigu with the aid of the local Naxi ferrymen. This monument commemorates this dramatic point in the epic Long March.

dispersed in confusion, and in gory celebration the champions decapitated nearly 3,000 of the enemy. The stone drum recounts it all: '...heads heaped like grave mounds, blood like rain...'

Another military event occurred here in recent times, a small but important chapter in the story of the Long March, Chinese communism's greatest ordeal. After breaking out of the Nationalist encirclement in eastern China at the end of 1934, the Red Army of 100,000 fled westward, embarking on an epic 6,000-kilometre (3,750-mile) march through some of the country's most bitter, rugged land before finding a temporary haven in the loess caves at Yan'an in Shaanxi Province. The main body of the army crossed the Yangzi several hundred kilometres east of Stone Drum, but 18,000 men crossed at this point. The citizenry rose to the occasion, ceaselessly ferrying troops to the northern bank in their boats, 40–60 men per trip. The entire crossing took four days and nights (24–28 April 1936) and is still remembered as the greatest event in the lives of the local Naxi. The prominent marble 'Chinese Workers and Peasants Red Army Second Route Army Long March Ferry Crossing Memorial', with a dramatic bronze statute of a soldier with a boatman, stands on a high promontory with a fine view over the Great Bend of the Yangzi.

Yongning and Lugu Lake

Northeast of Lijiang lies a gem of a lake, Lugu Hu, home to a number of different minority peoples—Moso, Tibetan, Pumi, Yi and others. Though only 110 kilometres away as the crow flies, the road is much longer, just over 280 kilometres, and takes most of a day if travelling by bus. The route passes through Ninglang Yi Autonomous County and a large town of the same name, a fascinating place to meet some of the Yi people and learn of their mountain life. Invitations to visit upland villages are sometimes given.

The lake straddles the Yunnan-Sichuan border, is approximately eight kilometres across and is dotted with five small islands, three of which are considered sacred and visited regularly for sacrificial purposes. The setting is stunning. Steep hills rise along two sides of the lake, whose surface lies at 2,685 metres above sea level, the highest in the province and the second deepest (90 metres) in China (the deepest being Fuxian Hu).

On the lake's Sichuan side, to the north and east, one finds a Babel where the children routinely speak three or four tongues—Moso, Tibetan, Mandarin Chinese and Pumi (Xifan). This region was historically an enclave of Bon, the archaic, pre-Buddhist religion of Tibet that relied heavily on magic and spells over nature. It is still possible to see peculiar towers, up to six metres tall, on the hills outside the main town of Luoshui.

At the top of a 'mast' sits a wooden offering tablet painted with a divinity surrounded by a green halo. Below is a jumble of wire, twine and yarn, looking like a damaged spider web. Amid the jumble one might find many tablets and cloth ties of varied colours. This type of tower is called *nya-ta*, a demon trap to catch and disarm evil forces and protect the crops below. It is also intended to prevent damaging hail. Bonpo monasteries survive as well; one fine wooden temple with murals stands at Zuosuo.

A mountain festival and a lake festival are the two main annual events for the Moso people. The former takes place on the 25th day of the 7th lunar month (usually in August or early September), the latter on the 15th day of the 3rd lunar month (usually late April).

The Plain of Yongning (2,900 metres) lies 20 kilometres west of the lake and is the cultural and agricultural centre of the Moso. Yongning town is unprepossessing, with a single main street, though the surroundings are memorable. To the east rises Lion Mountain (Shizi Shan), the dominant presence on the plain. To the north

(above) For the matriarchal tribe of the Moso, who live on the plain of Yongning, the women within a household reign over the family fortune and family names are passed down from mother to daughters. (opposite) Moso woman in the village of Ninglang, northeast of Lijiang.

stand the purple ranges of Sichuan and all round the verdant fields are crisscrossed with water channels.

It was here on the plain of Yongning that Kublai Khan massed his forces before the decisive, and victorious, battle against the Dali Kingdom in the year 1253. He marched his men southward through red mountains, visible today from the hill known as *La-ba-der*. He camped beneath the hill at a place called Ri Yue He, 'union of sun and moon'. It is possible to climb this steep hill southwest of town to view the famous meadow below, now a field of corn, rice and tobacco. Local legend says the Great Khan himself climbed the hill to review his troops.

Yongning is the home of the Moso, a group long considered a branch of the Naxi, who call these people 'Luxi'. The Moso consider themselves to be a separate group. Historically, the Moso called themselves Hlikhin and are known, somewhat sensationally throughout Yunnan, as a 'the last matriarchal tribe'.

Han Chinese find Yongning and Lugu Hu an intriguing area, based on the perpetuation of myths and tales about this matriarchal system. Prurience plays a part, too. The Moso practice a custom known as *A'xia*, whereby marriage is not announced formally, but rather a loose arrangement of cohabitation goes on for some time with various lovers. Children stay with the mother, as do the powers of decision making and control of money. Often children do not know the identity of their fathers. Men stay in their mother's households with sisters and children, helping to raise the nieces and nephews. The large houses are of wooden log construction and have many rooms for the extended family. Each home will usually have one son who is a monk and leads the family spiritual practices, after training at one of the local monasteries.

In former times the Yongning Monastery (Yongning Lama Si) was the most important building on the plain. It suffered badly during the Cultural Revolution, but was reconstructed with considerable care in 1990. A small chapel to the right of the main temple escaped damage and dates from the monastery's founding in the 17th century. The entire complex was, and remains, a Gelugpa (Yellow Hat) institution of Tibetan Buddhism.

An annual procession called 'Rounding the Mountain' is made in the midsummer to Lion Mountain overlooking Lugu Lake, and leads to the Ganmu Goddess Temple where young males and females go through a puberty rite, with the blowing of horns, beating drums and dancing around a bonfire in the night. The singing can be heard reverberating around the lake and mountains.

A Moso village of log clan houses on the shore of Lake Lugu below Lion Mountain. The lake, 30 kilometres east of the town of Yongning, straddles the Yunnan-Sichuan border. Approximately eight kilometres across, it is home to the Moso, a sub-group of the Naxi, a community which still adheres to its traditional matrilineal society.

A typical landscape of the Zhongdian area in autumn colours

A Tibetan family in Zhongdian

Tibetan Counties of Yunnan

ZHONGDIAN

Zhongdian is the name of both an extensive county and the town that is its capital, which is quickly finding its place on the tourists' map after being renamed Shangri-la, or Xiang-ge-li-la in Chinese, in 2001. (However, the name Zhongdian is still widely used.) It forms one of three counties that make up the Diqing Tibetan Autonomous Prefecture in northern Yunnan Province; Tibetans call their home Gyelthang. The prefecture adjoins Tibet in the northwest, Ganzi and Muli in Sichuan to the north, Lijiang to the south and Nu Jiang (Salween River) Lisu Autonomous Prefecture to the west. It has a population of more than 300,000 and is at the heart of the Hengduan Mountain Range that embraces the gorge systems of the great rivers that rush down from Tibet. The region has a huge range in elevation, from a 6,740-metre mountain on the border with Tibet to 1,480 metres in river valleys to the south. Plant hunters and naturalists during the first half of this century prized the area. Now many of the forests have been stripped, but still large tracts of virgin forest remain. Domesticated animals of the region include yak, *dzo*, sheep, goats, pigs and chickens; wild animals include the golden monkey, wild donkey, black-necked crane, lesser panda, leopard, muskdeer, pangolin, and many small mammals and birds. Hunting is universally loved here and guns are common; most of these rare treasures will struggle to survive.

Wheat, corn, barley and potatoes are the common staples; huge ricks (large wooden frames) for drying barley are a common sight in the harvest season. Mushrooms are prized, both for local consumption and for export, and the collection of herbs, roots and plant products for medicine play an important part in the local economy. Economic minerals—gold, silver, copper, iron, lead, zinc—and timber are major reasons for China's interest in this region.

Zhongdian is a long way from the major tourist destinations, but it should be considered seriously for a visit by anyone who is in northwest Yunnan. Until recently, the journey from Lijiang (200 kilometres) took five or six hours by bus, but an improved road has reduced the trip to around three hours. After Qiaotou and the entrance to Tiger Leaping Gorge, the road climbs steadily along the Xiao Zhongdian He (Small Zhongdian River), through large forests that occasionally give way to stunning vistas of distant mountain valleys enclosing isolated hamlets. Suddenly the bus goes over a final rise and one is miraculously transported onto the

Tibetan Plateau, over 3,000 metres in altitude and characterised by expanses of grass and grazing yaks. The transition from the hot and humid Yangzi River valley to the cooler and drier Tibetan highlands is as dramatic a way to approach Tibet as can be found.

Soon after reaching the plateau, a huge white stupa comes into view on the right. This marks the site where the previous Panchen Lama gave a speech and greeted the locals in the mid-1980s. Fine domestic architecture, fields of colour and rarified air give the run into Zhongdian a magical quality.

Many foreign visitors to the capital of the county (altitude 3,160 metres) are disappointed by what they see, as the reality bears little resemblance to the Shangri-la described in James Hilton's 1933 novel *Lost Horizon*—a pristine sanctuary of culture undisturbed by the turmoil of the outside world. In fact, tourism is growing as robustly here as in Lijiang, and local entrepreneurs have opened Internet cafés, restaurants serving Western food, and hotels with discos in what was once a dusty frontier town.

A single, very long main street holds all the major shops, offices and hotels. Most people here are Tibetans, though Chinese magistrates and lesser officials have resided in Zhongdian since the 18th century. Old Zhongdian, still in local Tibetan style, is situated to the south of the main street. The old town contains some interesting Tibetan-style houses, a walled monastery and a golden-yellow stupa on a hill. The park on the hill offers a panoramic view over the entire town.

The cynical view of the Shangri-la renaming is that it is a hollow marketing ploy designed to draw more tourist income to the region. However, there is also an optimistic view. By embracing the new name, the region has set itself a standard to strive towards: working to harness the forces of development and ecotourism to preserve and enhance both the Tibetan character and natural beauty of the land.

For better or for worse, many foreign travellers' disappointment in the area stems from the fact that they have not ventured far enough outside the city, because contained within the county are areas of pristine wilderness and stunning natural beauty. Such a vast and largely unmapped territory requires knowledgeable guidance, and some entrepreneurial ventures have set their sights on sustainable ecotourism as the future of Shangri-la. Some native Tibetans from the area whose families moved to India fleeing the Chinese Communists, have returned to contribute to the development of the region.

SONGZANLING MONASTERY

This large Yellow Hat (Gelugpa) Tibetan monastery has returned from the ashes and destruction that swept southeastern Tibet in the late 1950s and 1960s. Songsenlin, or Sumtseling Gompa in Tibetan, was founded in the 17th century during the reign

Bullfight at Tacheng, Weixi Lisu Autonomous Prefecture, northwest Yunnan. As part of celebrations for the Spring Festival, Lisu farmers bring their best bulls to compete in bull fights. As waiting bulls moan from the side-lines, two contestants bash heads until one is driven running from the field, often with the winner in hot pursuit.

The arrival of spring is celebrated among the Lisu with many festivities, including bullfights. These Lisu matrons are enjoying a bull fight and the first warm spring weather of February.

of the Great Fifth Dalai Lama, when the Yellow Hat school came to full ascendancy in Tibet. It lies a few kilometres beyond the north end of town and welcomes visitors who behave respectfully.

The monastery once had as many as 1200 monks, and now claims many hundreds, though most of these stay at home and work with their families, only coming together as a single body on rare festival occasions. In 1980 the second delegation sent by the Dalai Lama to investigate conditions in Tibet stayed in Zhongdian, and since then there has been steady reconstruction at this sacred site.

Also at the north end of Zhongdian, to the left of the main road that continues to Benzilan, is the Zhongdian Wooden Bowl Factory (Muwan Chagn). This site churns out thousands of small wooden tea bowls, favoured by Tibetans, as well as larger bowls and special lidded containers used in households to hold sweets, popped rice, seeds or other snacks to offer guests.

The Zhongdian area has a number of Buddhist sites. Red Hat Nyingma centre, outside to the east, is a wonderful secluded monastery in a bower. This second site is a few kilometres to the right of the road that leads southeast to Baidi (Sanba) and the limestone terraces of Baishuitai. The drive from Zhongdian to Baidi takes about three hours through impressive mountain scenery.

(left) Crossing the Yangzi by car ferry. Below the village of Xiaruo is one of the last car ferries across the River of Golden Sand. Plans have been made for a hydro-electric dam to span the river near this site. (right) Girl in Tibetan costume in Tacheng. In northwest Yunnan, where

XIAGEI HOT SPRING

About 12 kilometres to the southeast of Zhongdian is the Xiagei Hot Spring, which emerges from a natural arch below a steep limestone ridge. The turnoff from the main road is marked by a prominent concrete monument erected beside the road. A series of bathing pools have been constructed, surrounded by changing rooms, dormitories, and restaurants. The pools are reached by descending a long flight of concrete steps from the car parking area.

BAISHUITAI (WHITE WATER TERRACE)

In southeast Zhongdian County, across the Upper Yangzi from Daju, 108 kilometres southeast of Zhongdian, and two-days' walk from Tiger Leaping Gorge, is the area known variously as Bada, Baidi or Berder (Naxi). It consists of a broad valley that descends steeply to join the main river 20 kilometres away.

A narrow tributary valley emerges from between snow-capped peaks, dramatically widening and steepening as it enters the main valley above the Naxi village of Baidi. At this point there occurs a series of steep-fronted, yellow-white terraces that are arcuate in plan. Each terrace contains a semi-circular pool of water. The terraces, known as rimstone dams or tufa dams, were formed by the precipitation of calcium carbonate, which is carried in solution by the stream that flows over them. Deposition occurs where vigorous turbulence causes aeration of the water, resulting in de-gassing of the cold mountain waters. The resulting deposit is a solid and crystalline mass termed travertine. Similar alpine karst (cold climate limestone) terraces occur at Huanglong (yellow dragon) in northwestern Sichuan Province. Analogous features, but formed in warmer climates or by geothermal (hot volcanic) waters, occur at Pamukkale in Turkey, at Rotorua in New Zealand, and Yellowstone National Park in the United States.

Climbing up to the site from Baidi, visitors will notice that, below the glistening white terraces, there is a series of lower and shallower terraces to the right of the walkway. These features are a dull grey-white in colour, have a dry and crusty surface, and are no longer fed by the stream. The fact that these once more extensive terraces are now inactive suggests that either rainfall patterns or the characteristics of the feeder stream have changed since they originally developed.

This locality is considered to be a holy spring and is honoured by the local Naxi people, who have implanted painted wooden stakes around its edge. The flow of water, and consequently the extent of the saturated terraces, is at its greatest in March, when thousands of pilgrims and tourists come to picnic and drink the water. Many believe that the waters have curative powers and can help women conceive.

many cultures meet, Tibetan culture is often considered superior to all others. This proud girl is the daughter of a Tibetan father and Lisu mother, and has chosen to adopt the Tibetan costume she wears in preference to the Lisu costume of her neighbours.

BITA HAI AND NAPA HAI

These lakes and their surrounding nature preserves have become popular one or two-day trips for both local and foreign tourists. Bita Hai lies 25 kilometres east of Zhongdian; it is the smaller and more visited of the two. Approximately 23 kilometres from Zhongdian on the road to Baishuitai, there is a turnoff to the left. Take this road for 500 metres to a point where the trail to Bita Hai begins.

Napa is a huge lake situated by the main road north towards Benzilan, about seven kilometres from Zhongdian; the water spreads away far below while yaks graze at the shore. The Napa Hai Nature Reserve is home to a winter community of about 200 rare black-necked cranes.

BENZILAN

Benzilan, two hours by road to the north of Zhongdian, is a small town standing at 1,968 metres on a narrow strip of land on the right bank of the Upper Yangzi, perched on the valley side below sharply rising hills. It is a way-station on the main road north, halfway between Zhongdian and Deqen; the road passes above the farms, wooden houses and small temples of the town. The busy strip of Sichuan style restaurants is constantly visited by cars, trucks and buses. Sichuan Province and the village of Wake lie just across the water but can only be reached by a ferry.

A view of the River of Golden Sand (Jinsha Jiang) near the town of Xiaruo

Near the southern end of town, below the road, is Göchen Gompa, a small Tibetan temple with pretty murals. Walking north through the fields and lanes brings one to a stupa, regularly surrounded by old men and pious women, and another *gompa*.

DONGZHULIN MONASTERY

Twenty-two kilometres north of Benzilan on the main road is Dongzhulin Monastery (Dhondrupling Gompa), the second largest Yellow Hat centre in northwestern Yunnan. The old monastery, destroyed in 1959, stood ten kilometres from here on a remote mountain. It was rebuilt at this conspicuous spot for reasons of convenience; building materials could be brought to the site directly by road. Dongzhulin today has 300 monks and a *tulku* (incarnate lama) named Shumba Tenzing Chenling Choyöng.

DABAO SI

About ten kilometres to the north of Dongzhulin Monastery is Dabao Si, the only Tibetan nunnery in Yunnan. Built in the 1760s, the buildings were destroyed during the Cultural Revolution but restored in 1983. This Yellow Hat sect nunnery is reached by a pleasant half-hour walk up the hillside through a small village.

DEQEN

Deqen is Yunnan's northernmost county, most of which borders Sichuan, but a part in the west abuts Tibet. This border with Tibet is created by a massive mountain wall, running from north to south, known as the Kawa Karpo Range. Its tallest peak, called Meili Xue Shan in Chinese, is the province's highest point at 6,740 metres. The dramatic gorge of the Mekong River defines the range's eastern flank. Numerous mountaineering expeditions have assaulted the main peak, but all have failed. In early 1991, seventeen Japanese and Chinese climbers died in a single avalanche. Experienced mountaineers consider this region to be one of Nature's grandest displays, an enormous land cut by tremendous rivers that form some of the Earth's deepest gorges.

Deqen is also the name of the county seat, formerly known as Atuntze. Like most Tibetan towns, it has an old, traditional section and a new, faceless concrete section that mimicks Chinese settlements. The old town, to the north, is a pleasure to visit, with solid wooden houses and yaks in the alleyways. Deqen has 45 Moslem families; these are Tibetan Moslems, not Hui Chinese. They were mostly linked to the caravan trade that once transported tea, wool, gold, medicines and cloth to and from Lhasa and India. A 'fast' route from Deqen to Sadiya in Assam took only 18 days.

A visit to Deqen should be made for the grand landscapes, mighty mountains and spectacular descents to the river valleys. Buddhist monasteries still exist both close to town and in remote fastnesses.

NAKA TRASHI TEMPLE

Between Deqen and the Kawa Karpo lookout point is the important Tibetan temple of Naka Trashi. Chinese translate the name of this place as Fei Lai Si, 'the temple that flew from afar'. It is considered an eastern anchor of Tibetan religious civilization, and as such it is visited by thousands of pilgrims. Kawa Karpo, White Guardian of the holy mountain, is enshrined here as a statue, riding a white horse with the white mountain rising up under his steed.

DECHENLING MONASTERY

Dechenling is a newly reconstructed *gompa* (monastery) on the outskirts of Deqen, next to the road that descends to the Mekong and Yanmen. The incarnate lama from here is in exile in India. It is a Yellow Hat institution that suffered destruction in the late 1950s. A few fine murals remain, painted on boards that survived nearly four decades of neglect.

Dabao Si, the only Tibetan nunnery in Yunnan was restored in 1983.
The original buildings date from the 1760s.

NATURE AND WILDLIFE ALONG THE UPPER YANGZI

As the Yangzi winds its way from the highlands of Tibet to the sea, it passes a series of ecosystems in succession. At its source and for the first 813 kilometres of its path, it traverses the vast treeless Tibetan Plateau, a region of glacier-capped mountains, marsh-filled basins, grassland pastures, and sandy dune-fields. The source and upper reaches of the river are all inside the huge Snowlands Three Great Rivers Source Nature Reserve in Qinghai, approved as a national level reserve in 2002. In this reserve, where an estimated 25 per cent of the flow of the Yangzi is derived, are also found the sources of the Yellow and Mekong Rivers. Herds of Tibetan Wild Ass and Tibetan Antelope still migrate across the grassy basins here, and in the high mountain valleys herds of Wild Yak and Argali Bighorn Sheep can still be found. Extensive wetlands are breeding grounds for Black-necked Cranes, Bar-headed Geese and thousands of ducks.

As soon as the Yangzi leaves the high plateau, it is hemmed in by deep gorges as it flows south into the confines of the Hengduan Mountain Range. While the bottoms of the gorges are peculiarly dry and support only drought resistant shrubs and holy-leafed oaks, the mountain ridges above are densely forested with old-growth fir and spruce. In a narrow strip of the Hengduan Mountain Range, hemmed in by the Yangzi to the east and the Lancang (Mekong) River to the west, there occurs a unique species of monkey found nowhere else. It has been called the Yunnan Golden Monkey, although it is not golden, and does not only occur in Yunnan. A distant relative of the Hanuman Langur of India, it is better named the Pied Snub-nosed Langur (*Rhinopithecus bieti*), which captures two of its most distinctive characteristics. With long silky black hair on the back, a striking white rump, black limbs and tail, vivid pink lips and a choir-boy cowlick on top of its head, this monkey has become a charismatic symbol for conservation of these mountain forests.

The Pied Snub-nosed Langur is one of the rarest monkeys in the world. Scientists estimate that fewer than 2,000 individuals remain, making it almost as rare as the Giant Panda. The species has been recorded in northwest Yunnan and southeast Tibet, always between the Mekong and Yangzi. Two large nature reserves have been established for its protection, the Markham Nature Reserve in Qamdo Prefecture in Tibet, and the Baima

Snow Mountain Nature Reserve in Diqin Prefecture of northwest Yunnan. The Baima Nature Reserve is one of China's oldest, established in 1983 and made a national level reserve in 1988. With a total area of 2,816 square kilometres, it is also one of China's largest forest nature reserves.

While many nature reserves in China are closed to visitors, Baima Snow Mountain Nature Reserve has begun to encourage tourism as part of its conservation efforts. Nature tourism, it is hoped, can provide an alternative income for local communities living around the reserve, who have been deprived of income from logging and collecting forest goods inside the reserve.

Above Tacheng Village, Weixi Lisu Autonomous Prefecture, in the so-called Experimental Zone of the nature reserve, monkey tourism is being developed. By pre-arrangement, local Lisu guides can take adventurous visitors into the reserve to the beautiful Xianggu Valley. This is one of the few places where visitors can enter the deep forest and try to see the monkeys. Even if the monkeys are not cooperative, the valley boasts majestic views and beautiful forests. Huge forest giants, covered in hanging beards of lichens, loom up through the mist. Leopard, Red Panda, Black Bear, the goat-like Serow, Golden Eagle and White Eared-Pheasant all share these forests with the monkeys, which are also home to the endangered Handkerchief Tree, otherwise known as the Dove Tree (*Davidia involucrata*). In the villages below, local villagers are developing cultural attractions as well, including several examples of traditional Lisu log houses, now preserved as a museum of Lisu culture.

Monkey tourism may help the villagers of Xianggu Valley, but it could also have negative impacts to the monkeys. The slopes are steep and visitors must be in good shape to climb up to the monkeys' habitat and see them in their natural home. Unfortunately, the guides may also try to accommodate visitors who are less fit by chasing the monkeys down the slopes for a fee, disrupting the monkeys' behaviour and ranging. Eco-sensitive visitors should discourage the practice. Instead, they can arrange to stay high in the valley so that local trackers can find the monkeys and lead the visitors to them, rather than herding the monkeys down to the visitors.

Bill Bleisch has been working to conserve wildlife in China since 1987. Over the years, he has conducted research on several of China's most endangered species, including Western Black Gibbons in Yunnan, Grey Snub-nosed Monkeys in Guizhou and Tibetan Antelope in Xinjiang. He is currently China Programme Manager and Indochina Primate Programme Co-ordinator for Fauna and Flora International. When he is not travelling, he lives with his wife in Beijing.

A young Pied Snub-nosed Monkey (Rhinopithecus bieti) sits in a pine tree at Xianggu Valley above Tacheng. Also known as the Yunnan Golden Monkey, these monkeys are found only on the slopes of snow mountains between the upper Yangzi and Mekong rivers. They live in small family groups, each with a single male, one to four females and their off-spring. Family groups and all-male groups combine in large bands of up to 250 individual monkeys. Among the primates, they live in the highest and coldest conditions of any species besides man.

THE LAND OF THE BLUE POPPY

THE MEKONG VALLEY

*T*he weather had now set in fine, and nothing could have been more delightful than these marches up the Mekong valley, for we took matters fairly easily, making four stages from Hsiao-wei-hsi to Tsu-kou. Sometimes the narrow path was enveloped in the shade of flowering shrubs and walnut trees, the branches breasting us as we rode, the air sweetened by the scent of roses which swept in cascades of yellow flowers over the summits of trees thirty feet high; sometimes we plunged into a deep limestone gorge, its cliffs festooned with ferns and orchids, our caravan climbing up by rough stone steps which zigzagged backwards and forwards till we were out of ear-shot of the rapids in the river below; sometimes the path was broken altogether by a scree-shoot, which, dangerous as it looked, the mules walked across very calmly, though sending rocks grinding and sliding down through the trees into the river.

In one gorge through which we passed, large pot-holes were visible across the river between winter and summer water marks and yet others still higher up, forming a conspicuous feature of the otherwise smooth bare cliffs which dipped sheer into the river; but on the left or shaded bank dense vegetation prevailed wherever tree, shrub, or rock-plant could secure a foothold. The further north we went the more rich and varied became the vegetation of the rainy belt, though the paucity of forest trees, except deep down in the gullies, was always conspicuous.

Shales and slates, dipping at very high angles, and often vertical, alternated with limestone, through which the river had cut its way straight downwards; but at one spot, where an enormous rapid had been formed, huge boulders of a dark-green volcanic rock, like lava, with large included fragments, lined the shore and were piled in confusion below cliffs of slate.

It is at sunset that the charm of this wonderful valley is displayed at its best, for the sun having dropped out of sight behind the western range still sends shafts of coloured light pulsing down the valley, rose, turquoise, and pale-green slowly chasing each other across the sky till darkness sets in and the stars sparkle gloriously. It is long after dawn when the sleeping valley wakens to floods of sunlight again, and the peaks which stand

Cham Dance at the Dongzhulin Monastery (Dongdrupling Gompa) near Benzilan. An annual event to mark the end of the harvest season and banish evil spirits which culminates in the unfurling of a holy thangkha displaying sacred images rarey seen in public.

Yellow Hat monks at the Dongzhulin Monastery (Dongdrupling Gompa) near Benzilan, the second largest Yellow Hat centre in northwestern Yunnan.

sentinel over it, blotting out the views to north and south, lose the ghastly grey pallor of dimly-lit snow.

A TIBETAN FESTIVAL

*T*he Tibetan festival itself seemed more in accord with the usages of nat propitiation than with lamaism, except that it was eminently cheerful, and the people, led by their priests, went to the summits of the three nearest hills to east, north, and west in turn, in order to burn incense and pray; after which they ate cakes. The first day however was devoted entirely to the amusement of the children, for Tibetan mothers, as I frequently observed, are warm-hearted creatures with a great affection for their offspring.

Dressed in their best frocks, and wearing all the family jewels brought out for the occasion, they went up into the woods in the afternoon, picked bunches of flowers just as English children love to do, romped, made swings and swung each other, and finally sat down to eat cakes, which they had been busily making for a week past.

Just as the young of different animals more nearly resemble each other than do the adults, so too are children very much alike in their games the world over; picnicking is not confined to Hampstead Heath, nor picking flowers to botanists.

In the evening they all trooped back to the village to dance in the mule square, and skip. Three of four little girls would link arms and facing another similar line of girls advance and retreat by turns, two steps and a kick, singing, in spite of their harsh voices, a not unmusical chorus; the other side would then reply, and so it went on, turn and turn about.

THE LAST OF THE MEKONG

*T*his was the last we were destined to see of the great Mekong river. I was scarcely sorry to say goodbye, for the Mekong gorge—one long ugly rent between mountains which grow more and more arid, more and more savage as we travel northwards (yet hardly improve as we travel southwards)—is an abnormality, a grim freak of nature, a thing altogether out of place. Perhaps I had not been sufficiently ill-used by this extraordinary river to have a deep affection for it. The traveller, buffeted and bruised by storm and mountain, cherishes most the foe worthy of his steel. Nevertheless there was a strange fascination about its olive-green *water in winter, its boiling red floods in summer, and the everlasting thunder of its rapids. And its peaceful little villages, some of them hidden away in the dips between the hills, others straggling over sloping alluvial fans or perched up on some ancient river-terrace where scattered blocks of stone suggest the decay of a ruined civilization—all these oases break the depressing monotony of naked rock and ill-nourished vegetation, delighting the eye with the beauty of their verdure and the richness of their crops.*

Happy people! What do they know of the strife and turmoil of the western world? We wear ourselves out saving time in one direction that we may waste it in another, hurrying and ever hurrying through time as if we were disgusted with life, but these people think of time not in miles an hour but according to the rate at which their crops grow in the spring, and their fruits ripen in the autumn. They work that they and their families may have enough to eat and enough to wear, living and dying where they were born, where their offspring will live and die after them, as did their ancestors before them, shut in by the mountains which bar access from the outer world.

Frank Kingdon-Ward, Himalayan Enchantment, An Anthology, 1990

Frank Kingdon-Ward was born in 1885 in Manchester, where his father was a professor of botany.

After a two-year stint teaching in a Shanghai public school Kingdon-Ward was offered a place on a zoological expedition funded by the Duke of Bedford to journey up the Yangzi in search of new species in western China. On this trip he discovered a new species of mouse and two new shrews as well as sending back a small collection of plants to Cambridge.

In 1911 with the publication of his first book, On The Road to Tibet *he was elected fellow of the Royal Geographical Society and was commissioned to collect plants from Yunnan and Tibet to grow in English gardens. He brought back about 200 different species including 22 new to science, as well as making contributions to Kew Gardens herbarium. His book* The Land of The Blue Poppy *was written about this trip.*

Kingdon-Ward made numerous other expeditions, particularly to Burma, Assam and Tibet, almost until the time of his death in England in 1958.

Sichuan Province

In a half-forgotten local history a Chinese writer once set down these lines in praise of the richness of his homeland:

Both rain and drought follow the will of the people,
Famine is unknown.
Time has never seen a lean year;
Everyone knows it as Heaven on Earth.

'Heaven on Earth' (*Tian fu zhi guo*)—a description dating from the third century —referring to Sichuan, that unique province sprawled across a bit of central and much of southwestern China. From the yak-grazed slopes and scattered alpine meadows of its western plateau to the limestone gorges through which the Yangzi River tumbles eastwards into neighbouring Hubei Province, Sichuan covers a huge area. Slightly larger than France though only one-seventeenth of China's total territory, it is a populous province of more than 90 million people, even after the largest city of Sichuan, Chongqing, and its surrounding region, including the new Three Gorges reservoir area, were separated as a new 'national municipality'.

A glance at a relief map will show Sichuan divided naturally into two distinct parts, western and eastern. In the west, the rim of the Qinghai-Tibetan plateau projects into the province, giving way in its southern part to parallel mountain ranges enfolding deep chasms. One of these, the Great Snowy Mountains (Daxue Shan), soars to an average elevation of 4,420 metres. The snow-tipped Gongga Shan to the south is a thrilling sight for those who see it. From here, westwards and northwards, spreads the immense and empty land that early travellers called the Tibetan Marches. Between 1928 and 1955 it was a separate province, Xikang, a vast and wild region which retained its Tibetan chieftains and defied Chinese control until it was suppressed and incorporated into Sichuan. The western quarters of the province are still home to various groups including the Khampa Tibetans, who are strong and brave warriors, now pacified.

Eastwards, the land slopes gently down to the softer contours of low hills and rolling plains. Here is the 'rice bowl of China', first named as the Red Basin by German geographer Baron Richtofen. And here is the ancient writer's Heaven on Earth where, as an old saying goes, 'Drop anything and it will grow.' This hyperbole is readily explained. Some 60 million years ago, the basin was a vast lake which

Joseph Rock's encampment near Daocheng in southwestern Sichuan, near the Yunnan border, with Shenrezi, one of the main peaks of the Konkaling Range, in the background; photographed by Rock in 1928. Compare this with the recent photograph on pages 206–7.

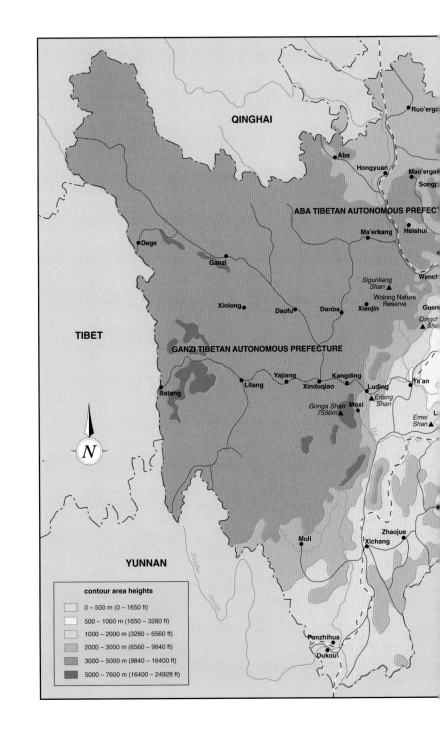

QINGHAI

Ruo'erga

Aba

Hongyuan

Mao'erga

Songp

ABA TIBETAN AUTONOMOUS PREFEC

Ma'erkang

Heishui

Dege

Ganzi

Sigunliang
Shan ▲

Wench

Wolong Nature
Reserve

Guan

Xinlong

Daofu

Danba

Xiaojin

Qingc
▲ She

TIBET

GANZI TIBETAN AUTONOMOUS PREFECTURE

Yajiang

Kangding

Batang

Litang

Xinduqiao

Luding

Ya'an

▲ Erlang
Shan

Gonga Shan
7556m▲

Moxi

Emei
Shan ▲

L

Muli

Zhaojue

Xichang

YUNNAN

Jinsha

Jinsha

Panzhihua

Dukou

contour area heights

0 – 500 m (0 – 1650 ft)

500 – 1000 m (1650 – 3280 ft)

1000 – 2000 m (3280 – 6560 ft)

2000 – 3000 m (6560 – 9840 ft)

3000 – 5000 m (9840 – 16400 ft)

5000 – 7600 m (16400 – 24928 ft)

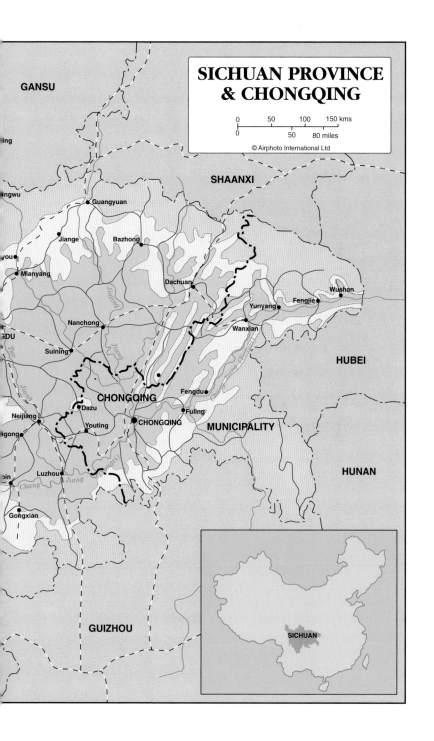

SICHUAN PROVINCE & CHONGQING

0   50   100   150 kms
0   50   80 miles
© Airphoto International Ltd

GANSU

SHAANXI

Guangyuan

Jiange   Bazhong

Mianyang

Dachuan

Wushan

Fengjie

Yunyang

Nanchong   Wanxian

HUBEI

Suining

CHONGQING

Fengdu

Dazu   Fuling

Neijiang   CHONGQING   MUNICIPALITY

Youting

HUNAN

Luzhou

Gongxian

GUIZHOU

SICHUAN

became drained when the Yangzi cut its course to the east and left a land covered with a crust of soft sandstone and shale, rich in minerals with rock brittle enough to crumble into a purplish-red soil. Coaxed by ample rainfall and subtropical warmth, rice, wheat, maize and other food grains burgeon irrepressibly out of this fertile soil.

This is the very heart of Sichuan. And within it, swarming with life and industry, is its largest expanse of level land—the alluvial Chengdu Plain. Intensively cultivated and supporting an enormous population, the plain is crisscrossed by one of the oldest irrigation systems in the world, so that, here and there, the landscape flashes vivid green and silvery grey, a mosaic of paddy fields and water channels. Poorer provinces traditionally looked to Sichuan for a share in Heaven's largesse. To Sichuan's discredit, this largesse used to include the opium poppy, whose crop was so valuable that its widespread cultivation displaced grain in the last century.

Violent tectonic upheavals in China's geological past created Sichuan's phenomenal landforms. Uplifting, faulting and subsidence on a massive scale caused the tilting of the terrain in a series of steps from the towering Tibetan tableland in the west to the soft valley floors of the east. Large tributaries of the Yangzi—the Min, Tuo, Wu and Jialing—dissect the eastern part in parallel swathes roughly from north to south. These main tributaries, it is said, gave Sichuan (meaning 'four rivers') its name.

On this wild and fecund land prehistoric man lived 30,000 to 50,000 years ago, as evidenced by a skull fossil unearthed in Ziyang, southeast of Chengdu, in 1951. Recent finds in the Wushan area of proto-human remains from over a million years ago suggest a cradle of human development. Little else is known of the area's early history. Painted pottery discovered at Daxi in Wushan, similar to the Yangshao ware of the Yellow River basin, suggests that in around 2500 BC the civilization of north China penetrated down to the upper Yangzi valley. Nevertheless the region remained peripheral to the rest of China, no more than a barbarous fringe inhabited by aboriginal tribes. Of these, peoples known as the Ba and the Shu are thought to have established kingdoms between the 16th to the third century BC. In 1985, this period dramatically emerged out of archaeological obscurity when workers digging near a brickworks in Guanghan, north of Chengdu, broke through to a pit filled with thousands of bronze, gold, jade and ceramic artefacts. There were stylized masks cast in the image of a grotesque face, with butterfly-wing ears, a scrolled nose, goggling cylindrical eyeballs and an ear-to-ear grin; life-size figures; wine vessels and other decorated ritual objects. These finds point to a sophisticated Shu culture distinct from that of north China. Little information about the excavations has so far been released, although two or three of those spectacular masks have now been put on display at the Museum of Chinese History in Beijing.

A nomadic way of life is still practised on the high-altitude pastures of Sichuan

The Ba and the Shu were in time subjugated; when the First Emperor of Qin, Shihuangdi, unified the empire in 221 BC, the territory which is present-day Sichuan was incorporated into the Chinese polity. Subsequent Han Chinese immigration and settlement reinforced its integration with China proper. But the region's geographical isolation, cut off as it was from the rest of China by mountain chains, as well as its economic self-sufficiency, encouraged separatist tendencies throughout its history. Sichuan was to demonstrate, time and again, that it was very much a world of its own. During the period of war and disunity known as the Three Kingdoms (AD 220–265), it became the independent Kingdom of Shu under the general Liu Bei. This name is still used as a name for the region, with obvious pride in its long heritage.

Remoteness and inaccessibility bred resistance to control by central political authority, typifying the old expression, 'the mountains are high and the emperor is far away.' The province's size and primitive communications made internal unity also elusive. "When the Empire is at peace, Sichuan is the first to have disorders; after peace is restored, Sichuan is the last to be stabilized" is often said of the province's volatile political record. At no time did this saying seem more appropriate than when, hot on the heels of the Republican Revolution of 1911, Sichuan became a battleground for local strongmen and their private armies. In the scramble for power, military leaders fought each other for domination of the province, until it simply fell apart and fragmented into warlord fiefdoms.

Sichuan's history during the first three decades of the Republican era was a dark period of military strife, unbridled power-grabbing and economic disruption. Any semblance of an orderly provincial administration was swept aside by the ambitions of army commanders who rose and fell in a confusion of shifting alliances and internecine squabbling. Once secured of a power base, a commander would control the territory held by his forces as its *de facto* ruler; he would become, in other words, a warlord. Independent of the national government, warlords abrogated to themselves such functions as defence and revenue collection; and so insatiable were their growing armies that taxes had to be levied in advance of the incomes earned. By 1934, for example, Guanxian county was paying taxes that would fall due in 1991. Beset with crushing debts, small landowners saw their meager acres forfeited, and tenant farmers, unable to meet spiralling rents, drifted into crime and vagrancy. Thus the stage was set for Sichuan to be one of the leading sources for revolutionary leaders, including Deng Xiaoping and Zhao Ziyang.

Some of the warlords in Sichuan hung on to power into the 1930s; others threw in their lot with the Guomindang (Nationalist Party), led by Chiang Kai-shek, to fight the communists, who were proving more of a thorn in Chiang's side than the Japanese and their incursions in Manchuria. Determined to achieve 'Unity before resistance', a policy aimed at eliminating communist ascendancy in the rural areas, Chiang pressed on with his campaign to squeeze the Red armies out of their soviet base in Jiangxi province in southeastern China. Thus began the Long March, an epic trek which started as a retreat from Chiang's pursuing troops and ended as a triumph of endurance and survival. About a third of the route cut through Sichuan from south to north. Countless marchers died ascending the icy precipices of the Great Snowy Mountains and crossing the treacherous marches of its deep valleys and high grasslands. Of the some 100,000 who participated in the Long March, only around 10,000 made it all the way to the wartime refuge of Yan'an in the northern province of Shaanxi, becoming hallowed heroes of the Communist era.

The Sino-Japanese War, which was finally declared in 1937 despite Chiang's passive stance, thrust Sichuan into unforeseen prominence. When Nanjing fell to the enemy, the inland port of Chongqing was adopted as the Nationalist capital. Entire factories and colleges were moved up from the coastal area to be out of the reach of Japanese depredations. Hundreds of thousands of refugees flooded in. Such wholesale immigration gave Sichuan an industrial impetus.

Present-day Sichuan is engulfed, like the rest of China, in a modernization spree. Some of the visual aspects of this seem harsh and ugly—the pollution of the cities, for example—yet the countryside remains immemorially agricultural. It was from Sichuan that Zhao Ziyang, local Party chief from 1975 to 1980, directed experiments in the privatization of agriculture that have led to greater productivity, diversity and rural prosperity.

For the traveller, Sichuan is an adventure of observing Chinese society in flux. But in more than one sense is the province a microcosm of China. For, unlike many other provinces, whether they boast Buddhist mountains, open grasslands, neat chessboard fields, venerable monuments or minority communities, Sichuan possesses all of these spectacles plus the bonus of the best cuisine in China. Much of the province remains little explored by the Western traveller. Having visited the more accessible sights, strike off into the fringes of those wilder areas, and the province reveals itself to you in all its glorious diversity.

FOOD IN SICHUAN

Sichuan cooking enjoys immense popularity in the West—deservedly so, yet some people still consider its most salient characteristic to be its ability to sear the mouth, bring tears to the eyes and a sweat to the brow. Sichuan food is undeniably hot and spicy, but those gourmets who have developed a taste for it also like it for its earthiness and robustness—insipid it is not.

Probably the most distinctive feature of the Sichuan cooking style is its leaning towards strong and even extreme flavours. Local people attribute the development of their cuisine to the weather in Sichuan. They say that chilli- and pepper-flavoured food stimulates sweating, which cools them down in the hot summer, while in the damp cool winter, it produces the opposite effect of warmth and comfort. But the chef is undoubtedly also helped by the prevalence of many local ingredients to salt, pickle and spice the food. For example, the Sichuan peppercorn, known as *huajiao*, thrives in the Minjiang valley. Unlike the black peppercorn, this reddish brown berry from a shrub (*Zanthoxylum bungei*) imparts an anise flavour and aroma and a mild spiciness when roasted and ground. From this one humble spice alone, the Sichuanese chef can conjure some half a dozen different flavours by blending it with other ingredients. A classic one is *mala*, obtained when Sichuan pepper, chilli and soya sauce are added to a nutty base such as ground sesame or sesame oil (*mayou*). Its effect on the lip and tongue is a tingling sensation, which has given rise to a play on the word *ma*, meaning to be numb or to have pins and needles. Another is *chenpi*, a blend of seasonings dominated by the fruitiness of tangerine peel. *Chenpi niurou*, a preparation of matchstick-shaped beef slivers deep fried to a dark brown crispiness and finally glazed with seasoning and tangerine peel, is chewy and delicious and makes and excellent hors d'oeuvre.

Perhaps at a loss for words—for how does one describe a flavour that is at once peppery, salty, vinegary and sweet?—Sichuan chefs call a third classic relish 'peculiar taste' (*guaiwei*), as in *guaiwei ji*, a cold dish of shredded chicken tossed in a thick sesame-based sauce.

This method of combining different flavours also yields *suanla*—sour and hot—and *yuxiang*—fishy fragrant, which owes nothing to fish but much to fermented soyabeans, garlic and wine.

In Sichuan, as elsewhere in China, Western visitors often find it difficult to avoid eating in hotel dining rooms and established city restaurants which have at least an English language menu. Yet it is possible to try the streetside eateries now that private enterprise and family-owned restaurants have burgeoned everywhere, run by proprietors eager to be helpful. In many of these places raw ingredients are laid in full view, so that, having made your selection, you can leave the cook to make up his own combinations. There will be a preponderance of vegetables, for meat, sliced or chopped up into bite-sized pieces, is frequently treated as an adjunct for flavouring rather than as the basis of a dish. Some of the vegetables will be familiar, such as cabbage, spinach, broad beans, potatoes, aubergines, cucumbers, kale and carrots. Others are more exotic to the Western palate, like *qingsun*, Chinese mushrooms, white radish and bamboo shoots.

Garlic, chives and spring onions are liberally employed. There is nothing so appetizing as a plain dish of blanched chives with slices of pork, or mustard greens sautéed with minced garlic. A classic Sichuanese dish is *mapo doufu*—cubes of

Noodle makers at work, photographed by Cecil Beaton (1904–1980) in the countryside of Sichuan. The noodles were made by hand, then strung out on a rack to dry. In his record of wartime China in 1944, Beaton has left a collection of photographs which reveal the essential dignity of the ordinary Chinese patiently carrying out their appointed tasks in the part of China still free from Japanese occupation.

beancurd strewn with minced pork and chopped red capsicums and glistening with chilli oil. The inventor of this dish is said to be Pockmarked Grandma Chen, who ran a famous inn in Chengdu, some 400 years ago. Another classic dish is *guoba xiaren*, whose distinctive ingredient—golden crispy rice crackling scraped from the bottom of the pot—is softened with a sizzling broth of shrimps poured over it in front of the guest at the table. There are several variations on this theme, such as combining the rice crackling with a broth of chicken, pork or eel. But the Sichuanese dish that is most widely eaten and loved for its classic simplicity and depth of taste is Viceroy's chicken (*gongbao jiding*), a quick-fried ensemble of diced chicken, crunchy peanuts and green capsicums said to be named after a late-19th-century provincial governor by his obsequious host at a banquet in Chengdu.

At a more sophisticated level, returned-to-the-pot pork (*huiguo rou*), camphor and tea smoked duck (*zhangcha kaoya*), and beef steamed in ground rice (*fenzheng niurou*) usually feature on restaurant menus. As its name suggests, (*huiguo rou*) is twice cooked. The pork (always of a cut with both lean and fat meat) is first boiled, left to cool before being thinly sliced, and then stir-fried in a piquant sauce in which

soyabean paste, sugar, chilli, ginger and garlic predominate. Finally stems of spring onions are scattered at the end both for extra flavouring and to add colour. Smoked duck is a banquet dish in which the oily taste of the bird is subtly palliated by smoking it over camphor wood and tea. In (*fenzheng niurou*), the ground-rice coating over previously marinated beef, subjected to hot blasts of steam in a bamboo container, becomes soaked by the meat juices, with the result that the concoction is at once aromatic and succulent.

The city people of Sichuan are proud of their 'fast food', which has a long tradition of being sold by vendors on the streets. As those vendors dispensed their snacks from mobile kitchens carried on shoulder poles (known as *dan*), the noodles (*mian*) they popularized came to be called (*dandan mian*). Into a bowl the vendor would put a spoonful or two of a seasoning of Sichuan pepper, soya sauce, chopped spring onions, vinegar and hot oil rendered a bright red by chillies, pour steaming stock on this, fill up the bowl with separately cooked noodles and top the whole concoction with a sprinkling of crisply fried minced pork. Nowadays this dish is more widely available in restaurants, where it is either eaten on its own as a snack, or served to round off a meal as a last course. Of dumplings and ravioli, there is a great variety, the most distinctive of which may well be the sort first sold off a Chengdu stall by a man named Lai Ruanxin. A helping of Lai (*tangyuan*) consists of four dumplings each stuffed with a different scented sweet filling, osmanthus blossom being a favourite. The dumpling itself is made of glutinous rice flour. It is customary, besides, to dunk the dumplings into sugar and sweet sesame paste before consumption.

Sichuan has its own version of the fondue. The original source being attributed to Chongqing, it is better known as the Chongqing hotpot (*huoguo*). This '10,000 people shared pot', so called because the hotpot sauce is left for the next customer, is now a communal pleasure for diners across China. The cuisine is said to have its origin with boatmen of the Yangzi who would boil up the assorted leftovers from the market over open fires along the shore of the river. The stock in which the ingredients are simmered is uniquely Sichuanese. A powerful consommé turned dark by (*huajiao*), fermented soybean and hot bean paste, and laced with rice wine. Into the communal chafing dish set over a spirit flame are thrown thinly sliced raw meats, fish, vermicelli and cut-up portions of vegetables, although the favourite ingredients by far, certainly among those who hail from Chongqing, are tripe and other offal. Other specialities include male parts from various animals to provide vigor for men. Opium pods have been placed in the sauce for extra flavor and attraction, though this is now illegal. Some restaurants have taken to providing individual hotpots, a boon for vegetarians and those who prefer milder flavours and wish to dilute their own stock. Either way a hotpot dinner is invariably a jolly and entertaining occasion, particularly on a cold winter evening.

Serving noodles and steamed dumplings from a roadside food stall, photographed by Cecil Beaton in 1944. An almost identical scene can still be found on many city streets in China today.

Western Sichuan

Tibetans had been settled for many centuries in the territory which now forms part of the provinces of Qinghai and Sichuan before the Sino-Tibetan political frontier was formally defined during the reign of Qing emperor Kangxi (1662–1722). By this agreed demarcation the territory west of the upper Yangzi, a section known as the Jinsha Jiang (the River of Golden Sand), was formally acknowledged to be governed by Lhasa, while all that lay to the east of it became the domain of the Chinese empire. Even so, in practice the frontier was a fluid one; semi-independent Tibetan tribes in the border regions more or less carried on as before, submitting to the authority of their chieftains rather than to the Chinese officials appointed over them. Although Chinese garrisons were stationed at Kangding (formerly Tachienlu) and other points along the road to Lhasa, domination of the rugged highlands west of the Sichuan Basin remained tenuous. There were sporadic Sino-Tibetan conflicts, inter-tribal skirmishes and nomad raids on Chinese settlements. This state of affairs continued despite the creation of a buffer province, Xikang in 1928.

Xikang has disappeared from the maps but western Sichuan still seems a world apart. Geographically it is a grand and savage region made up of tremendous mountain ranges and deeply eroded canyons. Three great rivers and their tributaries cut through it roughly from north to south—the Jinsha Jiang, the Yalong Jiang and the Dadu He. Culturally it is Tibetan: the 1,000-kilometre (620-mile) highway from Chengdu to the border of Tibet passes through the heartland of Kham, one of Tibet's three traditional regions.

The nomads here, known as Khampas, are great fighters: it has long been said that of all Tibetans the Khampas make the best killers and the greatest saints. Not so long ago they were divided into clans and tiny kingdoms only loosely controlled by Lhasa, and were feared throughout Tibet and the border regions as unruly bandits. Since then Kham has been subsumed by Sichuan: the present Ganzi Tibetan Autonomous Prefecture corresponds in area to a large portion of the original tribal territory. In the 1950s, smouldering resentment of the Chinese government's collectivization programme—anathema to a spirited, independent people such as the Khampas—flared up in violent armed resistance. A wave of guerrilla warfare rolled across Kham and into central Tibet, sparking a popular uprising in March 1959. Many Tibetan-Buddhist monasteries were destroyed in the fighting. As the world knows, this revolt was suppressed and the Dalai Lama—put to flight from Lhasa to India—remains in exile.

Khampas still wrest a living from their wild and desolate enclave. They can graze their yaks, sheep and horses on the high-altitude pastures, but much of the terrain is unfit for human habitation. The landscape consists of long stretches of wilderness broken by frozen rivers, and lofty mountains whose deforested slopes are covered with shale and rock. Against this backdrop a lone rider on a caparisoned horse may suddenly appear on the horizon, as proud and dashing a figure as one imagines his bandit forebears to have been. Khampa men are tall and muscular, wearing their hair in braids over which wide-brimmed hats are pulled down on foreheads. Feet are shod in brightly coloured boots, and a knife dangles from the belt securing a voluminous sheepskin coat worn, Tibetan-style, with one sleeve hanging loose from the shoulder. If at first all this looks intimidating, a flashing smile revealing a single gold front tooth soon dispels the effect. The Khampa are proud and dashing, but offer a cheerful hospitality to visitors.

Few places on earth are as difficult to visit as the Ganzi hinterland. Much of the area has only been officially open to foreigners since 1999. Travellers have penetrated it by public bus, or by hitching rides on trucks—it is mostly convoys of trucks that make that journey across western Sichuan. The drivers of these trucks are tough, spending as they do hour after hour jolting and slithering all over the road. From time to time the highway is put out of action by avalanches.

Tibetan tribesmen are renowned for their horsemanship, taking great pride in their mounts, and at every opportunity they love to display their skill, particularly at festive occasions

DEGE

If the road is passable, Dege, the last town on the highway before it enters Tibet, can be reached in five days. This highland settlement has two monasteries belonging to the Saskyapa sect, whose early exponents were particularly active in translating Buddhist literature from Sanskrit. Dege's Bakong Scripture Printing House has been reproducing copies from the pages of the 333 volumes of the Tibetan Buddhist canon, the *Kanjur* and the *Tanjur*, for over 270 years. Besides Buddhist classics, these volumes contain all the commentaries as well as works on medicine and astrology. Printing is done by hand from wooden blocks, more than 210,000 of them, on which the text is carved. Catalogued and numbered, this collection of blocks is stored in an enormous building lined with shelves. Printed sheets are stacked as loose leaves between wooden slates that are often decorated with carvings or paintings. There is an increasing demand for the 'books', and pious devotees come to buy them and to touch the ink dripping from the roller presses.

KANGDING

Kangding has a most dramatic geographic situation. This interesting town is cradled in a narrow fold between steep, dark green mountains and lies at an elevation of over 2,500 metres. A swift, foaming stream roars through its centre, sending up a constant rumble as the sound reverberates round the amphitheatre of hills. Frequently in deep shadow, for the mountains shut out sunlight, Kangding seems at once starkly grim and full of mystery.

Its approach from the west is heralded by village houses tucked into the hill slopes on which neat terraces have been cut to support a little cultivation. Barley is grown, and here and there you come upon cherry trees and peppercorn bushes. Ragged prayer flags and obelisk-like watchtowers can be seen en route. From Chengdu, the road to Kangding goes through Ya'an.

At the beginning of the Republican period (1911), there was still a Tibetan king resident in Kangding. He was monarch of the Chala kingdom, but in reality no more than a Chinese puppet. When Zhao Erfang, commanding officer of the Manchu campaign to annex eastern Tibet, overran western Sichuan, the king was stripped of even his nominal powers. Kangding's motley population at that time also included French priests; in fact it was the seat of the bishop of the Mission Etrangères, a Paris-based organization. Many famous Frenchmen passed through Kangding, not least of whom was the Lazarist Père Huc, whose account of a remarkable

Bakong Scripture Printing House in Dege has been reproducing copies of the Tibetan Buddhist canon for over 270 years. Printing is done by hand from wooden blocks, more than 210,000 of them, on which the text is carved.

expedition, *Souvenirs d'un voyage dans la Tartarie et le Tibet*, electrified France when it was published in 1850. Of the missionaries who later went there, most pursued their largely vain task of proselytization with great zealousness, dedicating their lives with very little expectation of ever returning to France again.

To early European observers Kangding marked the limit of China. Once out of its west gate, Tibet began. Indeed the outpost was for many of them the starting point of a journey to Tibet. They called it Tachienlu or Tatsienlu, a corruption of its Tibetan name, Dar-tsen-do. The very atmosphere of the town was Tibetan, for its importance resided in its being the emporium for brick tea, wool, hides, medicinal herbs and cloth, and there was a constant throng of muleteers, yaks, emissaries from Lhasa and red-robed lamas in the market square.

As the administrative centre of the Ganzi Tibetan Autonomous Prefecture, Kangding retains something of the civic importance it enjoyed when it was the capital of Xikang. Industrial progress has come in the form of textile and tea-processing factories and a hydroelectric plant. The inhabitants are mostly Han Chinese, although Tibetans still wander its streets.

The French fathers did not labour entirely in vain, judging by the small Catholic church on the south side of the river, easily found once you catch sight of the cross mounted on its roof.

Khampa Tibeten tribesmen adorn their much treasured horses with elaborate stirrups and horse-blankets

A herding family travels through the marsh meadows north of Kangding, Sichuan Province.
Yaks, sheep and goats make up their flock and provide most of life's necessities.
Kangding is the traditional gateway into Tibet from China.

Kangding's lamasery, Ngachu Gompa (or Anjue Si in Chinese), is towards the southern end of town at the end of Yanhe Xilu. Its series of double roofs with upturned eaves rise above the low stone buildings in front. In an anteroom just inside the entrance a large painted prayer wheel waits to be rotated; while devotees file around it, they can gaze upon the pictures of the late Tenth Panchen Lama, who visited Kangding in 1986, stuck all over the walls.

The high point in Kangding's calendar is the fair on Horse Race Hill (Paoma Shan) every year on the 18th day of the fourth lunar month (sometime between May and June). As the day draws near, tents and stalls spring up all over the slopes and Tibetans from far and wide converge for an exuberant round of trading, wrestling matches, tug-of-war contests, folk dancing and, of course, horse racing.

Kangding is known widely in China by virtue of the lilting, romantic Tibetan duet *Kangding Love Song*, which is a staple of the karaoke culture.

In May 1935, Mao led the Red Army north across the Yangzi River and on to seize the vital bridge at Luding across the Dadu River, thus escaping the pursuing National Party Army

LUDING

Luding is hallowed in Chinese communist history for the crucial battle fought here to gain control of its bridge.

The Dadu He (River), a tributary of the Min Jiang, plunges south between the precipitous walls of Sichuan's northwestern mountain ranges and then swings eastwards to merge with the Min waters at Leshan. In the reign of Emperor Kangxi (1662–1722) an iron chain bridge, constructed to a design that presaged the modern suspension bridge, was thrown across this turbulent river. It spans 101 metres and consists of nine stout iron chains forming the bridge deck, across which is a plank walkway, with two more chains on either side acting as handrails. All 13 chains are sunk into stone abutments on the banks, above which simple pavilions with curved eaves stand on brick foundations rising from the river floor. A billboard in the bridgehouse at the western end recounts the action at Luding Bridge on 29th May 1935, when 22 soldiers from the Fourth Regiment of the Second Division of the First Front Red Army captured the crossing from Guomintang troops and secured the communists' escape route through northern Sichuan.

Control of the bridge was imperative for the Red Army, pinched as it was between the Dadu River ahead and the Jinsha Jiang behind, while Guomintang troops were pressing closer to stop the Long March in its tracks. In a 24-hour forced march that covered an incredible 120 kilometres, the Red regiment raced enemy

School children race acros the iron chain bridge at Luding in 1981. Built in the Ming dynasty, the bridge was the site of an important battle between the communists and Guomintang in 1935.

reinforcements to Luding Bridge and took its western back approaches. It found that half the planks had been removed from the span, so that the assault party, the 22 heroes, could make it across only by swinging from the links hand over hand. Machine-gun fire from the eastern bank swept them as they slowly moved forward, while the men behind them had to lay down planks at the same time as providing cover. As those that were hit fell into the river, more men replaced them; accounts vary as to how many of the vanguard died. At last the assault party landed on the opposite bank, followed by the plank-layers and the rest of the regiment. The battle that ensued was a short and decisive one. With Luding Bridge taken, Mao Zedong, Zhou Enlai and commander-in-Chief Zhu De arrived soon after to lead the Red Army across the Dadu River.

GONGGA SHAN AND HAILUOGOU

Gongga Shan or, to call it by its Tibetan name, Minya Konka, is one of the highest peaks in the world. This 'Sublime White Mountain', as its Tibetan name translates, soars 7,556 metres above the eastern extension of the Tibetan Plateau, a spellbinding sight for anyone who sees it. Travellers to Kangding pass quite close to it, but the town lies so low in relation to its surrounding hills that any view of Gongga is blocked by the nearer peaks. You are far more likely to see its eastern face from

Part of the Konkaling Range in southwestern Sichuan, in mountainous Daocheng county. The main peak of Shenrezi stands 6,032 metres above sea level. Tibetan Buddhists believe the Dalai Lama to be the incarnation of Shenrezi, the all-compassionate one. Along with Chanodorji to the east and Jambeyang to the south, both 5,958 metres high, the three sacred snow peaks represent deities of the Buddhist pantheon. Named by the Fifth Dalai Lama, these holy

mountains attract countless pilgrims, who circumambulate the base of the mountains. The county town of Daocheng lies to the north on the south bank of the Daochu, a tributary of the Yangzi which flows south to merge with other tributaries. American explorer and botanist Joseph F Rock travelled extensively in the Sichuan borderlands during the 1920s for National Geographic *magazine and photographed these same peaks (see page 186).*

the summit of Emei Shan, the pass over Erlang Shan or at Hailuogou. If the skies are clear Gongga appears as a graceful, slightly blunted pinnacle of white ice scintillating against a background of deepest blue. The simple purity of its outline is unforgettable, a shining summit rising over a sea of mountains.

Gongga has proved difficult to climb. There have been two successful attempts, one in 1939 by two Americans and another in 1957 by six Chinese mountaineers. In 1981 a group of Japanese climbers were foiled in their attempt when eight of them were killed by an avalanche. The were within 300 metres of the top. One of the survivors was later saved by some Yi herdsmen.

Mount Gongga has four glaciers: Hailuogou, Yanzigou, Dagongba and Xiaogongba. Hailuogou (Conch Gully), its largest and most impressive, reaches down Gongga's eastern flank through a belt of conifer forests and terminates at an elevation of 2,850 metres, arguably the lowest glacier in Asia. The glacier, believed to have been formed some 1,600 years ago, is considered 'modern' by geological standards. In the late 1980s the area was opened as the Hailuogou Glacier Park.

Accessibility from the attractive town of Moxi (which is serviced by buses from Luding), and the mild weather prevailing through much of the year, made the area attractive to adventurous travellers. Although trekking to the top is still possible for the physically fit—you are only likely to get a little breathless as the air becomes thinner the higher you ascend—the paths are generally poorly maintained and difficult to follow. The authorities, instead, now prefer visitors to use the minibus up to Camp No 3 together with the compulsory services of a guide. From Camp No 3, the highest camp at 2,940 metres, where there are hotels and restaurants, it is a three kilometre walk to the cable car station for a ride over the glacier.

In early summer, the slopes splashed with blooming rhododendrons present a magical sight. Hailuogou is 1,800 metres below the snowline and endowed with a mild climate which means that the approach to the glacier passes through lush forests and abundant ground cover. Thousands of species of flora and fauna, some of them quite rare, are found here.

The viewpoint for the tongue of the glacier is an easy hike (two kilometres) from the third campsite. Down at your feet is a stupendous drift of ice and debris tumbled into a deep chasm edged with hardy firs. It is a greyish-blue expanse which belies the treacherous flow beneath. To see the ice fall, caves and seracs—huge irregular boulders of ice created by the intersection of crevasses—as well as the peak of Gongga Shan itself, one must walk down to the glacier tongue and follow it around to the right, a trek of around two hours to be undertaken with care and only with a guide.

The glacier, though spectacular, is only one of the many stunning sights one catches wherever one looks in Hailuogou Park. Gongga is part of an enormous range that includes 45 other snow-tipped peaks towering over 6,000 metres.

Hailuoguo (Conch Gulley) glacier, the largest of the four glaciers on Gongga Shan, is believed to have been formed some 1,600 years ago

EMEI SHAN: SACRED MOUNTAIN OF BUDDHISM

Emei Shan is more than a mountain; it is a frame of mind. That is not just because looking up at monumental heights induces in the beholder a sense of his own frailty and insignificance. It is also because for centuries Chinese belief has endowed Nature with a mystical influence on man's character, and Nature is supremely exemplified by mountains. Mixed up with this tradition was the ancient folk belief that mountains were the magical habitations of immortals. Although Taoist in origin, these ideas have been gathered into the Chinese Buddhist's view of the universe as a Chinese synthesis of philosophy and imagery.

China has several famous sacred mountains, both Buddhist and Taoist. Why they came to be venerated no longer matters; their sacred character has been thoroughly institutionalized by the many temples and places of pilgrimage established on their slopes since antiquity. Emei Shan's first temples were Taoist; later it became known as one of the four most holy mountains of Buddhism, the others being Jiuhua in Anhui Province, Wutai in Shanxi and Putuo in Zhejiang. Taishan in Shandong and Huangshan in Anhui are famous, but not Buddhist retreats.

There are at least two interpretations of the mountain's name. Some people say that 'Emei' derived from the first two syllables of 'Amituofo', the deity invoked in the Pure Land Buddhist prayer in which the repeated utterance of the holy name is supposed to help speed the pious to paradise. But since legends cling to practically every cave, streamlet and pinnacle, so the entire mountain has spawned a fable of its own. Emei means 'moth eyebrows', a poetic term for beautiful women, and the peaks of Emei, it is said, were originally four celestial maidens.

As the story goes, there used to be a temple outside the west gate of the town. A monk of this temple once gave shelter to a painter, who repaid his hospitality with four pictures, each one of an elegant and lovely young girl. The artist imposed one condition, however. Those paintings, he said, must be put away in a trunk for 49 days after his departure. Too impressed and delighted to heed the artist, the monk hung them on the wall. When he returned in the evening, he was astounded to find four girls chatting and giggling away in the hall, while the pictures were, of course, completely blank. As the truth dawned on him, he saw the girls run out of the room. Giving chase, he was only quick enough to grab hold of the skirt of the youngest girl. The desperate girl escaped his clutches by instant transmogrification into a pinnacle. Her sisters, loath to abandon the youngest, did likewise—which is why Emei Shan has three peaks close together, while the fourth stands a little distance apart.

Wanfo Ding (Myriad Buddhas Peak), the highest point on Emei Shan, is 3,099 metres above the sea. Below it the western face of the mountain slopes down in a series of inclines while eastwards the drop is almost perpendicular. Topped by a curiously truncated summit, the mountain with its ungainly silhouette is exactly the sort of geographical oddity which appeals to the Chinese, whose appreciation of Nature is often tinged with a particular fondness for its freakier aspects.

Travellers' reports of climbing Emei Shan have varied from enthusiastic recollections to a catalogue of woes. Much hinges on the weather. While the cooler heights make for a welcome interlude from the summer humidity and heat of the Chengdu Plain, frequent rain and low hovering clouds can turn the experience into a sodden endurance test. Early winter, when the mountain top is transformed by the first dusting of snow, can be a superb time to visit provided that you come armour-plated against the cold.

To climb to the top and witness Buddha's Aureole (see below) is the fulfilment of a Buddhist's dream. Inevitably, alongside the pilgrims, there are large numbers of tourists. One of the nicest aspects of the excursion may be the acquaintances you make on the way. There is a tendency for visitors who climb at the same speed to cluster together; after some hours of keeping pace, or resting at the same monasteries, you are likely to start swapping not only snacks but life stories as well.

For the convenience of less than ardent hikers there are buses to Wuxian Gang (for Qingying Ge), Jingshui, where there is a cable car (for Wannian Si) and Leidong Ping (for Jieyin Dian), where there is another cable car to Jinding (Golden Summit). Believe it or not, for those who are really averse to physical exercise, there is now a monorail from Jinding to the summit at Wanfo Ding.

ROUTES

If you are fit and properly-shod, and assuming that you are prepared to cheat a little (by taking a bus to Jingshui), the ascent and return can be done in two and a half to three days. You are the best judge of whether to add to this timetable by staying overnight near the Golden Summit in order to see the sunrise from the peak. The trail is paved with some quite steep steps in places. A common route from Jingshui is: Wannian Si–Changlao Ping–Huayan Ding–Xixiang Chi–Leidong Ping–Jieyin Dian–Jinding, probably with an overnight stop at Xixiang Chi. This route has been estimated at 30 kilometres.

A longer route loops round from Wannian Si to Qingyin Ge, then proceeds as follows: Hongchun Ping–Jiulao Dong–Xianfeng Si–Yuxian Si, merging with the previous route at Huayan Ding below Xixiang Chi. Total distance is about 52 kilometres. This is the more scenic route. Alternatively, a bus plies between Baoguo Si and Wuxian Gang, close to Qingyin Ge, so you can start your ascent from that point without going via Wannian Si. The majority of climbers choose to ascend by the first route and descend by the second.

Those who want a taste of the mountain without knocking themselves out may like to consider this compromise: take the bus to Wuxian Gang for Qingyin Ge, walk up to Hongchun Ping and stay the night. The next day, simply walk down the same way again, after which a bus and cable car can be taken to the summit. Since the monastery at Hongchun Ping is not strategically positioned for a climb up the entire mountain, it is generally not crowded with tourists. The monastery has well-preserved architecture and a serene courtyard.

For those who want to go the whole way and start from the bottom, the route is Baoguo Si–Fuhu Si: one kilometre; Leiyin Si–Huayan Si–Chunyang Dian–Qingyin Ge: ten kilometres; from there walk on to Wannian Si and then follow either of the routes above to the top, about 48 kilometres in total.

FOOD AND LODGINGS

As pilgrims have done for centuries, today's hikers must accept the spartan accommodation and vegetarian fare offered by Emei Shan's temples if they lodge overnight on the mountain. While some travellers complain about the sometimes primitive and damp condition, others have found the sensation of waking up at dawn to tolling bells and the muffled chants of monks more than adequate compensation for the discomfort of the night.

The main places on Emei Shan providing meals and lodgings are: Baoguo Si, Fuhu Si, Leiyin Si, Wannian Si, Chunyang Dian, Qingyin Si, Hongchun Ping, Xianfeng Si, Xixiang Chi, Jieyin Dian, Woyun Binguan and Jinding Si. Most of these provide dormitory-style accommodation with rudimentary plumbing and electricity. It is advisable to pack a torch, or even candles, and toilet paper. However, Woyun Binguan, located just below the cable car station at Jieyin Dian, provides both hot water and heating and is consequently more expensive. Be aware also that, especially during the high season, there are large numbers of tourists and pilgrims and many of the better places soon fill up.

Although you may like to bring along a pack of your own favourite trail mix or snack to eat during the climb, there are many wayside stalls, teahouses and restaurants selling all kinds of food and drink. Bottled water is also widely available. Remember, too, the higher you climb the more expensive things tend to become.

After a night or two on the mountain, the hot baths and clean sheets at Hongzhushan Guesthouse, back at base, will make one feel the most pampered of sybarites. This hotel, a short walk from the bus terminal at Baoguo Si, sprawls in its own grounds in a villa-style complex of buildings, including Number Four, which was once occupied by Chiang Kai-shek but is now open to guests despite its proclaimed status as an historical monument.

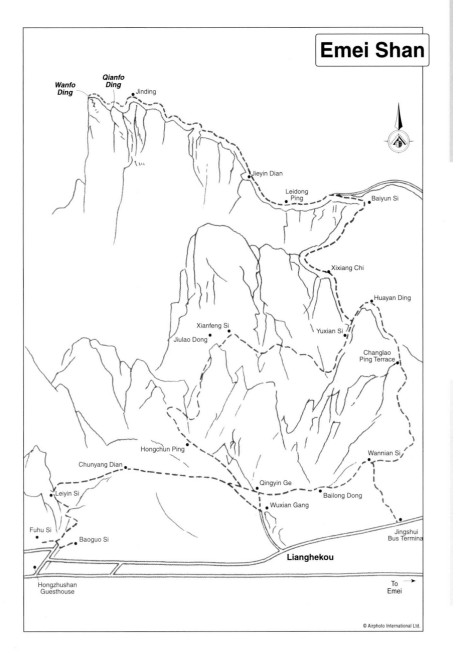

Emei Shan

Wanfo Ding

Qianfo Ding

Jinding

Jieyin Dian

Leidong Ping

Baiyun Si

Xixiang Chi

Huayan Ding

Xianfeng Si

Yuxian Si

Jiulao Dong

Changlao Ping Terrace

Hongchun Ping

Wannian Si

Chunyang Dian

Qingyin Ge

Leiyin Si

Bailong Dong

Wuxian Gang

Fuhu Si

Jingshui Bus Termina

Baoguo Si

Lianghekou

Hongzhushan Guesthouse

To Emei

© Airphoto International Ltd.

TEMPLES AND SIGHTS

Baoguo Si and Fuhu Si are the most frequently visited temples around the foothills. Before their ascent climbers can be seen inspecting the variously decorated walking sticks sold beside the road. A staff seems as much part of the image of the toiling pilgrim as the straw overshoes and rosary beads, numerous strings of which are also for sale. You can equip yourself with a map of the trails here.

Baoguo Si (Temple of Dedication to the Country), is the gateway to the holy mountain. Founded in the 17th century, Baoguo Si was extended in the early Qing period (1866) and is fairly typical of all the temples on Emei Shan. Four imposing halls snuggle into the hill slope one behind another, the last being a library for sutras. Through the gate pavilion, you come to a large courtyard flanked by the monks' quarters with its upper-storey gallery more than likely festooned with drying towels. The main hall of the temple stands at the far end, its roof rearing up above huge wooden beams. Beyond it is the Seven-Buddha Hall dedicated to the six Buddhas of the past and Maitreya, the Buddha of the future. The most treasured relic of this temple is found behind Seven-Buddha Hall: this is the porcelain Buddha, a 2.4 metre figure fired in the kilns of the capital of chinaware, Jingdezhen in Jiangxi Province, in 1415.

'Sea of Clouds', Emei Shan

Puxian Hall is the centrepiece of this temple complex. Incense smoke and the swelling chant of monks from some concealed recess greet you as you reach the entrance. Inside, pennants and draperies dangle from the rafters. Many of them are of red silk, embroidered or appliquéd with figures of monks, dragons and Chinese characters. A red silk drum like an enormous lampshade hangs between tasseled pennants sewn with tiny copper bells. The crimson of the silk is echoed in the lacquered pillars flanking the altar, and in the faded satin kneelers in front of it. Spreading his benevolence about him, Puxian glitters from inside a glass case, looking more Indian than Chinese with his gilt headdress. The tutelary deity of Emei Shan, Puxian (Samantabhadra in Sanskrit) is sculpted in his customary pose, sitting cross-legged on a white elephant.

Further uphill is **Fuhu Si** (Subduing Tiger Temple). A legend relates how a fierce black tiger once terrorized the neighbourhood. One day three sisters, a little bored with studying Taoism on the mountain, came to the stream. Being Taoist novices, these girls were rather eager to wield their magic on the notorious tiger, but their powers proved unequal to the task, and it was their brother, dropping from the sky at an opportune moment, who finally tamed the beast. A bridge was later built to mark the tiger's defeat.

Up a flight of stairs and beyond a spacious courtyard, the nicely-kept main hall is dominated by three Buddha figures. A few worshippers sink to their knees, but most of them perform a quick triple bow from the waist. Joss sticks in their clasped hands smoulder and give off a musty fragrance. In the dark, hushed hall (much less of a tourist trap than Baoguo Si), two oil lamps do nothing to lift the gloom, although a pair of enormous drums on either side of the altar stand out clearly enough.

Fuhu Si was founded during the Southern Song dynasty (1127–1279). However, the Huayan Pagoda to the left of the main hall, an unusual 13-tier bronze structure whose surface is covered with 4,700 Buddha images and the text of the Huayan Sutra, dates from the end of the 16th century (late Ming dynasty).

Other mountain streams meander between rocks down the wooded slopes. Past **Leiyin Si** (Thunder Temple), a mid-19th-century establishment, and **Chunyang Dian** at 940 metres, you drop down to **Shuang Feiqiao** (Double Flying Bridges) straddling two little rivers which, tumbling down a miniature waterfall just above, meet at an outcrop of rock called **Niuxin Shi** (Ox Heart Stone). Named for the 'singing' waters, **Qingyin Ge** (Clear Sound Pavilion) stands above the bridges among luxuriant vegetation at the junction of two paths, one to Hongchun Ping, the other to Wannian Si. As there is a bus service to Wuxian Gang, an easy two-kilometre (just over a mile) walk from Qingyin Ge, this is a busy crossroads for climbers.

LIGHT AT THE END OF THE TUNNEL

*T*he railway halt at Emei was at the end of a long muddy road, and a market nearby sold fruit and peanuts to the pilgrims waiting patiently, leaning on their walking-sticks, for the train. And then, above the sound of sparrows and the whispers of bamboos, a train whistle blew. I like these country stations, and it seemed perfect to sit there among the rice fields in the hills of Sichuan until, right on schedule, the big wheezing train arrived to take me away, south into Yunnan. It was twenty-four hours to Kunming, and the train was uncharacteristically empty: I had a compartment to myself, and this one—because of the intense and humid heat—had straw mats instead of cushions.

'There are 200 tunnels between here and Kunming,' the conductor said when he clipped my ticket. No sooner had he got the words out of his mouth than we were standing in darkness: the first tunnel.

We were among tall conical hills that were so steep they were terraced and cultivated only half-way up. That was unusual in China where land economy was almost an obsession. And the day was so overcast that waterfalls spilled out of the low clouds and paths zigzagged upwards and disappeared in the mist.

So many tunnels meant that we would be among mountains the whole way—and hills and valleys, and narrow swinging footbridges slung across the gorges. The ravines were spectacular and steep, and the mountains were close together, so the valleys were very narrow. All of these magnificent geographical features had meant that the railway line had been difficult. In fact many of the engineering problems had been regarded as almost insurmountable until the early seventies when, with a combination of soldiers and convicts—a labour-force that could be shot for not working—the line was finally finished.

The line could not go through the mountains of the Daxue range, and so it crept around their sides, pierced their flanks, and rose higher and circled until it had doubled back upon itself. Then you looked down and saw the tunnel entrances beneath you and realized that you had not advanced but had only climbed higher. Then the train was in a new valley, descending to the river once again. The river was called the Dadu He, 'Big Crossing'. It was wide and greyer than the sky above it. For most *of its length it was full of boulders. Fishermen with long rods or ancient fish-traps sat on its banks.*

These were the densest, steepest mountains I had seen so far, and the train was never more than a few minutes from a tunnel. So, in order to read or write, I had to leave the lights burning in the compartment. One moment there was a bright valley with great white streaks of rock down its sides, and gardens near the bottom and vegetable patches sloping at an angle of forty-five degrees, and the next moment the train would be roaring through a black tunnel, scattering the bats that hung against the walls. This was one of the routes where people complained of the length of the trip. But it was easily one of the most beautiful train-trips in China. I could not understand why tourists went from city to city, on a forced march of sightseeing. China existed in all the in-between places that were reachable only by train.

'What do you want for lunch?' the chef said. This dining-car was empty, too.

'This is a Sichuan train, right?'

'It is.'

'I will have Sichuan food then.'

*He brought me Sichuan chicken, hot bean curd, pork and green peppers, green onions stir-fried with ginger, soup and rice—a four-*yuan *lunch—and I went back and had a siesta. There were countries where train-journeys were no more than a period of suspense, waiting to arrive; and there were countries where the train-journey was itself an experience of travel, with meals and sleep and exercise and conversation and scenery. This was the latter. When I woke up in mid afternoon I saw that the mist and cloud had dispersed. The long hooting train had passed from low steep mountains into higher broader ones. I sat by the window and watched the world go by.*

Paul Theroux, Riding the Iron Rooster, *1988*

Paul Theroux *has written several volumes of highly-praised fiction and numerous successful travel books, including* The Great Railway Bazaar, The Old Patagonian Express, The Kingdom by the Sea *and* The Pillars of Hercules.

Wannian Si, 1,020 metres in altitude, is where most visitors start their ascent, since about a 40-minute bus ride from Baoguo Si to Jingshui takes you quite close to it. From the bus terminus it is only a three to four kilometre walk to the temple if you do not want to wait for the cable car.

Founded in the third century, **Wannian Si** (Temple of a Myriad Years) is probably the oldest surviving monastery on Emei Shan. The holy mountain's patron saint, Puxian, is honoured here in the most arresting religious building on Emei Shan. This is a square brick hall surmounted by a stupa-decorated dome. Rather more suggestive of Indian shrines than of Chinese ones, the hall is composed of brick and stone only, and is beamless. Its purpose is to enclose a magnificent bronze statue of Puxian and his mount, a six-tusked elephant with its feet planted in lotuses. At least three disastrous fires have demolished Wannian Si since the statue was wrought in the tenth century, and each time this image has escaped more or less unscathed. The hall is not very large, so that Puxian and his elephant, together measuring more than eight metres high, seem to fill it all. If you peer more closely, however, you will see that the interior walls are shelved and set with a multitude of fired-clay Buddha figures. Emperor Wanli's mother, who came to Emei Shan on pilgramage, is supposed to have ordered the shrine to be built in 1580. It is also said that twice a year, at the solstices, the sun shines through a hole in the dome and strikes the bodhisattva's forehead.

In a side hall, four other treasures belonging to the monastery are normally locked safely away. The unspoken condition for taking them out is a generous donation to the temple funds. The treasures are: a small jade Buddha from Burma; a manuscript, closely written with scriptures, consisting of a sheaf of more than 400 narrow palm-leaf pages; a Ming-dynasty imperial seal; and a tooth of the Buddha. The last is a most curious relic, about 30 centimetres long, rather less in width and some eight centimetres thick, a lump of smooth veined yellow ivory which came into the temple's possession during the Southern Song period (1127–1279).

A tough haul up a winding trail, and the next stop for bearings is **Huayan Ding**, where two routes converge. Downhill to the left, as you face the summit, are **Xianfeng Si** (Immortal Peak Temple) and **Jiulao Dong** (Nine Ancients Cave), sites formerly revered by Taoists. A Chinese version of the Rip van Winkle story is told about these sites. One day an abbot of Xianfeng Monastery met nine old men near the cave. Invited to join them for a game of chess, the abbot whiled away a few pleasant hours. Only when he returned to the monastery did he realize that the few hours were actually 60 years—had he stayed, he would have achieved immortality. He rushed back to the cave at once, but no trace of the immortals remained.

Emei Shan's notorious and ferocious monkeys lurk around here, scampering out of the undergrowth to extort food from passers-by. Local people say that you should

In the main hall of a Buddhist temple on Emei Shan

show your empty palms to them if you want to avoid their importunate pestering. They bite, too, so give them a wide berth. To the right the path goes up to **Xixiang Chi** (Elephant Bathing Pool), a popular overnight stop for climbers before their assault on the summit. Climbers have now reached the temperate zone, and will notice the subtropical vegetation of the lower slopes giving way to rhododendrons and other species of deciduous shrubs and trees. The temple at Xixiang Chi, in a lofty position on the edge of a precipice, is named after the legendary wash of Puxian's white elephant, although it would be hard to imagine anything of that size having much of a bath in the meagre tank of water here.

Above Xixiang Chi, the path zigzags up to a plateau at the rear of the summit. At this altitude the air is perceptibly colder, and in winter the slopes are blanketed with snow. It can be startlingly beautiful at that time, when all around the branches of trees are frosty sheaths of ice, while at your feet the undergrowth thrusts out fingers of sparkling crystal. Every puff of wind sends a tremor through the trees, sweeping the ice and snow to the ground with a faint whispering rustle.

Four hours' hike from Xixiang Chi, **Leidong Ping** (Thundering Cave Terrace) marks the end of the motor road (the drive up from Hongzhushan Guesthouse

SICHUAN PROVINCE

takes around two hours). *Huagan* porters press their litters on elderly visitors for the last 15-minute lap to the cable car. From **Jieyin Dian** (Reception Hall) the cable car (for which there may be a long queue) lurches over treetops to deposit you at an elevation of 3,077 metres. It starts operating early enough for the sunrise, a glorious spectacle of orange gaudiness if you catch it. Unfortunately this is such a popular attraction with most visitors and pilgrims, and all the vantage points so crowded, that it is impossible to witness the moment with the peace and solitude one might feel appropriate.

The path from Leidong Ping to the summit (a climb of about an hour and a half) includes two very steep flights of stairs. Once at the top, you can walk on to **Wanfo Ding** (Myriad Buddhas Peak) on the western edge, the highest point on Emei Shan.

Except in clear weather, the summit is something of an anticlimax. The original **Jinding Si** (Golden Summit Temple), which by all accounts was as resplendent a structure as one can imagine, was gutted by fire in the 1880s. Financed by subscriptions from provincial officials as well as Tibetan Buddhists, it was a shining monument clad in tiles of iron and bronze and ornamented with thousands of Buddha figures covered with gold. These days Tibetans still regard the mountain as holy, coming on pilgrimages and leaving a few scattered prayer flags fraying on poles.

Besides sunrise and sunset, the celebrated sights of Jinding are the **Sea of Clouds** and **Buddha's Aureole** (also called Buddha's Glory). Clouds are all too prevalent on the summit, sometimes robbing climbers of their hard-earned views by enveloping everything in an opaque whiteness. On a sunny afternoon, though, when the clouds hug the lower slopes, leaving the summit clear, a curious effect of light can be see, most often between two and four o'clock. Then, shadows cast by objects on the summit upon the clouds below take on a bright halo of rainbow colours. Although the mirage is a natural phenomenon, caused by the rays of sun being refracted through water-laden air, pilgrims in the past thought it a manifestation of the Buddha and some of them would leap from the cliff in ecstatic wonder. This practice was frowned upon, and chain railings and walls were put up at Self-Sacrifice Crag to forestall further losses of life.

Fan Chengda (1126–93), a poet and scholar from Jiangsu Province, came to worship on Emei Shan and left this record of his impressions: 'The rounded gauze cloud spread out below the cliff, rose brilliant and beautiful, came within a few *zhang* (a Chinese measure of length) of the cliff, and stood there. It was unbroken and shone like polished gems. At the time minute drops of rain were falling, as at the finishing of a shower. I leaned forward and gazed upon the centre of the cliff; there was a great aureole resting upon the level cloud; outside this was a triple halo, having the colours of ultramarine, yellow, red and green. The glory was in the centre, like bright space, serenely clear. Each person looking saw the image of himself in the empty place exactly as in a mirror, and there was not an infinitesimal part obscure. If I lifted my hand or moved my foot the image followed the motion, but I could not see the person standing by my side.'

The greatest sight of all, though, is not one of the traditional vistas of Emei Shan. To the west the land lifts towards the Tibetan plateau, and the distance before it is filled with mountains. At first feathery clouds hide the farthest peaks; as the sun rises higher, the scene is gradually tinged with blue. Bluer and bluer it becomes, and then the white incandescent crest of Gongga Shan appears. Two plateaux flank the pinnacle to the right and left, absolutely flat as if the tops had been sliced off. Momentarily the view is shut out by clouds being drawn up by the sun, but just as suddenly it re-emerges, this time more sharply in focus. To Fan Chengda the snow on the mountains of the 'western countries' was bright as polished silver. 'The mountains extend into India and other foreign countries, and beyond I know not how far,' he wrote, 'but they are seen as distinctly as though upon the table before me—marvellous and incomparable sight; a diadem for a whole lifetime.'

LESHAN: THE GREAT BUDDHA

Overlooking the Min River waters from 71 metres high and 28 metres broad, the Great Buddha of Leshan (Leshan Dafo) is unquestionably enormous. In fact it is the largest carved Buddha in the world and as Sichuan's most famous man-made curiosity it should not be missed.

Leshan, a growing city of more than 200,000, 31 kilometres east of Emei town, nestles at the confluence of three rivers—the Min Jiang, the Dadu He and the Qingyi Jiang. The town was a prosperous centre of silk weaving and white wax production. White wax trees (*baila shu*), which abounded in the area, were the basis of an extraordinary industry. Farmers engaged in it used the trees as repositories for the eggs of a scaly insect which, once hatched, secreted a wax that coated the branches. The wax was then scraped off, melted in boiling water and collected, to be used in the manufacture of candles and as a polish.

The days of silk and wax are over, but Leshan remains a lively and prosperous town, now cashing in on its status as a UNESCO World Heritage site and major tourist attraction. It is also home to new semi-conductor factories.

Most visitors make only a perfunctory call at Leshan itself, going straight to the pier for a boat trip to Wuyou Shan. This takes them past the Great Buddha in his rocky niche for a full-frontal view. Leaving from the pier on Binjiang Lu, regular ferry boats make the 25-minute trip to Wuyou Shan until about 5.30pm. This short ride gives passengers plenty of time, while the boat dawdles in front of the Great Buddha, to take photographs of themselves with the Buddha in the background.

There are three approaches to **Lingyun Shan**, on whose cliff face is carved the Great Buddha. You can cross the bridge from Wuyou Si, take a direct ferry from Leshan or reach the back of it by road. The road ends close to the 13-tiered **Lingbao Pagoda**. From here it is only a short walk to **Dafo Si** (Great Buddha Temple), entered from a spacious courtyard off which an unpretentious hotel, Nanlou Binguan, is located. Through Dafo Si's hall of Guardians, in which Maitreya (the Buddha to Come) is depicted in the traditional image of a fat-bellied, grinning deity, you come to an open area level with the Great Buddha's right ear. It teems with photographers' stands. To meditate upon the poetry of Su Shi, also known as Su Dongpo (1036–1101), unquestionably the presiding genius of Leshan and its

environs, go to the part of the hill around the Dongpo Studio. There are gardens, walkways, and old buildings decorated with intricate woodwork. Su Dongpo, who was born in the town of Meishan, some 60 kilometres north of Leshan, is said to have come here to drink and contemplate the moon. One of his poems, written in the night of the Mid-Autumn Festival in 1076, chastises the moon in one verse:

Rounding the red pavilion,
Stooping to look through gauze windows,
She shines on the sleepless;
The moon should know no sadness;
Why, then, is she always full when dear ones are parted...

The Zaijiu Ting pavilion overlooking the river and Leshan City is dedicated to Su Dongpo as his 'drinking pavilion'. On the pillar columns is inscribed one of his poems:

At the feet of the Great Buddha of Leshan (above)
Descending by the Nine-twists Stairway alongside the Great Buddha (below)

Though great to be governor of Leshan, better to drink on Lingyun Mountain.

Descend by the **Nine-Twists Stairway** (Jiuqu Zhandao), past numerous carved niches, along the Buddha's right side. The steps, cut into the cliff, are quite steep in places, but a solid metal railing prevents people from falling off onto Buddha's toes below. Small shrine images carved into the soft red sandstone have been worn bare by countless visitors over the thousand years of pilgrimage.

From the Buddha's feet, more steps to the left wind uphill between bamboo, banana trees and caves (in one of these Haitong apparently lived after blinding himself). These steps will take you back to Dafo Si. Along the way, the river Min Jiang is always in view, its surface broken by floating logs and sampans midstream. A haze often hangs over it, but the outline of Wuyou Shan in the near distance, lacy with foliage on the cliffs, is usually visible.

From the top of Dafo Si, drop into the Forest of Steles (Beilin) if you are interested in Chinese calligraphy. There are many steles here covered with rows of Chinese characters in various scripts.

Back in the eighth century, the turbulent waters of the three rivers converging just below Leshan made navigation so difficult that many a boat capsized in the current. Haitong, a Buddhist monk, conceived the idea of carving a Buddha figure above the spot to protect river craft from danger. One of those fanatic Buddhists who resorted to self-mutilation to demonstrate their piety, Haitong went so far as to blind himself. The sculpture was a labour of nearly a century. Down the years there has been some erosion of the reddish-brown sandstone in which the seated Buddha is carved, but considering that it is well over a thousand years old the statue is remarkably intact. This can be attributed to the hidden drainage network incorporated into its design. Still, some water does seep through, and lichen and weeds sprout grotesquely from the cracks. A fuzz of grass covers the Buddha's lap, his chest is green with ferns, while some yellow flowers struggle for existence on his lap. The statue was restored in the mid-1990's with donations from a Thai Buddhist association.

Sitting with his back against Lingyun Shan, the Great Buddha is flanked by two guardian figures, much smaller at eight metres high, while behind him the hill is dotted with pavilions. The most stunning—raised as it is on the crest—is Longbao Pagoda. A ladder-like staircase coils up the cliff-side to the Buddha's right. From the front the statue looks clearly out of proportion. Its nose is said to be 5.6 metres long, and a hundred people can sit in a circle on one foot. Visitors like to be photographed standing by one of the Buddha's toes, but the crowds are now kept at a respectful distance, not longer allowed to climb up onto his feet.

A quiet inn and restaurant serving vegetarian specialties is at Bijin Luo Tower, overlooking Wuyou Shan Mountain. Along the south flank of Lingyu Mountain is a unique construction of a 'fisherman's village'—a group of wooden buildings and central pavilion built on a stone foundation over 200 meters long shaped like an ancient ship, with staircase entrances at bow and stern. Small restaurants offer fish meals from the river.

Wuyou Shan, once part of the mainland, was cut adrift when and an overflow channel was dug to divert the Dadu River floods in the third century BC. It is now linked by a suspension bridge to Lingyun Shan, although it can also be reached by boat. From the pier, a shaded pathway leads to **Wuyou Si**, a Chan Buddhist temple founded in the eighth century, whose elaborate pavilions afford nice views of the river from its terraces. The Luohan

A type of junk known as a laohuaqiu *passes the Great Buddha at Leshan. A photograph taken in the mid-1980s.*

Hall is filled with 500 newly rebuilt and painted statues of the Buddha's followers, or arhats—no two are alike—together with an impressive statue of Avalokiteshvara, the Bodhisattva of Mercy.

From the temple, one can follow the walkway down and reach a rear gate to the park. A dock has a direct ferry back to Leshan passing the Great Buddha offering a view of the eroded guardians on the outer cliff sides.

TRAVELLERS IN A BOTANICAL PARADISE: PLANT HUNTING IN SICHUAN

Tea roses, peonies, chrysanthemums, azaleas, camellias—flowers familiar in European and American gardens—were unknown outside the Far East until introduced from China by plant collectors in the 18th and 19th centuries.

The first European plant collectors were missionaries and merchants, notably officers in the service of the British trading concern, the East India Company. As foreign commerce in China was initially confined to the southern port of Guangzhou (or Canton, as it was known then), their shipments contained only subtropical plants that were cultivated in local gardens. The situation changed dramatically when, in the second half of the 19th century, as a result of treaties terminating a series of wars, other ports in China were opened to foreign commerce and residence. Subjects of the European treaty powers were then allowed to travel to the interior. Many sailed up the Yangzi River to Chongqing. From there they penetrated western Sichuan, northwest Yunnan and beyond. A vast temperate region with a wealth of wild flora unequalled elsewhere in the world lay before them. That region became the hunting ground of botanists.

Sichuan particularly compelled botanic exploration because of its highly diverse topography. Between its basin and its peaks, the province presented vertically demarcated zones of vegetation from the cultivated crops of warm, wet farmlands to the myriad varieties of herbs and flowers of alpine meadows. Much of it was virgin territory undefiled by the hand of man. Primitive communications meant, though, that plant collectors faced near-insuperable obstacles in reaching the most rewarding areas. They walked enormous distances or, at best, bumped along in a bamboo chair, known as *huagan*, borne on the shoulders of coolies. At night they either camped or slept in stinking shacks, sharing them with cattle. Bad weather could set all their efforts at nought, for unless kept clean and dry, specimens could be easily destroyed by mould. Sometimes they found themselves fording raging torrents, hacking through impenetrable forests, plodding up rugged mountains, and even being set upon by bandits and hostile tribesmen.

They rose to the challenge. Some of them had the opportunity anyway, being stationed on the spot as consular officials or missionaries; others were specialists in natural history who made the long journey and stayed at least a whole season so that they might gather seeds for planting at home. They are remembered through the plants that bear their names. Augustine Henry (1856–1930), a medical officer with the Chinese Maritime Customs in Yichang on the Yangzi, took to plant-collecting out of boredom with expatriate life. During periods of leave he wandered in Hubei and Sichuan, sending the herbarium material and seeds gathered with the help of Chinese assistants to the Royal Botanic Gardens at Kew in London. Towards the end of his tenure in China Dr Henry was posted to Yunnan, another province rich in flora. He was instrumental in introducing such garden plants as *Rhododendron Augustinii* and *Viburnum Henryi*. He also reported sighting the dove tree, an ancient plant growing wild only in China.

At that time the French Catholic missionary effort was gaining a foothold in western China. Dedicated priests of the Mission Etrangères spent long lonely years in the interior, hardly ever seeing another European. Père Jean Pierre Armand David (1826–1900) was an assiduous botanist and zoologist. During a two-year expedition from Chongqing through Chengdu to Sichuan's northwestern corner, he found his first specimen of the dove tree, growing at an altitude of 1,830 metres. It was subsequently named after him—*Davidia involucrata*. This tree, besides being rare, is exceptionally ornamental. Two large pure white bracts sprout under each tightly-packed flower-head, so that, when in bloom, a tree conjures the illusion that a flock of doves with outstretched wings has alighted on its branches. David did not stay long enough in the area to collect any seeds; that was left to E H Wilson, the most outstanding plant-hunter of western China (see below).

Jean André Soulié (1858–1905) was another missionary. From his base in Kangding (or Tachienlu as the town was designated in early European travelogues) this plant-collector sent to the Museum of Botany in Paris a prolific harvest including *Primula Souliéi* and *Buddleia variabilis*. Later he went farther afield towards Tibet, and it was near the frontier, at Batang, that he was captured and shot by Tibetan monks in 1905.

Although better known for his studies of the Naxi tribe in western Yunnan, Joseph F Rock (1884–1962) also travelled extensively in the Sichuan borderlands and introduced innumerable plant species to the Western world. An Austrian born in Vienna, he went to the United States in 1905 and later proceeded to Honolulu where, in between teaching Latin and natural history at a school, he made himself an expert on the flora of the Hawaiian islands. His first expedition to China, in 1922, was under the auspices of the US Department of Agriculture. Not only did he collect plants; the bird life and the peoples of western China also fascinated him. Before long his insatiable curiosity had taken him into regions hitherto unexplored by foreigners—the corners of Sichuan, Yunnan, Gansu and Qinghai provinces inhabited by Tibetans. In time Rock's activities in botany were displace by an interest in ethnological research. He never published anything on Chinese flora, but he did leave an invaluable written and photographic record of the minority peoples among whom he lived.

Such was the European rage for new exotic species that the field covered by amateur botanists was soon invaded by professional collectors, thanks to their sponsorship by private nurseries, botanical gardens and institutions like the Horticultural Society of London. Ernest Henry Wilson (1876–1930) was both by training and temperament the epitome of the

Rhododendrons, which grow best on high ground,
cover the hillsides of Sichuan from late May

meticulous plant collector. In 11 years of travelling in central and western China he sent to England and America a botanical and horticultural cornucopia comprising 65,000 specimens of some 5,000 species and the seeds of about 1,500 different plants.

Wilson, born in the English county of Gloucestershire, left school very young and became an apprentice in a nursery garden. Later he attended botany classes at a technical college in Birmingham. His bent for botany was recognized by the Director of Kew Gardens, and it was while Wilson was there that his name was put forward to the nursery firm of James Veitch & Sons to go to China on their behalf. Besides a general brief to search for plants to introduce into English gardens, his main quest was to be, quite specifically, the elusive dove tree.

On his first expedition (1899–1901) Wilson travelled by way of the United States, where he called on Professor C S Sargent at the Arnold Arboretum in Boston. In China he made a detour to consult Augustine Henry in Yunnan, and then embarked upon a thorough survey of the mountains and valleys along the Hubei–Sichuan border, which indeed yielded not only *Davidia involucrata* but a veritable bounty of seeds, herbarium material, bulbs and roots.

Wilson made four journeys to China altogether. During his second sojourn the patch he made uniquely his own was Sichuan. He covered an enormous area, from present-day Leshan to the far northwest, going twice to Songpan. He also made a thorough investigation of the flora on Emei Shan.

In 1907 he was again in Hubei and Sichuan, this time for the Arnold Arboretum, concentrating on woody plants. It was on his last visit to China that he made his greatest discovery—the Regal Lily. His description of the flower reveals nothing of the excitement he must have felt on finding it, yet it is typical of his factual style: 'In the Min Valley the charming *Lilium regale* luxuriates in rocky crevices, sun-baked throughout the greater part of the year. It grows three to five feet tall, and has slender leaves crowded on stems bearing several large funnel-shaped flowers, red-purple without, ivory-white suffused with canary-yellow within, often with the red-purple reflected through, and is deliciously fragrant.'

(following pages) Logs are floated on the Min Jiang, a major tributary of the Yangzi, down to saw mills near Chongqing. (pages 232–3) Originally a goat path, this road is hacked out of the rock above the Min Jiang in Sichuan Province.

CHENGDU

Sooner or later, the visitor to Chengdu comes upon the wide boulevard (Renmin Nan Lu) which slices through the city centre and ends in a colossal statue of Chairman Mao, one arm raised in greeting. Local residents were wont to compare Chengdu with Beijing, but the only point of resemblance to have survived is the straight north–south main street, divided into six lanes by lines of trees. The city walls with their four gates at the compass points, enclosing a Chinese as well as a Manchu district, were pulled down in the 1960s, though by then they were very damaged, and consisted merely of broken embankments of masonry. (A gate of the old wall is left in the north of the city, down a rutted road—Xitu Lu—but it is enclosed within a military area and cannot be inspected at close quarters.)

To the left of the statue of Mao on his high platform, one block from the square in the angle made by Dongyu Jie and Yanshikou, is the People's Market (Renmin Shangchang), which was burnt down in the aftermath of student demonstrations in June 1989, but has now risen from the ashes as one of the largest and most modern department stores in China.

Roads radiate outwards from this central square, spanning the rivers that formed three sides of the original city. Of course Chengdu is no longer confined within these watery boundaries. Since becoming provincial capital in 1938, it has developed rapidly into the cultural, transportation and industrial centre of China's southwest region, and its population has grown.

The city is believed to have been founded more than 2,300 years ago, emerging from obscurity when the Qin dynasty (221–206 BC) established the County of Chengdu after China was unified under one empire. It became the capital of Shu Han, the independent kingdom of Liu Bei, in AD 221. By the tenth century its commercial importance was something to be reckoned with, so much so that the earliest form of paper money was introduced by its merchants to oil the wheels of trade. Commodities centred on the products of Chengdu's surrounding farmland and the more distant frontier regions, but a touch of luxury was provided by *jin* (brocade), woven in the area since the third century. An earlier name for the city, Jincheng (Brocade City), was derived from this.

To some people Chengdu still seems like an overgrown town; others boast that it is a cosmopolitan metropolis. It might sound patronizing, though it would be true, to say that it is very much a provincial city. It lacks the character of, say, lowering grey Chongqing, with its hilly location, its proximity to a bustling waterways and its winter fog. Chengdu seems more intimate by comparison. It has many modern high-rise buildings, but they are still surrounded by warrens of side streets

Chairman Mao's statue, Chengdu

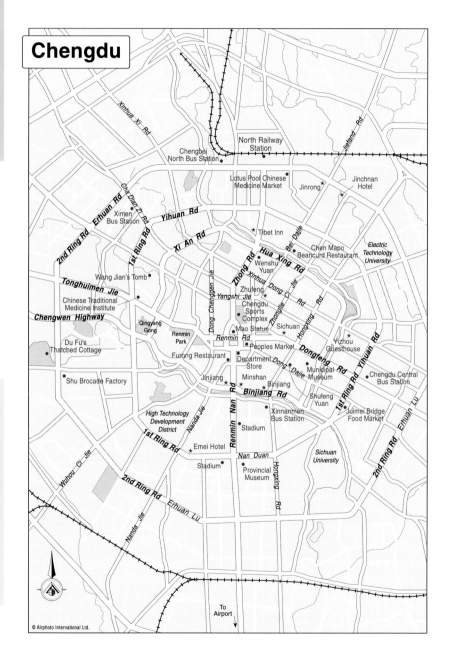

Chengdu

Ximen Bus Station

Cha Dian Zi Rd

Erhuan Rd

2nd Ring Rd

1st Ring Rd

Xinhua Xi Rd

Yihuan Rd

Xi An Rd

North Railway Station

Chengbei North Bus Station

Lotus Pool Chinese Medicine Market

Jinrong

Jinchnan Hotel

Jiefand Rd

Tibet Inn

Chen Mapo Beancurd Restaurant

Electric Technology University

Bei Dajie

Hua Xing Rd

Zhong Rd

Xinhua Dong

Wenshu Yuan

Dong Chenggen Jie

Wang Jian's Tomb

Tonghuimen Jie

Chinese Traditional Medicine Institute

Chengwen Highway

Qingyang Gong

Renmin Park

Yangshi Jie

Zhufeng

Chengdu Sports Complex

Sichuan

Zhongjia

Hongxing Rd

Yizhou Guesthouse

Mao Statue

Renmin Rd

Dongfeng Rd

Yihuan Rd

1st Ring Rd

Du Fu's Thatched Cottage

Furong Restaurant

Peoples Market

Department Store

Dong Dajie

Municipal Museum

Chengdu Central Bus Station

Shu Brocade Factory

Jinjiang

Minshan

Binjiang

Binjiang Rd

Shufeng Yuan

Juimei Bridge Food Market

Wuhou Ci Jie

High Technology Development District

Nanda Jie

Renmin Nan Rd

1st Ring Rd

Emei Hotel

Stadium

Xinnanmen Bus Station

Xinnanmen

Stadium

Nan Duan

Hongxing Rd

Provincial Museum

Sichuan University

2nd Ring Rd   Erhuan Lu

Erhuan Lu

2nd Ring Rd

Nanda Jie

To Airport

© Airphoto International Ltd.

with their neighbourhood markets and stores. In appearance and feel it is similar to many other regional centres in China.

Not all of them, though, have as interesting a street life. Dashing Khampas from western Sichuan, knives glinting from the folds of the *chubas*, sweep through the streets; suddenly a group of Yi, distinguishable by their fringed woollen capes over workaday clothes, materialize at the entrance of a hotel or restaurant. In Binjiang Park, by the banks of the river which wends across the southern half of the city, the Jinjiang (on some maps called the Nanhe), vendors stir their 'Chongqing hotpots' in winter and sell ice-cream in summer, while elderly citizens huddle over cards or mahjong tiles in pools of shade under dusty trees. Early in the morning, these retired folk from the neighbourhood gyrate to the scratchy strains of modern dance music.

Shangliu international airport is 18 kilometres to the west of the city and serves many regional destinations, including Bangkok, Hong Kong, Lhasa, Seoul and Singapore, as well as all the major internal cities.

SIGHTS IN CHENGDU
WENSHU YUAN

This Tang-dynasty temple is located about one and a half kilometres south of the railway station, down Wenshu Yuan Jie running east off Renmin Zhong Lu. The narrow approach, lined with a mumble of stalls purveying all the paraphernalia of worship—incense, 'hell money' for burnt offerings, red candles, firecrackers—is a fascinating manifestation of the popularity of religion in China today but also its more down-to-earth commercial possibilities. Mahjong sets, far from striking an incongruous note, seem perfectly in keeping with the other wares on sale.

Wenshu the God of Wisdom or, by his Sanskrit name, Manjusri, does not seem to be the pre-eminent object of worship at the eponymous temple. The principal shrines are dedicated to Maitreya (the Buddha to Come), Sakyamuni and Avalokitesvara (or Guanyin, the Goddess of Mercy). The devotion of Chinese Buddhists to their favourite bodhisattva, Guanyin, has been exhibited in many ways, but perhaps none more ardent than the masochistic act of an 18th-century adherent, who embroidered a picture of the goddess, not with silk thread but with hair pulled from her own head; this piece of embroidery is among the treasured relics at Wenshu Yuan.

Those shrines take up three of the five halls built along a central axis stretching from the temple entrance, the last two being used for preaching and for the storage of sutras (Buddhist scriptures), of which there is quite a collection. The temple is particularly proud of the three books written by fanatic monks in their own blood around 1836. Apparently the authors used to sit down to their task every morning by dipping their brushes in blood from their self-lacerated tongues.

Forming a rectangular enclosure around the central halls are long monastery buildings, for Wenshu Yuan is the Sichuan headquarters of the Chan (Zen) Buddhist sect and an active seminary. Novices and monks eat in a gloomy refectory furnished with rows of trestle tables and benches all facing a central aisle.

Although the monastery was founded earlier, its buildings date from 1697–1706 and are typical of architecture of their time.

LOTUS POOL CHINESE MEDICINE MARKET

One of the most interesting places to visit in Chengdu, when historical monuments pall, is the Lotus Pool Chinese Medicine Market (Hehua Chi Zhongyao Shichang). There, in the north of the city, close to the railway station, is a vast hangar-like building, open at the sides and heaped with every ingredient of the Chinese pharmacopoeia, both animal and vegetable. The temperate slopes of Sichuan's high mountains abound in herbs, roots and plants with a variety of curative properties, and, judging from what is available here, huge supplies of these find their way to this wholesale emporium. Gunnysacks surround each stall, their contents pungent with a mixture of sweet, woody, or sharply acrid aromas. The most extraordinary things spill from them: there are whole monkey skeletons, slabs of tree bark and sticks of twigs, porcupine quills, deer antlers, shiny green and matt-brown striped snakes coiled and tied, dried seahorses and black knobbly slug-like caterpillar fungus. More appealing to the eye are the bright red seeds of Chinese wolfberry, claret-coloured dried jujubes, orange peel and the pearly kernels of different fruits. Then there are the more familiar cinnamon, liquorice and ginseng. At the back of the building, clinics are conveniently located to provide on-the-spot prescriptions.

ZHAOJUE MONASTERY

Zhaojue Monastery was founded in the seventh century and harboured many an eminent monk. The monks were adherents of various sects, although the monastery is now closely associated with Chan Buddhism and, given its location in southwest China, with the Yellow Hat sect of Tibetan Buddhism. The monastery is certainly large enough to accommodate all kinds of practices and rites.

Behind the red painted walls are several courtyards and shrines. With an ancient tree and an iron bell tower in front of it, the main hall rises two storeys on a framework of painted pillars and carved beams. Restoration work on this huge hall was completed in 1990. Inside, a massive Buddha seated on a lotus and displaying a swastika on his chest is flanked by two other Buddhas.

Before reaching the main hall, a small shrine behind a courtyard, the Guanyin Ge, is worth a look. This is heralded by a small iron bell tower; like the one in front of the main hall, the clappers hanging from the bells are fish-shaped. To the left and right of the gate are grottoes dedicated to Guanyin, the Goddess of Mercy, filled with smouldering incense sticks and faded flowers and Buddha figures galore.

WANG JIAN'S TOMB

Wang Jian (847–918) was a local ruler during one of those recurrent periods of disunity in China's imperial past when a centralized state broke into short-lived regional kingdoms. In this case it was the interval between the fall of the Tang and the rise of the Northern Song known as the Five Dynasties period (907–960). Wang Jian's tomb, discovered in 1942, lies in a cold, damp, arched vault under a grassy mound. The raised stone grave is supported by 12 effigies; along three sides of the platform is a frieze of dancing girls and musicians performing on lutes, clappers and drums. The redeeming feature of this depressing site is the pretty garden below the mound, where there is a popular teahouse.

DU FU'S THATCHED COTTAGE

Du Fu (712–770) is regarded by most Chinese scholars as China's greatest poet. In the year 759, with help from a relative, Du Fu came to Chengdu. There, by a small stream in the west of the city, he built himself a cottage and off and on for the next four years passed one of the most peaceful and carefree periods of his hard life, tilling the land, tending his fruit trees and writing some 240 poems. One of the poems refers to his rural retreat by a limpid brook, with its wicket gate opening onto a rutted country lane, where, living in remoteness, he could be nonchalant about his shabby gown. The poetry he wrote here is full of leisurely observations of the changing seasons—the red earth after spring rains, swallows chasing in and out of his house, the scent of loquats ripening on a tree, dewdrops on the tips of bamboo leaves, autumn gales tearing the thatch off his roof. A vein of sadness, about ill health, disappointments and life's brevity, also runs through it, but there is serenity, too, as when he watches his wife cut paper for a chessboard, and his son fashion a fish hook from a needle.

Du Fu's cottage has long since vanished. Instead, a symbolic thatched pavilion— the Shaolin Caotang—stands amidst the luxuriant greenery of a commemorative park. The very stream by which Du Fu built his humble house faces the park entrance. It was in the 11th century that a shrine to the poet was first established. Today the grounds embrace several buildings, some containing exhibitions of the poet's work. But most people seem to come here to stroll in the gardens and sit in the teahouse near the entrance.

(above) A traditional teahouse typical of Chengdu
(below) The dazzling costumes and make-up of Sichuan opera

WUHOU CI

Lost to a fire in the 17th century, Wuhou Ci was completely rebuilt in the early Qing dynasty. Its grounds in the southwest corner of the city now form the Southern Suburbs Park (Nanjiao Gongyuan).

Engraved steles line the approach to a series of halls, one behind the other. The first hall commemorates Liu Bei, whose statue looks out to a Ming-dynasty iron cauldron, embossed with dragons, in the centre of the paved courtyard in front. Two corridors, one filled with the sculpted figures of 14 civil officials and the other with 14 military commanders, enclose the courtyard to the east and west. Liu Bei's tomb is to the west of the lotus pond.

The hall to Zhuge Liang stands at the rear, framed by the graceful upturned double roofs of a bell tower to its right, and a drum tower to its left. Within the hall, the gilded statues of three generations of the Zhuge clan sit side by side. The biggest of the three bronze drums in front of them, its lid studded with six crouching frogs, is said to date from the seventh century.

PROVINCIAL MUSEUM

From the skull fossil of Ziyang Man (c. 30,000 BC) to the photograph of communist leaders Deng Xiaoping and Liu Bocheng in conference during the southwest liberation campaign in November 1949, the collection at this museum gives a useful overview of Sichuan's long history. The museum is situated just south of the city ring road (Yuhuan Lu Nan San Duan).

Cultural relics from the area's earliest settlements include pottery from Daxi and bronzes dated to the Ba and the Shu kingdoms. From the Han empire the earthenware tomb figures and stone bas-reliefs are probably the most striking exhibits. Also on display is an enormous loom constructed almost entirely of bamboo and wood. This early 19th century machine stands four metres high and measures five metres from end to end. Sichuan's celebrated brocade used to be woven on it. The revolutionary struggles of the Communist Party, including the Long March, are recorded in photographs and documents.

Southern Sichuan

Southern Sichuan is mountainous with crowded and growing cities, most of them industrial centres. The city of Panzhihua, for instance, situated on the Jinsha Jiang in the province's southernmost tip close to the Yunnan border, is southwest China's largest iron and steel producer, shrouded in a haze of air pollution. Besides iron ore and associated metals, coal is also mined, for the region as a whole is rich in mineral resources, which is good news for the local economy but holds limited interest for the traveller. The relatively few tourists who penetrate southern Sichuan usually go little further than Xichang. One other city stands out from the rest. Zigong, famed capital of salt, is a gem of a place.

Southwestern Sichuan is also home to one of China's largest ethnic minorities, the Yi, who cluster around the foothills of Daliang Shan (Great Cool Mountains), a range of highlands to the south of Emei Shan. It is in the Liangshan Yi Autonomous Prefecture, where more than 1.3 million of them live, that their largest single community is found. The rest of the Yi, whose total population exceeds 5.5 million, are distributed among the provinces of Yunnan, Guizhou and Guangxi.

Formerly known to the Hans (ethnic Chinese) as Lolos, the Yi came from the eastern Tibetan highlands and had retreated southwards as Chinese colonization spread to the peripheral tribal territories. They were mentioned in Chinese historical records two millennia ago, in which their customs were described in some detail, including that of arranging their hair upright on their crowns in a horn-like protrusion supported by a sheath of black string. The Yi believed that their hair conducted spiritual impulses and forbade anyone to touch it.

Holed up in remote inaccessible mountain areas after giving up their original territory to the Chinese, the Yi resisted foreign control and kept their traditional society alive up until recent times. Until 1958 they practised a caste system, with the nobility (known as the 'Black Bones') lording it over serfs (the 'White Bones'). Of Han Chinese and other tribal stock, the White Bones were most probably captured in raids and later enslaved. Since the aristocrats disdained menial work, agriculture and animal husbandry were undertaken by these slaves. They cultivated mainly corn, buckwheat and vegetables (although, like their Chinese neighbours, they also grew opium), and they raised cattle and ponies. The Black Bones inclined to more pugnacious pursuits, and one which particularly suited their independent spirit and bellicose temperament was banditry. Yi bandits accosted the first of the Long Marchers when they arrived in southern Sichuan in May 1935, demanding money and weapons and killing some of the men. The main force, however, were allowed to pass through unmolested as the result of a safe conduct agreement negotiated between commander Liu Bocheng and the Yi chieftain. There is another well-known story told of the Yi, about a US air-force pilot who was captured and kept by one of the tribes as a slave for 12 years. The events were later dramatized in a Chinese-made film.

The Yi ethnic minority is divided into many sub-groups with differences of customs and dress, but they share a common Tibeto-Burman tongue and have their own script. In appearance the Yi are tall, dark-complexioned and distinguishable from the Han Chinese by their aquiline noses. While nowadays the pressures of modernization are prompting people everywhere to adopt functional Western-style clothes, Yi men have not yet abandoned their poncho-like woollen cloaks, nor Yi women their bits of embroidered accessories like colourful bags and belts. On festival days all their attractive jewellery is displayed. The women are adorned with silver collars and hooped and pendant earrings made of gold, silver or bone. Some men also wear earrings, often of a large lump of amber or coral, which dangles from just one ear. Quite complicated hairstyles are sometimes worn, including the horn mentioned in Chinese historical literature 2,000 years ago. Yi women also wear a necklace with a bronze mouth harp, which they play traditionally to express their sorrow when separated from their parents after an arranged marriage. It is considered private music played only at home.

XICHANG

Although this city is officially the seat of Liangshan Yi Autonomous Prefecture, Xichang's population is mostly Han Chinese. (Zhaojue to Xichang's northeast is a predominantly Yi town.) Lying at a relatively high altitude, Xichang enjoys a pleasant climate, with frequent spells of clear skies and beautiful moonlit nights—hence its epithet, 'Moon City'. Every year, on the 24th of the sixth month by the lunar calendar, the Yi people celebrate their torch festival with a programme of horse racing, dancing and general merry-making.

A remaining section of the city wall, including the old south gate, lies to the northeast. What remains of the old town is in this area. A market sits by the riverside and a number of old wooden teahouses can also be found here.

The few foreign travellers who venture as far as Xichang are directed to Qionghai Lake, the city's scenic resort five kilometres to the south. Here is the site of Xichang's fanciest hotel, here was once held a national water-skiing competition, and here is located a lakeside park under a lushly forested hill. On the western shore of the park is the fascinating Liangshan Yi Slave Society Museum. It has more than 2,000 exhibits which are unfortunately labelled in Chinese only. Among them are ancient books covered in the distinctive Yi script, murals, exquisite costumes, jewellery, weapons, saddles, household utensils and some gruesome photographs of slaves being tortured. Continuing up the hill from the museum, you find yourself among the ancient trees of Lushan (Mount Lu). There are cypresses planted in the Han (206 BC–AD 220), crape myrtle and fir. The cypress in front of the Bright and Prosperous Temple (Guangfu Si), the biggest of the religious establishments on Lushan, is said to be more than 2,185 years old.

Xichang is one of the centres of China's space programme. Xichang Space Flight Centre, where satellites are launched on the back of Long March rockets, is located 65 kilometres to the north of town. The launch station, which may be visited, consists of a lift-off ramp and a computer-equipped control room in addition to various technical installations and assembly plants. Some 1,200 technical and support staff live and work at the base. However permits for foreigners can take several days to arrange.

ZIGONG

In the early days of the People's Republic there were only three centres in Sichuan large enough to be designated for administrative purposes as cities, and Zigong was one of them, sharing the honours with Chengdu and Chongqing.

Zigong's prominence goes back a long way. It used to be called Ziliujing (Self-Flowing Wells), which just about sums up the cause of its prosperity. When early travellers approached the site of Self-Flowing Wells, they never failed to note the array of tall wooden derricks, festooned with ropes, that stood on the ridges of surrounding hills. These contraptions enabled underground brine, of which Ziliujing had a seemingly inexhaustible supply, to be drawn to the surface. In the heyday of salt production around the late 18th century, there were as many as 3,000 salt wells in Sichuan, and a majority of them were concentrated in the Ziliujing area.

The southwestern hinterland, so distant from the sea, relied for the bulk of its salt on the brine wells of Ziliujing. Salt played a key role in China's economy in imperial and republican times. As an essential commodity, it was a reliable source of revenue and its distribution and sale had long been a favourite means by which the central government levied taxes. To this end various methods to control the trade were devised, spawning a considerable bureaucracy in the process. During the Qing dynasty (1644–1911), the government simply took the whole industry under its wing and ran it as a state monopoly, dividing the country into

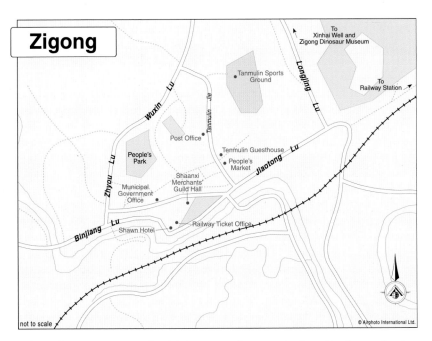

Zigong

To
Xinhai Well and
Zigong Dinosaur Museum

Tanmulin Sports
Ground

To
Railway Station

Wuxin Lu

Longjing Lu

Tanmulin Jie

Post Office

People's
Park

Tenmulin Guesthouse

People's
Market

Jiaotong Lu

Shaanxi
Merchants'
Guild Hall

Municipal
Government
Office

Zhyou Lu

Binjiang Lu

Shawn Hotel

Railway Ticket Office

not to scale

© Airphoto International Ltd.

salt-producing regions each with its own sales organization. On the production side, a fixed quota of output had to be delivered to the government, while marketing was placed in the hands of licensed wholesalers who in turn distributed the commodity to designated retail agents. This led to huge fortunes for many a salt merchant, including wily Shaanxi traders who carried the precious salt along the 'salt road' to Xi'an and north China. Their splendid guild hall still graces Zigong. Such a system also yielded quite a few opportunities for abuse: corrupt officials enriched themselves by indiscriminate granting of licences which, once secured, were passed on within a family as if it were some kind of hereditary right. Thus it was that the salt, when finally bought by the consumer, came to fetch very high prices and that production workers were harshly exploited to maximize profits for the middlemen involved.

The statue of a salt worker in the **Zigong Salt History Museum** is an evocative representative of the innumerable labourers who spent their lives in the shadow of the looming derricks. On the walls around, murals record the myths which had grown up to explain the discovery of the wells. One tells of a shepherdess who, following her flock, found their favourite spring to be oozing water which tasted salty. Li Bing, the pioneer of irrigation in Sichuan, is credited with sinking the first salt well in the third century BC. Systematic exploitation of brine wells began in the

Eastern Han period (AD 25–220). Natural gas was discovered to issue from some of the borings as well as brine. These 'fire wells', when the technology was eventually perfected to separate the gas, conveniently provided the means by which brine could be boiled.

The West first learned about mechanical deep-well drilling techniques from China, where 'percussion' drilling was developed at centres such as Ziliujing in the 11th century. It could take decades to drill a well but the tools, crude though they were, bore through solid rock to depths of 1,000 metres and more. The museum's comprehensive collection of drilling instruments, well repairing tools, iron drill-heads and plummets conveys a fascinating picture of the ingenious if primitive technology employed.

Old photographs of Ziliujing show derricks with bamboo ropes dangling from them. Ropes were passed through a pulley at the top and then coiled round an enormous windlass turned by oxen. The buckets of brine thus lifted were emptied into vats and conducted along a maze of bamboo aqueducts, which either ran along the ground or meandered on a framework of stilts like some flimsy roller-coaster, to boiling factories where hundreds of pans would be bubbling away to evaporate the water. If there was gas in the well, another series of pipes was installed to tap it for use as fuel.

A final section of the museum shows how modern technology was introduced to the industry in the 1920s. The city acquired its present name in 1939, when Ziliujing merged with neighbouring Gongjing. Today Zigong continues to benefit from its ancient industry, extracting natural gas and manufacturing a variety of chemical products from soda and ammonium chloride to monosodium glutamate. It produces 40 per cent of the nation's well and rock salt. At present rates of extraction, its salt reserves are expected to last 5,300 years.

Turning from past and present developments of Zigong's salt industry, spend some time looking at the museum itself. This is none other than the **Shaanxi Merchants' Guild Hall**, known as Xiqin Huiguan. It seems entirely appropriate that this exuberantly ostentatious structure, located in the middle of Shawan—Zigong's commercial district—should now preserve the relics of an industry which had enriched its sponsors.

In the late imperial age (end of the 19th to early 20th centuries) Shaanxi natives were active in commerce; for whatever reason, they became particularly adept bankers and merchants, and like all successful businessmen before and since, they succumbed to the urge for acquiring status symbols. What they came up with was at once traditional, opulent and conducive to their own pleasure and comfort. They built a string of *huiguan* (literally meeting houses) in the cities in which they had business. These were lavish affairs, containing function rooms, shrines to patron saints and large courtyards in which to hold festive gatherings.

At Ziliujing, the salt merchants of Shaanxi excelled themselves. Their guild hall, 16 years in the building (1736–52), fully attested to their power and wealth. Its magnificent gate house, which rises on red pillars to layers of exaggeratedly upturned roofs, incorporates an architectural conceit: although it is a four-storeyed structure, the second floor (which is taken up by a stage) cannot be seen from the front, while at the back, as viewed from the courtyard inside, it is the fourth floor which is cleverly hidden.

Through the courtyard and an antechamber, a flight of steps leads to a raised reception hall. Panels of bas-reliefs illustrating the theme of filial piety have been let into the walls on either side of the staircase. The airy reception hall, open on all sides, straddles a fish pond. Behind this is a more formal hall; besides two rows of thick red pillars made of Shaanxi stone, its most prominent feature consists of wall tablets inscribed with the names of the building's sponsors. Both halls are decorated with intricate painted carvings of dragons and phoenixes on the beams and brackets.

Both the guild hall and the museum collection are beautifully maintained. Most of the buildings of **Wangye Temple**, though, have been pulled down. A short distance south of the guild hall, at a bend of the Fuxi River which swirls past the edge of the city, this late 18th-century temple was local resident's antidote to the outflow of wealth into Shaanxi pockets. Since salt left the city by river, a temple on its bank, it was thought, would guarantee that the city's revenues would remain where the money was made. Unfortunately the temple had to give way to a riverside thoroughfare—Binjiang Lu and Jiaotong Lu—when that was widened. All that is left is a two-storeyed pavilion topped by a splendid roof encrusted with carved figures. Like the Shaanxi guild hall, the upper floor contained a stage, which now serves as a dance hall. Below it is a traditional teahouse.

Zigong's distinctive buses, run on natural gas which is carried in huge floppy bags on their roofs, weave along the main thoroughfares. Each bag holds enough fuel to drive a bus for 80 kilometres.

The **Xinhai Well** was the first well in the world to exceed a depth of 1,000 metres. It was drilled in 1835. There is not much to the site apart from a derrick, a rough shed under which the well and windlass are sheltered, and a workshop for boiling brine, but in those humble exhibits the whole process of Zigong's backbone industry is interestingly illustrated. Rickety lath-and-plaster houses sagging under grey-tiled roofs still line the streets.

The **Zigong Dinosaur Museum** at Dashanpu, is located in Da'an district 11 kilometres northeast of the city center. Dinosaur fossils and skeletons have been excavated in some 70 sites around Zigong since the 1920s. The richest finds were at Dashanpu. In fact more than a hundred skeletons of dinosaurs, mammal-like reptiles, turtles, amphibious animals and fishes were found piled together in a mass which scientists believe must have been washed down by a flood in the middle of the Jurassic period, 160 million years ago. Ten years after the discovery in 1972, construction of the Zigong Dinosaur Museum over the excavation site commenced. The museum opened in 1986. Its centrepiece is the Hall of Specimens where ten varieties of Jurassic fauna are displayed. They include several species of *Shunosaurus* and two skeletons of the huge *Omeisaurus tantuensis*. These are over 20 metres long. The original creatures, weighing about 40 tonnes, would have been herbivores. Not so the *Yandusaurus multidens*, a small dinosaur with needle-like teeth, which suggest that it was omnivorous, feeding on insects and small mammals. Excavations also yielded the skeleton of a flying bat-like creature, the *Angustinaripterus longicephalus*, as well as of *Sinopliosaurus*, the first of its kind to be unearthed in southern China.

A rear hall contains the spectacular Fossil Burial Site, two partially excavated pits in which the curved spines of several dinosaurs are clearly discernible.

The building itself is shaped like a giant stegosaurus, with metal ridge plates along its arched roof line. It is a cartoon architecture, but iconic of the research still underway. A new 'Dinosaur Kingdom' amusement park is being built nearby, to the west, as a new entertainment attraction. All this may be reached via the new highway or train from Chongqing or Chengdu.

Zigong Dinosaur Museum

ISABELLA BIRD
LADY TRAVELLER IN SICHUAN

Isabella Bird (1831–1904), daughter of a clergyman, seemed destined to become one of those Victorian invalids whose mysteriously debilitating illnesses kept them confined at home to a life of sickly spinsterhood and occasional good works. Yet she was to turn into one of the most adventurous and celebrated travellers of the 19th century.

She was born in the north of England and grew up in Cheshire. Wracked by a chronic spinal disease, she took to travelling to improve her health. Wandering in remote places and writing about them became a lifelong pre-occupation. Her last great journey was to China (started in January 1896 and concluded in the summer of the following year), and her account of it, *The Yangtze Valley and Beyond*, was published in 1899.

When Isabella Bird Bishop set off for China, she was a 64-year-old widow (she had married an Edinburgh doctor, John Bishop, in 1881). Starting in Shanghai, she steamed up the Yangzi as far as Yichang. There she transferred to a 'native boat' and continued to Wanxian. In her passage through the gorges, she observed the trackers closely and later described their 'inhuman work' with vividness. They were a rough lot, she thought, but as the journey went on their courage, endurance, and good nature won her sympathy and admiration. She regretted their addiction to opium but showed remarkable tolerance of it. Although her river voyage was free of accidents, it was not without excitement, and she would have been fully alive to the dangers that lurked when she saw on two occasions down-bound junks being tossed in rapids, hit rocks and vanish in smithereens of timber.

The towns along the Yangzi captivated her, especially those with fine temples roofed in glazed green and yellow tiles. She thought the Zhang Fei Temple magnificent, and was only sorry that the crowds of curious locals who surrounded her camera, trying to peer through its lens and shaking its focusing cloth, prevented her from taking a photograph of the pavilions. The countryside of the river valley was, to her eye, alternatively grand and picturesque. Above Wind Box Gorge, she gazed upon distant forest-covered or snow-crowned mountains, and, below, clusters of villages with 'white-washed, black-beamed, several-gabled, many-roofed, orange-embowered farmhouses', around which every slope and level was 'cultivated to perfection, the bright yellow of the rape-seed blossom adding a charm to greenery which was never monotonous.'

From Wanxian Isabella Bird went upcountry, venturing into towns in the Jialing Valley, across to Wenchuan and out towards the fringes of Manzi (barbarian) territory—a land journey on foot and by sedan chair of nearly 2,000 kilometres. This foray took her to Chengdu; then she floated down the Min Jiang to Suifu (today's Yibin), where she rejoined the Yangzi. It was, even by today's standards, a formidable voyage. Throughout, her fascination with every detail of alien customs and surroundings never flagged. There was always a bounciness in her approach to new experiences. She never whined about the discomforts or dangers encountered, and continually displayed an immense resourcefulness that is the mark of all great travellers.

Chongqing waterfront, photographed by Cecil Beaton in 1944 in the course of several months' travelling in China as official photographer to the British Ministry of Information

STAGE II

THE SICHUAN BASIN AND THE THREE GORGES: YIBIN TO YICHANG

From about the 27 degrees north parallel, the Yangzi, flowing north–northeast for some 800 kilometres, forms the borders between the provinces of Sichuan and Yunnan, finally reaching the Sichuan or Red Basin. After Yibin, the river, now called the Chang Jiang, is joined by the Min Jiang and Jialing Jiang from the north and the Wu Jiang from the south. Thus originates the name of Sichuan Province—'Four Rivers'. The 500-metre high Sichuan Basin, with its mild winters and long rainy season, has long been agriculturally rich; in the late Han dynasty, Chengdu (today's capital of Sichuan) was even bigger than the then imperial capital of Luoyang. Sichuan has remained one of China's most important 'bread-baskets', producing cotton, hemp and silk as well as grain. On the large, flat Chengdu plain, the Min Jiang was harnessed for irrigation as early as 250 BC by the Dujiangyan irrigation system, which has been the basis of the region's prosperity ever since.

Near the confluence of the Dadu and Min rivers is the great sacred Buddhist mountain of Emei, studded with ancient temples. Not far distant, at Leshan, the river actually laps near the stone feet of the world's largest carved Buddhas. The 70-metre high Tang-dynasty (618–907) statue took 90 years to complete, from 713 to 803. The monk Hai Tong, who spent his life working on the project, believed such a grand effigy would prevent the flooding that would occasionally afflict the area.

The huge city of Chongqing stands at the confluence of the Jialing and the Yangzi. Below this city the river continues its progress through Chongqing Municipality, and on through the famous Yangzi Three Gorges into Hubei Province where, at Yichang, its flow sharply checked by the Three Gorges and Gezhou dams, it enters the flat lands of its middle reaches.

A sailing sanpan prepares to negotiate the Wu Dou Bridge, which dates from the Ming dynasty, in Wu Gorge; wu dou translates as 'no struggle'. The bridge has now been submerged by the Three Gorges Reservoir.

Chongqing

The bustling 'Mountain City' of Chongqing is centred on a promontory on the north bank of the Yangzi and rises above the confluence of the Yangzi and a major tributary, the Jialing Jiang, around the busy docks at Chaotianmen. The city has long since outgrown its original site and spilled over to the adjacent banks of both the Yangzi and Jialing. Cable cars glide across to opposite banks and giant bridges carry the city's burgeoning traffic. Caves perforate the steep hills, once built as bomb shelters and now busy as garages or naturally cool restaurants and hair salons.

For centuries it has been the main commercial and transportation centre for Sichuan Province. Hundreds of ships lined the muddy banks below the remaining old city wall at Chaotianmen—rusty ferries packed with commuters and barges heaped with goods plied the Three Gorges to the rest of China. Chongqing is the destination for most of the bulk transport that passed through the Gorges, which is likened to an eyedropper feeding the elephant of the populous region of Sichuan. The port bustle was impressive and sweat-soaked. Thousands of porters known as the *bang bang jun*—the help army—line up with their bamboo poles and ropes to carry supplies up the staircases from the river into the heart of the city. These cheerful troops, some 200,000 on any given day, are generally laid-off workers nowadays professionally organized by agencies. Many also work on the construction sites, camping in the muddy disarray of the crowded city.

Chongqing has undergone a rapid transformation. This is mainly due to the city being granted national status in 1997 as a municipal region similar to Beijing, Shanghai and Tianjin with an administrative region that includes the eastern Sichuan counties down river, encompassing a total population of some 31 million people. Chongqing is now the world's largest metropolitan region. The city itself has a population of around six million. It is expected to grow to 10 million in the next decade, gobbling up nearby farmland for apartment complexes. Rural people can now move into the city and with the purchase of an apartment, become full city citizens.

This area will bear the brunt and possible benefits of inundation by the construction of the Three Gorges Dam, the world's largest dam project, that has displaced over 1.3 million people. Chongqing has seen an enormous amount of reconstruction, with the demolition of many old neighbourhoods that had previously been bombed by the Japanese and reconstructed into the traditional ramshackle warrens laced with sandstone staircases. These squalid conditions gave close quarters to the city residents, who are known for their cheerful pleasure in sitting outside on cool summer nights.

The traditional lifestyle of Chongqing is being transformed by giant shopping and residential complexes that all but eliminate the spicy street life into glitzy boutiques for the parade of newly flush consumers. The centre of the city is the Jiefang Bei, or Liberation Monument—a modern tower built in the 1950's to memorialize the martyrs of the civil war. The plaza area is now closed to cars, making a vast pedestrian refuge for shoppers. Another large development, the Three Gorges Plaza, has been built at the center of the Shapingba area, west of the older downtown center. This marble-paved complex, surrounded by tall office and residential buildings, features a large bronze expressionist sculpture and a scale model of the great dam, with inscriptions from its chief advocate and a former resident, ex-Premier Li Peng.

The dam project has initiated construction of massive new walls along the river shores and although the rise in water level has reduced the flight of steps to a minimum, some of the *bang bang jun* still scurry eagerly to assist passengers with their luggage when they board or disembark from their cruise ships. Although improved road and rail connections with the rest of the country have reduced the importance of relatively slow river transportation and curtailed the frenzy of activity around the port, there are still a total of 80 docks lining the banks, some 20 of which are dedicated to handling passengers.

New express highways soar overhead and road tunnels penetrate the mountains in an effort to alleviate the thick crawl of traffic through the city. A new monorail line, running the length of the peninsula, is due to open later in 2004.

As the main industrial centre for southwest China, Chongqing is a major producer of iron and steel and boasts the largest aluminium smelter in China, as well as being an important pharmaceuticals centre. Chongqing Longcin, established in 1993, is one of the largest motorcycle manufacturers in the country and in 2002 moved to a newly built industrial park, where it employs over 5,000 people and has a production capacity of one million motorcycles and two million engines annually. The popularity of the motorcycle has more than a little to do with the almost total absence of bicycles in this hilly city.

This landlocked port is plagued by some of the worst air pollution in China, as industry and traffic jams spew toxins into the still humid air. However, the local government is taking steps to improve the situation, including the introduction of LPG-fueled public buses.

The folk cuisine of outdoor sidewalk dining is the *huo guo* or hot pot. These are basins filled with bubbling chili oil and *hua jiao*—flower pepper that causes the mouth to tingle—into which are dipped all kinds of meats and vegetables. Once the river boatmen's campfire meal of leftovers from the day's market, *huo guo* is now the local favourite, sometimes because opium pods are sometimes placed in the brew.

HISTORY OF CHONGQING

In the fourth century BC, Chongqing (then called Yuzhou) was the capital of the State of Ba, whose men were renowned for their prowess in battle and their military successes. In the Southern Song dynasty (1127–1279) the city's name was changed to Chongqing—meaning 'double celebration'—to mark the princedom and enthronement of Emperor Zhaodun in 1189. He was himself a native of the city.

Chongqing had always been an important port, bustling with junks from Sichuan's hinterlands and neighbouring provinces, and acting as the collection point for the abundant produce of the region, including hides and furs from Tibet, hemp, salt, silk, rhubarb, copper and iron. Under the Qifu Agreement of 1890, Chongqing was opened to foreign trade. This marked the beginning of the exciting history of steamboat navigation from Yichang through the treacherous gorges to Chongqing, a development aimed at opening up the riches of Sichuan to trade with the outside world. By the early part of this century, a massive trade in opium grown in southwest China had sprung up, abetted by warlord factionalism and greed.

Visitors to the city in the 1920s and '30s commented on its 30-metre high city wall, and the rough steps from the river up to the city gates 'dripping with slime from the endless procession of water carriers'. At that time, Chongqing, with a population of over 600,000, had no other water supply. Between 10,000 and 20,000 coolies carried water daily to shops and houses through the steep and narrow lanes of the city. All portage was done by coolies as there were no wheeled vehicles in

The 'dragon back' ridges, visible at low water as the Yangzi passes the downstream docks at Chaotianmen, Chongqing. The ridges will be permanently submerged once the Three Gorges Dam reservoir reaches its full height in 2006–7.

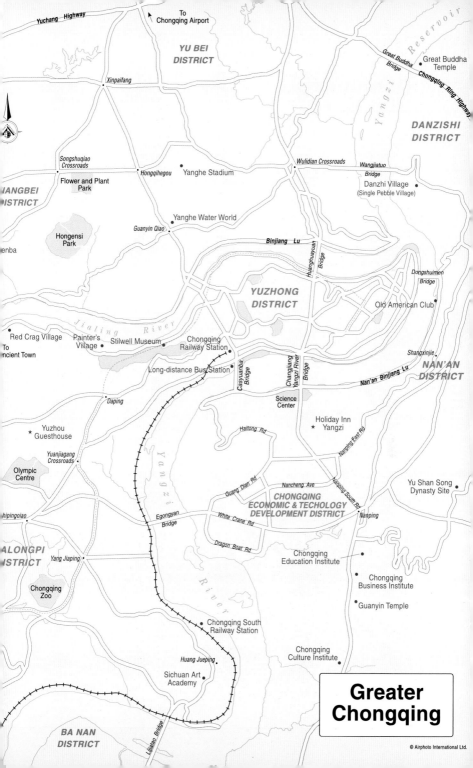

Greater Chongqing

© Airphoto International Ltd.

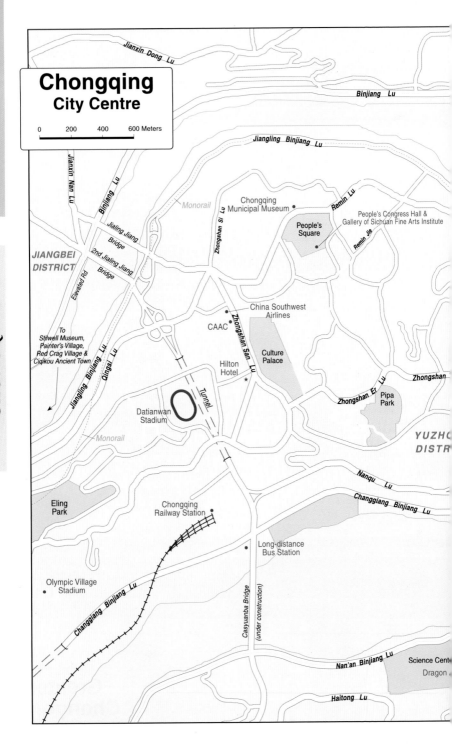

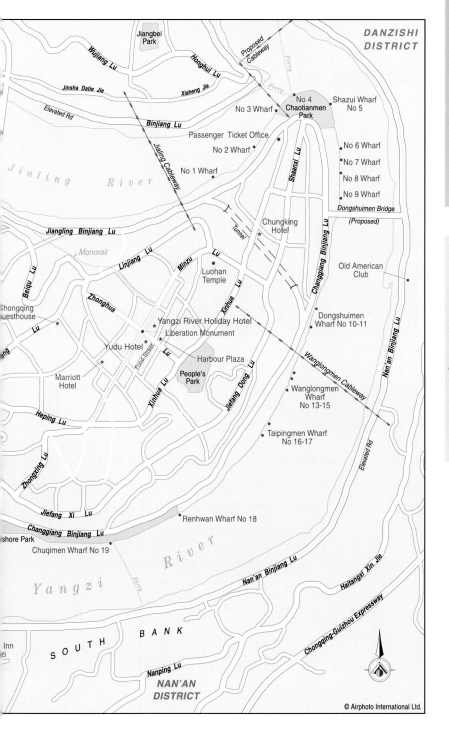

DANZISHI
DISTRICT

Jiangbei
Park

Wujiang Lu

Honghui Lu

Proposed
Cableway

Ferry

Jinsha Datie Jie

Xiaheng Jie

Ferry

Elevated Rd

Binjiang Lu

No 4
Chaotianmen
Park

No 3 Wharf

Shazui Wharf
No 5

Passenger Ticket Office

Jialing Cableway

No 2 Wharf

Shaanxi Lu

No 6 Wharf

Jialing   River

No 1 Wharf

No 7 Wharf

No 8 Wharf

No 9 Wharf

Jiangling Binjiang Lu

Tunnel

Changqiang Binjiang Lu

Dongshuimen Bridge

(Proposed)

Monorail

Linjiang Lu

Lu

Chungking
Hotel

Old American
Club

Belu Lu

Zhonghua

Minzu

Lu

Luohan
Temple

Xinhua Lu

Chongqing
Guesthouse

Lu

Yangzi River Holiday Hotel
Liberation Monument

Dongshuimen
Wharf No 10-11

Yudu Hotel

Food Street

Lu

Harbour Plaza

Jiefang Dong Lu

Wanglongmen Cableway

Nan'an Binjiang Lu

Marriott
Hotel

Xinhua Lu

People's
Park

Wanglongmen
Wharf
No 13-15

Heping Lu

Taipingmen Wharf
No 16-17

Zhongxing Lu

Elevated Rd

Jiefang Xi Lu

Changgiang Binjiang Lu

Renhwan Wharf No 18

shore Park

River

Chuqimen Wharf No 19

Ferry

Yangzi

Nan'an Binjiang Lu

Haitangxi Xin Jie

Inn
zi

SOUTH   B A N K

Chongqing-Guizhou Expressway

Nanping Lu

NAN'AN
DISTRICT

© Airphoto International Ltd.

A member of the bang bang jun, *or 'help army', awaits with bamboo pole and rope to assist passengers on and off the cruise ships at Chongqing*

Long staircases were a common sight along the Yangzi where people had to bear huge loads between the waterfront below and the streets above. This was particularly true in Chongqing. The closure of the Three Gorges Dam and the rise in water level over the coming years means many of these staircases will disappear.

THE BOMBING OF CHONGQING

The bombing by the Japanese which began in 1939 continued in 1940 and in 1941 with increasing ferocity. As soon as the winter fogs lifted the planes came, and through the gruelling hot summer, until late in autumn, being bombed was part of the normal process of living. Our daily activities were geared to this predictable occurrence: one rose early, and since the nights were an inferno of heat and sweat, the rock exuding its day-stored heat, it was easy to wake when the sun rose, for dawn did not mean coolness, but another raging hot day. Quickly the fire was lit with sticks of wood and a fan to spurt the flame, water boiled for morning rice, and by nine o'clock the day's first meal (the before-the-bombing meal) had been consumed. The first alert then started. One went to the dugout, with some luggage in hand, kettle and iron pan (irreplaceable after 1940, as metal became almost non-existent); and there one spent the day. Sometimes the bombs fell very near and we came to know the peculiar whistling sound they made. At other times the drone was further away, and the explosions faint. Sometimes the bombers came over five or six times, on occasion up to twenty times a day. And once, in 1941, they continued without let for seven days and nights, and many people died, both in the bombings and also in the air-raid shelters, especially babies, from heat and exhaustion and diarrhoea.

The shelters were scooped-out tunnels in the rock, and since Chungking was all rock, with juttings and small hollows and hillocks almost everywhere, the bowels of these promontories could easily be utilized. But some of the common shelters had been dug in softer earth, and were unsafe. They caved in after a while. There was no ventilation in them, and the people who sat deep inside, away from the one and only outlet, the mouth of the tunnel, became anoxic if the raid was prolonged. They started to thresh about, or to faint. In between the explosions, there was respite. While awaiting the next batch of bombs, everyone would come out of the dugout, sit round the mouth of the cave, fan, gulp the hot air; but this was almost as gruelling as sitting inside the dugout because there was hardly any shade, and if there was a single bush, it was monopolized in its thin narrow coolness by some police squad or some self-important official and his family.

Han Suyin, *Birdless Summer, 1968*

CHONGQING—A PERSONAL VIEW

Chongqing may be largely unknown abroad, except by wartime historians and China watchers. But for those who do venture here, a little effort to get to know Chongqing is amply rewarded. Yes, there are smokestack industries and at times the top of the high-rise buildings which now dominate the city centre will disappear into the fog, which is a common feature throughout the winter. Residents and tourists alike would no doubt like clearer skies more often, but poor and challenging weather notwithstanding, the city has a certain charm which doesn't take much effort to uncover.

City planners have done a lot to improve the image of urban Chongqing in recent years; the pace of change and the scale of modern development has been amazing to witness. Transport links have been improved and many outlying areas can now be reached through an emerging network of good road links to the centre. In recent years I have heard many people liken the downtown Liberation Monument pedestrian and shopping area to parts of Hong Kong, with its high-end malls and shopping centres and acres of neon signs. Chongqing people certainly like the new heart of Chongqing and have taken to strolling around the area in the evening, rather like in Mediterranean countries. A visit to the revolving restaurant at the top of the Yudu Hotel in the very heart of Chongqing will help to give you a good perspective on the massive scale of the city and provides an ever-changing view of the city's never-ending hustle and bustle. The food's pretty good too!

Aside from the new, a lot of Chongqing's heritage too is still evident. Modern luxury office buildings and hotels sit right next door to older housing, most of it wooden and a little ramshackle. Some of this has historical value. While the old British Consulate building has unfortunately gone, there are still some vestiges of the time when Chongqing, as wartime capital, had many foreign embassies here. A major project to restore a complex of old guild halls and merchant houses, the Hu Guan Hui Guan, has the support of the World Bank and promises to provide Chongqing with a major tourist destination in years to come. There are truly some hidden delights, like the Painters' Village, where revolutionary artists, many now in their 80s, share stories of their time on the Long March, or with Chairman Mao in Yan'an.

And, if you look carefully, not all Chongqing's trademark ladder streets, built up and down its hills and on to the docks, have gone. Chongqing still has its other trademark, *bang-bang* men, who carry huge loads of shopping or even sofas and safes across their shoulders on bamboo poles.

Perhaps the best thing about Chongqing is its people. With fewer Western faces around, local people are less used to visitors and, as a result, we have a certain novelty value which can take some getting used to. But Chongqing people are as hospitable and warm-hearted as they are curious, always urging you to try some of the traditional Chongqing hotpot (guaranteed to burn the roof off your mouth) and anxious to ensure that you are getting to know the real Chongqing beyond the new five star hotels and glitzy malls.

That, for me, is the real attraction of Chongqing: the open welcome you receive from the city's people and a genuine desire to see you back again soon.

Carma Elliot served as British Consul-General in Chongqing from 1999–2004, and in that time became a great fan of the city and its people.

A cable-tram takes people from the piers at Chaotianmen up to street level. Chongqing stands at the confluence of the Yangzi and Jialing rivers.

the city, only sedan chairs. The staircase streets have virtually disappeared, and all that remains of the city wall is the odd outcrop of masonry that props up a house here, or abuts a path there. The former gate of Chaotianmen, at the tip of the promontory overlooking the harbor, has been rebuilt into a plaza park. A funicular railway still descends to the docks below for passengers boarding the many boats to destinations near and far.

In 1939, during the Sino-Japanese War, the Guomindang government of China moved the capital from Nanjing to Chongqing, and on the south bank of the Yangzi foreign delegations built substantial quarters, which can be seen from the river. The airstrip used then can still be seen on the Shanhuba sandbar as one crosses the Yangzi River Bridge. The Guomindang government headquarters is now the People's City Government Offices (only the gateway is left of that period), situated just opposite the Renmin Hotel.

During the Sino-Japanese War (1937–45), Chongqing's notorious foggy weather conditions probably saved the city from complete devastation, for only on clear days could the Japanese bombers, which flew over in 20-minute waves, succeed in accurately dropping their thousands of bombs. One survivor from that era is the old American Club located along the south-bank boulevard of the Yangzi. This elegant building from the early 1900s, with its wide porticos and view of the city, is constantly under threat from developers.

WHAT TO SEE IN CHONGQING

Chongqing, always a trading city, was never noted for its cultural heritage or architecture. However, unlike most northern Chinese cities, Chongqing and other Yangzi River towns are very lively at night. On summer evenings residents stroll about in the hope of a refreshing breeze, and dancing often takes place in People's Square, in front of the People's Congress Hall. Street markets and sidewalk restaurant stalls can be found along Xinhua Lu and Shaanxi Lu towards Chaotianmen. A bright and cheerful strip of restaurants and bars has sprung up along the south bank, on Nan'anbin Lu, just east of the Yangzi River Bridge.

Most visitors are taken to Eling Park at dusk to view the city. It is an attractive sight of steep lamplit streets sweeping down to the dark waters of the river below. First thing in the morning, walk down to the Chaotianmen docks; at the waterfront, a busy panorama unfolds—cruise ships, tugboats, rows of pontoons, even a cable tramway to ease the ascent from shore to street of passengers as they disembark from their upstream cruises.

The Jialing cable car starts its journey from Cangbai Lu to Xinlongqiao Jie on the north bank (Jiangbei). The five-minute ride is fun on a clear day. Another cable car, at Wanglongmen, on Xinhua Lu, spans the Yangzi to the south bank on Shangxin Jie.

As one strolls around the city take note of the Chongqing banyan trees that line many of the streets. This large-leafed banyan (*Ficus lacor*, or *huang jiao shu* in Chinese) has been adopted as the city tree. It has no aerial roots as the traditional Chinese banyan, but instead its main roots twist around each other and are said to signify the united spirit of the Chongqing people, particularly during the war. The city flower is the camellia.

THE LUOHAN TEMPLE

This 19th-century temple is glimpsed through an ornate passage whose walls are encrusted with rock carvings in the manner of Buddhist grottoes. Luohan are Buddhist saints; they traditionally number 500, although in this temple there are actually 524 statues of them. They are of recent vintage, the last of the originals having been destroyed in the Cultural Revolution (1966–76). The present statues were made by the Sichuan Fine Arts Institute in 1985.

PEOPLE'S CONGRESS HALL AND GALLERY OF SICHUAN
FINE ARTS INSTITUTE

Sometimes known as the Renmin Hotel, it was originally built as the administrative offices for southwest China in the early 1950s. Parts of it are now a three-star hotel, but with an auditorium with seating for over 4,200 people it is also the city's main venue for performances and meetings. The architectural style is a combination of the Temple of Heaven and the Forbidden City. It is certainly the most spectacular building in Chongqing and worth a look inside, if only to visit the gallery of the Sichuan Fine Arts Institute (Sichuan Meishu Xueyuan), which is housed in the two rooms either side of the entrance lobby. This is highly recommended, even for those with only a passing interest in Chinese art.

The Institute is the only residential undergraduate- and graduate-level fine arts college in southwest China, with a student enrolment of around 300 a year. Students come from all over China as well as from abroad. The college was founded in 1950, and has departments of sculpture, painting, crafts (including lacquerware, textile design, packaging design and ceramics) and teacher training. The institute itself is located at Huangjiaoping, on the northern bank of the Yangzi, about half-an-hour's drive from the centre of the city. The city-centre gallery is therefore far more convenient for visitors and displays the best work of its students teachers and professors. The work, which includes traditional Chinese, contemporary oil, water colour and some woodcuts, comes in all sizes and styles, to suit a wide range of tastes. Helpful guides are on hand to answer questions and explain about the paintings and artists. There are frequently demonstrations of the various painting techniques.

The People's Congress Hall, beside People's Square, bears a striking resemblance to the Temple of Heaven in Beijing

Most of the items are for sale and prices are negotiable. Visitors are welcome to browse even if they have no intention to buy; the atmosphere is relaxed and thankfully free from the usual uncomfortable pressure to purchase that seems all too pervasive among arts and crafts shops frequented by tourists. Another reassuring difference is that the origin and quality of the artwork is guaranteed. It may even be possible to meet the artist who painted the work you wish to buy.

NEW CHONGQING MUNICIPAL ART MUSEUM & YANGZI THREE GORGES GALLERY

This museum, located on Renmin Lu opposite the People's Congress Hall, across from People's Square, is due to open at the end of 2004. The existing Chongqing Museum, located at 72 Pipashan Zhengjie, will be closed about six months beforehand while the artefacts are transferred. The new building is planned to have an exhibition area of some 42,000 square metres and be divided into two main sections. These will cover the development and culture of Chongqing itself, and the Three Gorges and its history and culture, and will display some of the archaeological treasures rescued from the Gorges before the rise in water level.

The new ground floor gallery exhibiting the history and culture of the Yangzi's Three Gorges consists of seven primary exhibition halls. The latter include a foyer followed by halls featuring the antiquity of the Three Gorges, legends and the history of ceramic writing, the mysterious Ba people, the power of Qin and Han, the cultural heritage of Jin and Tang, 1,000 years of cultural phenomena and the legacy of the Three Gorges.

The various subjects exhibited include the geological structure of the Three Gorges, natural scenery, famous sites, myths and legends, historic events, utilizing 500 photographs and reconstructed images, electric-powered maps, and various computerized programs.

Of the 116 groups of objects on exhibit, the majority come from what had been accumulated in storage from excavations and collecting as of 1997, with the remainder from the old collections of the Chongqing Cultural Relics and Three Gorges units. The collection will also contain some of the objects recovered from the Three Gorges area before it was flooded. The relics include early Neolithic ceramics, Ba cultural bronzes, Han mythical birds and a Han-Wei period ivory chessboard, a Southern Song gold belt, and Song and Yuan porcelain caches.

Some of the highlights of the collection are: 1) a 7,000-year-old ceramic *fu* basin excavated in 1999 from the lower strata at Yuxi in Fengdu county—the earliest intact Neolithic artifact from southwestern China; 2) a bronze *hu* fermented-beverage container with swing handle and coiled dragon décor from the Warring States period, excavated from a Ba person's tomb at Lijiaba in Yunyang county in 2000; 3) an exquisite two-sided bird-decorated bronze sword from the Warring States period, excavated in 1997 from a Ba person's tomb at Lijiaba in Yunyang; 4) a unique Ba Yue ceramic bird holding a pearl in its mouth, with displayed tail feathers, unearthed in 2001 from a burial site in Fengdu; 5) an inscribed ceramic and ivory chess board, predating the earliest of its kind (Song dynasty), dating to the Han-Wei period; 6) an exquisite gold belt, 107 centimetres long, of 14 pieces featuring grape motifs dating from the Song dynasty, excavated in 1986 from a burial site at the Nanquan People's Hospital; and 7) a Qinliang jade crowned helmet, called *hu*, that belonged to Ma Qiansheng, a person of high rank from Zhongzhou, who died in 1595 at the end of the Ming dynasty.

Ground floor exhibition halls of seven rooms are as follows:

Room 1: Ancient Three Gorges exhibits include: a) the history of the formation of the Three Gorges; b–c) geological views of the walls of the gorges; d) reconstruction of Early Man; e) distribution map of the Three Gorges; f) site remains of Wushan Man; g) site distribution map of Paleolithic settlements in the Three Gorges; h) discovery of the Gulf of Gaojiazhen.

Room 2: The Goddess Legend and the history of ceramic writing exhibits including: a) the cultural type of Shaopengzui; b) reconstruction of a Shaopengzui culture village; c) representative Neolithic artifacts; d) Yuxi culture; e) Daxi culture (see page 321); f) the legend of Great Yu; g) bronze vessels of the Ba people; h) photographs of Lijiaba (see page 320); i) the excavation of Lijiaba; j) Excavated objects from Lijiaba; k) views of Wu and Qutang gorges; l) Wu Gorge's Goddess Peak and its legend; m) site remains at Shaopengzui.

Room 3: The mysterious Ba people exhibits include: a) sketch map of the Ba realm; b) Shuangyantang site (see page 320); c) legends of the Ba people; d) excavation of Shuangyantang; e) site of Zhongba; f) Zhongba and dragon kilns; g) cultural relics; h) brine springs; i) Chujiao burial and Chu culture; j) Ba Yue dancing and Ba music; k) replicas of Ba burials.

Room 4: Qin and Han exhibits include: a:) Zhang Fei Temple; b) excavations at Jiuxianping; c) Ziyang City site; d) the Spirit Bird; e) Qutang Gorge; f) Baidi City; g) excavations at Zhuque; h) excavations of Han burials; i) excavated artifacts.

Room 5: The culture of Jin and Tang exhibits include: a) Precious Pagoda site; b) contents of burial sites; c) Buddhist images; d) the Yu River and tracking roads of the Western Jin; e) the myth of Guicheng (Ghost City); f) Iron Pillar at Kuimen (Qutang Gorge); g) representative poetry and scenic arts; h) remains at the Tang site of Yuxi; i) remains at Mingyueba; j) two Jin burials and artifactual remains from Dayuba; k) questions concerning salt and its health value.

Room 6: Cultural exhibits spanning the last 1,000 years include: a) tracking roads of the Three Gorges; b) the large stele at Kuimen; c) remains of the Yuan dynasty; d) excavation of a Song city; e) views of the Precious Stone Fortress (Shibaozhai); f) peoples of the Three Gorges; g) Xinjia and Changshou Huoshenmiao kilns; h) ceramics and kilns from Zhongba and Kaixian; i) conservation of White Crane Ridge; j) preservation of the Three Gorges cultural relics; k) new cities of the remaining peoples; l) diagram of the storage areas of the Three Gorges.

Room 7: Legacy of the Three Gorges exhibits include a) People's Hall and People's Auditorium; b) background of the Three Gorges Museum; c) map of China and Chongqing; d) relocation of Zhang Fei Temple; e) preservation of Precious Stone Fortress (Shibaozhai); f) preservation of Dachang residences; g) the historical and cultural legacy of New District cities.

PAINTERS' VILLAGE (HUAJIA ZHI CUN)

Painters' Village was established in the 1950s to nurture artists who would create paintings and lithographs to glorify the revolution. These state-sponsored artists came from all over China and included members of minority nationalities. They were paid a salary and their work was taken for use as propaganda, to exhibit overseas, or to give to foreign dignitaries as gifts. During the Cultural Revolution the artists were driven away and many of their works destroyed.

One of the few remaining artists at the Painters' Village, 84-year-old Lin Jun has worked there since its establishment in the 1950s and still enjoys showing visitors around. Many of his works are in the collection of the China National Art Gallery as well as in overseas museums

In 1984 the government established a gallery and invited overseas artists to visit and exchange ideas. Some of the work produced at the Village has been purchased by overseas museums for their collections. There are only six surviving artists today—the youngest being 55 and the eldest, Lin Jun, is a sprightly 83—and they enjoy what, for China, are excellent conditions. They have their own studios and produce an impressive range of work. Lin Jun is particularly well known for his incredibly detailed and powerful woodcut images, especially his early work that supported the revolutionary ideal.

Since China embarked on economic reforms, however, the artists have had to become commercial, since the government no longer buys all their work. The artists received a small percentage from what it sold to supplement their meagre salaries. There is a wide variety of work on display and as with the gallery of the Fine Arts Institute, the visitor feels under no pressure to make a purchase as the artists proudly show them around.

STILWELL MUSEUM

The museum, which was established in conjunction with the Stilwell Foundation in the USA and the Foreign Affairs Bureau in Chongqing, is dedicated to General

In the name of the people of the
United States of America,
I present this scroll to the
City of Chungking
as a symbol of our admiration for its brave men,
women and children.
Under blasts of terror from the air, even in the
days before the world at large had known this horror,
Chungking and its people held out firm and uncon-
quered. They proved gloriously that terrorism
cannot destroy the spirit of a people determined
to be free. Their fidelity to the cause of freedom
will inspire the hearts of all future generations.

—Franklin D. Roosevelt
May 17th, 1944

譯 文

我以美利堅合衆國人民的名義致意
重慶市，以表達我們對英勇的重慶市民
的敬意。

還在全世界人民了解空襲恐怖之
前，貴市人民在多次殘暴的空襲面前，
表現出堅毅鎮定、英勇不屈的精神。還
光榮地證明：決心爭取自由的人民，其
意志决非暴力恐怖所能摧毀。你們對自
由事業的忠誠將永遠鼓舞子孫後代。

富蘭克林 D·羅斯福
1944年5月17日

This memorial outside the Stilwell Museum bears an inscription from Franklin D Roosevelt in which he praises the 'brave men women and children' of Chongqing. 'They proved gloriously that terrorism cannot destroy the spirit of a people determined to be free.'

A bust of Joseph Stilwell, affectionately known as Vinegar Joe by his troops, stands outside the Stilwell Museum, overlooking the Jialing River, with the burgeoning Jiangbei District in the background

Mao Zedong and US envoy Patrick J Hurley at the start of the 1945 Chongqing coalition talks. Just one of many archive photographs in the Stilwell Museum.

Joseph Stilwell (1883–1946). Stilwell was sent to China in 1942 by US President Roosevelt and served as Chief of Staff to Chiang Kai-shek and Commander-in-Chief of the American forces in the China-Burma-India theatre until 1945 when the threat of the Japanese Imperial Army was finally overcome. General Stilwell was instrumental in ridding Asia of that threat.

The museum is located at 63 Jialingxin Lu in the actual house occupied by General Stilwell during the war. The house is a tribute to his daughters, Alison and Nancy, who devoted so much time and effort in bringing this project to fruition in 1992. The building was reopened in March 2003 after extensive renovation. The ground floor is a reconstruction of the layout during Stilwell's residence. Downstairs in the basement are several rooms displaying a wealth of archive photographs documenting such achievements as the Hump Flight Route over the Himalayas, the Dixie Mission, the exploits of the Flying Tigers, and the participation of Merrill's Marauders in the Burma campaign.

RED CRAG VILLAGE (HONGYAN CUN) AND GUI YUAN

Both these are now memorial museums to the 1949 revolutionary activities in the city. In the 1930s and '40s, during the period of co-operation between the Guomindang

Scenes around the narrow streets of the ancient town of Ciqikou,
beside the Jialing River in the northwest of Chongqing

government and the Chinese Communist Party against the aggression of the Japanese, these buildings were the offices of the Communist Party and the Red Army. Mao Zedong stayed in Gui Yuan House during his brief stay in Chongqing in 1945.

ANCIENT TOWN OF CIQIKOU

Situated on the south bank of the Jialing Jiang, in Shapingba District, about a half an hour's drive from the city centre, is the ancient town of Ciqikou (literally meaning 'porcelain mouth', or more accurately, port). The town used to be a centre for porcelain production and was located beside the river to facilitate its transportation.

Formerly known as Longyin (Hidden Dragon) Town, after the emperor's family fled here at the demise of the Ming dynasty, the town has its origins in the Song dynasty, although the present buildings date from the late Qing. It is very rare in modern China to find such a well-preserved example of an old town within a big city environment. What makes Ciqikou so interesting is that it is not a reconstruction or a tourist theme park, but a living town whose residents go about their daily lives, albeit under the gaze of visitors as they wander the tree-lined, flagstone streets. It is inevitable that some of the shops should turn their attention to the tourist market, but there are just as many teahouses and restaurants that are clearly patronized by the local population.

SIGHTS AROUND CHONGQING

DAZU BUDDHIST GROTTOES

Dazu is famous for its monumental religious sculptures. This unassuming county town, 165 kilometres northwest of Chongqing, has 40 Buddhist grottoes secreted among its terraced hillsides containing about 50,000 carvings. The remoteness of the location has protected the caves from vandalism and the painted sculptures are in excellent condition.

None of the carvings date before the last two decades of the Tang dynasty (618–907), when the more famous cave temples in northern China—at Dunhuang, Yungang and Longmen—had long since been completed. By that relatively late date, Buddhist sculpture had broken away completely from the Indo-Hellenistic influences so evident in the earlier Buddhist caves, and evolved a distinctly Chinese style. This development is amply illustrated in the grottoes at Beishan and Baodingshan, the two most stunning petroglyphic sites at Dazu.

Local legend has it that 'Dazu'—literally Big Foot—commemorates an outsize footprint left on the bed of a Baodingshan pond by Sakyamuni (the historical Buddha). 'Dazu' also means Great Sufficiency, and the county town is set amidst lush fields where grain, fruit, fish and pigs are farmed. Half the rolling, verdant, timeless landscape is water, with ribbons of irrigated terraces broken by spindly trees. The most comfortable way to reach the caves is to hire a car. The ride over hilly country will take about two hours, and the return journey can be easily made in one day.

BEISHAN

The Beishan (North Hill) sculptures owe their existence to a rebellion in AD 881. When the rebel leader Huang Chao reached the then imperial capital, Chang'an (Xi'an), Emperor Xizong fled to Chengdu. Loyalist generals and their armies followed, and this so outraged local sentiments that one of the provincial commanders, Wei Junjing, dispatched his own troops to Beishan to forestall further encroachment. Perhaps to make sure that his actions would be blessed, he later had Buddha images carved on the sandstone cliff faces around his military base. Begun in 892, this meritorious exercise was to be continued by others for a quarter of a century afterwards.

The iconography consists of statues and high reliefs set in caves and grottoes or cut into the face of a crescent-shaped cliff known as Buddha Bend (Fowan). Each grotto or shrine has a painted number, but there are no explanatory labels (the shrines are identified by the same numbers in the descriptions below). The southern section, containing work from the Tang (618–907) and Five Dynasties period (907–960), should be seen first. Considering the severe persecution of Buddhism between AD 843–5, when foreign religions were proscribed by imperial decree, it is remarkable that the faith remained sufficiently tenacious for piety to be flaunted on such an unbridled scale, as it was in these shrines. One reason for this was undoubtedly Sichuan's remoteness from the imperial capital.

Even so, the northern sculptural style persisted, as can be seen in the rendering of the disciples and saints that flank the Buddha (Sakyamuni) in **Shrine 10**. In this relic from the later Tang, the modelling of the figures is sensual and imposing, but the plump, bland faces suggest absence of emotions. There is little emphasis on drapery: garments fall in folds delineated unfussily by intaglio lines. On the right, Bodhisattva Mahasthama with his golden crown and lotus bud is an incomparably fine representation of serenity and detachment.

'Western Paradise' or 'Pure Land' is illustrated in **Shrine 245**, the pride of the small Tang collection. Diverse schools of doctrine held sway in China at various times. The Pure Land school arose during the sixth century and became immensely popular. Although based on interpretations of an Indian sutra (scripture), it dispensed with the more obscure teachings of the original religion and believers were encouraged to strive not for Nirvana, but for Pure Land, a happy paradise. Presiding in paradise is Amitabha Buddha (Amituofo in Chinese). In a previous existence he was a monk named Dharmakara who had spent millions of years practising meditation and performing acts of charity. As it is only by the grace of Amitabha Buddha that men will be led to salvation, constant recitation of his name is an essential element in the Pure Land form of worship. It is said that Emei Shan, Sichuan's holy mountain, was named from the first two syllables of this invocation.

Here, then, is Amitabha Buddha in his Western Paradise, the centrepiece of the ensemble. Seated under a lotus, he is flanked by the bodhisattvas Guanyin (see below) and Mahastama. Altogether, though, there are more than 500 figures in this intricately wrought work. It is also full of surprising detail. The top third of the shrine is a rollicking composition of cranes and parrots wheeling between canopies of clouds, of bodhisattvas and urchins, and of many-storeyed pavilions and lotus ponds. A veritable celestial orchestra is suggested by depictions of Chinese zither, *pipa*, conch and cymbals. The use of colour, particularly aquamarine blue and gilt, heightens the richness of effect. Below Amitabha Buddha, running across the base and along the sides of the shrine, are narrative bands of bas-reliefs that recount how Vaidehi, the mother of a prince, is led through renunciation to the way of truth.

About a third of Beishan was carved in the Five Dynasties, a transitional period between the decline of Buddhism and a brief revival of influence in the Song dynasty (960–1279). Note the androgynous representation of Avalokitesvara (**Shrine 273**), whom Chinese Buddhists later transformed into Guanyin, the Goddess of Mercy and bestower of sons. At this point the feminization of the bodhisattva was clearly still incomplete. By the Song dynasty, as we shall see, this bodhisattva had become— at least as far as the plastic arts were concerned—an unequivocally female deity inspiring enthusiastic devotion and her sculptors' most ardent energies.

Song-dynasty sculptures cluster in the northern section of Buddha Bend. If Tang sculpture was vigorous and unadorned, that of the Song dynasty reflected a tendency towards refinement and a greater concern with decoration. By the 11th century, although certain sects still had their adherents among the populace, Buddhism had lost its prominence. This decline in spiritual conviction is manifestly reflected in religious iconography, where the concern with expressing otherworldliness was overtaken by an urge to portray deities naturalistically. Certainly the figures carved here appear rather more human than divine. Some of them are elaborately clothed; several representations of Guanyin, for example, are richly draped, bejewelled and crowned with ornate headdresses (see Shrines 136 and 180). This bodhisattva's transformation from Avalokitesvara into the Goddess of Mercy is now complete: there is no mistaking the femininity of this matronly, double-chinned figure, who resembles, as one Chinese writer put it, 'a lady of noble birth'.

As a whole, **Shrine 136** is known as 'The Revolving Wheel'. It is the largest cave in the complex and took four years to carve (1142–6). The Wheel of Law, balanced on eight carved columns, is sculpted in the round. This solid piece in turn supports the roof of the cave. On the wall behind and to the sides of this centrepiece are ranged a statue of Sakyamuni Buddha and more than 20 bodhisattvas, guardians and donors in various poses. Two seated and two standing images of Guanyin apart, there is Puxian (Samantabhadra) mounted on an elephant (Puxian, the Bodhisattva of Universal Benevolence, is particularly associated with Emei Shan). Like Guanyin, Puxian is here portrayed in female form, with a gentle expression, downcast eyes and the merest hint of a beatific smile. In a parallel composition to the left of the wheel, the Bodhisattva of Wisdom (Manjusri) rides cross-legged on a lion.

There is nothing matronly about the Guanyin with a Rosary (**Shrine 125**). Here she cuts an altogether more delicate figure, trailing ribbons and framed by an elliptical aureole. There is movement and grace in the twist of her body and the tilt of her head—a refreshing contrast to the stillness of other Guanyin figures at Beishan and an astonishing departure from the restraint traditionally exercised in religious sculpture. It is an unashamedly romantic image. Sadly, it has not weathered the centuries without some damage, although the lissom young goddess has come through with her enigmatic smile intact.

A similar absence of solemnity characterizes Guanyin Gazing at the Reflection of the Moon (**Shrine 113**). Although the lower part of this piece has crumbled away, it is nonetheless possible to discern in Guanyin's relaxed pose an almost playful mood, as if she is splashing a foot in water. The same cannot be said of the rigidly seated goddess in **Shrine 133**; she, too, is gazing at the reflection of the moon, but she does so in a posture which somehow exudes disapproval and severity.

Shrine 155 exemplifies the thousand-buddha cave, a favourite motif in Buddhist iconography whereby countless tiny figures are chipped out in niches over an entire wall. A surprising number of the ones here have been preserved. They wrap round the gorgeous figure of the Peacock King (Mayurasana-raja) on his blue and russet-coloured throne.

BAODINGSHAN

Echoing an earlier tradition of Buddhist iconography, the rock sculptures at Baodingshan (Precious Summit Hill) form a series of narratives based on Buddhist scriptures. This stupendous project was launched by a monk, Zhao Zhifeng, an adherent of Tantric Buddhism, in the Southern Song dynasty (1127–1279). By the time Zhao was preaching in Sichuan, Buddhism was in retreat in northern China. Nevertheless he was able to collect sufficient donations to have more than 10,000 icons chiselled out of the hillsides here. They are mostly concentrated at Great Buddha Bend (Dafowan), a U-shaped valley reached by a stone staircase from the south. Along the sweep of the craggy surfaces sacred and secular images erupt out of the ochreous background like some phantasmagoric vision of heaven and hell. They were the last of their kind, for no known cave sculpture on such a huge scale was carved anywhere in China after 1249, when Dafowan was completed. The scale, nevertheless, is rather

Rock sculpture at Dazu Buddhist Grottoes, (above) the 'Revolving Wheel', Beishan;
(below) Buddha bearing the coffin of his father, Baodingshan

Rock sculpture at Dazu Buddhist Grottoes, Baodingshan, (top left) a drunk behaves improperly to his mother; (top right) a disciple of the Buddha; (below) the keeper of hens

less daunting than that of the cave temples in the north of the country, where the harshness of the terrain itself lent awesomeness to the sculptures wrested out of it. Nor, in comparison, do these sculptures have the polish and spiritual force of great art, but their very coarseness does give them a certain rough-hewn grandeur.

Zhao Zhifeng's creation was a brilliant stroke of proselytization: the message of some of the stories-in-stone, whether it is retribution for unfilial acts or the evils of drink, would have been quite explicit to all manner of believers. When the whole spectacle is plonked down in the open countryside so that it is easily accessible (unlike, for example, the caves in the high cliffs of Yungang), the crowds of pilgrims gathered here every spring, to burn incense at the Sacred Longevity Temple (Shengshou Si) and to take in the sideshows, would have been large indeed.

Visiting the temple today, you are more likely to be greeted by souvenir and drinks hawkers than by any vendor of incense. A path leading from the temple winds its way to the entrance to Dafowan. Thirty tableaux, each numbered, unravel as you proceed round the amphitheatre of rock. The nine demonic Guardians of the Law (**Shrine 2**), some brandishing swords, all of them snarling, prepare one for contemplating the Revolving Wheel (**Shrine 3**) in a suitably subdued frame of mind. The wheel symbolizes the Six States of Transmigration through which all living beings pass. Depending on their moral actions, living beings may be reborn into any of these states: as gods in paradise, as men in a world of prosperity, as gods and 'hungry ghosts' (tormented spirits) joined in battle, as animals, as hungry ghosts, or in hell. As the wheel is ever revolving, so the cycle of rebirths in infinite, and only the attainment of Nirvana through the practice of Buddhism brings it to an end.

Next comes the rock sculpture's creator, the monk Zhao Zhifeng, in youth, midlife and old age (**Shrine 4**). The three characters for 'Baodingshan' are in the calligraphy of an official in the Southern Song. Also commemorated is Vairocana Buddha, believed to be the founder of Tantric Buddhism (**Shrine 5**). He is flanked by the Bodhisattva of Universal Benevolence (Samantabhadra) and the Bodhisattva of Wisdom (Manjusri), and together they are known as the Three Saints of the Avatamsaka School (Huayan to Chinese Buddhists). This lowering triad, seven metres high and inclined slightly forwards, is plainly designed to be viewed from below.

Just before the curve of the valley doubles back upon itself there is a pavilion (**Shrine 8**) whose precious occupant is an amazing seated statue of Guanyin, the Goddess of Mercy, characteristically endowed with a thousand arms (actually 1,007, according to a monk who counted them by pasting a numbered gold leaf on each hand). It is a magnificent object, a gleam of burnished gold, blue and turquoise in the opaque half-light of its modest shelter. Arms flare out behind the seated goddess and give way to a coiling tangle of hands, some clutching a rosary, others balancing a miniature pagoda. Each upturned empty palm is carved with an all-seeing eye.

A reclining Buddha (**Shrine 11**) marks the eastern end of Dafowan. So massive are the head and torso that they fill the entire surface; thus, chopped off at the knee, the Buddha lies on his right side in the position of final deliverance, at the moment of entering Nirvana. With his enormous head and foreshortened body, he is a mildly grotesque figure. The Birth of the Buddha is the theme of the relief (**Shrine 12**) on the corner. As recounted in scriptures and legends, the Buddha was born to the king and queen of Sakyas, a state at the northern edge of the Ganges plain, in around 563 BC. He was named Siddhartha. His birth was foretold in his mother's dream, in which a white elephant entered her womb through her side; Brahmins summoned by her to interpret the dream took it to be a sign that the child, when born, would become either a universal monarch or a Buddha. This extraordinary boy grew up in luxury, was eventually married to a cousin and fathered a son. But he was to renounce all this out of compassion for the suffering in the world. Adopting the life of an ascetic, the prince (now known as Gautama) wandered from place to place in a quest for the truth. After years of intense study and many struggles, the truth was revealed to him as he meditated one evening under a tree in a place which has come to be called Bodhgaya. As night turned into dawn, Gautama's '…mind was emancipated… Ignorance was dispelled, knowledge arose…darkness was dispelled, light arose.' This account of Gautama's life, amplified by the legends and myths that have developed around the man, is retold in countless works of sculpture and painting. Here, at Baodingshan, the legend invoked in the corner grotto has a distinctly

Seated statue of Guanyin with 1,000 arms, Baodingshan, Dazu Buddhist Grottoes

Chinese flavour. It relates how nine dragons appeared out of the sky at the moment of Siddhartha's birth, their mouths spewing warm and cold water for the baby's bath. The choice of subject was probably dictated by the existence of a natural spring nearby; by channelling the water through the dragons' heads to flow over the bust of the infant prince the ancient craftsmen neatly devised a means of drainage.

Past the images of the Peacock King, Vairocana, bodhisattvas, devotees and flying *apsaras* or angels (**Shrines 13–14**), you come upon a touching illustration of how traditional Confucian thought was fused with Buddhist beliefs. Filial piety is the virtue advocated in Parental Kindness (**Shrine 15**): lest undutiful children forget, the pains of childbirth, the suckling of an offspring, a mother's care and other scenes of parental tenderness which are vividly depicted in 11 panels should induce a proper sense of gratitude.

So serious is the sin of filial ingratitude to the Chinese mind that yet another huge relief (**Shrine 17**) is devoted to condemning it. Perhaps the awful warning represented by the deities of the wind, thunder, lightning, clouds and rain (**Shrine 16**) is designed to put the pilgrim in a suitably chastened mood; at any rate, the next tableau will reassure him that the wrath of gods is not visited upon the world of men if human relationships are conducted with propriety, particularly relationships between children and parents. The Buddha himself (the bust in the centre of this relief) has convincingly demonstrated his filial piety, even in his previous births—as related in the Jataka stories—for all that the Six Heretics (bottom row) may jeer and point the finger. There is no clearer refutation of their slander than the vignette (bottom left) in which the Buddha is shown bearing the coffin of his father. Any contradiction between Siddhartha's renunciation of his family and the Confucian ideal of the dutiful son (as exemplified by the figure, lower right, dangling his aged parents from a shoulder pole) appears to have been resolved. The whole ensemble provides an interesting gloss on the intellectual temper of the times, for by the 12th century, various earlier attempts to syncretize indigenous cults with Buddhism had given way to a resurgence of the influence of Confucianism. From reinterpretations of the Sage's teachings, which actually drew on Buddhist and Taoist ideas, an ethical and metaphysical system emerged to supplant Buddhism as the prevailing orthodoxy.

Before moving on, take a look at the girl playing a flute in a niche just above the heretics. This lovely figure seems an aberration, as irrelevant to a sermon on filial piety as the girl feeding chickens is to the punishments of hell (**Shrine 20**). We can only imagine her as a flight of fancy on the sculptor's part, a whimsical re-creation of a farmer's pretty daughter once glimpsed briefly in the countryside.

What distinguishes **Shrine 18**, the story of Amitabha and his Pure Land, is not so much its scale, nor the configurations of its many elements, but its groups of some 60 cherubic children straddling balustrades, playing music and lolling in lotus blooms. They symbolize the happiness promised by rebirth in the Western Paradise (see Beishan, shrine 245).

All the same, the halls of heaven look very much like a scene on earth. Not so the lower depths of hell (**Shrine 20**). Here one sinner is protrayed on the point of dismemberment; there another lost soul, hair and haunch gripped by a demon with a horse's head, is seconds away from being boiled in a cauldron of oil. Repugnant ghosts writhe and grimace in torment, ravaged by hunger, fire and cold. Above and to the right, cautionary tales signal dire warnings against the iniquity of drink: a drunk kills his father and rapes his mother; a wife, a brother and a sister are spurned by their unrepentant boozy relative; shifty-looking characters tempt with bowl and pitcher of wine; an inebriated father fails to recognize his son.

It is with some relief that one turns to the keeper of hens, whose sin is the taking of life but who looks, for all that, entirely undeserving of terrible retribution, so lovingly has she been rendered in her wholesome comeliness.

The western end on the same side of the valley is dominated by **Shrine 21**, dedicated to Master Liu, Zhao Zhifeng's teacher. Master Liu's asceticism took the form of self-mutilations including gouging out an eye and severing his left arm. If the disciple was inspired by reverence for his mentor, though, he failed to give it expression in this clumsily executed and rather static ensemble. Besides the details of Master Liu's austerities, the shrine is studded with secular figures from scholars to warriors. Strung out below the gilded figure of the master are the Ten Great Vidyarajas—manifestations of the Buddha and bodhisattvas in their combat with evil; they are unfinished pieces.

Across the bridge, look in on the Cave of Complete Enlightenment (**Shrine 29**). In a classic composition three images of the Buddha are ranged against the back wall while a dozen bodhisattvas line the walls on either side. The disciple kneeling in front is carved in the round. The artisans responsible for this cave have thought-fully improved the natural lighting of the vault by cutting an opening above the entrance. To stall erosion by seeping moisture, they carved a dragon on the left wall to trap the water that trickles in and to conduct it, drip by drip, into a bowl held aloft by the figure of a monk. The water then flows through the monk and out of the cave.

Finally, a parable with a rustic touch (**Shrine 30**). The tale unfolded in this relief suggests that, just as cattle are gradually tamed into quiescence, so the clamours of earthly desires may be eventually overcome through the practice of Buddhism. First the recalcitrant buffalo tries to run away. A few lashes of the whip later, it submits to being led to a stream for a drink. The herdsmen relax as the cattle feed. A flute is produced for a spot of music. The last scenario showing man and beast at rest hints at the blessed state in which all cravings are extinguished.

BIG BUDDHA AT SINGLE PEBBLE VILLAGE

by Elizabeth Childs-Johnson

The area of the Three Gorges on the Yangzi is important to China's cultural heritage for two primary reasons. Firstly, it belongs to what I and many archaeologists in China identify as China's southern cradle of civilisation. Secondly, this area is extremely rich historically from imperial times to the present, but little data has been collected that would help put it solidly on the map of China's cultural framework. The whole area suffers from an overwhelming lack of archaeological, art historical or cultural study. Excavations indicate that this area was settled in pre-Han times by a relatively unknown people called Ba, and to a certain extent by others including the Shu and Chu on the western and eastern flanks. Although western Sichuan and Hubei through Jiangsu and Shanghai, where the Yangzi empties into the sea, are currently better known archaeologically than the Three Gorges area, it is evident that this region was a vital ingredient in the formulation of Chinese civilisation and personality.

Anyone who has travelled by boat through the Three Gorges will be familiar with various monuments dating from the Han through to the Qing dynasties. These sites include the Precious Stone Fortress and Pagoda (Shibaozhai) near Zhongxian, the White Emperor City (Baidicheng), the Zhang Fei Temple at Yunyang, Qu Yuan's Memorial Hall at Zigui, Temple of the God of the Underworld at Fengdu, the hanging coffins on the Daning tributary that runs south into the Yangzi at Wushan and the late Warring States Ba cemetery at Fuling. All of these monuments have been affected by the new dam and most have already been physically moved to a higher location or else preserved through defensive foundations and protective flood walls. Many other monuments virtually unknown to the China watcher and Sinophile have also been affected by the rise in the water level.

One of these is the Buddhist monument at Single Pebble Village (Danzishizhen), just east of Chongqing where the Yangzi makes an abrupt turn to flow south to north. A large niche, 8.5 metres tall by 5.5 metres wide and 2.5 metres deep, hugs a cliff on the south bank of the river and encloses a monumental 7.5-metre-tall seated Future Buddha, Maitreya, flanked by the standing disciples, Ananda and Kasyapa and carved by the artist Zou Xing. A flight of stairs rises 20 to 25 metres from what used to be the shore of the Yangzi to the stone platform of the Buddha; this has now been largely submerged.

When the river is in flood the water laps the base of the Buddha; one may observe water marks on the Buddha's feet, legs and lower body. This Buddha, once protected by a wooden temple awning, now hangs as if suspended on the cliff's edge. Carved out of the wall's yellowish sandstone, the figure was probably once painted. The Future Buddha is seated on a dais with legs pendant. The face is square to round and the head is covered by spiral curls characteristic of a Buddha. The eyes are almost closed with a serene look that penetrates the ever flowing waters of the Yangzi. The left hand rests on his knee and the right hand is held up in the fear-not gesture. Flanking disciples hold their hands in prayer mudra.

According to in situ inscriptions and a Ba county gazetteer, the niche is dated to the late 14th century—the late Yuan and early Ming periods. At this time the area approximating what is today known as Ba county was controlled by a military general named Ming Yuzhen who set up his own dynasty, which he named the Great Xia in 1363, although he had controlled this area since 1357. He died in Chongqing in 1366 and his son, Ming Ao, succeeded him. By 1371 the area was recovered by Ming dynasty founder Zhu Yuanzhang's military forces.

The sculptor of this group, and of an earlier phase of sculpture belonging to the partially preserved temple complex behind, was Zou Xing, a cadre general under Ming Yuzhen's leadership. Ming Yuzhen was apparently a farmer who founded the 'Farmers' Righteous Military' party in this part of Sichuan province. This party had ties with the White Lotus faith who subscribed to the idea that Maitreya Buddha, the Future Buddha, would descend from Heaven as the World's New Leader, thus politically ending the foreign, Mongolian dominated dynasty of the Yuan and inaugurate the Bright, Ming dynasty (1368–1644). After Ming Yuzhen named himself emperor, he declared that 'Maitreya would descend, the Ming king would appear, and All under Heaven would be in peace.' This heroic sculpture of Maitreya Buddha looming over the Yangzi at Single Pebble village is testimony not only to great Buddhist sculpture, especially rare in this part of the south during the Yuan, but to Chinese politics that depended on Buddhist belief to promote political salvation. There is no question that the military leader, Ming Yuzhen, considered himself, as with dowager empress Wu Zitian of the earlier, mid-Tang period, a Maitreya Buddha incarnate. This cave temple sculpture in essence is comparable to the great big stone-cut Tang Buddha at Longmen, the early Tang Buddhist cave temples on the Yi River in Henan province.

The Buddhist Temple site at Single Pebble continues to be the object of local worship and a gathering point on Buddhist holidays. Incense burns in front of all Buddhist images, whether they include the big Future Buddha or a remnant piece of sculpture or inscription from this site. John Hersey wrote the book A Single Pebble about the life of a well-known head tracker and a foreign engineer interested in dam hydraulics in the Three Gorges. The dedicated and heroic, lifelong head tracker Single Pebble in the end loses his life while running the rapids, and the engineer is even more convinced of the need for dam control. The major theme of the book is the conflict between modernization and the profundity of Chinese tradition. The question begs itself, does one still have to make this choice between tradition and modernisation, or is there some way of accommodating both?

Elizabeth Childs-Johnson, Ph D, is an art historian and archaeologist focussed on ancient China of Neolithic through Han periods, and on the cultural preservation and heritage of these periods. She currently holds an ACLS (American Council of Learned Societies, National Endowment for the Arts) research fellowship while completing a study of Shang ritual art and is a research associate at the International Center for Liangzhu Studies in Yuhangxian, Zhejiang Province, while completing a study of the Late Neolithic Chinese 'Jade Age'.

The 7.5-metre-tall seated Future Buddha, Maitreya, flanked by the standing disciples, Ananda and Kasyapa, at Single Pebble Village (Danzishizhen), near Chongqing, dating from the late 14th century

BOATS GREAT AND SMALL

The traditional Chinese boats that navigated the Yangzi were *sampan* (meaning three planks), the larger-sized *wupan* (five planks) and junks. Their sails were tall to capture any welcome breeze, and stiffened by bamboo battens. The sculling oar, or *yulo*, was extremely long with normally four men working it. Mats overhead provided shelter for passengers; decks were covered with coils of bamboo rope. Local pilots were hired to negotiate the most difficult rapids. Their instructions were relayed to the harnessed trackers pulling the long hauling ropes—often far ahead of the boat—by a drum beaten at different rhythms. Large freight junks often required 300 or 400 trackers as well as groups of strong swimmers who would loosen the ropes should they snag on rocks along the way.

An eighth-century poem gives a compelling picture of the gruelling drudgery of a boat puller's life:

> A Boatman's Song
> *Oh, it's hard to grow up at the way-station side!*
> *The officials've set me to pullin' station boats;*
> *Painful days are more, happy days are few,*
> *Slippin' on water, walkin' on sand, lake birds of the sea;*
> *Against the wind, upstream, a load of ten thousand bushels—*
> *Ahead, the station's far away; behind, it's water everywhere!*
> *Midnight on the dykes, there's snow and there's rain,*
> *From up top our orders: you still have to go again!*
> *Our clothes are wet and cold beneath our short rain cloaks,*
> *Our hearts're broke, our feet're split, how can we stand the pain?*
> *Till break of dawn we suffer, there's no one we can tell,*
> *With one voice we trudge along, singing as we pull;*
> *A thatch-roofed house, what's it worth,*
> *When we can't get back to the place of our birth!*
> *I would that this river turn to farm plots,*
> *And long may we boatmen stop cursing our lots.*
> Wang Qian (768–833)

They were truly beasts of burden, as observed by an American, William L Hall, and his wife, who spent several weeks on a small Chinese cargo-boat in 1922:

If the boat happens to turn about when it is struck by a cross-current, a call from the pilot brings all the trackers to their knees or makes them dig their toes into the dirt. Another call makes them either claw the earth or catch their fingers over projecting stones. Then they stand perfectly still to hold the boat. When it is righted, another call makes them let up gradually and then begin again their hard pull.

Passengers usually took *kuaize*—large *wupan*—and paid for the Yichang–Chongqing trip 185 cash for every 100 *li* (18 cents for every 50 kilometres). They would also supply wine for the crew, and incense and fireworks for a propitious journey. Going upriver, this journey used to take as long as 40–50 days in the high-water period and 30 days in low water, depending on the size of the boat, while the downriver trip could be completed in five to12 days. At the end of the journey the passengers might buy some pork as a feast for the crew.

River life was varied along the Yangzi and its tributaries. Big junks, fitted out as theatres, sailed between the towns to give performances of Chinese opera or juggling. Some boats were built as hotels, offering accommodation to travellers arriving too late at night to enter the city gates. Others were floating restaurants and tea-houses, not to mention boats which were a source of livelihood as well as home to the numerous fisherfolk and their families.

Peasants along the lower and middle Yangzi first set eyes on foreign men-of-war and steamers when Britain's Lord Elgin journeyed as far as Wuhan (Hankou) in 1842. Although the Chinese had in fact invented the paddle wheel (worked probably by the treadmill system) for driving their battleships as early as the eighth century, paddle boats were not widely used. In an incident on Dongting Lake in 1135, they were proved positively useless when the enemy threw straw matting on the water and brought the paddle wheels to a stop. They seem not to have been used since.

With the opening up of the Yangzi ports to foreign trade in the latter half of the 19th century, foreign shallow draught paddle steamers and Chinese junks worked side by side. But the traditional forms of river transport slowly became obsolete, and were confined to the Yangzi tributaries for transporting goods to the distribution centres.

Early Western shipping on the Shanghai–Wuhan stretch of the river was dominated by Americans, whose experience of paddle steamers on the Mississippi and other rivers had put them to the fore. The American firm of Russell and Company was the leading shipping and trading concern in those years. A fifth of the foreign trade was in opium shipped up to Wuhan. By the late 1860s, British companies such as Jardine & Matheson and Butterfield &

Swire had successfully challenged the American supremacy. Accommodation on the companies' river boats was luxurious, and trade was brisk.

The Wuhan–Yichang stretch was pioneered by an English trader, Archibald Little, who established a regular passenger service in 1884 with his small steamer Y-Ling. In his book *Through the Yangtse Gorges*, he described the bustling scene on the river:

> *The lively cry of the trackers rings in my ears, and will always be associated in my mind with the rapids of the Upper Yang-tse. This cry is 'Chor-Chor', said to mean 'Shang-chia', or 'Put your shoulder to it', 'it' being the line which is slung over the shoulder of each tracker, and attached to the quarter-mile-long tow-rope of plaited bamboo by a hitch, which can be instantaneously cast off and rehitched. The trackers mark time with this cry, swinging their arms to and fro at each short step, their bodies bent forward, so that their fingers almost touch the ground… Eighty or a hundred men make a tremendous noise at this work, almost drowning the roar of the rapids, and often half a dozen junks' crews are towing like this, one behind the other. From the solemn stillness of the gorge to the lively commotion of a rapid, the contrast is most striking.*

Other companies soon followed, but none dared travel this route at night. Again, it was Archibald Little's perseverance that brought about steamship navigation through the gorges above Yichang to Chongqing. Acting as captain and engineer, he successfully navigated his 17-metre *Leechuan* up to Chongqing in 1898, though he still needed trackers to pull him over the worst rapids.

During the heyday of the Yangzi in the 1920s and 1930s, travel by steamer from Shanghai all the way up to Chongqing was luxurious though not entirely safe. Halfway, at Wuhan, passengers had to change to smaller boats for the rest of the journey.

After the establishment of the People's Republic of China, priority was placed on making the Yangzi safe for navigation all year round, and major rock obstructions were blown up in the Gorges. The Yangzi today is the vital economic artery of central China, with a highway network and many new bridges complementing the traditional port activites. Thousands of regular ferries and small river boats, offering a range of accommodation, overflow with passengers. The great lumbering river liners of the old 'East is Red' fleet are now mostly idle or scrapped, as air and bus transport is faster and competitive in price. There are now many luxury river cruise ships which ply the route from Chongqing to Wuhan or Yichang, with a few going to Nanjing and Shanghai.

Laohuaqiu, *Sichuan's largest type of junk*

Type of crooked-stern junk (wai pigu), specially designed to negotiate sudden twists and turns in the river

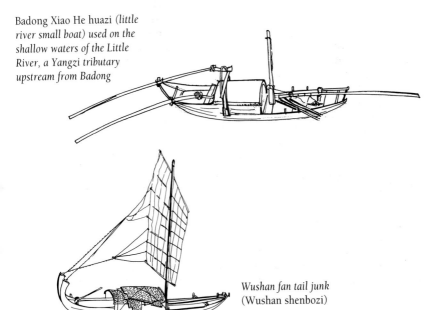

Badong Xiao He huazi (*little river small boat*) *used on the shallow waters of the Little River, a Yangzi tributary upstream from Badong*

Wushan fan tail junk (Wushan shenbozi)

Houseboats or kuiaze under full sail on the Yangzi River in 1971. Prior to the steam ship these vessels were the main means of transport for passengers travelling between Yichang and

Chongqing. The upstream journey could take as long as 40 to 50 days during periods of high water. The downstream journey, on the other hand, could take as little as five to 12 days.

IN THE BEGINNING
A personal reflection by Audrey Ronning Topping

I have had a sentimental attachment to that mystical force known as the Yangzi River since childhood. My father, born on the banks of it's largest tributary, the Han, regaled us with Chinese folklore and supernatural legends. No other river in the world has touched so many lives. The lore of the river itself embodies the mythic image of Old Cathay—the celestial, five-clawed dragon—symbol of the emperors. Lung Wang, the four-clawed Dragon King, still resides in a castle under Goose Tail Rock in Wind Box Gorge [Qutang Gorge]. I know this to be true because my father showed me his tail swishing and I saw it with my own eyes.

It all started back in the mists of time, when the gods were manoeuvering for power over the Celestial Kingdom and Emperor Yu-wang seized control of the rivers. After meditating on Tu-san Mountain and studying the markings on nine tortoise shells he determined that the 'River to Heaven' should run eastwards, through the mountains to the sea—but the spirits of the mountains refused to budge. The Emperor appealed to the Wizard Wu-tze. She appeared to him as a great ape and with one mighty blow from her nostrils blasted a gorge halfway through the reluctant mountains. Exhausted, she retired in a cave where she lives to this very day. The canyon enabled the river, now furious about the hold up, to rage through Wind Box Gorge and halfway through Witches Gorge before the mountains blocked it again. Modern geologists claim that the gorges were excavated during the past 250 million years or so by the impact of the hurtling waters, but the ancients relate that Emperor Yu himself hacked out the rest of the gorges with a cosmic ax and unleashed the torrents that now coil and hiss like mischievous dragons through the heartland of China into the Pacific Ocean.

* * * * *

My missionary grandparents, Halvor and Hannah Ronning, fell in love while sailing up the Yangzi in a junk from Shanghai to Hankow where they were married on Christmas Day 1891. The next spring they sailed in a *kuiaze* (houseboat) up through the Three Gorges to Chongqing.

They journeyed in a three-roomed *kuiaze* or houseboat. It took over three weeks compared to my recent trip of three days and four nights. In those days the boats anchored every night and the Ronnings would go ashore for food supplies. When the *kuiaze* arrived at the rapids they disembarked via a slippery gangplank and walked along the rocky banks. I have seen photos of my elegant grandmother in her bustled skirt and high-buttoned boots and grandfather in his Prince Albert suit walking along the rocky banks. Not recorded were the nearly naked trackers in red turbans and straw sandals high above on the narrow towpath, their shoulders harnessed to braided bamboo hawsers, pulling their boat, often straining on all fours, inch by inch up through the rapids.

The houseboat carried four adult passengers and my grandparent's adopted Chinese son who was tragically swept overboard and drowned. The junk required a crew of 26 including the skipper and his wife, two pilots, a cook with a charcoal burner, four deck hands, and two swimmers to clear the lines and sixteen trackers. More trackers were hired below each rapid. Sometimes it took up to thirty men to pull the *kuiaze* while a big junk required over two hundred. Grandpa often talked about the pandemonium created as the trackers strained to the rhythm of clashing gongs and banging drums. 'Gangers' ran along the lines of men shouting curses and cracking whips. Behind the trackers two men were positioned to clear the towline when it caught on the rocks. At the foot of each rapid red lifeboats were stationed to rescue survivors.

The missionaries always reached their destination on foot long before the boat arrived. They would sit on the rocks and watch their houseboat at the end of the towline slowly forging ahead, the bow barely bobbing above the white water. The 'laopan' was perched on top of the deck house hanging onto the mast with one arm while waving his other arm, stamping his feet and raving at the trackers who were chanting so loudly they couldn't hear him anyway. At the foot of the mast squatted the drummer who banged out signals when the towline was caught so the trackers could stop pulling. Grandpa explained that the chaos was created to drive away the evil spirits and distract the trackers from thinking about their precarious positions. Everyone knew that a slippery hitch or one false maneuver could result in the boat tearing loose and crashing. One stumble could mean total disaster with loss of both the ship and trackers. If anyone fell off the track it was often necessary to cut him loose to fall to certain death rather than risk bringing the whole line of men down with him. Grandpa expressed great admiration for these fleet-footed trackers even though he failed to convert them to Christianity. They believed their very lives depended on the benevolence of the river gods. Although my grandparents later sailed the rivers of China by junk, steamer and gunboat they always maintained that the only way to appreciate the great gorges was from a *kuiaze*. No wonder that years later I felt guilty sailing in a spacious, air-conditioned luxury cruise ship.

Audrey Ronning Topping and her family have lived and worked in China for four generations. As a writer and photographer she has witnessed and recorded the transformation of China in leading publications including the National Geographic *and* The New York Times. *She is author of five books.*

胜 利 的 航 程

Mao meeting several peasants on the deck of his cruiser Kunlun *on a boat trip along the Yangzi River. The title of this poster "A Journey of Victory" was a metaphor of the Cultural Revolution.*

A JOURNEY UPSTREAM ON THE 'EAST IS RED NO.36'

It is easier to climb to heaven
Than take the Sichuan road...

Peak follows peak, each but a hand's breathe from the sky
Dead pine trees hang head into the chasms
Torrents and waterfalls outroar each other
Pounding the cliffs and boiling over rocks,
Booming like thunder through a thousand caverns,
What takes you, traveller, this long weary way
So filled with danger.

Li Bai (701–62) *The Sichuan Road*

A voyage up the Yangtze in November 1979 was very different to today—no pleasure steamers or tourists then. The imprimatur of Maoism was very much in evidence with the local population still dressed in their blue or grey Mao suits, although one might spy the occasional flash of brightly coloured long johns poking out below the blue cotton trousers. Or the monotony of blue might be broken by a passing kindergarten bus—in other words a pedicab with a large box on the back, stuffed with babies in coloured jackets and ribbons like a flower seller's cart.

The East is Red No 36 was to be our home for the four-day trip upstream from Wuhan to Chongqing. Our travelling companions were a group of good friends and 'old China hands'. The night before boarding the boat was spent in Wuhan (formerly the treaty port of Hankow) at the Victory Hotel. A disturbed night with our sleep shattered by the dawn chorus of a barge and boat symphony floating up from the nearby Yangtze. This racket started at 4.30 am, once the night prowling cats left off. At 7.30 am bleary eyed we piled into the bus and drove the short distance down to the river. Our lauban, a long-time resident of China had organised a supply of extra provisions—champagne, coca-cola (then not widely available in China) and of course Cooper's Oxford marmalade. As our entire luggage was transferred from the bus onto the floating quay and then hauled up the steep gangplank this group of 'foreign friends' caused a huge amount of amusement and interest to all the passengers hanging over the rails.

Probably as much amusement as Thomas Cooper had caused in 1868 when preparing to travel up the Yangtze. He had been advised, for security's sake, to dress as a Chinese scholar: 'To all outward appearances indistinguishable from veritable Chinese, I set to work for my own metamorphosis, and began to accustom myself to the tail and petticoats, walking in which required considerable practice before a proper gait could be attained.' No simple task the 'barber shaved my head and made, by judiciously interweaving false hair with the natural growth, a capital pigtail, transforming me at once into a fairly respectable looking elderly Chinaman, and I spent my last night in Hankow (Wuhan) in all the discomfort of pigtail and petticoats.'

The East is Red No 36 was a bulky 20-year-old steamer with some 800 berths and operated by the Yangtze River Board. We were very elegantly accommodated on the deck below the bridge, with a sitting room running horizontally across the bow of the boat leading onto an outdoor deck (a fine place for early morning tai-chi). Four inner cabins opened onto a glass-covered passageway and the four outer cabins onto a good wide metal deck, very comfortable for sitting out on. The cabins themselves were fitted modestly with black silk velvet curtains around each bed. Once 'under way' we discovered that the plumbing arrangements were interesting. Every half an hour or so a great rush of water would flush through the communal bathrooms, day and night. Our dining room was the other end of the 71-metre-long vessel and ran horizontally across the stern. So three times a day we were shepherded from one end of the vessel to the other—this was the only time that officially we rubbed shoulders with our fellow passengers—sometimes they were hurried into their cabins ahead of us.

We steamed off up river swiftly and remarkably silently—under the Wuhan rail and river bridge. Floating docks and brick buildings gave way very soon to wide flat banks with very misty hills beyond. We passed small tugs and lines of big sampans chugging upriver together. One small junk with tattered sails was being pulled upstream by a strong young man with a shoulder rope—seemingly with little effort. As the river narrowed we steamed close to the right bank giving loud boops on the horn from time to time. Along the banks a wide, lovely band of trees had been planted and billowed thickly, parallel to the river. Sparrows perched on the loading beam in the bow of the ship sunning themselves. Our private deck on the bow was a perfect spot to watch the passing scene except for the dreadful din issuing forth from the loudspeakers—sometimes music, sometimes chat explaining 'points of interest'. A few carefully chosen words from our lauban got it turned off!

The scene flowing by was much the same as the one experienced by Victorian travellers such as Isabella Bird in the 1890s and Thomas Copper in the 1860s though the atmosphere was not at all the same. Steamers had been an unwelcome introduction on the river by foreigners in the 1800s. Isabella Bird explains how the distaste of foreigners affected her. 'To get to deep water we were often close under the right bank, and had the divertissement of being pelted with mud and such names as 'foreign devils' and 'foreign dogs', an amusement which one would have supposed would have palled upon the peasants in the years which these steamers have been running.'

The river continued to wind in huge coils through wide flat land all misty in the sun. We headed diagonally across the water, following the deep-water channels. Water buffalo waded in the shallows below steep muddy banks the trees had moved further back. High reeds on the bank were cut and made into stooks to dry. By the afternoon the river began to narrow, the banks became steep and rocky.

We awoke at 3 am on the second night to find the boat tied up at Ichang [Yichang] which marks the eastern end of the gorges. An hour or so later we set off into the black moonlit night and the first gorge. The searchlights from our boat illuminated the steep rocky walls of the Xiling gorge—now very close by. We all stumbled onto the deck wrapped in coats and blankets, the light gradually dawning outlined layered mountains rising sharply around us and the Yangtze as a narrow smooth brown torrent swirling by. The river bends through sloping grass and rock hills and we zigzagged across it steering diagonally from bank to bank at what appeared to be great speed. Grey marker buoys guided our path which took us sometimes right in on the banks—so close it seemed we could lean out and snatch at the boulders. About 20–30 feet above the present surface a line of stripped rock and layered steps of silt mark the high water mark. Above that we began to make out some simple farmhouses, thatched, sometimes tiled, on the hillsides. Thin terraces stepped up beside them and scraggy trees ran up the brows of the hills behind them like the hairs of a crew cut. Above, behind and in front, the high grey peaks of mountains threw jagged, saw-toothed outlines against the breaking

SICHUAN BASIN

dawn. We saw a few small junks with sails being rowed upstream by four standing rowers in front and two behind. Later the hillsides were covered in a mass of orange trees, bushy green and laden with fruit. Or as Isabella Bird noted, 'oranges appear in splendid groves, mixed up with persimmons: the soil absolutely destitute of weeds, looks as if it were cultivated with trowels and rakes… tilled with a pencil instead of a plough.' There were occasional patches of bright green grass and little plots of vegetables. There also was a form of mining—dark grey coal dust stained some of the rocks below small industrial buildings. Despite the narrowness of the river (some 500 feet) it was as smooth as a lake, reflecting the slopes of the hills as they zigzagged away from us in front and behind.

Our boat 'blows and blares' every ten minutes or so, which must be shattering for the villages on the slopes. By 7 am smoke rose from all the houses and many people were out—some fishing with long nets, one walking with three dogs, some more trekking up the terraces with large wicker panniers on their backs. At one largish settlement many people streamed down to boats which were loading a great quantity of tree trunks: pit props?

The Xiling gorge though still very dramatic was, until many rocks were blasted in the 1950s, famous for treacherous rapids. Each year the rapids claimed many lives as witnessed by Robert Payne during the Second World War: 'it [the sampan] suddenly stopped and began to sway backwards and forwards, caught against the rocks, swinging like scissors, until suddenly the roar of the river came to our ears and at that moment the sampan broke in two, spilling the occupants into the white river. For two or three seconds—certainly not more than five seconds—we watched three or four small black heads bobbing up and down against the smooth rock: then they disappeared, following the boat which was already disappearing downstream.'

We reached the second gorge at around 11 am which coincided with lunch. As we had now been aboard for several days some of us had chatted to the fellow passengers whose cabins we passed as we walked along to the dining room. Little did we realise this would have unpleasant consequences for them. Each meal was delicious Shanghainese food except perhaps for the breakfast with the well-known solid 'welded eggs'. The main attractions of this gorge were pointed out to the passengers via loudspeaker and we were spoilt as a young lady came to tell us what not to miss—the 12 peaks of the Wu gorge, a lone boulder shaped like a Tang lady visible just below a peak on the horizon and so on. The Wu mountain peaks are some of the most famous in China, constantly invoked in poetry and paintings.

The gorge itself has steep-sided cliffs falling sheer into the river with upper slopes sparsely patterned with grasses and puffs of feathery trees. On the right bank (north) at one place a huge semi-circular rift had split off an amphitheatre of pink-brown cliffs with six or seven tiers, each with a flat grassy top descending into the water. We passed many little hamlets, sometimes only seemingly 20 foot above the high water mark that in every case here was as high or higher than the top of our boat. Our lauban remembers that one of his company's river steamers, which ran the Chungking–Hankow route in the old days, once went aground on a rock in this gorge at high tide. The water fell 20 feet in two hours and left it stranded in mid-air till the high water returned the next year.

That afternoon we followed the river sharply round to the right and into the top Qutang gorge. A river police building above us in silhouette signalled the beginning of the gorge. Above high mountains sloped sharply down in triangular flanks to a water-line of diagonally twisted rock in layers as fine as do-fu. Way above us the rock faces were patterned with honey-gold streaks of colour that made them seem lit up in the sunlight. As we came further into the gorge the slopes became narrower and more sheer; huge slabs of cliffs watermarked in grey and honey-gold streaks, with, on the right side an incredible path cut into the rock wall like a shelf. The Yangtze water here is especially deep and fast: small boats cannot come up here in late summer. Giant characters are carved into the rock faces on both sides—much of it very new, some record losses of ships here during the Japanese war. Our ship's hooter echoed back and forth between the rocks—an eerie sound. Little white goats are speckled over the patches of grass, seemingly stranded on impossible cliffs and peninsulars.

At the end of the gorge we saw, on the right a lou and small ting in a garden—the place where King Lui Bai lay dying of rage after loosing a great battle and gave his son into the safe keeping of Zhuge Liang. Then the boat turned, and the whole river broadened out into a choppy brown sea edged with mountains all misty in the path of the sun, now out as it began to set, casting a magic pink glow. Looking back we cannot see the river's path through the mountains, which have closed in behind us. It looked as if we were sailing west on a great pink lake.

Out of the gorges and a quick stop at the town of Fengjie marking the western end of the gorges—the home of the poet Du Fu during the Spring

SICHUAN BASIN

and Autumn period (722–481 BC). We tied up and streams of people poured down the long steps to the quay carrying bamboo poles and baskets whilst a mass of our passengers fought their way off. Teams of young men unloaded bundles of planks on their shoulders and more baskets of tangerines were brought on board. It was here that the group of professors we had befriended, as we walked to and fro for our meals, were whisked off the boat by a group of grim looking men. A frisson went around our group when we realised their new companions were plain clothed Public Security Bureau officials.

Our first and only long stop was at the ancient city Wanxian only recently opened to tourists. From our steamer the town was a vast rampart, with a grand stairway from the river all the way up to the main street: and high grey dour warehouse buildings rising from immensely elongated stiff pillars. Hundreds of people poured down to the ship as we docked. A herd of sampans nestled up to our boat, their occupants proclaiming their various wares at the top of their voices. Some with hot food on offer others just piles of oranges loose in the bottom of the craft. A similar scene was recorded by young Tan Shi-hua travelling down river in the 1920s: 'A stuffy steam rose over charcoal stoves on which greasy meat cakes and noodles were being cooked. The hungry passengers bought eggs, sausage and cold jellied soup. Floating restaurant boats with semicircular awnings, lighted with kerosene lamps, bumped against the side of our craft…' Tan Shi-hua went on to describe the gambling and brothel boats alongside—not openly on display in 1979! Here we were allowed off our boat, though heavily chaperoned, to walk through the winding streets. Markets bustling with customers and little shops filled the winding streets. On the side-lines groups of old men smoked strange longs pipes whilst playing chess or just gossiping. Grannies sitting on their doorsteps in elegant bamboo chairs knitting as they kept an eye on the children skipping rope. We walked round a park, bought some trinkets and ate delicious juicy local pomelo at a reception in an old hotel whilst listening to the history of the Wanxian. Back at the East is Red a real opera of unloading cargo was going on. A series of gigantic crates were heaved onto the first jetty, then manhandled by almost unbelievably strong dockers across and up a plank onto the next jetty for storage. The whole thing done by hand, two old men with cloths tied round their heads like open-topped turbans, carried crates three times their own size, unaided on their backs.

We set sail again into the sunset, a magic time on the river. Plumes of smoke rose from the boats tied up as the evening meal was cooked; a majestic old junk was rowed towards the shore, the soft light illuminated her huge flat rectangular sail. Behind, the distant hills rose in increasingly paler layers of blue grey against the pink sky—a peaceful timeless scene.

Shibaozhai was our last surprise of the trip. We saw the building in the far distance and did not believe it possible: nine stories of a pagoda-shaped building plastered up against the rocky walls of a small flat-topped boulder hill which rose up on all sides some 100 feet or so from a small town. The pagoda—not in fact a pagoda at all, but a staircase, rose in nine tiers against the hill, each roof twirled up at the edges into a long horn. The whole thing painted scarlet with fresh new paint that was so startling in the misty greyness all around. Above it, on top of the cliff, and immediately behind it, sat a further three-storied lou or viewing platform also painted scarlet and in the same style, so it looked as if it had jumped off the pagoda and landed slap behind it on the rock. This whole elaborate building was the means of getting from the town up onto the table top, where a Confucian temple, white and spacious took up almost the whole flat space with courtyards and trees. It all caused us much excitement and many rolls of film.

We awake very early the next morning to find that, far from being just outside our destination Chongqing, we were anchored in thick gleaming fog and could not even see the riverbanks—eventually the fog cleared and we docked, bidding farewell to the East is Red No 36.

Caroline Courtauld
Excerpts from the diary of Maggie Keswick

Maggie Keswick *was educated in Shanghai, Hong Kong and Scotland, and on P&O ships between the two. She first visited China at the age of four and returned there in 1961 with her parents for the first of many trips. Her great grandfather, William Keswick, was a great nephew of Dr William Jardine who, together with James Matheson, in 1832 founded the firm that still bears their name today. She is the author of the much acclaimed book* The Chinese Garden.

(above) A fishing junk on the lower river in 1979. (below) One of the East is Red river liners with capacity for up to 3,000 passengers in 1985. Nowadays passengers wishing to travel through the Three Gorges can do so on one the modern five-star cruise ships.

SAILING THE YANGZI

I sailed 1,500 miles downstream, from Chungking to Shanghai. Every mile of it was different; but there were 1,200 miles I did not see. It crosses ten provinces, 700 rivers are joined to it—all Yangtze statistics are hopeless, huge and ungraspable; they obscure rather than clarify. And since words have a greater precision than numbers, one day I asked a Chinese ship captain if he thought the river had a distinct personality.

He said, 'The mood of the river changes according to the season. It changes every day. It is not easy. Navigating the river is always a struggle against nature. And there is only one way to pilot a ship well.' He explained—he was smiling and blowing smoke out of his nostrils—'It is necessary to see the river as an enemy.'

Later a man told me that in the course of one afternoon he had counted nine human corpses bobbing hideously down the river.

The Yangtze is China's main artery, its major waterway, the source of many of its myths, the scene of much of its history. On its banks are some of its greatest cities. It is the fountainhead of superstition; it provides income and food to half the population. It is one of the most dangerous rivers in the world, in some places one of the dirtiest, in others one of the most spectacular. The Chinese drink it and bathe in it and wash clothes in it and shit in it. It represents both life and death. It is a wellspring, a sewer and a tomb; depthless in the gorges, puddle-shallow at its rapids. The Chinese say if you haven't been up the Great River, you haven't been anywhere.

They also say that in the winter, on the river, the days are so dark that when the sun comes out the dogs bark at it. Chungking was dark at nine in the morning, when I took the rattling tin tram on the cog railway that leads down the black crags which are Chungking's ramparts, down the sooty cliffs, past the tenements and billboards ('Flying Pigeon Bicycles', 'Seagull Watches', 'Parrot Accordions') to the landing stage. A thick, sulphurous fog lay over the city, a Coketown of six million… Doctor Ringrose, who was from Leeds, sniffed and said, 'That is the smell of my childhood.'

Paul Theroux, Sailing Through China, 1984

THE STORY OF THE THREE KINGDOMS

If one wishes to understand China, one must have some familiarity with the history of the Three Kingdoms and with the lore that surrounds it. Above all this is true on the middle and upper Yangtse where it seems every bend in the river leads to another site associated with this epoch and to the stories that have grown around it like the layers of a pearl around its grain of historical fact. If the events seem complicated and the stage crowded with unfamiliar actors, that too is part of China's reality. One might as well seek to know the Greeks without the Trojan War or the English without Shakespeare.

Lyman P Van Slyke, *Yangtse: Nature, History and the River,* 1988.

By AD 150 the Han dynasty (206 BC–AD 220) was already rotting from within, the result of a series of weak emperors. The uprising of peasant rebels known as the Yellow Turbans (AD 184) gave three strong warlords (Cao Cao, Liu Bei and Sun Quan) the opportunity to amass their own independent armies. They gradually set up rival territories within the Empire and fought it out for the control of China. The history of their struggle formed the basis for the 14th-century popular novel *The Romance of the Three Kingdoms,* a compilation of fact and fiction taken from the repertoires of 12 centuries of storytellers. It is a rambling saga of heroism and treachery, of larger-than-life heroes and villains against the backdrop of the dying dynasty. Tales from this era are also the subject of many Chinese operas.

The three kingdoms were:

The Kingdom of Wei: North China, comprising the Yellow River basin; the base of the Qin and Han dynasties. Its ruler was Cao Cao, Duke of Wei, characterized in the novel as the archetypal Chinese villain, a brilliant but ruthless general. 'Speak of Cao Cao and he is there' is the Chinese equivalent of 'Talk of the devil'.

The Kingdom of Shu: the area that is now called Sichuan. It was established by Liu Bei, pretender to the throne by virtue of being a distant relation of the Han emperor. Although a rather weak and insignificant personality himself, his royal blood attracted gifted followers, the most famous of whom are Zhuge Liang and Liu's two sworn blood-brothers Zhang Fei and Guan Yu.

Zhuge Liang was Liu's premier strategist and has been held up as an example of military genius ever since. There are numerous stories of how he defeated Cao Cao's larger armies by guile and bravado rather than strength. For instance, there was the time he was staying in an unprotected city when Cao Cao's army arrived unexpectedly. As the troops approached, they saw that the city gate was wide open and that Zhuge Liang, accompanied only by one young servant boy, was perched on top of the city wall calmly playing the harp. Convinced that they were about to walk into an ambush, the enemy withdrew.

Guan Yu was so revered for his loyalty that he was gradually turned into a god. Given the honorary title Guan Gong, and also known as Guan Di, God of War, Justice and Righteousness, until recently nearly every large town in China had a temple dedicated to him. His statue can be recognized by its distinctive red face, signifying bravery and goodness.

The Kingdom of Wu: The rich and fertile lower Yangzi region, as far as the sea. This was controlled by the treacherous Sun Quan, whose family was the most influential in the region. Between Shu and Wu was the middle Yangzi basin, a no-man's land of marshes and lakes. From here one could threaten either Shu or Wu and it was here that some of the most crucial battles took place. On the run from Cao Cao's army, Liu Bei took refuge in this area and Zhuge Liang persuaded Sun Quan, the ruler of Wu, to ally with them against the powerful Cao Cao. Although their combined forces were still far less than Cao Cao's, together they routed him in the critical battle of Red Cliff, at a site upriver from modern Wuhan.

Now it was Cao Cao's turn to flee for his life. Although Guan Yu actually cornered him and could have killed him he let him go, as Cao Cao had done the same for him in an earlier encounter.

But the alliance between Liu Bei and Sun Quan did not last long. Sun Quan tried to persuade Guan Yu to betray Liu Bei and join him. When Guan Yu refused, Sun had him beheaded and sent his head to Cao Cao, hoping for an alliance with him. The grief-stricken Liu Bei ignored Zhuge Liang's advice and launched a disastrous campaign against Sun. Before the fight even began, his other sworn brother Zhang Fei was murdered by two fellow officers who planned to surrender to Sun. Liu was ignominiously defeated and retreated to Baidi Cheng, where he died a few years later.

Cao Cao also died without achieving his ambitions. Although his son succeeded in conquering the other two Kingdoms, it was a short-lived triumph, as he was toppled in a *coup d'état*. So none of the three realized their dream of ruling over the whole of China.

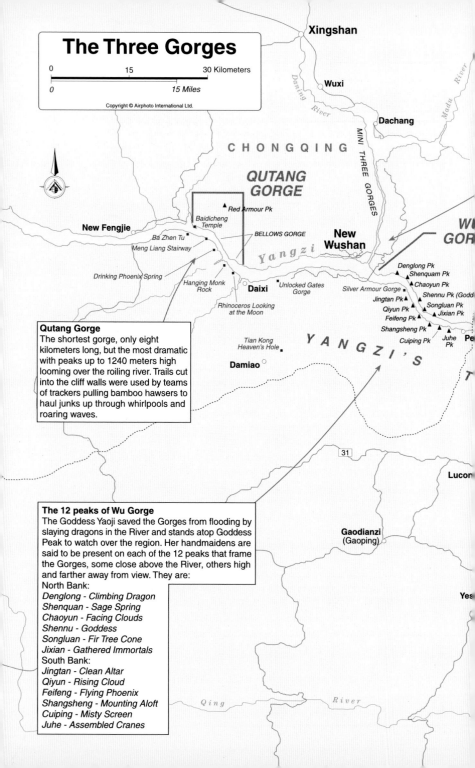

The Three Gorges

0   15   30 Kilometers

0   15 Miles

Xingshan

Wuxi

Dachang

Madu River

Daning River

C H O N G Q I N G

QUTANG GORGE

▲ Red Armour Pk

New Fengjie

Baidicheng Temple

Ba Zhen Tu

Meng Liang Stairway

BELLOWS GORGE

New Wushan

W GOR

MINI THREE GORGES

Yangzi

Drinking Phoenix Spring

Hanging Monk Rock

Daixi

Unlocked Gates Gorge

Silver Armour Gorge

Denglong Pk ▲
▲ Shenquam Pk
▲ Chaoyun Pk
Shennu Pk (Godd
Jingtan Pk ▲ ▲
Qiyun Pk ▲ Songluan Pk
Feifeng Pk ▲ ▲ Jixian Pk
Shangsheng Pk ▲
Cuiping Pk ▲ ▲ Juhe Pk

Pe

Rhinoceros Looking at the Moon

Tian Kong Heaven's Hole

Damiao ○

Y A N G Z I ' S

T

Qutang Gorge
The shortest gorge, only eight kilometers long, but the most dramatic with peaks up to 1240 meters high looming over the roiling river. Trails cut into the cliff walls were used by teams of trackers pulling bamboo hawsers to haul junks up through whirlpools and roaring waves.

31

Lucon

The 12 peaks of Wu Gorge
The Goddess Yaoji saved the Gorges from flooding by slaying dragons in the River and stands atop Goddess Peak to watch over the region. Her handmaidens are said to be present on each of the 12 peaks that frame the Gorges, some close above the River, others high and farther away from view. They are:
North Bank:
Denglong - Climbing Dragon
Shenquan - Sage Spring
Chaoyun - Facing Clouds
Shennu - Goddess
Songluan - Fir Tree Cone
Jixian - Gathered Immortals
South Bank:
Jingtan - Clean Altar
Qiyun - Rising Cloud
Feifeng - Flying Phoenix
Shangsheng - Mounting Aloft
Cuiping - Misty Screen
Juhe - Assembled Cranes

Gaodianzi
(Gaoping) ○

Yes

Qing   *River*

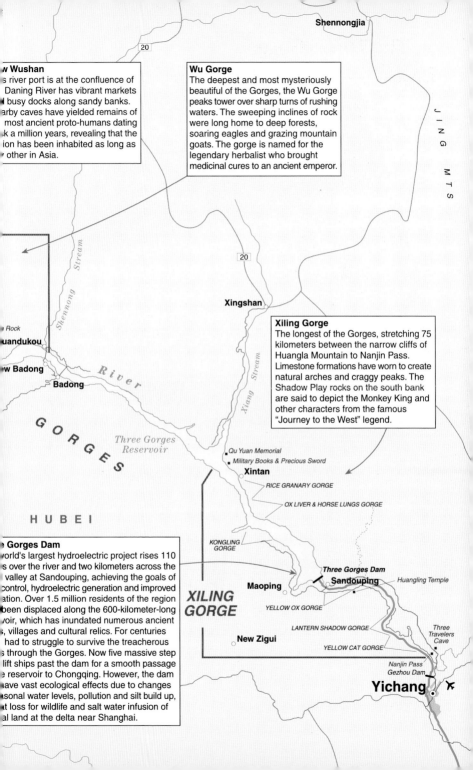

Shennongjia

20

w Wushan
s river port is at the confluence of
Daning River has vibrant markets
d busy docks along sandy banks.
arby caves have yielded remains of
most ancient proto-humans dating
k a million years, revealing that the
ion has been inhabited as long as
other in Asia.

Wu Gorge
The deepest and most mysteriously
beautiful of the Gorges, the Wu Gorge
peaks tower over sharp turns of rushing
waters. The sweeping inclines of rock
were long home to deep forests,
soaring eagles and grazing mountain
goats. The gorge is named for the
legendary herbalist who brought
medicinal cures to an ancient emperor.

J I N G   M T S

20

Xingshan

Shennong Stream

Xiling Gorge
The longest of the Gorges, stretching 75
kilometers between the narrow cliffs of
Huangla Mountain to Nanjin Pass.
Limestone formations have worn to create
natural arches and craggy peaks. The
Shadow Play rocks on the south bank
are said to depict the Monkey King and
other characters from the famous
"Journey to the West" legend.

Rock
uandukou

w Badong

Badong

R i v e r

Xiang Stream

G O R G E S

*Three Gorges
Reservoir*

Qu Yuan Memorial
Military Books & Precious Sword
Xintan

RICE GRANARY GORGE

OX LIVER & HORSE LUNGS GORGE

H U B E I

KONGLING
GORGE

e Gorges Dam
vorld's largest hydroelectric project rises 110
s over the river and two kilometers across the
valley at Sandouping, achieving the goals of
control, hydroelectric generation and improved
ation. Over 1.5 million residents of the region
been displaced along the 600-kilometer-long
voir, which has inundated numerous ancient
, villages and cultural relics. For centuries
had to struggle to survive the treacherous
s through the Gorges. Now five massive step
lift ships past the dam for a smooth passage
e reservoir to Chongqing. However, the dam
ave vast ecological effects due to changes
sonal water levels, pollution and silt build up,
t loss for wildlife and salt water infusion of
al land at the delta near Shanghai.

Three Gorges Dam
Sandouping

Huangling Temple

Maoping

YELLOW OX GORGE

*XILING
GORGE*

LANTERN SHADOW GORGE

Three
Travelers
Cave

New Zigui

YELLOW CAT GORGE

Nanjin Pass
Gezhou Dam

Yichang

(above) The Yangzi is navigable from Shanghai to Xinshezhen in Sichuan—a distance of over 3,000 kilometres. Before the construction of the Three Gorges Dam, Yangzi captains would have to keep a constant vigil and considered the Great River far more hazardous than mere ocean navigation. (below) Sailing junk in Sichuan.

The Three Gorges

Note: The following are the riverside towns and historical sites as they would appear on the downstream journey from Chongqing. Although some description and background is retained for historical interest, bear in mind that most of these towns are in the process of being completely or at least partially submerged by the new dam. In some cases entire new towns have been constructed nearby, above the final projected water level. The giant sluices of the Three Gorges Dam (San Xia Ba) were closed on 1st June 2003 and within about two weeks the water had reached the interim level of 135 metres. Construction work on the Dam continues and it is anticipated that between 2007 and 2009 the waters will rise once more, a further 40 metres to the final height of 175 metres. Meanwhile, the remaining old buildings that lie below this level are in the process of being demolished so they will not become submerged hazards to shipping.

FULING

The river Wu rises in Guizhou, and at its confluence with the Yangzi, on the great river's south bank, stands the ancient city of Fuling. Some 2,000 years ago Fuling was the political centre of the Kingdom of Ba (fourth to second centuries BC) and the site of its ancestral graves. Fuling is the connecting link in water transportation between northern Guizhou and eastern Sichuan. The town and its surrounding area are rich in such produce as grain, lacquer and tung oil, and the local specialities are hot pickled mustard tuber, Hundred-Flower sweet wine and pressed radish seeds. In 1972 archaeologists excavated graves from the Kingdom of Ba, and among the finds were ancient musical instruments. Today the city has a population of over one million, and its lower levels are being submerged by the rising water. A high wall faces the reservoir holding the waters back.

The most important archaeological site in Fuling is a set of ancient carvings and inscriptions on what is known as **White Crane Ridge**. This lies about one kilometre west of the town, near the south bank of the river. Although now below the new water level, it has been preserved *in situ* in a specially constructed, 250-metre long, underwater museum. At writing, this project is not yet realized.

On the ridge of hard, purple sandstone are carved ancient water level marks in the form of 14 scaled fish and inscriptions of nearly 30,000 characters referring to the hydrology of the river at this point. There is also a sculpture of Guanyin, the Goddess of Mercy. The earliest of the stone fish, two of which are carps of over one metre in length, were carved in the Tang dynasty (618–907). They used to be visible only at the lowest water level, which occurred perhaps once every decade or so. It was said that when the eye of the carps appeared there would be a bumper harvest. Other inscriptions date from the Song dynasty. The inscriptions contain valuable hydrological data covering a span of 1,200 years, from the first year of the Tang dynasty to the early 20th century, and describe 72 different years when the water in the Yangzi River fell to record levels.

In 1996, a 26-year-old American named Peter Hessler arrived in Fuling to begin a two-year stint as a Peace Corps volunteer teaching English at the local college. He writes about his experiences and observations during his time in the city in the book, *River Town: Two Years on the Yangtze* (see Recommended Reading).

FENGDU

Fengdu, on the north bank of the river, 172 kilometres east of Chongqing, was in the past more popularly known as the 'City of Ghosts'. There is a temple here dedicated to the God of the Underworld.

The origin of the town's extraordinary reputation dates back to the Han dynasty (206 BC–AD 220) when two officials, Yin and Wang, became Daoist (Taoist) recluses here and eventually Immortals. When combined, their names mean 'King of the Underworld'. For many centuries, Fengdu was well known as a pilgrimage site, especially for the deceased, some of whom were said to be able to walk zombie-like to Fengdu for their judgment and rebirth. Less ambulatory souls would fly over the clouds and land at the 'Looking Back Pavilion' (Huijing Lou), to watch the funereal rites of their family. They would then drink a 'tea of forgetfulness' to erase all human memories before being reborn. The tea is still served in the tower, but without much effect on the living.

Today the town is thronged with tourists attracted by temples and shrines dedicated to the demons of the underworld. There is a cable car to the original temple complex on **Minshan**, overlooking what remains of the old town which is in the process of being demolished. The area will be completely submerged between 2007 and 2009. However, the historical temples located on Minshan will remain accessible beside the river. A large new town has been established opposite, on the south bank.

A pilgrim to the old temple used to be able to purchase, for the sum of one dollar, a 'Passport to Heaven', stamped by the local magistrate and the abbot. Landmarks in the temple complex bear horrific names—Ghost Torturing Pass,

The new 'King of the Underworld' pavilion at Fengdu, which overlooks the ancient Minshan temple complex and the old town, which has been prepared for final demolition

Last Glance at Home Tower, Nothing-to-be-done Bridge. Fengdu's temples display instruments of torture and wild demon images. Shopkeepers kept a basin of water into which customers threw their coins: if they sank they were genuine, but if they floated the coins were ghost money and unacceptable. Boats would anchor in midstream rather than by the bank in case of attack by ghosts.

A large building in the likeness of the God of the Underworld rises over the old town, with a restaurant in his head. This monument overlooks the old temple complex on Minshan hill, soon to become an island. An amusement park in the higher valley gives cart tours of the ghoulish imagery of the underworld, with automaton animation. It is pure kitsch, a daily Halloween, Chinese style. The town government has also initiated a new attraction, the largest rock carving in the world, on a mountain slope 15 kilometres northeast of the old town. This new carving of the God of the Underworld is some 400 meters high, such that one can walk in one ear and out the other in the low-relief sculpture, which has been hand cut from the red sandstone. A statue of the Goddess of Mercy stands on the top of his head, as if to keep away the ill omen of such an immense demonic visage. Boats will sail from the Yangzi to this new attraction after 2006 when the full reservoir waters rise.

DINGFANG TOWERS

Just before reaching the town of Zhongxian, on the north bank, are the Dingfang Towers, or *que*. This monument was constructed during the Eastern Han dynasty (25–220). A *que* is a kind of ornamental tower, not uncommon during this period, and was usually constructed in front of religious buildings or royal tombs to show a person's status. The monument at Dingfang is a double *que* with two eaves and is of particular archaeological importance. It is planned to move the towers before they are inundated by the river. There are only 31 *que* still in existence in China, mostly in Sichuan and Chongqing.

ZHONGXIAN

There are two moving stories about how Zhongxian (Loyal County) got its name. In the Warring States period (475–221 BC), Ba Manzi, a native of Zhongxian, became a general in the army of the Kingdom of Ba. Towards the end of the Zhou dynasty the Kingdom of Ba was in a state of civil war, and Ba Manzi was sent to the Kingdom of Chu to beg military assistance to put down the rebellion. The price demanded by Chu was the forfeit of three Ba cities. Once Chu's troops had helped restore stability to Ba, the King of Chu sent his minister to demand the payoff. Ba Manzi, however, said: 'Though I promised Chu the cities you will take my head in thanks to the King of Chu, for the cities of Ba cannot be given away', whereupon he cut off his own head. Receiving his minister's account, the King of Chu sighed: 'Cities would count as nothing had I loyal ministers like Ba Manzi.' He then ordered that Ba Manzi's head be buried with full honours.

The second tale is of another man of Zhongxian, the valiant general Yan Yan, who served the Minor Han dynasty (AD 221–63). Captured by the Shu general Zhang Fei, he refused to surrender, saying boldly: 'In my country we had a general who cut off his own head but we do not have a general who surrendered.' Enraged, Zhang Fei ordered Yan's beheading. The doomed general remained perfectly calm as he asked simply, 'Why are you so angry? If you want to cut off my head then give the order, but there is no point in getting angry and upsetting yourself.' Zhang Fei was so deeply moved by Yan's loyalty and bravery in the face of death that he personally unbound him, treating him as an honoured soldier.

Traditionally, the thick bamboo hawsers used to haul junks over the rapids were made in this area, as the local bamboo is especially tenacious. Bamboo handicrafts are still a thriving industry today, while the local food speciality is Zhongxian beancurd milk. Part of the original town will be submerged by the rising waters.

The red pavilion of Shibaozhai (Precious Stone Fortress)

SHIBAOZHAI (PRECIOUS STONE FORTRESS)

Shibaozhai represents the first gem of Chinese architecture to be encountered on the downstream journey. From afar, the protruding 220-metre hill on the north bank can appear to resemble a jade seal, and is so named. The creation of the hill is attributed to the goddess Nuwo, who caused a rock slide while she was redecorating the sky after a fierce battle between two warring dukes.

A red pavilion hugs one side of this rock. Its tall yellow entrance gate is decorated with lions and dragons and etched with an inscription inviting the visitor to climb the ladder and ascend into a 'Little Fairyland'. The temple on top of the hill was built during the reign of Emperor Qianlong (1736–96) and access to it was by an iron chain attached to the cliff. A nine-storeyed wooden pavilion was added in 1819 so that monks and visitors to the temple would not have to suffer the discomforts of the chain ascent. In 1956 three more storeys were added. Each floor is dedicated to famous generals of the Three Kingdoms period (AD 220–265), local scholars and renowned Chinese poets. The rising waters of the river will eventually surround the pagoda, which will be preserved on an island behind a small dam of its own.

In front of Ganyu Palace at the top of Jade Seal Hill is the Duck Hole. It is said that as spring turns to summer, if you take a live duck and drop it through the hole, it will quickly reappear swimming in the Yangzi. In the past the monks apparently drew their drinking water from this hole by using a pipe made of bamboo.

The spirit wall in the temple's main hall is constructed of excavated Han-dynasty (206 BC–AD 220) bricks. The hall behind is dedicated on the right to Generals Zhang Fei and Yan Yan of the Three Kingdoms (see pages 304–5), and on the left to General Qin Liangyu (1576–1648) who fought bravely against the Manchu forces. A mural shows the goddess Nuwo repairing the sky.

In the rear hall are the remains of the Rice Flowing Hole. Legend has it that long ago just enough husked rice would flow up from the small hole each day for the needs of the monks and their guests. One day a greedy monk, thinking he could become rich, chiselled a bigger hole, and the rice flow ceased forever. His effigy may be seen in the last room of the temple complex.

Tourist cruise ships usually dock at Shibaozhai for a few hours' visit. A gaunlet of souvenir stands greets visitors off the docks. The new town of Shibaozhai is located directly above the site of the old town, which has largely been demolished and will be submerged by the next rise in the water level.

The Shibaozhai pavilion pictured in 1983. The surrounding village was demolished in preparation for the closure of the Three Gorges Dam in 2003. Prior to the final rise in water level between 2007–9 a protective coffer dam will be constructed around the pavilion and the rock against which it stands, thus creating an artificial island. Cruise vessels will still be able to dock and visit the site.

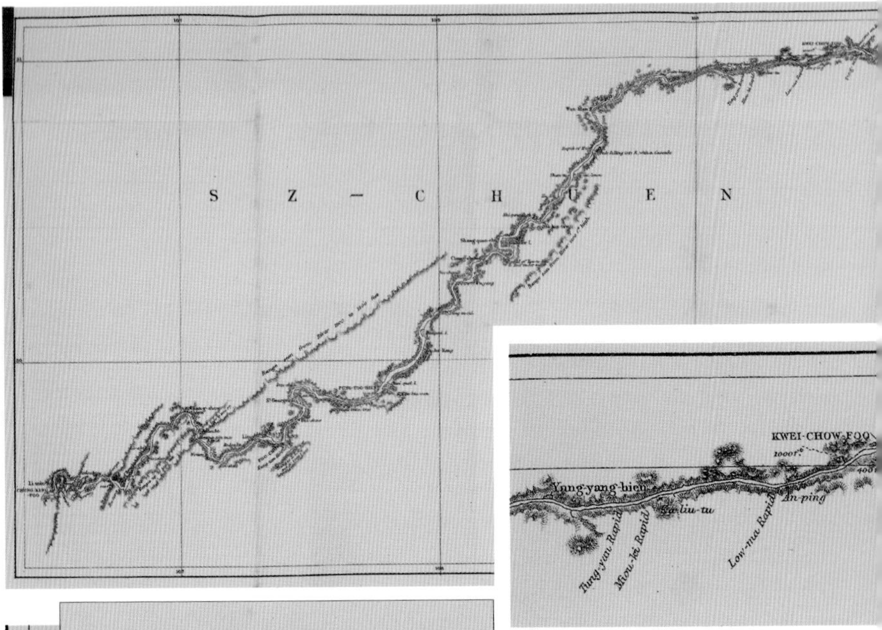

SICHUAN BASIN

THE THREE GORGES

S Z — C H U E N

KWEI-CHOW-FOO

1000 ft

400 ft

Yang-yang-hien

Tung-yuen Rapid

Moou-tsï Rapid

liu-tu

Lin-ping

Low-ma Rapid

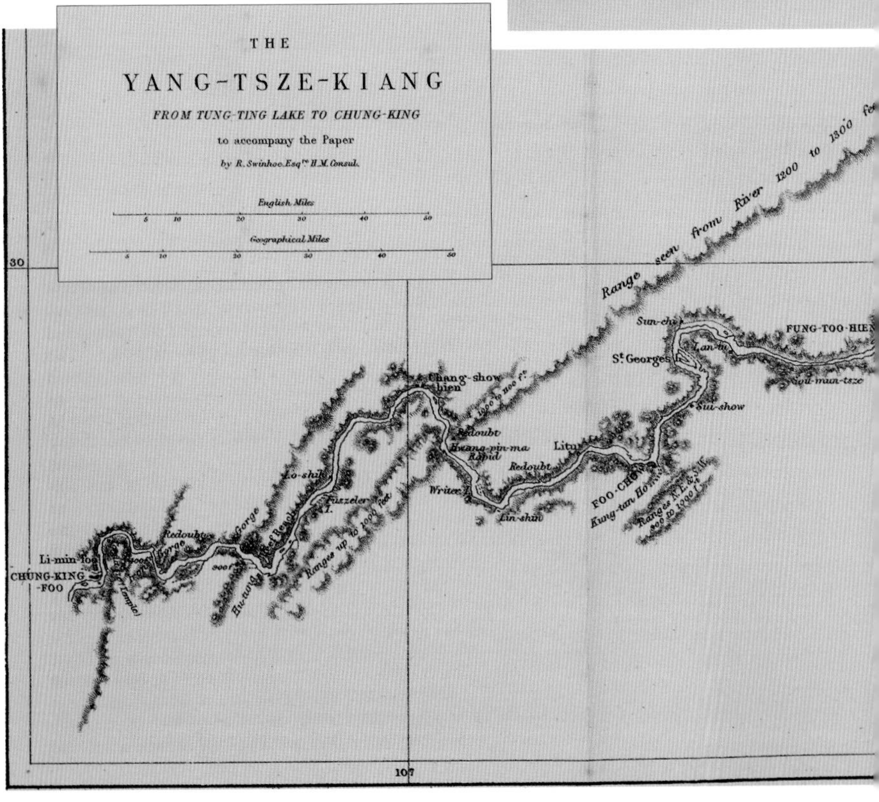

THE

YANG-TSZE-KIANG

FROM TUNG-TING LAKE TO CHUNG-KING

to accompany the Paper

by R. Swinhoe, Esqre H.M. Consul.

English Miles

5   10   20   30   40   50

Geographical Miles

5   10   20   30   40   50

Range seen from River 1200 to 1300 feet

30

Range seen from River 800 to 900 ft.

FUNG-TOO-HIEN

Sun-chi

Lan-ni

St Georges

Tsui-mun-tze

Siu-show

Chang-show-hien

Redoubt

Swang-niu-ma Rapid

Litu

Writer

Lin-shui

Lo-shih

Fuzzeler

Gorge

Redoubt

Li-min-ho

CHUNG-KING-FOO

Redoubt

Gorge

Euang

Rapid

FOO-CHOW

Kung-tan-Horse

Range seen from River 800 to 900 ft.

107

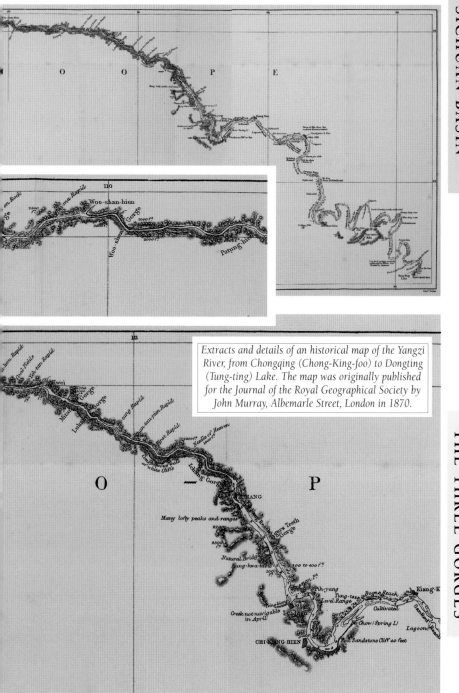

Extracts and details of an historical map of the Yangzi River, from Chongqing (Chong-King-foo) to Dongting (Tung-ting) Lake. The map was originally published for the Journal of the Royal Geographical Society by John Murray, Albemarle Street, London in 1870.

THREE GORGES ARCHAEOLOGY

At the beginning of June 2003, the gargantuan, 600-kilometre-long reservoir behind the Three Gorges Dam at Sandouping was filled to a height of 135 metres above sea level. Some 1,208 sites of historical and archaeological importance along the Yangzi River were inundated.

Archaeological discoveries made during the salvage efforts have recently identified the area as one of the most culturally important in China. As a result, local museums have been greatly enriched and Chinese archaeology has advanced both technically and financially. Unfortunately for the future of serious archaeological research in the region, it is all too little too late.

In 1992, when the dam's construction was approved by China's National Peoples Congress, not a single archaeologist was among 412 experts consulted. After a hurriedly commissioned UNESCO report a year later identified key sites and made various recommendations, the government appointed Yu Weichao, then director of the Chinese History Museum, as director of the Planning Group for Cultural Relic Protection of the Three Gorges Reservoir and Dam Construction.

Salvage archaeology and cultural heritage preservation carried out between 1997 and 2003, from a global or national point of view, were unprecedented in terms of style of execution, scale, and time. Not only was the work arduously complicated and revolutionary in pursuing China's new 'market economy' style of management, but it applied, for the first time, scientific technology and analysis (for example, DNA testing, satellite photography, CAD computer software) never used before in these areas, where archaeology is relatively pubescent or modern cultural heritage preservation non-existent.

Exploiting only 339 million yuan (US$38 million) in government funds, some 110 different departments or institutes from 20 provinces and autonomous areas, involving some 7,000 people, offered various levels and types of aid from architectural relocation, architectural repair, under-water calligraphy preservation, archaeological excavation, cultural relic protection, to scientific and material value analysis.

Yu Weichao and the academic institutions involved tried to advance work on the most important sites, their plight and findings increasingly publicised outside China by scholars such as Elizabeth Childs-Johnson. As sites were uncovered, looting thrived and artefacts of dubious origin surfaced on the international market.

By 2000, with increasing pressure from the archaeological community inside and outside China, substantial funds were finally allocated and a salvage operation was launched with 100 teams of archaeologists from more than 20 provinces and cities working on 120 of the most important sites. It was all far too late, and despite the introduction of high-tech equipment, in archaeological terms there was hardly time to scratch the surface. Over 6,000 significant artefacts unearthed represent only a tantalising hint of the rich potential of the region. Indeed, so little time was left when the money arrived that many of the museums, institutes and university departments involved, while frustrated, have found themselves richer than ever before.

The archaeological findings have established that the Three Gorges region was one of the main meeting places between East and West in ancient China. Excavations have unearthed material contributing to a revised picture of the early human cultures in the region. Extensive late-Neolithic remains in the principal Three Gorges region are from the Daxi culture (ca. 5000–3200 BC) and the Chujialing culture (3200–2300 BC), but it is the Ba culture sites that have most excited archaeologists. The Ba people can be traced from late-Neolithic origins until the Warring States period of the Eastern Zhou (481–221 BC).

Important early sites, all now submerged, are at Lijiaba at Yunyang, Shuangyantang on the Daning River, and at many places within the Xiling Gorge. Later sites were discovered in the Wu Gorge and at Wushan. Finds of this period are characterised by distinctive works of art such as decorated bronze weapons, large musical instruments such as drums and gongs, and boat-shaped wooden coffins, many sharing similarities to the contemporary Shu culture of western Sichuan.

According to Elizabeth Childs-Johnson, recent archaeological work has uncovered what little we know about the elusive Ba and their relationship to Shu and Chu cultures before and after the Warring States and Han periods.

Flooded remains from later periods include the extensive Tang dynasty (618–907) ruins at Mingyueba on the southern bank of the Xiaojiang River which runs into the Yangzi. Also permanently submerged are many of the area's distinctive 'low-water calligraphies', engraved into the limestone walls of the gorges to record safe water levels for the passage of boats, and dating from the Han and Eastern Jin period (317–420) to the Qing period (1644–1911). Most important of these is Baiheliang or White Crane Ridge, near Fuling, which has unique carvings dating back to the Tang period, where there are plans to build an underwater museum.

The standing monuments of the area are the most visible archaeological casualties although some were relocated, such as the famous Zhang Fei temple complex opposite Yunyang town, built in the Northern Song period (960–1126), which was rebuilt 32 kilometres away. The Qing temple built at Zigui as a memorial to the romantic poet Qu Yuan (338–278 BC) has being moved to Maoping near the dam.

Other monuments have been protected by rampart walls. One example of this is the Ming period fortified treasury of Shibaozhai at Zhongxian—a wooden tower built into the cliff face by the Jiaqing emperor in 1800. A similar defense has been erected for the 7.5-metre high sculpture of Buddha at Single Pebble Village (see pages 283–5).

Discovered in 1987, **Lijiaba** was excavated intensively since 1993 by the archaeological unit of Sichuan University's department of history. The 50-acre settlement has yielded artefacts from the Shang through Han periods (ca. 1700 BC–220 AD). Weapons from the Warring States period (476–221 BC) were identified as Ba because of their unusual shapes. Ceramic evidence points to settlement by both the Ba and their eastern neighbours the Chu, during the Spring and Autumn period (771–476 BC). Discovery of a cemetery and excavation of some of its tombs reveal a strong Ba cultural presence and may tell us more about its origins, historical development and relations with the Chu.

Sichuan Museum site surveys of **Shuangyantang** in 1957 and 1958 were continued in 1987 and 1992 by the Sichuan Unit of the Chinese Academy of Social Science and by the Sichuan Archaeological Institute. Excavations uncovered ceramics contemporary with the Xia, Shang (ca. 1700–1100 BC), and Western Zhou (1100–771 BC) periods. Most recently excavation yielded a ritual bronze wine vessel dating to the early to middle Shang period. Tall for this type of container (78.7 centimetres), the vessel is locally made and decorated with relief images of animal masks and seated birds identical to those on vessels found in hoards in Sichuan, Anhui and Shaanxi provinces. The vessels provides new evidence of a thriving bronze-casting culture that stretched across all of Sichuan and southern China. Yu Weichao believes that ancestors of the Ba people made this 3,500-year-old bronze vessel.

Xiaotianxi, the burial centre of Ba nobility and royalty during the late Eastern Zhou period (771–221 BC), was excavated by three provincial museums in 1972. They unearthed bronze weaponry unique to the region (including a boot-shaped ax and a revolver-shaped dagger-ax), a sword, a short-handled gong, a drum, examples of Ba writing (including an inscribed spearhead), and boat-shaped coffins carved from wood, all dating to third century BC. Many of the weapons are decorated with images of growling tigers shown in profile, a common Ba emblem.

The Daxi (ca. 5000–3200 BC), the Three Gorges' earliest Neolithic culture, and its successors, the Chujialing (ca. 3200–2300 BC) and Shijiahe (ca. 2300–1800 BC), created elegant ceramics and jades. Site surveys at **Daxi** began in the late 1950s and excavations were later conducted by the archaeological unit of Sichuan University's history department. Archaeologist Lu Depei of Wuhan University believes that all three cultures were centred in the Wu Gorge area. Salvage excavations have yielded many new discoveries. The Daxi and Chujialing produced ceramic drinking goblets and bowls, polished red on the outside and black on the inside, that are more varied in shape, colour and decoration than the red-painted pots made by contemporaneous Neolithic cultures in the Yellow River Valley. The Daxi also crafted jade into arc-shaped ornaments, slit-disk earrings, and beads. Shijiahe jades, which were probably used as religious symbols, feature perforated images of mythological birds and shaman heads. At Zhongbaodao, a site at Yichang in Xiling Gorge, Sichuan University archaeologists found artefacts of the Daxi and Chujialing cultures as well as those contemporary with the later Xia period (ca 2200–1700 BC). Archaeologists speculate that Xia artefacts, including a three-legged pitcher with a long pipe spout, are early examples of the Ba culture.

Excavated in 1995 by the Sichuan Fengjie County Museum and the Baidicheng Cultural Relics Institute, the late Neolithic–Shang (ca. 3500–1100 BC) settlement and cemetery at **Laoguanmiao** has yielded stone tools and potshards belonging to an otherwise unknown Neolithic culture. The earliest shards are associated with handmade red-clay ceramics decorated with diamond patterns that date between 3500–3000 BC.

WANXIAN

About two hours below Shibaozhai the boat reaches Wanxian, which is guarded by two nine-storeyed pagodas for good fortune. Of the three major regions affected by the proposed Three Gorges Dam, Yichang, Wanxian and Chongqing, Wanxian will lose the most. Two-thirds of the total population of 1.2 million are being relocated in Wanxian prefecture and the reservoir will inundate 60 per cent of the city. Over 900 factories are located below the new waterline, and many have already been replaced on higher ground.

Wanxian has a number of silk-weaving and spinning factories supported by intense silkworm cultivation—operated on a family basis—which continues year round in Wanxian County. Other light industries include tea, bamboo and cane goods, cotton clothing, leather and Chinese medicines. The local paper mills utilize wheat and rice straw from the surrounding countryside.

HISTORY OF WANXIAN
Known as the Eastern Gate to Sichuan, the city is 2,000 years old, receiving its present name during the Ming dynasty (1368–1644), and becoming a foreign treaty port in 1902. In 1926 two British gunboats bombarded the city, causing massive fires, when the local warlord commandeered foreign vessels for the transport of his troops. This became known as the Wanxian Incident. Following this event which angered the local populace, a boycott on the loading and unloading of British vessels was enforced for several years. The city later suffered aerial bombardment by the Japanese in their unsuccessful attempt to conquer the region.

As the halfway city between Yichang and Chongqing, Wanxian was a main port for East Sichuan merchandise (including large quantities of tung oil, used in treating wooden junks). The town once had a thriving junk building industry; the boats being constructed from cypress wood found in the nearby hills. Early travellers commented on the huge number of junks anchored at Wanxian.

WHAT TO SEE IN WANXIAN
The town is famous for its rattan and cane market where buyers and sellers mingle in a frenzy of bargaining for handmade summer bed mats, fans, hats, straw shoes, furniture and basketry. Small, round, red-trimmed baskets with lids are the most popular item and are well known throughout China. Roadside stalls trade in spicy noodles and cooling, opaque soyabean jelly and fresh fruit. In the mornings, local produce and seasonal delicacies such as mountain mushrooms or live eels can be found in the market.

Two buses await the arrival of tourists at the ancient city of Wanxian in 1979. These buildings have now been demolished in preparation for the flooding of the Three Gorges reservoir.

An assortment of boats and barges crowd the docks at Wanxian in 1985, the city has always been a busy river port

There was a community of foreign missionaries in this region (formerly Sichuan Province) before 1949, and two churches—Catholic and Protestant—continue to draw sizeable congregations of country folk.

In 1983 a small workshop was set up, employing two teenage boys and a few part-time workers to paint and varnish river stones from the Three Gorges. These make attractive mementos and can be bought at the Arts and Crafts Store. Visitors may also visit silk-weaving and cane-furniture factories.

LU POND AND XISHANPAI PAVILION
This small pool, originally dug by a locally revered Song-dynasty official, Lu Youkai, was once a very large lotus pond surrounded by decorative pavilions. Now it is not much more than a traffic roundabout. Nearby stands an ancient two-storey, yellow-tiled pavilion which houses a huge rock carved by the calligrapher Huang Tingzhen. Around the Xishanpai Pavilion once flowed a winding freshwater channel. Local literati would spend their evenings here, floating full wine cups along the channel. When a wine cup stopped in front of one of them his forfeit would be to compose a poem.

WESTERN HILL PARK
A clock tower, which dominates the town's skyline from the river, was built in this large park in 1924. The upper part was damaged by Japanese bombs in 1939. There is a memorial to a Russian volunteer pilot whose plane crashed in the river in the same year. During the summers, people would relax in bamboo deck-chairs under the leafy trees, sipping tea and listening to Sichuan-style opera. The new water level will reach the base of the tower, which will be preserved by a small isolation wall in similar fashion to Shibaozhai.

TAIBAI ROCK
The poet Li Bai (701–62) lived here for a time; in the Ming dynasty a memorial hall was built to commemorate him. Stone inscriptions dating back to the Tang dynasty are still to be seen.

THE THREE GORGES MUSEUM, WANGZHONG HIGHWAY
This small museum, on the Wanzhong Highway, is a repository for some of the artefacts that were collected in advance of the flooding of the area upon completion of the new dam. Han tomb effigies and a Ba period hanging coffin are featured. The museum's exhibits are rudimentary, but the shop is extensive—the usual tourist trap with no local products.

YUNYANG

The original county town of Yunyang (Clouded Sun) used to be situated 64 kilometres below Wanxian, on the north bank. This is already completely underwater, and a new town has been constructed three kilometres upstream on the same side.

The Tang-dynasty poet, Du Fu (712–70), banished to a minor position in Sichuan, fell ill while travelling through Yunyang and stayed for many months, recuperating and writing poetry.

ZHANG FEI TEMPLE

Zhang Fei, the 'Tiger General' of the Kingdom of Shu during the Three Kingdoms period (AD 220–65), is revered as a man who kept his word (see pages 304–5). In 221, Guan Yu, Zhang Fei's sworn brother, was killed by the armies of the Kingdom of Wu. The Tiger General, then an official in Langzhong County, swore revenge and prepared to attack Wu with his army arrayed in white armour and pennants—white being the colour of mourning. He ordered Commanders Zhang Da and Fan Jiang to lead the attack and avenge his brother, under pain of death.

The two pusillanimous officers got Zhang Fei drunk and cut off his head. They then fled by boat to Yunyang, intending to surrender to Wu. Here, however, they heard of a peace settlement between Wu and Shu, and threw Zhang Fei's head into the river, where it circled a fisherman's boat. Zhang Fei appealed to the fisherman in a dream to rescue his head and bury it in Shu. The fisherman obeyed, and the head was interred on Flying Phoenix Hill. A temple was built to commemorate the bold warrior on the south bank of the river, opposite the site of the original town. It is said that, before internment, the head was placed in a vat of oil, and when copper cash was thrown into the vat, the head would float up to give advice to the lovelorn and childless.

The temple was partly damaged in the flood of 1870, so most of the present ensemble of buildings dates from the late 19th century. It was extensively restored. Sixty per cent of the temple's rich collections of paintings, tablets and inscriptions were lost during the Cultural Revolution. In front of the main hall are giant statues of the three famous sworn blood brothers—Liu Bei, Guan Yu and Zhang Fei. Inside the hall sits the wild-eyed, red-faced Guan Yu; on either side are scenes from his life. The Helpful Wind Pavilion contains steles and huge portraits of the general and his wife. It is said that his spirit, in the form of a helpful wind, frequently assisted passing boats. Junkmen used to stop at the temple to light firecrackers and burn incense in appreciation.

The whole temple has had to be relocated to save it from inundation. It now sits opposite the new town. Piers have been built to accommodate tourist ferries from Yunyang and it is possible that some cruise ships may also dock here.

A Tang dynasty pagoda that has stood alone, high above the Yangzi River, for over 1,000 years is now joined by a section of the new town of Fengjie

Temple entrance at Baidi Cheng, White Emperor City

FENGJIE

Fengjie stands on the north bank, just above the western entrance to Qutang, the first of the three great Yangzi gorges. Fengjie town, the county seat for the area, was an attractive town, with part of its Ming-dynasty city wall intact and stairways from the ferry pontoons leading up through three old city gates.

Fengjie was typical of many of the Yangzi River towns. Its markets were filled with local produce, clothing, mountain herbs and fruits—especially peaches, pomelos and snow-pears—for which it was famous. Leafy trees and traditional whitewashed two-storeyed houses lined the main street. Outside the city wall, above the river, used to be makeshift mat-shed teahouses where the local men and travellers would relax in bamboo deck-chairs, drinking tea and eating sunflower seeds or eggs boiled in tea.

Sadly much of the old town has had to be demolished in preparation for the rise in water level. However, the town is still very lively with Chinese tourists who have come to visit the famous historical site of Baidi Cheng nearby (see below).

HISTORY OF FENGJIE

The ancient town was called Kuifu in the Spring and Autumn period (722–481 BC), but became known as Fengjie after the Tang dynasty (618–907). It has long been famous as a poets' city, as many of China's greatest poets commemorated their visits here with verses. The Tang-dynasty poet Du Fu (712–70) wrote some 430 poems while serving as an official here for two years.

Liu Bei, the King of Shu during the Three Kingdoms period (see pages 304–5), died of despair in the Eternal Peace Palace after he was defeated by the armies of Wu. According to two ancient tablets unearthed in recent years, the Fengjie Teacher Training Institute now stands on the site of the palace. On his deathbed, Liu Bei entrusted his sons to the care of his loyal adviser, Zhuge Liang, entreating him to educate them in wisdom and to choose the most talented one to succeed him as king.

It was here that Zhuge Liang trained the troops of Shu in military strategy. He constructed the Eight Battle Arrays, 64 piles of stones 1.5 metres high erected in a grid pattern, 24 of which represented the surrounding troops. The principles of Zhuge Liang's manoeuvres have long been studied by China's military strategists and continue to be relevant to present-day concepts of Chinese warfare.

Nearby was the small village of Yufu (now submerged), which means 'the fish turns back' and relates to the legend of Qu Yuan, China's famous poet and states-man of the third century BC. During his service at court, the country was riven by factions and discord. His political enemies had him exiled; eventually, in despair, he drowned himself in Dongting Lake. His body was allegedly swallowed by a sacred fish which then swam up the gorges to Qu Yuan's birthplace, near Zigui, where the fish intended to give Qu Yuan an honourable burial. However, so great were the lamentations and weeping of the mourners along the shore that the fish also became tearful and swam past Zigui. It was not until it reached Yufu that the fish realized its mistake and turned back. (See the section on Zigui on page 355 for more about the legend of Qu Yuan.)

BAIDI CHENG (WHITE EMPEROR CITY)

The local ferry from Fengjie takes about 20 minutes to reach Baidi Cheng on the north bank of the river, passing several pagodas on the surrounding peaks.

Because of its strategic position the town was chosen in the first century AD by Gong Sunshu, an official turned soldier, as the site of his headquarters. The legend goes that in AD 25 white vapour in the shape of a dragon was seen rising from a nearby well. Taking this as an auspicious omen, Gong declared himself the 'White Emperor' and the town 'White Emperor City'. Remains of the city wall can still be seen on the hill behind Baidi Mountain. The 12-year reign of the White Emperor was regarded as a time of peace and harmony, so after his death a temple was built to commemorate his reign. This temple dates back over 1,950 years.

The climb up the wooded Baidi Mountain to the temple complex used to involve a flight of several hundred steps. The rise in the water level of the river means that this climb has been greatly reduced; it has also turned Baidi Mountain into an island. Fine views of the entrance to Qutang Gorge can be seen from the temple.

The **Western Pavilion** on the slope is believed to have been occupied by the great poet Du Fu, who wrote numerous poems at this site. The pavilion (at one time known as Guanyin Dong) overlooks what Du Fu described as 'the limitless Yangzi'. Further up the hill is a *stupa*, marking the grave of a much-loved literary monk who served at the temple during the Qing dynasty (1644–1911).

A red wall with an imposing yellow dragon-head gateway surrounds the temple complex. Though the temple was originally dedicated to Gong Sunshu, the White Emperor, his statue was removed in the Ming dynasty (1368–1644) and replaced with images of Liu Bei, Zhuge Liang, Guan Yu and Zhang Fei, heroes of the Shu Kingdom during the Three Kingdoms period. The present halls date from the Ming dynasty.

The front hall contains large modern statues which depict Liu Bei on his deathbed entrusting his sons to the care of Zhuge Liang. To the left is the handsome, winged **Observing the Stars Pavilion** (Guanxing Ting), where a large bronze bell can

Hanging coffins of the Ba people who once roamed this area. Records of this minority tribe ended in the Ming dynasty almost 400 years ago. How and why these coffins were put on such precipitous cliffs still baffles scholars today.

be seen hanging in the upper storey. From this pavilion Zhuge Liang observed the stars and made accurate weather forecasts which helped him plan his victorious battles. The two Forest of Tablets halls contain several rare engraved stelae, some of which are over 1,300 years old. The Phoenix Tablet is particularly finely engraved. The Bamboo Leaf Poem Tablet is one of only three in China. It is considered a fine work of art, combining as it does poetry and calligraphy, for the tablet is engraved with three branches of bamboo, each leaf forming the Chinese characters of a poem.

The **Wuhou Hall** is dedicated to Zhuge Liang, his son and grandson. The bodies of the statues are of the Ming dynasty (1368–1644), but the heads, smashed in the Cultural Revolution (1966–76), are new. **Mingliang Hall** is dedicated to Liu Bei, who is shown surrounded by four attendants, as well as the black-faced Zhang Fei and the red-faced Guan Yu on one side, and Zhuge Liang on the other. Adjoining rooms display furniture, scrolls, porcelain and other cultural relics.

In 1987, several buildings were converted to form a museum displaying the many cultural relics found within the area, including two coffins from the Ba culture. One of these dates back to the Western Han dynasty (206 BC–AD 8).

At the foot of Baidi Mountain, Yanyu Rock—over 30 metres long, 20 metres wide and 40 metres high—used to be a constant hazard to boats riding the swift current and heading into the narrow entrance of Qutang Gorge. Over the ages, countless vessels perished. In 1959 it took a work team seven days to blow up this gigantic rock.

QUTANG GORGE

Immediately below Baidi City is **Kuimen**, the 'Dragon Gate' entrance to the first of the three gorges of the Yangzi River—the eight-kilometre long Qutang Gorge (also known by early Western travellers as the Wind Box Gorge). The shortest at eight kilometres, but grandest of them all, the gorge's widest point is only 150 metres. Mists frequently swirl around the mysterious limestone peaks, some nearly 1,500 metres high.

Prior to the Three Gorges Dam this gorge was a particularly dangerous stretch during high-water seasons and had been known to rise to 50 metres. It was as if, in the words of the poet Su Dongpo, 'a thousand seas were poured into one cup'.

An upper Yangzi steamboat captain recalled how in September 1929 the level of water was 75 metres, and likened the passage to a trough, with the water banked up on both sides. His ship became quite unmanageable, and was carried down, broadside on, only coming under control again at the lower end. He would never, he vowed, try to negotiate it again at such a level.

Kuimen, the entrance of Qutang Gorge, with White Salt Mountain (Baiyan Shan) looming above, appears on the reverse of the latest issue of the ten yuan note

Two mountains—**Red Armour Mountain** (Chijia Shan) to the north, once compared to a celestial peach, and **White Salt Mountain** (Baiyan Shan) to the south—form the Kui Men entrance, their steep precipices like the wings of a giant door guarding the tumultuous waters. It is a picture of the entrance to Qutang Gorge that appeared on the reverse of the old five yuan banknote (which are still to be found in circulation), and now decorates the latest ten yuan note.

In the Tang dynasty (618–907) chains were strung across the river as an 'iron lock' to prevent the passage of enemy boats. In the Song dynasty (960–1279) two iron pillars nearly two metres tall were erected on the north side, and seven chains, some 250 metres long, were used to block the river passage. Although the original purpose was defensive, the chain locks were later used to enable local authorities to gather taxes from all boats travelling downriver. This system continued until the middle Qing dynasty (1644–1911). The iron posts are now placed at the entrance to the viewing pavilion on the north bank.

On the precipice of Bai Yan Shan (south side) are a series of holes nearly a metre apart and about one-third of a metre deep, forming a 'Z' shape. These are known as the **Meng Liang Stairway**. According to legend, Yang Jiye, a Song-dynasty general, was buried on a terrace high up on the mountain. His loyal comrade-in-arms, Meng Liang, decided secretly to take the bones back for burial in Yang's home town. In the dead of night he took a small boat into the gorge and began to hack out a pathway to the terrace. Halfway up the rock face he was discovered by a monk who began

*Grooves etched into the wall of Qutang Gorge by the ropes of trackers
hauling barges along the river over several centuries*

crowing like a cock. Meng Liang, thinking that dawn was breaking and fearing discovery, abandoned his task. When he later discovered the monk's mischief, he was so provoked that he hung the monk upside down over a precipice. The rock below Meng Liang Stairway is known as **Hanging Monk Rock** (Daodiao Heshangshi). History records, however, that General Yang was not buried here and the steps are probably the remains of an ancient river pathway. Sections of a city wall, 1,400 years old, have been found on top of Bai Yan Shan so it is possible that the pathway led to this early settlement. Another theory about the stairway suggests that it was built to provide access to the rare medicinal herbs which grow high on the cliff faces.

At the highest point above Hanging Monk Rock one can see **Armour Cave** (Kuangjia Dong) where it is said a Song-dynasty woman general hid her weapons. In 1958 the cave was explored and found to contain three 2,000-year-old wooden coffins from the Kingdom of Ba, in which were bronze swords and lacquered wooden combs.

Nearby used to be the **Chalk Wall** (Fenbi Tang) where 900 characters, dating from the Song dynasty, were carved by famous calligraphers on the rock face. The site derived its name from the limestone powder which was used to smooth rock surfaces before being carved. Although this site has now been submerged, copies can be seen nearby on a higher cliff face.

Across on the north bank is the **Bellows Cave**, which is a large, deep cave which resembles a blacksmith's bellows. A Ba hanging coffin may be seen in the cliff crevice to the east of the cave.

East of Armour Cave (on the south side), on the top of a black rock, is a huge stone which the Chinese say resembles the body of a rhinoceros looking westwards as if forever enjoying 'the autumn moon over the gorge gate'. They call this rock 'Rhinoceros Looking at the Moon'. As one sails by the formation, seen directly from the side, it is said to resemble Liu Bei, King of Shu during the Three Kingdoms period, sitting on his throne.

From Baidi Cheng to Daixi through the whole length of Qutang Gorge, visitors may see, high up on the northern face, the old towpath, hand-hewn in 1889 by the local people. Prior to this there existed a smaller towpath which was often submerged at high water. Travellers had to abandon their boats and climb over the peaks, a dangerous and time-wasting detour. Boats going upstream had to wait for a favourable east wind; if the wind was in the wrong quarter, boats could be stranded in the water for ten days or more.

The sandstone walls of the gorges have become pitted by natural erosion, causing lines of holes, some of which are several metres deep. The town of **Daixi**, at the mouth of a stream bearing the same name, marks the eastern end of Qutang Gorge. Over 200 burial sites have been found here, and excavations have revealed a rich

(following pages) Precarious footpath along the cliffside of Qutang Gorge offered the only land access to this stretch. The path will be submerged once the reservoir reaches its full height.

collection of bone, stone and jade artefacts and pottery as well as various burial forms of the middle and late New Stone Age period (see pages 318–21).

Below Daixi the river widens out. About five kilometres downstream, on the south bank, are two sharp, black peaks which form the **Unlocked Gates Gorge** (Suokai Xia). On the west side of the gorge, midway up the mountain, is a semi-circular stone shaped roughly like a drum—this is the **Beheading Dragon Platform** (Zhanglong Tai). Facing this on the opposite side of the gorge is a thick, round stone pillar, the **Binding Dragon Pillar** (Suolong Zhu). Once upon a time, the Jade Dragon, a son of the Dragon of the Eastern Sea, lived in a cave on the upper reaches of the Daixi Stream. One season he decided to visit his family by way of the Yangzi, but shortly afterwards found himself lost. Changing into the form of an old man, he asked his way of a herder boy. The boy pointed north with his sickle. The dragon rushed off in that direction but again got lost, whereupon he flew into a mighty rage and rushed at the mountains, causing them to crumble and dam up the river; farmlands were flooded, earthquakes toppled houses, and men and animals perished. At this moment the Goddess Yao Ji rushed to the spot on a cloud. She rebuked Jade Dragon, but he was unrepentant. She flung a string of pearls into the air; it changed into a rope that bound the dragon to the stone pillar. Yao Ji then ordered the great Da Yu, controller of rivers, to behead the murderous dragon on the nearby platform. He then diverted the river by cutting the gorge. The people of this valley have lived happily ever since.

WUSHAN

Wushan County is situated above the Yangzi on the north bank and embraced by lovely mountain peaks where flourishes the tung tree, whose oil was used for the caulking, oiling and varnishing of junks and sampans. A two-million-year old fossil of an ape man was discovered in a cave in these mountains in the 1980s. This important archaeological find is now in the Beijing Museum of Chinese History.

The town of Wushan dates back to the latter part of the Shang dynasty (c. 1600–1027 BC). In the Warring States period (475–221 BC), the King of Chu established a palace west of the city. During the first century, the faith of the Buddha had reached China and many temples were built here; almost all the temples have been destroyed over the years. The name of the town originates with Wu Xian, a successful Tang-dynasty doctor to the imperial court, who was buried on Nanling Mountain, on the south bank opposite Wushan. A winding path—with 108 bends—leads from the foot of the mountain to the summit where there is a small temple. This path was an official road through to Hubei Province in ancient times.

Much of the original town was situated on a low-lying flood plain on the north bank of the river and has been demolished in preparation for the final rise in water level. A new road bridge arches over the river and leads to Wu Mountain, scarring the entrance to the Wu Gorge.

The energetic visitor may climb to the summit of **Wushan** (Witches Hill), a two-hour hike. Worshippers still come to a small shrine here, built within the ruins of an old Buddhist monastery. From the summit the views of Wu Gorge and the river are spectacular. A less strenuous outing may be made to the newly opened limestone cave complex in Wu Gorge high up on the cliff face above the north bank of the river. This involves a short boat ride from Wushan town, an easy scramble up the rocky slope and then a walk along the old towpath. Around the cave complex there are the usual teahouse and ornamental pavilions. The cave complex, **Luyou Dong**, is named after a Song-dynasty official who visited Wushan and left an appreciative record of his stay. The lower parts of this cave are now submerged.

Wushan was, until its demolition in 2002, a rough market town with worn steps from the mud flats and docks to the narrow streets packed with farmers selling their produce. A lively market was built along the remains of the old city wall. Old homes were crowded with families and 'beauty salons' catered to the visiting sailors. It was the epitome of a steamy and spicy river port. Today all that has gone, with the large new boulevards and pretentious buildings of the new town cut higher into the mountain slopes. The park which runs from the new dock area to the government center high up the hill is the future site of the world's largest 'people mover', a 400-metre escalator that will make the climb up to town an attraction.

DANING RIVER EXCURSION: THE LITTLE THREE GORGES

Some of the cruise ships stop at Wushan to allow their passengers to take a trip up the crystal-clear Daning River through its magnificent Little Three Gorges (Xiao Sanxia), whose total length is only 33 kilometres. However, a similar excursion is now possible along the Shennong Stream, a tributary at the eastern end of Wu Gorge, and other cruise operators have added this to their itineraries (see page 350 for more details).

The Daning River excursion is undertaken in low motorized sampans or aboard new larger excursion boats. About three kilometres from the mouth of the river, at its confluence with the Yangzi, the entrance to the first of the gorges is reached. This is the **Dragon Gate Gorge** (Longmen Xia), three kilometres long. The mouth of the gorge is like a massive gateway through which the river rushes like a green dragon, hence its name. The gateway appears to shut once one has passed through. On the east side is **Dragon Gate Spring** (Longmen Quan) and above it **Lingzhi Peak**, topped by the Nine-Dragon Pillar. On this peak, it is said, grow strange plants and

the fungus of longevity (*lingzhi*), guarded by nine dragons. On the western bank, two rows of 15-centimetre square holes, continuing the entire length of the small gorges and numbering over 6,000 are all that remain of an astonishing plank walkway, which was first constructed in the Han period and recorded in the Annals of Wushan County in 246 BC. Wooden stakes inserted into these hand-hewn holes supported planks and large bamboo pipes, which stretched for 100 kilometres along the river. This pipeline conveyed brine, while the planks provided an access for maintenance. In the 17th century the pathway, used by the peasant leader Li Zicheng in his uprising against the Ming dynasty, was destroyed by the imperial army.

After leaving the gorge the boat passes the Nest of Silver Rapid (Yinwo Tan). In the past, rich merchants trading in the hinterland often came to grief here; perhaps there are caches of silver under the bubbling surface still! In 1958 work began on clearing major obstacles from the river.

The Daning then meanders through terraced hillsides before entering the ten-kilometre **Misty Gorge** (Bawu Xia), with its dramatic scenery of rocks, peaks and caves, including Fairy Maiden Cave, Fairy Throwing a Silk Ball, and Guanyin

(opposite) View into one of the Little Three Gorges. (above) Sampans on the Daning River tributary. (following pages) Trackers haul a sampan through the rapids.

Seated on a Lotus Platform. A long, layered formation, like a scaly dragon, can be seen on the eastern cliff. Suspended upon the precipice is a relic of the ancient inhabitants of eastern Sichuan 2,000 years ago, an 'iron' coffin (which is actually made of wood that has turned black with age). This gorge is accordingly also known as **Iron Coffin Gorge**.

The former village of Double Dragon or **Shuanglong** (population 300), above Bawu Gorge, was the halfway point. The village, with houses dating from the 1700s, during the early Qing dynasty, was demolished in 2002. The lush valley is now inundated. Excursion boats currently proceed upstream to visit Dachang, the Ming era village now being emptied prior to the second level inundation in 2006.

Emerald Green Gorge (Dicui Xia), 20 kilometres long, is inhabited by wild ducks and covered with luxuriant bamboo groves from which rises a deafening cacophany of bird-song. There are also many types of monkey still to be seen if you are lucky. Once their shrill cries resounded throughout the Yangzi gorges, but today they can be seen and heard only along some of the tributaries. River stones of an extraordinary variety and colour can be gathered.

In 2002, an old man sits among the ruins of his house in the village of Shuanglong (Double Dragon) and sings aloud from a cartoon booklet of classic mythology, as if singing could stop the demolition

WU XIA (WITCHES GORGE)

Below Wushan the river approaches the entrance to the 40-kilometre long Wu Gorge, the middle Yangzi gorge which straddles the boundary between Chongqing Municipality and Hubei Province. So sheer are the cliffs that it is said the sun rarely penetrates. The boat passes, on the south side, the **Golden Helmet and Silver Armour Gorge** (Jinkuang Yinjia Xia) shaped, it is said, like an ancient warrior's silver coat of arms crowned by a round golden helmet. Ahead are the 12 peaks of Wu Gorge, famed for their dark and sombre grace. Poets have attempted to evoke both their bleakness and beauty:

Autumn Thoughts
Jade dews deeply wilt and wound the maple woods;
On Witch Mountain, in Witch Gorge, the air is sombre, desolate.
Billowy waves from the river roar and rush towards the sky
Over the frontier pass, wind and clouds sink to the darkening earth.
These clustered chrysanthemums, twice blooming, evoke the tears of yesteryear;
A lonely boat, as ever, is moored to the heart that yearns for home.
To cut winter clothes, women everywhere ply their scissors and foot-rulers
Below the White Emperor's tall city is heard the urgent pounding of the evening wash.

A marker on a hillside in Wu Gorge indicates the height of 175 metres,
the level the water will reach once the Three Gorges reservoir is fully filled in 2009

*(opposite) Fir Tree Cone Peak (Songluan Feng), one of the 12 sentinel peaks of Wu Gorge
(above) As dusk settles over Wu Gorge, a game of Chinese chess helps to pass the time
at a navigation station*

A navigation control station with one-way arrow markers for traffic in the Three Gorges.
This system was established by British customs officials to provide safe passage when
the first steamboats came up the Gorges in the 1890s.

Six peaks line the north side:
Climbing Dragon Peak (Denglong Feng)
Sage Spring Peak (Shengquan Feng)
Facing Clouds Peak (Chaoyun Feng)
Goddess Peak (Shennu Feng)
Fir Tree Cone Peak (Songluan Feng)
Gathered Immortals Peak (Jixian Feng)

Three peaks flank the south side:
Flying Phoenix Peak (Feifeng Feng)
Misty Screen Peak (Cuiping Feng)
Assembled Cranes Peak (Juhe Feng)

Three more peaks may be glimpsed behind these:
Clean Altar Peak (Jingtan Feng)
Rising Cloud Peak (Qiyun Feng)
Mounting Aloft Peak (Shangsheng Feng)

More often than not these green-clad peaks are hidden by swirls of cloud and mist, and are difficult to distinguish, though each has its own characteristics and posture.

The most famous is the **Shennu Feng** (Goddess Peak)—also referred to as Observing the Clouds Peak—which resembles the figure of a maiden kneeling in front of a pillar. She is believed to be the embodiment of Yao Ji, the 23rd daughter of the Queen Mother of the West. Yao Ji, at the age of 18, was sent to oversee the Jade Pool of the Western Heaven, accompanied by 11 fairy handmaidens. But she found life there lonely and cold, and took to rambling among the mountains and rivers of the mortal world. Wushan became her favourite place, and there she established a small palace.

Once, returning from a visit to the Eastern Sea on her floating cloud, she came upon 12 dragons playing havoc with the river and the mountains, and causing flooding and hardship in their wake. She summoned Da Yu the Great from his work on the Yellow River and, alighting from her cloud, presented him with a heavenly supernatural book. This endowed him with powers to call upon the wind, rain, thunder and lightning to move the earth, thus enabling his sacred ox to slash open the gorges (which is why all oxen have bent horns), and permit the waters to drain into the Eastern Sea. Yao Ji resolved to stay here with her 11 maidens to protect the boats from the dangerous rapids, the peasants' crops from damage, the woodcutters from wild animals, and to grow the fungus of longevity for the sick. Eventually these 12 maidens became the 12 sentinel peaks of Wu Gorge. There are, of course, many variations to this story. For example, it was said that if the Goddess can be seen from the river the journey will be safe; or if she is veiled in mist or rain, this is because she is bathing and shy.

As the river twists and turns, a mountain comes into view, appearing as if it will block the way. This is **Gathered Immortals Peak**. Five kilometres below this peak is a small tributary which marks the boundary between the municipality of Chongqing and Hubei Province.

Just above the north-bank town of Guandukou—marking the end of Wu Gorge—was the site of the Flint Rapid (Huoyan Shi), which was very violent at high water, with limestone rocks jutting into the river like huge stone gates beckoning helpless craft. These, along with all the dangerous rocks in the shipping channel, were blown up in the 1950s.

BADONG

Badong, the county seat and the westernmost county town of Hubei Province, is being rebuilt three kilometres upstream on the south bank, as its predecessor is being submerged by the rising waters. The town now stands opposite Guandukou and is linked to it by means of a new cable-stay bridge which is part of the newly constructed Hubei–Sichuan trunk road that runs through the Gorges.

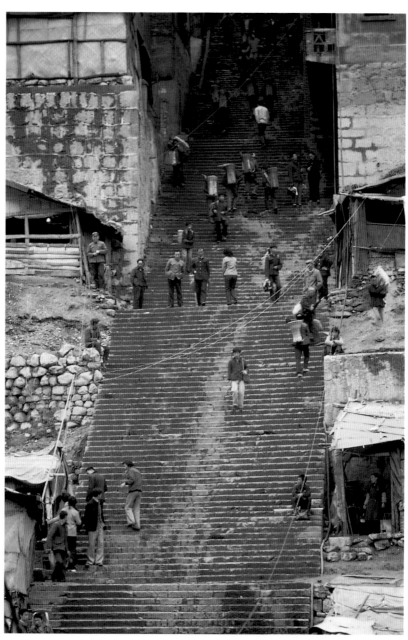

In this photograph from 1985, labourers can be seen carrying baskets up one of the long stairways that led from the river into the old town of Badong. This was the traditional method of loading and unloading the boats calling at this busy river port.

The old town of Badong prior to the Three Gorges Dam. Houses in the river towns had to be built high up the bank due to the extreme fluctuations in water levels during wet and dry seasons.

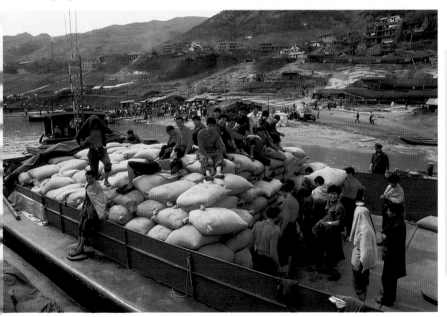

Loading a river barge at the old town of Badong in 1985. Many of the old buildings have now been demolished in preparation for the final rise in water level behind the Dam and a new town has been constructed three kilometres upstream.

In ancient times, Badong was situated on the other side of the Yangzi and belonged to the State of Ba; in the Song dynasty (960–1279) the town was moved to the southern bank. Local products include tung oil, lacquer, tea, medicinal herbs and animal skins. Labourers, pitch black with coal dust, used to be a common sight in Badong as they loaded and unloaded river lighters, negotiating the steep steps above the river with staff in hand, humping baskets of coal. Houses with wooden balconies huddled together on pillars embedded in solid concrete foundations above the bank of the river.

SHENNONG STREAM EXCURSION

Guandukou lies at the mouth of the Shennong Xi (stream), a tributary of the Yangzi that rises in the Shennongjia. This mountain basin hosts a variety of unique flora and fauna, the source of many traditional herbal medicines. Great slopes of arrow bamboo in snowy valleys used to support many pandas, together with white-furred bear, fox and rabbit. A legendary primate, *ye ren*, a nocturnal vegetarian which nests in high trees, is said to inhabit the thick cloud-wrapped forests.

Since the completion of the dam, the water level has risen from about one metre deep to about 40 metres deep, meaning the Shennong Stream is navigable further up its course. Some cruise ships now moor beneath the suspension bridge at Guandukou, at the mouth of the tributary, where passengers disembark and transfer to a smaller vessel for a journey upstream to Bamboo Gorge.

A short distance after leaving Guandukou a single coffin belonging to the Ba people can be seen perched in a small cave high up on the right-hand side. Some distance beyond, as the river meanders through tranquil scenery of verdant river cliffs and terraced fields, is a large cave on the left-hand side called **Swallow Cave**. The entrance is 100 metres high and 40 metres wide and extends for eight kilometres into the mountain. Well-developed rectilinear joints in the rock control the vertical sides and horizontal roof of the cave, and a number of large stalactites hang above the entrance. The cave is populated by a very unusual species of bird, the Himalayan swiftlet (*Aerodramus brevirostris*), called in Chinese *duan zui jin si yan*, literally short-billed, gold silk swallow. Normally only found in coastal areas in Southeast Asia, it is for some unexplained reason also to be found in caves on the Shennong Stream and its source mountains, the Shennongjia.

The region is famous for rare medicinal herbs and it is not uncommon to see local tribesmen in their boats gathering plants growing among the rocks at the edge of the river.

On reaching **Bamboo Gorge**, passengers board small, traditional wooden boats known as *wan dou jiao*, or peapod boats, due to their shape. The boats are 13 metres long, 1.8 metres wide and 0.7 metres deep. Teams of trackers—local Tujia tribesmen

—skillfully paddle the boats upriver through the narrow, steep-sided limestone gorge. Stalactites are suspended from overhanging walls and large-leafed Chinese parasol trees shade the water, by now running almost clear. As brown dippers hop from rock to rock, butterflies sip nectar from pink hibiscus flowers. Eagles can sometimes be spotted soaring overhead.

The stream gradually becomes shallower and before long the boats reach stretches of fast-flowing rapids. Here the boatmen jump into the water and haul the craft using traditional bamboo ropes, accompanied by the chants used for centuries by trackers on the Yangzi, their cries echoing around the gorge above. A rare species of yellow lily can be seen clinging to the rock walls. Flowering only during the autumn months, their habitat is restricted to the limestone cliffs of the Three Gorges. The flowers, growing on a single stem with no leaves, are shaped rather like a bulb of garlic, hence the local name 'stone garlic'. They are used as a snake-bite remedy. In the quieter reaches of the gorges, golden monkeys (*Rhinopithecus roxelana*) still roam in chattering bands. These are a very colourful, bright orange-yellow, hence the name. Since it shares its habitat with the panda, it is well-protected and happily not an extremely rare species.

After a short rest for the boatmen and a chance for passengers to stretch their legs, the boats turn around and rush back downstream, aided by the skilful use of the long *yulo*, a heavy steering oar placed over the bow to guide the boat through the swirling rapids. Once on the more placid stretches the boatmen are able to relax

The closure of the Three Gorges Dam has meant that the Shennong Stream, at the downstream end of Wu Gorge, has become navigable for a much greater distance and a number of cruise operators are offering excursions that explore its waters

SICHUAN BASIN

THE THREE GORGES

(top left) The 110-metre-high Swallow Cave on Shennong Stream (see page 350); (top right and bottom) on reaching Bamboo Gorge passengers board traditional, small, wooden peapod boats to travel further upstream, paddled by local Tujia boatmen

(top left) Unusual birds and plants are glimpsed in the narrow, steep-sided limestone gorge; (top right and bottom) as the stream becomes shallower the boatmen jump into the water to haul the boats through the rapids using traditional bamboo ropes

Local Tujia tribesmen, their calls and chants echoing around the canyons, track boats through the rapids of Bamboo Gorge much as trackers have hauled vessels through the Yangzi's Three Gorges of the for centuries. This is the only place that trackers can still be seen in action.

Traditional rope sandals, which give grip on the slippery stones, are still worn by the trackers on the Shennong Stream. It is customary for each boatman to make his own. Clothes were formerly not worn by trackers on the main river in case they were swept off by the strong currents.

On the downstream journey, a heavy steering oar known as a yulo *is placed over the bow to guide the boat through the rapids*

and it is a customary for them to sing Tujia trackers' songs or, if there are women aboard, to sing love songs that echo in the canyons.

The peapod boats are solidly built and very stable in the water, each carrying 12 passengers and five or six crew. Although passengers are obliged to wear lifejackets as a precaution, the deftness of the boatmen leaves you in no doubt you are in safe hands.

ZIGUI

Qu Yuan, one of China's greatly loved patriotic poets, was born in 340 BC in the Qu family village very near Zigui. The fame of the walled town that stood on the north bank dates from this period long ago. **Qu Yuan's Memorial Hall**, with its distinctive white gateway and walls edged in red, has been relocated to a higher site above the final projected water level. It contains a Ming-dynasty (1368–1644) statue of the poet, as well as stone inscriptions. The old town has been demolished and its residents moved to New Zigui near Maoping on the south side of the river, not far from the Three Gorges Dam site.

The great poet served as a chancellor to King Huai of the Kingdom of Chu, with special responsibility for the royal clans. The king had complete trust in him until

discord developed among the clans and Qu was falsely slandered. Banished from the capital, he wandered about in Hubei Province, deeply sad and bitter. His poetry and essays reveal his romanticism, loyalty and patriotism. Qu had vigorously advocated that the State of Chu stand firm against attack by the Qin state, but his advice had gone unheeded, and in May of the year 278 BC, he drowned himself in Dongting Lake at the age of 62.

According to historical records, the local people scoured Dongting Lake for his body, beating drums and racing their boats in the course of their search. This event came to be commemorated each May, and to this day the Dragon Boat Festival (Duanwu Jie) is held in the river towns up and down the Yangzi and in many other parts of China. *Zongzi*—packets of glutinous rice steamed in leaves and tied with reeds—were thrown into the water as a sacrifice to Qu Yuan. The tradition of eating *zongzi* at this festival continues in Chinese communities the world over.

There are many fairy tales about Qu Yuan. East of Zigui is a bay named after him. It is said that when he died, a huge fish swallowed him up and swam all the way from Dongting Lake past Zigui to Yufu and back again, where it disgorged the body, amazingly still intact (see also pages 327–8). It is said that he never forgot his ancestral home; to the farmers there he introduced a jade-white rice which was soft and fragrant. Locals remember him at each new rice harvest.

XIANG XI (FRAGRANT STREAM)

A small stream just below Zigui and above the entrance to Xiling Gorge is well known to all Chinese as the home of the beautiful Han-dynasty (206 BC–AD 220) heroine Wang Zhaojun. Her story is the quintessence of virtuous patriotism.

Zhaojun, a maid of honour to the emperor, refused to bribe the painter from whose portraits of court ladies the emperor traditionally chose his concubines. In revenge, the painter portrayed her as quite hideous, and so imperial favour was denied her. In 22 BC the emperor, wishing to make a marriage alliance with the northern Xiongnu king, chose Wang Zhaojun. Only then did he set eyes on her; he was captivated but it was too late. Married to the Xiongnu king, Zhaojun was able to exert a good influence on relations between the Xiongnu and Han peoples, which gained her great respect. The emperor, in his rage at having lost her, decreed the beheading of the corrupt court painter. Local people say that before her marriage, Wang Zhaojun returned to her home town and, when washing in the stream, dropped a precious pearl which caused the stream to become crystal-clear and fragrant. Tradition names a pavilion-topped mound to the south of Hohhot in Inner Mongolia as her burial site.

Zhaojun's ancient courtyard home overlooks the Xiang Stream above the town of Xingshan. Trees line the opposite shore, with guest cabins built in the branches.

Mr Hu Zhenhao, one of the last of the Xiling Gorge trackers, famous for his performances of old boat songs, with his troupe based in Zigui, the original home of dragon boat races

XILING GORGE

Xiling Gorge starts at Xiang Xi and zigzags for 76 kilometres down to Yichang. It is the longest and historically the most dangerous of the Yangzi gorges. Before the passage was made safe in the 1950s, 'the whole surface of the water was a swirling mass of whirlpools sucking the froth they created into their centres'. Xiling comprises seven small gorges and had two of the fiercest rapids in the stretch of the Yangzi between Chongqing and Yichang.

On entering the western entrance the boat passes through the four-kilometre long **Military Books and Precious Sword Gorge** (Bingshu Baojian Xia). The name of the gorge refers to a stratified layer of rock, now underwater, that resembled a stack of books. There are two stories told of these formations, both concerning heroes from the classical novel *Romance of the Three Kingdoms* (see pages 304–5).

One legend has it that Zhuge Liang (181–234), military adviser to the King of Shu, became seriously ill while passing this way. Unwilling to entrust his valuable military treatises to any member of his entourage, he placed them up here on this inaccessible ledge, to be kept safe for later generations. The second tale is also about Zhuge Liang. It was he who devised the stratagems which enabled Liu Bei, the king, to defeat the Kingdom of Chu and establish the Minor Han dynasty (AD 221–63). Afraid that he would eventually fall out of favour, Zhuge Liang retired from official life and went into seclusion, hiding his military writings and sword here.

A large cleft rock stands at the mouth of a ravine—Rice Granary Gorge (Micang Xia)—on the south side. Fine sand, blown by river winds, piles up on this rock, and slowly sifts through a hole underneath. People call this Zhuge Liang's Granary.

Further on was the site of the perilous Xin Tan (new rapids) that rushed over submerged rocks. In 1524, rock slides from the northern mountainside created this 3.2-kilometre long, triple-headed rapid. The fall of the riverbed was estimated at about six metres. When the water level was low, junks would unload their cargo and be hauled over by 100 or more trackers. Passengers would join their boat beyond the rapid after walking along a winding mountain track and passing through the village of Xintan. In 1941 the steamboat Minxi came to grief and several hundred people perished. The swift current carried boats downriver through Xin Tan at the rate of seven metres per second.

In 1854 a local merchant collected subscriptions from river traders and built three life-saving craft to patrol the Xin Tan rapids, and to salvage boats and survivors. This was the beginning of the Yangzi River Lifeboat Office, which eventually maintained its Red Boats on all the danger spots along the Chongqing–Yichang stretch until the 1940s (see page 367).

Steep field cultivation by the upper Yangzi, a major cause of soil erosion and river silt

The village of Meirendao in Xiling Gorge as it was in 1985. Its population has since been relocated by the government and the site submerged following the closure of the Three Gorges Dam in June 2003.

An earthquake in 1984 slid half of the ancient town of Xintan into the current. A new town has been constructed higher up on the north bank above the projected water level. In the town and visible from the river is an obelisk, which is a memorial to Cornell Plant, an Englishman who lived here for about 20 years during the early 20th century. He served as river inspector for the Chinese Imperial Maritime Service and was responsible for setting up the navigation system on the Yangzi. This system continues today, with over 500 new buoys being placed in the reservoir, following Plant's original marking plan of white–north shore and red–south shore.

Beyond Xintan the channel winds east and then south, towards **Ox Liver and Horse Lungs Gorge**, apparently named after yellow stalactite formations that used to be on the north side. These have now been removed to save them from the rising waters and are on display in the museum in New Zigui. One of the 'Horse's Lungs' was said to be shot away by British gunboats during the reign of Guangxu (1875–1908).

In the middle stretch of Xiling Gorge, the strange and lovely **Kongling Gorge** towers above the iron-green rocks of the 2.5-kilometre long Kongling Tan, which were the worst of all the Yangzi rapids. Seventeen catastrophes involving steamships occurred here between 1900 and 1945. The larger boulders choking the channel had names such as 'Big Pearl', 'Monk's Rock' and 'Chickens' Wings', but the deadliest of all was known as 'Come to Me'. Apparently the only way for riverboat captains to successfully negotiate this rock was for them to sail straight for it and then turn at the last possible moment; the current would carry the boat safely past. But should the skipper be too timid and turn too soon, the boat would be dashed on the rocks.

Thankfully for the modern day traveller, the rise in water level behind the Dam has made such experiences a thing of the past. One can only try to imagine the drama and terror of the past while sailing along the new 'peaceful lake' of the reservoir.

Downriver from the Dam, the boat enters **Yellow Ox Gorge** (Huangniu Xia)—said to look like a man riding an ox. Here the passage widens out and sweeps past the ancient **Huangling Temple** (Huangling Miao) on the south bank, nestling amid orange and pomelo trees. The great poet Du Fu wrote of his journey through this gorge:

Three dawns shine upon the Yellow Ox.
Three sunsets—and we go so slowly.
Three dawns—again three sunsets—
And we do not notice that our hair is white as silk.

RIVER RITES

Life on board a junk was hard and dangerous work. Cornell Plant, River Inspector for the Chinese Imperial Maritime Service in the 1900s, wrote about the risks of travelling through the Three Gorges: Chinese say that one junk in ten is badly damaged, and one in 20 totally wrecked each trip. Probably not 20 per cent reach Chungking unscathed, and never one without experiencing some hair's-breadth escape.

It was common for trackers to fall from the towpaths to their deaths or to break a limb and be left behind by their junk. Thus Yangzi boatmen had a wealth of rites and taboos that had to be observed to ensure a safe passage.

At the beginning of a voyage and also before entering the Three Gorges, the most dangerous stretch of the river, it was the cook's task to light incense, set off firecrackers and, most importantly, to kill a rooster and sprinkle the blood on the bows of the junk. Writing in 1880, Captain Gill described how to get through the Xintan Rapids safely. The junk could hire a shaman who would come on board with a yellow flag inscribed 'Power of the Water! A happy star for the whole journey'. As the boat ploughed through the waves dragged by the straining trackers, the shaman would stand at the bow, waving the flag in a regular motion to appease the powers of the water. It was also essential to sprinkle rice on the water all the way through the rapids.

Like fishermen everywhere in China, many Yangzi boatmen still believe that it is very bad luck to turn over a fish at table: 'capsize fish, capsize boat'. Another taboo is resting chopsticks on top of a rice bowl in a position that suggests a junk ran aground. Unlike Western sailors, however, there is no taboo against women aboard ship and junk owners usually brought their wives along.

Sometimes fish swimming upstream used to jump onto the decks. They were considered demons and had to be taken ashore and buried. Boatmen also had to contend with the ghosts of the drowned, who would string themselves in a line behind a boat, preparing to board the vessel and cause trouble. The way to shake them loose was to cut quickly in front of another boat, so that the ghosts would lose their grip and attach themselves to the boat behind. Not a very neighbourly thing to do! Describing this to explorer Wong How Man in 1986, a boat captain recounted that, 'In the past, it was a game that often left the trailing boat's owner jumping, cursing and shooting off firecrackers to pacify his increased string of ghosts.'

Meanwhile those living on shore had floods to contend with. The lovely pagodas all along the river were built for flood prevention. It was believed that floods were often caused by dragons (since they have the power to control the waters), or by evil demons. A pagoda built on top of the hill inhabited by one of these creatures could prevent him from coming out and causing trouble. A pagoda could also prevent the wealth of the nearby town from being swept away by the current.

After the disastrous flood of 1788, which inundated over 30 counties in Hubei Province, the Emperor ordered nine iron oxen to be placed along the banks of the river. According to the court record: 'The Sea Dragon submits to Iron and the Ox belongs to Earth, Earth controls Water, the Iron Ox can suppress the flood.' This was following Chinese theories of the properties of the elements: fire, metal, earth, water and air.

Teams of trackers looking strangely like penguins on an iceflow as they haul heavily laden cargo junks through the treacherous rapids of the Three Gorges in this historical photograph taken in the late 19th century

TRACKING THROUGH THE RAPIDS

*T*hough the junk was now apparently safe, for it breasted the smooth, swift water of the second sluice and was no longer being thrown from side to side, the heaviest work still remained to be done. I turned to watch the trackers, for theirs was now the heavy work of making many tons of cypress go uphill on a fiercely resisting roadway of water. It was a moving sight—horribly depressing, to see more than three hundred human beings reduced to the level of work animals, blind-folded asses and oxen; yet thrilling too, to see the irresistible force of their co-operation, for the three hundred and fifty cloth shoes of their each step up the slope were planted in the same moment, and the sad trackers' cries, 'Ayah!... Ayah!,' were sung in a great unison choir of agony and joy, and the junk did move.

It moved, however, more and more slowly, as the last and hardest test of the trackers' labor began—heaving the junk over the head of the rapid, over the round, swift crest of the sluice. The bow of the junk seemed to dig into the water there. The rope grew taut. The great crowd of towing men hung for a long time unable to move. I saw the cook look down toward the junk, obviously at a loss what to do.

Then suddenly from midstream, from the very center of danger, came a lovely, clear, high-pitched line of song.

It was Old Pebble. I looked out and saw him standing on the deck, himself leaning as if to pull, hurling a beautiful song at the crowd on the bank.

On the proper beat the many trackers gave out a kind of growl and moved their feet forward a few inches, and the bow of the junk dug deeper into the head of the sluice. They took a second, firmer step. And a third, and a fourth.

I had never heard Old Pebble sing such a haunting melody. I saw that he was in a kind of ecstasy. His face shone in a grimace of hard work and happiness. I remembered my doubts about his credo of 'simplicity', which he had recited to me in our first evening on the river, and I remembered my distress that such a sturdy young man did not avow personal goals of wealth, love, honor, and fame. Now I saw from his face that this was his life's goal; this instant of work, this moment's line of song, this accord with his poor fellow men, this brief spurt of useful loyalty to the cranky, skinny, half-mad owner of the junk on which he had shipped, and above all this fleeting triumph over the Great River.

At last the junk raised its head, shivered, and shot suddenly forward into the still water of the pond above the rapids.

When it was over, and the junk was pulled up to the loading platform, Old Pebble was streaming sweat, but he looked very happy.

I walked down to the river's edge to see what he would say. He jumped ashore and bent down to the river and scooped up double handfuls of the brown water and washed his face, sloshing and snorting like a small boy. I moved near him. He looked up. All he said was, 'Ayah, this river is a turtle.'

John Hersey, A Single Pebble, 1914

The present Huangling Temple was constructed during the Ming dynasty, although the original is thought to have been built in the Spring and Autumn period (770–476 BC). As the temple is downstream of the Three Gorges Dam it will not be affected by the rise in water level.

HOW MUCH FOR A LIFE?

In 1854, a rich merchant living near Xin Tan, one of the most dangerous of all the rapids in the Three Gorges, raised subscriptions to build three life-boats. Painted red to distinguish them from regular craft, they soon became known as the Red Boats. More money was raised over the years to increase the fleet and in the 1880s the running of the service was taken over by the government, although funds still came from public subscription. By the early 1900s there were almost 50 boats stationed along the river. In 1800 alone they saved 1,473 lives from 49 wrecked junks.

A Red Boat would accompany each vessel on the most perilous parts of the journey—being dragged upstream by the trackers over the different sets of rapids. Downstream voyages were not as dangerous, so a special escort was not deemed necessary. When a wreck occurred a gun was fired as the summons for all Red Boats to come and help.

The life-boats were not allowed to salvage cargo from the wrecks. However, there was a reward system for the salvaging of human beings. W E Geil, who travelled along the Yangzi in 1904 on his way to Burma, describes how it worked:

On life-saving the Chinese have curious notions. While eating cakes cooked in lamp oil in a tea house in Chintan village [Xintan], the skipper of the Red Boat came in and I asked him certain questions about the pagoda for destitute souls. He told me that for the recovery of a dead body from the water, a reward of eight hundred cash is given by the emperor. It used to be eight hundred cash for saving a live man and four hundred for a dead one. but it was soon discovered that this did not pay, so it was reversed, and now four hundred cash are given to save a live man and eight hundred to recover a dead one. This allows four hundred cash to bury the man if he dies after being taken out of the water. This interesting fact was further explained to me by another of the Red Boat men—that the dead man involves funeral expenses and the live man none! This is good Celestial reasoning. It would be more profitable to drown a man before pulling him out. I found out afterwards that the reward of four hundred cash is given provided the rescuer gets his clothes wet; otherwise he gets but two hundred.

W E Geil, A Yankee on the Yangtse, 1904

Huangling Temple, said to have been first built during the Spring and Autumn period (770–476 BC), is dedicated to the great Da Yu who, with his yellow ox, controlled the flood waters and dug the gorges (see page 347). The present hall was built in the Ming dynasty (1368–1644) and houses a statue of Da Yu, as well as stone inscriptions. Zhuge Liang is also said to have dug the Yellow Ox Spring (or Toad Rock, as it is sometimes called) nearby. Its clear water, according to the Tang-dynasty *Book of Teas*, was excellent for the brewing of tea, and Yellow Ox was classified as the Fourth Spring under Heaven.

After one passes below Huangling Temple, on the south bank, a natural stone arch bridge may be seen with a white 'aspara' angel statue on top near a pavilion. From here downstream is the last stretch of natural scenery of the Gorges—the **Bright Moon Gorge** (Mingyue Xia) and the **Lantern Shadow Gorge** (Dengying Xia) loom ahead. The latter is overlooked on the south side by peaks in the shape of four figures from the 16th-century Chinese novel, *Pilgrimage to the West* (also known as *The Monkey King*). When the evening sun's rays fall upon these peaks, the figures do appear lifelike—Xuan Zang standing on the precipice edge; Monkey (Sun Wukong) peering into the distance; Sandy (Sha Heshang) carrying the luggage; and Pigsy (Zhu Bajie) riding a horse, all silhouetted against the fading light like characters in a shadow play.

At the last turn of the Xiling Gorge is the village of Shibei with a prominent pillar—a memorial to the 1939 battle with Japanese troops who were stopped here during their invasion. Just upstream, below the Lantern Shadow rocks, is a new guest house in traditional style, 'Home of the Gorges' (Sanxia Ren Jia), with a clear stream flowing out of a canyon and some wooden junks tied at a dock. This small enterprise is a new piece of nostalgia in the face of nearby massive developments.

The last of the smaller gorges is **Yellow Cat Gorge** (Huangmao Xia), so named from the yellow cat-shaped rock on the riverside. Qi Taigong Fishing is the name given to a rock beside a cave on the south face, because of its fancied resemblance to a bearded old man wearing yellow trousers.

Now the boat reaches the strategic **Southern Crossing Pass** (Nanjin Guan), with Three Travellers' Cave above (see page 392), marking the end of Xiling Gorge and the three great Yangzi gorges. The river widens dramatically and ahead lies Gezhou Dam and Yichang.

The Gezhou Dam, impressive if first seen coming up-river, is now an anticlimax for those coming down. Nevertheless, it was China's largest before the construction of the Three Gorges Dam and is still the third largest dam in the world and the world's largest low-water dam. It produces 2.715 million kilowatts of electricity per hour. A single stage lock allows ships to descend to the level of Yichang.

THE YANGZI RIVER DAMS by Raynor Shaw

The concept of damming the Yangzi River is not new. In 1919 Dr Sun Yat-sen published a paper titled *A Plan to Develop Industry*. The paper contained a section on *Improvements to Navigable Rivers and Canals*, which recommended the construction of several large dams to enhance flood control, provide irrigation, and to generate electricity. Geological surveys to determine suitable locations for a dam in the Yangzi valley began in the 1930s. By 1947 a team of 50 American geologists and engineers were working at one of the potential sites. Following the Communist victory in 1949, work was suspended.

During the 20th century most of the large rivers in the world were dammed—the Ganges, Indus, Nile, Niger, Danube, Zambesi, and Parana. Only the Congo, Amazon (although the Tocantins tributary was dammed) and Yangzi remained un-dammed. The first dam across the Yangzi, the Gezhou Dam, was constructed between 1970 and 1989. However, plans for a larger dam across the Yangzi River were still being made.

Many of the Yangzi tributaries have already been harnessed by smaller dams and diversion structures. The power of the waters falling from the Tibetan Plateau are an inducement to build electrical industrial complexes such as the large Ertan Dam on the Dadu River feeding the extensive smelting and metal refining centre at Panzhihua in Sichuan Province. The Chinese Ministry of Water Resources has proposed eight more dams in the upper Yangzi. Two are under construction near Lijiang and the Great Bend of the Yangzi.

The Gezhou Dam

Where it leaves the confines of the Xiling Gorge at Nanjinguan (the Nanjin Pass), the Yangzi River dramatically widens from 300 metres in the gorge to 2,000 metres, and abruptly turns to the south. Three kilometres downstream, near the city of Yichang, the Gezhou and Xi islets formerly divided the main river channel into three channels: the southern Dajiang (Grand Channel); the central Erjiang (Second Channel); and the northern Sanjiang (Third Channel) between Gezhou Islet and the north bank of the river. This locality was selected for the first dam across the Yangzi River, the Gezhou Dam.

Construction of the Gezhou Dam took 18 years, employed 100,000 workers, and cost 4.85 billion yuan. The ground breaking and foundation laying ceremony was held on 26 December 1970, Mao Zedong's birthday, and the completed dam was finally commissioned in October 1989. Work was carried out under three projects.

The Sanjiang (Third Channel) Project began in May 1971 and was commissioned in April 1985. This project comprised two ship locks, one silt-flushing sluice, and a man-made navigation channel. During construction a total of 2.7 million cubic metres of material were excavated to house the machine hall and two million cubic metres of concrete were poured. Phase 2, the Dajiang (Grand Channel) Project, was carried out between 1982 and May 1986. This project comprised erecting a 989.4-metre-long section of the dam, a silt-flushing sluice, Lock No 1, and the Dajiang Power Station. The 166.8-metre-long silt-flushing sluice, which contains nine openings with a discharge capacity of 20,000 cubic metres a second, is designed to continually flush the navigation channel and ship lock and also to dissipate flood discharges. The Erjiang (Second Channel) Project consisted of a 17-outlet flood-discharge sluice with a discharge capacity of 3,900 cubic metres a second and a seven-unit power station with a generating capacity of 4,900 Megawatts (MW). Excavated material amounted to 68.4 million cubic metres, and 6.3 million cubic metres of concrete poured.

Construction of the dam involved the removal of 55 million cubic metres of rock and earth to form the foundations. The finished dam, which is 2,606.5 metres long and 70 metres high, required the pouring of 11.3 million cubic metres of concrete, sufficient material to build a ten-metre-wide, 0.5-metre-thick road from Guangzhou to Beijing. In addition, 77,200 tons of steel structures and equipment were used. After the main channel was closed off on 4 January 1981, the original water level was raised by 20 metres to 62 metres above sea level. The resulting reservoir covers an area of one million square kilometres and contains 1.58 billion cubic metres of water. During the dry season, and prior to the construction of the Three Gorges Dam further upstream, the reservoir extended 110 kilometres upstream to Shangguan Ferry. During the wet season, it extended a further 70 kilometres to Fengjie. Maximum controlled water level variation is 18.6 metres. The completed Gezhouba ('ba' means dam in Chinese) Water Control Project includes flood control, power generation, improvements to navigation and a bridge.

Seasonal flood discharges (water volumes) of the Yangzi River pose a constant threat to the safety of both the dam and the inhabitants of the Yangzi valley. The average discharge of the river at Yichang is 14,300 cubic metres per second, although the flow can vary considerably. The lowest water flows of about 2,770 cubic metres per second were recorded in 1937 and 1979. In contrast, the largest water flows occurred in 1788 and 1870, when 86,000 cubic metres per second and 110,000 cubic metres per second, respectively, were recorded. Consequently, the dam includes a 27-bay spillway that can discharge 110,000 cubic metres of water a second, which is

A view of Gezhou Dam at Yichang. Construction began on 26 December 1970 and was completed 19 years later in October 1989.

equivalent to the discharge of the 1870 flood. On the 19 July 1981, the dam was tested during construction by a flood of 72,000 cubic metres a second. Two silt screening sluices and two silt prevention dykes were incorporated in the dam to allow sediment flushing, which will prevent, or at least reduce, siltation in the lower section of the reservoir behind the dam.

Power generation at Gezhouba began in June 1981. The Dajiang Power Station has an installed generating capacity of 14,700 MW from 21 sets of 700 MW turbine generators, all of which were manufactured in China. Electricity is primarily provided to Hubei, Henan, Hunan and Jiangxi provinces. The Dajiang 500 KV substation, with six-incoming and six-outgoing 500 kilovolt DC transmission lines, supplies electricity to east China, including Shanghai.

Three ship locks are located at the northern end of the dam. These were opened to navigation in June 1981. Locks No 1 and No 2, the two largest, have a 20-metre rise and can accommodate ships of 12,000 to 16,000 tons. These locks are both 280 metres long, 34 metres wide, and five metres deep. The large, electrically controlled lock gates that seal the chambers are 34 metres high by 19.7 metres wide and weigh 600 tons. Following closure of the gates, electrically controlled water valves allow the 280,000-cubic-metre chambers to fill in 15 minutes. Lock No 3, the smallest, is 120 metres long, 18 metres wide, and 3.5 metres deep and can accommodate 3,000 ton ships. The crest of the dam is crossed by a bridge, which can be raised by 18 metres to allow ships to pass.

The Three Gorges Dam

Following extensive surveys, two potential sites for a larger dam were selected at Sandouping and Taipingxi. Both are areas of granite in a region of folded sedimentary rocks. The site finally selected for the Three Gorges Dam is at Sandouping, 27 kilometres upstream from the Gezhou Dam and the widest point in the gorges, where the channel was 1,000 metres wide. Zhongbao Island, 1,000 metres long by 200 metres wide, was located in the middle of the channel.

Strong citizen opposition to the Three Gorges Project forced the People's Congress to temporarily suspend plans for the dam in March 1989. However, the project was swiftly resurrected by Premier Li Peng in the aftermath of the Beijing massacre in June 1989. In 1993, almost 75 years after Sun Yat-sen's paper was published, 49 years after site selection surveys were initiated, and four years after the Gezhou Dam was commissioned, work began on the Three Gorges Project.

Construction was planned in three phases over a period of 17 years between 1993 and 2009, at a total cost of 90 billion yuan. The Three Gorges Dam and associated infrastructure was estimated to cost 50 billion yuan. A further 40 billion yuan was allocated for resettlement of the population living below the final reservoir level of 175 metres asl (above sea level). During the peak of construction activity, the project occupied a security-controlled construction area of 15.28 square kilometres, employed 27,000 labourers working 24 hours a day in three shifts, and was overseen by 200 local and overseas engineers. The final phase employs 15,000 workers. When completed the Three Gorges Dam will be the largest hydroelectric dam in the world. The concrete gravity dam stretches for 2,309.47 metres across the valley, reaches a height of 185 metres asl, which is a maximum of 181 metres (equivalent to a 60-storey building) above the deepest part of the river bed, and is 80 metres wide at the crest. Water will be impounded to a final height of 175 metres asl, which is 113 metres above the level at the Gezhou Dam. Water storage will amount to 70 billion cubic metres in a reservoir extending for about 600 kilometres upstream to a point 65 kilometres above Chongqing.

During the First Phase, from 1993 to the end of 1997, the southern river channel was closed off with a reinforced concrete coffer dam. A diversion channel was excavated and a temporary ship lock was constructed on the north bank. The temporary lock was 240 metres long, 24 metres wide and four metres deep. Navigation continued through the middle channel, by-passing the main channel in which construction of the dam was carried out.

The Second Phase, between 1998 and 2003, involved constructing the second stage coffer dams and rerouting the river through the diversion channel. These works allowed the permanent five-step ship lock, the spillway, the intake dam and the northern power station to be constructed. Two flights of ship locks, each of five stages, have been installed. The northern flight for upstream vessels and the southern flight is for downstream vessels. Each lock measures 280 metres long, 34 metres wide, and five metres deep. They are designed to accommodate vessels up to 10,000 tons. Passage through the lock takes about two hours. The locks are closed at both ends by a pair of mitre gates. Each gate is 20 metres wide, 39.5 metres high and weighs 900 tons The lower sluice gate of the spillway has a slot for sediment flushing. Opening of the fifth step will coincide with raising the reservoir to the final height of 175 metres asl. Upon completion, passage through the five steps will take from three to five hours.

The Third and final Phase, between 2003 and 2009, commenced on 16 June 2003 with the closing of the diversion channel and temporary ship lock, rerouting the river through the spillway dam and raising the water level to 135 metres asl. Following the water level rise, the first four steps of the five-step permanent ship lock, the spillway and the sluice gate were opened on 16 August 2003. During this phase the ship elevator will be constructed. The lift will be 120 metres long, 18 metres wide and 3.5 metres deep to accommodate vessels up to 3,000 tons. Passage time will be between

The five-stage shiplock under construction

Installation of the first turbine in 2002

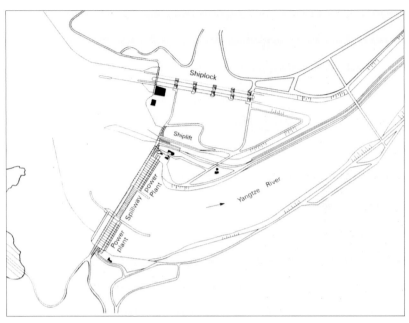

The general layout of the Three Gorges Project

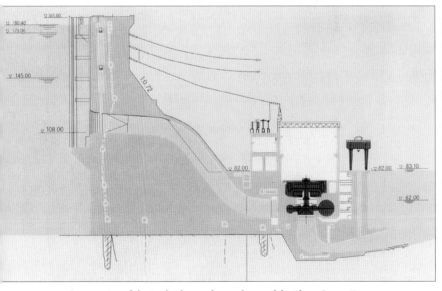

Cross-section of the intake dam and powerhouse of the Three Gorges Dam

Installation of the Francis-type turbines for hydroelectric generation

30 to 45 minutes. The third stage reinforced concrete coffer dam was erected, allowing construction of the northern power station that is 643.7 metres long and houses 14 generators. Work began in July 2003 and will be completed by 2009. A second power station, 584.2 metres long and housing 12 generators, is being constructed at the southern end of the dam.

Included in the project is a new 28-kilometre-long expressway, opened in 1996, connecting the Three Gorges Dam site with Yichang and the Gezhou Dam site. The road has five tunnels, the longest being 3.6 kilometres. Journey time is now reduced from two hours to 30 minutes. Immediately downstream from the dam is a 900-metre-span suspension bridge, built between 1994 and 1996. The bridge weighs 290 tons, cost 390 million yuan to build and is supported on two British-manufactured cables costing 100 million yuan each.

During the 16-year project, 102.83 million cubic metres of rock and soil will be excavated and 31.98 million cubic metres of earth and rock embankments built. A total volume of 27.94 million cubic metres of concrete will have been placed, incorporating 463,000 tons of reinforcing bars. In addition, 256,500 tons of steelwork will have been erected.

The four main objectives of the dam are flood control, electricity generation, and improvements to navigation and irrigation.

Because 70 per cent of the tributaries are in the upper reaches of the river the majority of the seasonal runoff from the Yangzi river basin can be intercepted at Sandouping, thereby protecting the flood prone lower reaches. The reservoir has a flood storage capacity of 22.15 billion cubic metres and is designed to accommodate the one in 100 year frequency flood, rather than the one in ten year flood of the Gezhou Dam. During normal years December, January and February are the main dry season months and July, August and September are the peak flooding season. The flood control strategy is based on this seasonal pattern. From early December to early February the reservoir will be maintained at the maximum 175 metre level, but between February and May the reservoir will be lowered to the 155 metre level, allowing a 20-metre flood control capacity to contain the initial flood. During May and June the reservoir will be lowered by a further ten metres to the 145 metre level, creating a 30-metre flood control capacity. The reservoir will be maintained at the 145 metre level during the flood season months of July to September.

With 33 per cent of China's 1.2 billion population concentrated in the Yangzi valley, the demand for electricity is high. Hydroelectricity will, in future, be generated within the region. This will avoid the need for expensive power transmission and reduce the current reliance on coal fired generation, which is polluting. Currently between 40 and 50 million tons of coal are used each year, transported from the Wei River valley in Shaanxi Province, or from Inner Mongolia.

Electricity generation will be carried out at two power stations. The 700 megawatt (MW) generators, driving Francis-type turbines, have been ordered from General Electric (Canada), ABB (Switzerland), Siemens (Germany) and Alstom (France). Total generating capacity from the initial 26 sets of generators will be 18,200 MW. An area on the south bank has been reserved for six additional generating sets. Four 700 MW generators will be commissioned each year until 2007. Eventually there will be a total of 40 power generators at the main dam, with a total generating capacity of 28,000 MW. When fully operational the Three Gorges plant will generate 84.7 Terawatt hours (TWh—one trillion or 1012 watt hours) or 15 per cent of China's electricity needs. Distribution will be by 15 transmission lines. Supply to Hubei and Sichuan provinces and Chongqing Municipality in central China will be by 500 kilovolt alternating current lines and to the cities of Shanghai and Guangzhou by 500 kilovolt direct current lines.

Because of the marked seasonality of the rainfall, prior to construction of the dams river levels fluctuated markedly. Thus navigation was very seasonal. When the dam is filled to the final 175 metre level the water level at Chongqing will be raised by 45 metres, allowing year round navigation to reach the city. The ship locks on the dam are designed for an annual one-way movement of 50 million tons.

Over recent decades North China has become drier, the discharge of the Yellow River has decreased to crisis levels, the problem of desertification has increased and Beijing has experienced severe water shortages. Related to the Three Gorges Project is a project known as the South to North Water Transfer Scheme (SNWTS), which is designed to convey surplus water from the Yangzi River north to the Yellow River and Beijing (See further Special Topic on page 383). This requirement was an important factor in designing the final height of the Three Gorges Dam.

Environmental and Social Concerns of the Three Gorges Project

Construction of the massive Three Gorges Dam clearly will have an immense impact on the regime of the Yangzi and on the surrounding region. Many of the potential problems have been addressed in wide-ranging environmental impact assessments and other studies carried out during the planning stages of the dam. Safety of the dam structure and ensuring water quality are the two overriding concerns.

Since the 1970s, earthquake studies have been carried out in the dam and reservoir area to assess rock characteristics, geological structures, fault activity, and potential water seepage. Rock stress measurements have been made in 300- to 500-metre-deep boreholes. These studies have concluded that both the dam site and the reservoir area are seismically stable. A magnitude six earthquake is the maximum predicted in the region. However, the dam has been designed to resist an earthquake of magnitude seven. Large landslides occur in the reservoir area, but studies have shown that most of the banks are composed of hard rock, major faults are few, and neotectonic activity (recent earth movements) is low. Therefore, it was concluded that the reservoir banks are stable and that landslides would not adversely affect navigation or the dam structures.

The annual average sediment load of the Yangzi River is about 490 million tons. Reduction of the current velocity caused by the dam could create undesirable sedimentation problems that would ultimately fill up the reservoir, rendering it worthless. For example, prior to the construction of dams along the Colorado River in the USA, the measured annual sediment load was 135 million tons a year at the mouth. This was reduced to 0.1 million tons a year after the dams were built, indicating retention of eroded sediments within the drainage basin. Consequently, studies of the Yangzi River began in the 1960s using observation, analogue analyses, mathematical modelling, and physical modelling to assess the optimum design for flushing the sediment through the dam. Altogether 14 physical models were built— five of the dam area and nine of the upper reaches—at scales of between 1/100 and 1/300. Modelling results concluded that because about 84 per cent of the annual sediment load is carried during the flood season from July to September the reservoir level should be kept at the lower level of 145 metres to allow the flood waters to flush the reservoir. In addition, several planned water conservancy projects on the major tributaries, including shelter-belt forestry schemes, will reduce incoming sediment loads. Calculations indicated that after 80 to 100 years of operation the reservoir will still have between 86 per cent to 92 per cent of its original capacity.

Regular flooding is a beneficial process that deposits silt over lowlands, replacing the soil and replenishing fertility. Flood control measures will prevent this natural process and artificial fertilization may need to be introduced to compensate. However, long-term, possibly detrimental, effects of flood control on soil fertility are difficult to assess. An overall reduction in flow in the lower reaches has raised concerns about possible saltwater intrusion in the delta area around Shanghai. Discharge in the lower reaches will have to be carefully managed.

Active measures taken to preserve water quality are many and varied. Slopes above 25 degrees in the reservoir catchment area must, by law, be restored to grassland. During the 1950s and 1960s, in order to achieve

The second stage of the Three Gorges Dam under construction in 2002. The spillway (centre river) and left-bank powerhouse are protected behind a coffer dam. At this stage of the project shipping passed the site by means of the diversion channel (left). Part of the

new town of Zigui can be seen in the distance, on the extreme left. The narrow channel on the right, running beside the river, leads to the shiplift in its early stages of construction. Beyond this the five-stage shiplock is being excavated through the hillside.

SICHUAN BASIN

THE THREE GORGES

national iron production quotas, large areas of trees were felled as fuel for furnaces. Today a ban has been imposed on tree felling, and tree planting is being promoted. Polluting factories have been closed down and the opening of new factories is strictly controlled. Measures have been taken to control the 1.35 billion tons of wastewater discharged annually into the Yangzi River.

Within the reservoir area 49 rare or endangered species were identified. Fish migrations through the dam have been considered and the ecology of the freshwater carp studied. The Gezhou Dam project included a study, between 1981 and 1988, of the effects of the dam on the freshwater sturgeon and the effects of changing water quality on the freshwater dolphins (see Yichang Sturgeon Research Centre on page 393).

Social consequences of the dam are wide reaching. Close to 1.9 million people living below the projected 175 metre final reservoir level have been forcibly displaced to places as far apart as Shanghai, Qingdao (in Shandong Province), western Sichuan Province and Guangzhou. Two cities, 11 county towns, and 116 townships will have been destroyed, along with 24,500 hectares of farmland. Studies for the resettlement scheme were conducted in an eight year, 237-million-yuan project, and 40 billion yuan was allocated to implement the resettlement plans. Almost 33 per cent of the population were moved to different provinces. About 60 per cent of the remaining rural population will continue in agriculture and 40 per cent will need to find new jobs.

A total of 44 archaeological sites and ancient monuments will be inundated by the reservoir. These have been the subject of rescue surveys and excavations, but the cultural and heritage losses to the nation, and to the world, are immense (see Three Gorges Archaeology on pages 318–21).

Environmental Benefits of the Dams

Fortunately, several tangible benefits will be derived from the Three Gorges Project, mostly in the middle and lower reaches of the river. About 1.53 million hectares of farmland on the Jingjiang Plain and in the Dongting Lake area will be protected from damaging floods, along with the lives and livelihoods of the 15 million residents of those regions. Silt deposition in Dongting Lake will be reduced, prolonging its life span. Dry season flow rates can be artificially increased in the lower reaches, improving water quality and providing a reserve for the planned South To North Water Transfer Scheme.

Power generation at the dam will reduce coal consumption by up to 50 million tons a year. Calculations suggest that this will eliminate the emission of 10 million tons of carbon dioxide, two million tons of sulphur dioxide, 370,000 tons of nitrous oxide, and 10,000 tons of carbon monoxide, as well as reducing the discharges of related waste water and solids such as fly ash.

THE SOUTH TO NORTH WATER TRANSFER SCHEME
by Raynor Shaw

China has water resources of about 28,000 billion cubic metres, the sixth largest national reserves in the world. However, China only ranks 88th in terms of water per head of population. Hindering the uniform development of the country is the fact that the water resources are not evenly distributed across the nation. Southern China and the Yangzi basin have about 80 per cent of the runoff, but only 40 per cent of the farmland. In contrast, the Yellow River and Hai River basins occupy about 50 per cent of the country, contain 45 per cent of the farmland and support 36 per cent of the population, despite possessing only 12 per cent of the national water reserves.

Clearly, there is a great disparity between the amounts of water contained in the catchments of the two great rivers of China. Even after considerable abstraction by agriculture, industry and the major population centres located along the river banks, the annual water discharge at the mouth of the Yangzi River is about 980,000 million cubic metres, with about 760,000 million cubic metres in drier years. This is about 17 times larger than the discharge of the Yellow River. In fact, the discharge of the Yangzi River at Yibin, which is only halfway along the course, is four times that of the Yellow River. Furthermore, 94 per cent of the Yangzi River runoff reaches the sea, in contrast to the Yellow River that suffers large evaporative losses. Remarkably the Min Jiang, a major tributary of the Yangzi River in the Sichuan Basin, has a drainage basin only 20 per cent that of the Yellow River, but has twice the annual water flow. This disparity in the relative discharges of the two river catchments has increased in recent years.

Three important groundwater-related problems affect the drier northern region. Firstly, the rivers that cross the dry expanses of the Loess Plateau all have relatively low discharges. With an increasing demand for water from a growing urban population, intensive agriculture, and expanding industry, water abstraction is further reducing the discharge of the Yellow River. Climatic patterns also appear to be shifting. Over recent decades annual rainfall totals have decreased and northern China is becoming drier. The Qinling

Mountain Range normally blocks a proportion of the moisture-bearing winds that are drawn in from the southeast by the monsoonal circulation, producing rainfall that swells the discharge of the middle reaches of the Yellow River. But circulation patterns are changing and less rainfall is passing the Qinling Range with the result that seasonal rainfall is lower, river discharges are decreasing and groundwater recharge is slower. Consequently, the groundwater table is being lowered to critical levels in several areas. Beijing is now experiencing severe water shortages as the water table below the city is lowered by the increase of groundwater pumping, coupled with a decrease in potential natural recharge. Underground water is being exploited beyond sustainable levels. Another consequence of the water deficit is that desertification is becoming a problem. The edge of the desert is advancing southwards by up to six metres a year in some areas, with sand sheets burying roads, villages and farmland, a phenomenon that is increasingly worrying planners.

Secondly, a major concern is the large sediment load of the rivers that cross the easily erodible Loess Plateau of northern China. Erosion rates are increasing as economic development places greater demands on these fragile deposits. Despite the considerably lower water discharge, the Yellow River carries an annual sediment load of about 1,600 million tons, which is about 3.5 times more than the sediment load of the Yangzi River. This high sediment concentration makes the water unsuitable for irrigation, for drinking and for other purposes without treatment.

Thirdly, salinization is an increasingly serious geological hazard in low-lying areas of the Yellow River floodplain, especially where the rate of evaporation of surface water exceeds the annual rainfall. During the hot summer months, ground water containing dissolved minerals is drawn to the surface by capillary rise, and intense evaporation results in a layer of surface salts. This saline crust decreases crop yield, and reduces local incomes. This problem is currently tackled by drilling numerous wells to regulate the water table.

During the past 50 years, scientists and planners have been seeking solutions to the problem of increasing droughts. Realizing that there is sufficient water in the Yangzi River basin to supply the needs of the parched north of the country, over 50 technical studies have been carried out to investigate feasible schemes for transferring water from the south to the north. The result is that an important, long-term component of the Three Gorges Dam Project is an ambitious scheme known as the South to North Water Transfer Scheme (SNWTS), a policy of *nan shui bei diao*—southern waters toward the north. The SNWTS is being designed to transfer water northwards from the more amply supplied Yangzi River catchment to the Yellow River, and particularly to Beijing, the capital. Essentially, the scheme has three components, comprising an open channel system in the lowlands of the east, a channel and aqueducts in the undulating topography of the centre, and a network of tunnels through the mountains of the west. Together these channels will link the Yangzi River basin with the Yellow, the Hai, the Huai, the Yalong and the Dadu rivers. However, the engineering challenges are immense.

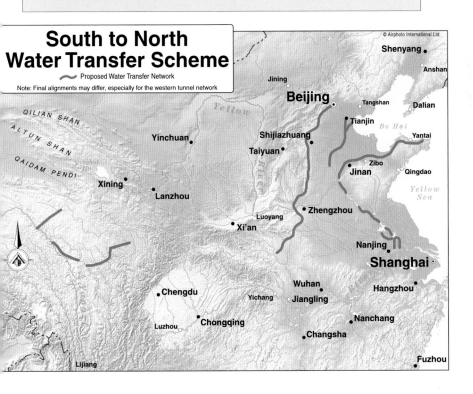

South to North Water Transfer Scheme

~ Proposed Water Transfer Network

Note: Final alignments may differ, especially for the western tunnel network

© Airphoto International Ltd.

Proposals for the eastern channel consist of widening the existing Yanzhuo Channel, the Grand Canal, to enlarge the current capacity. The new waterway will be called the Jing-Hang Channel, named after the terminal points of Beijing and Hangzhou. However, the major problem facing engineers is that the southern source is lower than the northern terminus. Overcoming this obstacle will involve raising the water level in the south by constructing a series of dams, and pumping water between them. A second problem is that the water in the eastern system is polluted and of poor quality. Therefore the eastern channel will not directly solve the drinking water shortage faced by Beijing. Planners envisage that, by the year 2050, this channel, with the second largest capacity of the three channels, will carry over 148 million cubic metres of water northwards each year.

Less formidable problems confront the engineers tackling the central channel, which is designed to transfer water from the existing Danjiangkou Reservoir, situated on the Han River near Wuhan. The Han River is the longest tributary of the Yangzi, and the dam controls about 60 per cent of the catchment, an area of 95,000 square kilometres. Although there is a slight northward gradient along this alignment, the latest plan involves raising the height of the existing dam crest (built in the period 1958–1973) to increase the head of water. However, it is anticipated that raising the water level in the reservoir will also raise the level of the regional water table, causing waterlogging of the surrounding land and resulting in the displacement of large numbers of people. This channel has the smallest design capacity, carrying about 130 million cubic metres of water each year.

Today, water use in the upstream reaches of the Yellow River is severely restricted by law to ensure a continuation of the flow. However, when the eastern and central channels are operational they will replace 30 to 40 million cubic metres of water that is currently abstracted by the inhabitants along the river, water that no longer passes down the channel to the lower basin. The planned additional water supply capacity will provide a valuable reserve to meet future requirements, both forecast and unanticipated.

The most ambitious section of the scheme is the western network of tunnels, which will involve tunnelling through the mountains for hundreds of kilometres to the upper reaches of the Yellow River, an immensely expensive operation. Runoff from the Tongtian River will be fed to the basins of the Yalong and the Dadu rivers. This network is designed to supply water to the six provinces of Qinghai, Gansu, Ningxia, Shanxi, Shaanxi, and Nei Meng (Inner Mongolia), but particularly to irrigate the Gansu Corridor, a rich agricultural area. Importantly, the western network will also be able to supply the middle and lower Yellow River basin, if necessary, as the design capacity of 170 million cubic metres of water a year will be sufficiently large. Forecasts indicate that the additional capacity of the western network will not be required until the year 2030, therefore construction of this part of the scheme will commence much later than the other components.

The Grand Canal in Jiangsu Province is still an important component of the transport network of the region, but may in the coming years become part of an ambitious new project to divert surplus water from the Yangzi River to the arid north of China

STAGE III

THE MIDDLE BASIN: YICHANG TO MA'ANSHAN

From Yichang the Yangzi enters its Middle Basin, flowing through Hubei, Jiangxi and Anhui provinces to Ma'anshan, on the border of Jiangsu Province, before entering its final Coastal Delta stage. The river, widening out abruptly from the narrow confines of Xiling Gorge and with a pent-up force out of Gezhou Dam, rolls through broad floodplains, fed by tributaries and lakes that used to be serious flood points during heavy summer rains.

Networks of dykes and embankments—obscuring the view—stretch the length of the river, which can be as wide as one and a half to two kilometres, and could cause widespread flooding during normal rainy seasons. In abnormal summer deluges the many lakes in the area, joining forces with the Yangzi and its tributaries, would inundate the land, forming great expanses of water. It is hoped that with the construction of the Three Gorges Dam these disastrous floods will become a thing of the past.

Up to the Sui dynasty (581–618) the middle reaches were sparsely inhabited, but from the Tang dynasty (618–907) on, waves of people migrated from the north, fleeing from civil wars, famines, heavy taxation and harassment from marauding Tibetans and Turks. With the sharp rise in population, dyke construction became more intense. But it was during the Ming and Qing dynasties (1368–1644 and 1644–1911) that treasury funds were allocated to the construction of dykes—mainly along the north bank of the Yangzi—which were built as high as ten to 16 metres in places. Once built, the burden of maintenance fell to local landowners and peasants, and upkeep was often neglected.

The meandering, looping course of the river created severe silting so that the raised riverbed required constant dredging. The wash of large boats crisscrossing the channel can churn into the embankment causing mini-landslides. The rich alluvial Jianghan Plain, between the north bank of the Yangzi and the Han River, is a major cotton- and grain-growing area and was very vulnerable to flooding. In 1952 the Jingjiang Flood Diversion Project was launched. Flood prevention measures

A large junk under full sail on the middle reaches of the Yangzi River in the mid-1980s. These magnificent craft have now sadly disappeared from the river.

included the strengthening of the 180-kilometre stretch of dyke along the Yangzi's northern bank (in the Shashi region), and the construction of flood-intake sluices, regulating dams and retention basins on the south side to divert the waters. On the Han River, the Danjiangkou Water Conservancy Project and dam draw the flood waters from this tributary to irrigate the more arid regions of northwest Hubei. The Shashi retention basin, covering an area of 920 square kilometres, took 300,000 workers some 75 days to construct in 1954.

Above Dongting Lake, the Yangzi forms the border between the provinces of Hubei and Hunan. The lake itself is the second largest in China. Fed by four rivers and emptying its waters into the Yangzi, it abounds in aquatic products. At Dongting Lake the river streaks northeastwards, beside hinterland dotted with numerous lakes, towards Wuhan, the largest city along its middle reaches. Here it is joined by the 1,532-kilometre long Han River, which gives the names of Hanyang and Hankou to the north bank parts of the sprawling Wuhan metropolis.

During the dry winters, exposed sandbars and low water levels pose serious hazards to shipping. At Wuhan, the navigation channel can be as shallow as two metres.

Freshwater fish abound—silver and big-head carp, Yangzi sturgeon and Wuchang fish, to name a few (for more on the sturgeon see the section on Yichang Sturgeon Research Centre below). Also native to the river are dolphins and a species of alligator. Although the Yangzi white dolphin, or *baiji*, is thought now to be extinct, the extremely rare Yangzi alligator still survives in the middle to lower reaches. The world's smallest alligator, it is a protected species and a research centre in Anhui Province is trying to ensure its survival.

Having crossed the entire width of Hubei Province, the river enters Jiangxi, forming its border with Anhui. Immediately below the city of Jiujiang and the cherished, beautiful mountain of Lushan, it is joined by the blue freshwaters of Poyang Lake, the biggest in all of China. From here on, the Yangzi enters its lower reaches.

YICHANG

Situated at the eastern mouth of the gorges, Yichang is the administrative centre of nine surrounding counties. Its population is engaged in light industry, chemical and steel production. The construction of the Gezhou Dam helped Yichang to grow from a small town of 30,000 into a city of over 500,000. The Three Gorges Dam is only 44 kilometres upstream via a new highway cut through steep mountains. The Yichang waterfront is lined with levees and docks busy with barges and passenger liners. The new Yiling Bridge crosses the Yangzi to the south shore over a charming riverside park.

History Of Yichang

History records that as early as 278 BC the town was razed to the ground in a battle between the armies of Chu and Qin. In the Three Kingdoms period (see pages 304–5) 50,000 Wu troops set fire to the encampments of the Shu army, utterly routing Liu Bei, who retreated upriver to Baidi Cheng.

Yichang became a treaty port in April 1877, in accordance with the Chefoo (Yantai) Convention of 1876 signed with Britain, and continued to be the furthest inland treaty port for many years, as large merchant and passenger vessels were not yet able to navigate the gorges upsteam to Chongqing. Here, cargo was unloaded from the larger boats plying the stretch of river between Yichang and Wuhan, and reloaded onto smaller ones running between Yichang and Chongqing.

An American traveller in 1921 described the port as 'crowded, incessantly busy, a perfect maelstrom of sampans, junks, lighters with cargo, steamers and gunboats.' Eventually technology enabled ships to continue the journey upstream and Chongqing itself became a treaty port in 1891.

The English trader Archibald Little, noting his expenses for a night's stay in the treaty port, showed how far four English pennies went in late 19th-century Yichang, and incidentally his solicitude for his servant:

> *Supper for self and coolie, 4 bowls of rice at 10 cash (copper cash),*
> *'fixings' of cabbage and bean curd free* *40*
> *Use of straw-plaited mattress for ditto, 2 at 10* *20*
> *Breakfast, same as supper*..*40*
> *Supper and breakfast for 'Nigger', my dog* *20*
> *Pair of straw sandals for coolie (his old ones being worn out)*............*12*
> *Total 132 copper cash, or, in English money, 4d* *132*

During the warlord years of the early part of this century, Yichang's revenue was greatly boosted by taxes imposed on boats carrying homegrown opium from Yunnan and Guizhou Provinces by its Opium Suppression Bureau.

During the war with Japan, the gorges above Yichang again acted as a barrier. When Wuhan fell to the Japanese in 1938, Yichang became the centre for shipping essential personnel, machinery, libraries and museum collections up the Yangzi to Chongqing. After the Battle of Yichang in 1940 the Japanese capture of Yichang marked their furthest westward advance. The Japanese also used Yichang as a staging area for bombing raids over Chongqing.

What To See In Yichang

The streets of the old town centre are lined with trees. Though the city wall was pulled down in 1929, the street names still indicate where it once stood (Eastern

Ring Road, Southern Ring Road and so on). The main market is found just off Jiefang Lu. Along the waterfront a few old foreign buildings of the treaty port days can be seen, but most are gone, replaced in the modern styles. One remnant of the past is the Zhenjiang 'Protect the River' pavilion, once part of a large temple, now a tea house and disco.

THREE TRAVELLERS' CAVE

Apart from the Gezhou Dam, tourists may also visit the Three Travellers' Cave, ten kilometres northwest of the city. In 819, three Tang-dynasty poets, Bai Zhuyi, his brother Bai Xingjian and Yuan Zhen, met up in Yichang and made an excursion to this site. While enjoying the spectacular scenery, they inscribed some poems on the cave walls. Afterwards they were dubbed the 'First Three Travellers'. In the Song dynasty (960–1279) the famous literary family of Su—the father and two sons—on their way to the capital to take the imperial examinations, visited the cave and added poems as well. All three passed the imperial examinations at the same time. People call these gentlemen the 'Second Three Travellers'. Throughout the ages, other visiting literati and officials have left their contributions on the cave walls.

A small spring trickles through the rock near the entrance; local superstition maintains that if women wash their hands in its pure water it will improve their culinary skills. The hill above the cave presents a fine view of the entrance to Xiling Gorge: The Zixi Pavilion contains a memorial stone to the 11th-century philosopher

Statue of Zhang Fei on the site where he is said to have beat his battle drum at Three Travellers Cave overlooking Nanjin Pass, the entrance to Xiling Gorge near Yichang

Xiu Ouyang, who lived in Yichang for three years. Nearby is a drum platform and fire watch station, said to be the site where Zhang Fei, a general of the third-century Kingdom of Shu, beat his battle drums. A large statue configures him looking east for trouble coming up the river into the Gorges.

A cable car ride crosses the Yangzi near Three Travellers Cave hill, for an aerial view of Nanjin Pass. The Tao Yuan docks just downstream from Nanjin Pass are the terminus for many river liners.

Visitors are sometimes taken on a short excursion along a mountain road offering stunning views of Xiling Gorge, and passing several peaks, including Filial Mountain and Camel Mountain. The road continues over a natural stone bridge, which was originally—

View of the entrance of Xiling Gorge from Three Travellers' Cave

so legend has it—a fairy's silken sash, thrown up to help her mortal husband ascend to heaven with her. The stone gateway and its steep stone steps delineate the ancient land route crossed by travellers to western Hubei and Sichuan.

Below Yichang lies the bluff known as Tiger's Teeth Gorge which, for travellers upriver, is the first glimpse of sights to come.

YICHANG STURGEON RESEARCH CENTRE

A visit to the Sturgeon Research Centre, established in Yichang in 1982, is recommended. It was set up to protect the giant Chinese sturgeon (*Acipenser sinensis*) whose breeding cycle was threatened by the construction of the Gezhou Dam. Previously this fish, that grows up to 500 kilograms in the East China Sea, would return to the upper Yangzi to spawn, swimming almost 3,000 kilometres inland to Yibin—coincidentally, the limit of safe navigation on the river, 370 kilometres

A dredger is on constant duty near Yichang to keep silt from blocking the Gezhou Dam. Many experts fear this could be an even greater problem for the Three Gorges Dam

A preserved specimen of the giant Chinese sturgeon (Acipenser sinensis) on display at the Yichang Sturgeon Research Centre. The lifecycle of these magnificent creatures, that can grow up to 500 kilograms and traditionally spawn 3,000 kilometres upstream in the upper Yangzi, has been disrupted by the construction of dams on the river.

upstream from Chongqing. In order to ensure the survival of this prehistoric species the Research Centre nets about 20 mature fish each autumn to breed artificially. It is hoped that the fish, which is now a protected species, will eventually adapt to breeding in the river below the dam. The Centre raise the young fish in tanks until they are six months old and then releases them back into the river to begin their long journey to the sea.

These enormous fish live up to 60 to 70 years, and grow on average to between three to four metres long, but have been known to reach five metres. The males take about nine years to reach maturity, and the females 14 years, after which they breed every four or five years. Because the fish feed only in the ocean, they will gorge themselves before setting off up the Yangzi to breed and will eat nothing during the one year it takes them to complete their mission and return to the sea. Each female is capable of producing around 25 kilograms of eggs.

As well as preserved specimens of fish at various stages of their life cycle, the Research Centre also keeps three or four large live specimens in a swimming tank so visitors can appreciate the size of these magnificent creatures. These fish have to be carefully hand fed as they are reluctant to eat in freshwater and cannot be kept in captivity for very long.

Although concentrating their work on the Chinese sturgeon, the Research Centre also breeds the smaller Yangzi sturgeon, a species that grows up to 200 kilograms, as well as studying and breeding species from overseas. Live specimens of a variety of these other species can be observed in display tanks.

The third species of sturgeon native to the Yangzi, the white sturgeon, is thought to be extinct. A more aggressive species than the other two, it proved too difficult to breed artificially, and there have been no reports in recent years of any being caught on the river.

JINGZHOU

Jingzhou, previously the famous city of Jiangling, has now been somewhat absorbed by the sprawling growth of Shashi, but it is still surrounded by its 16-kilometre long and nine-metre high city wall. Jingzhou is visited from Shashi, now a surrounding city referred to as Shajin.

Jingzhou was the capital of Jing, one of the nine great regions into which Emperor Yu, founder of the Xia dynasty (2200–1800 BC), divided China. From Jingzhou the emperor received as tribute exotic gifts of gold, ivory, cinnabar, silver and feathers. In the Spring and Autumn period (722–481 BC) the city was the capital of the Kingdom of Chu. Its walls, according to tradition, were first built in the third century by Guan Yu, a hero of the Three Kingdoms era. Guan Yu was renowned for his strength, height and valour. A thousand years after his death he was deified as the god of war, and his fierce red-faced image appears in many Chinese temples throughout Asia. Stories of his exploits and battles over the city are vividly told in the novel, *Romance of the Three Kingdoms*.

WHAT TO SEE IN JINGZHOU

Since Jingzhou was the capital of 20 kingdoms during both the Spring and Autumn and Warring States periods, it is not surprising that valuable artefacts have been found buried in the many tombs on Phoenix Hill. These relics, in particular an important collection of lacquerware, 2,000-year-old silk garments and fabrics are exhibited at the fine Jingzhou Museum, also an important research centre, and well worth a visit. Also on display is an almost perfectly preserved male 'wet mummy' of a Han-dynasty official, named Sui, floating in a herbal fluid under a glass cover. Not a sight for the squeamish, but he leaves a lasting impression.

SHASHI

Shashi is situated on the north bank of the Yangzi, and its cotton mills are supplied with raw cotton from the rich Jianghan Plain on which it stands. Shashi's workforce is principally employed in its many light-industrial enterprises—machinery, durable consumer goods, printing, dyeing and textiles. The city sits some ten meters below the tops of the protecting levees. An old saying goes, 'Look down to see your path, look up to see ships sail by.'

The city was the port for the ancient city of Jiangling and a distribution centre for produce from surrounding towns and Dongting Lake, which was trans-shipped mostly to Wuhan. This trade was in cotton, beans, grain and aquatic products. In the Tang dynasty (618–907) it already enjoyed a reputation as a prosperous city, but its peak was reached during the years of the Taiping Rebellion, in the mid-19th century. After the rebels captured Nanjing in 1853, river trade on the Yangzi between Shashi and Shanghai more or less came to a standstill, so Shashi became vital to the distribution of products coming downriver from Sichuan.

The Sino-Japanese Treaty of 1895 opened the city to foreign trade; Japanese engaged in the cotton-seed trade formed the majority of the resident foreigners, though this community was never large.

There is a story that the army of Communist General He Long captured Swedish missionaries here in 1931. The women were released following negotiations with the Swedish Consul General, but the release of a doctor was delayed until a ransom was paid. The ransom demanded was: four dozen Parker fountain pens, four dozen watches and 60 or 70 cases of medical drugs!

West of the city, the seven-storeyed Wanshoubao Pagoda, built in the Ming dynasty (1368–1644), stands directly on the waterfront. Bas-relief figures of Buddha, set into niches, and inscriptions by the donors adorn its brick facade. A temple once adjoined it.

Below Shashi the river winds tortuously towards Dongting Lake for about 320 kilometres. Villages dot the south bank of the river and water buffalo graze in the paddy fields. The north embankment is often too high for a view of the surrounding country.

DONGTING LAKE

The beautiful Dongting Lake is rich in fairy tales and legends. On its eastern shore stands the graceful three-storey Yueyang Tower of Yueyang City, one of the Three Great Towers south of the Yangzi (the other two being Yellow Crane Tower in Wuchang, and Prince Teng Pavilion in Nanchang). From its terraces and from pleasure boats on the lake, many famous Chinese poets have been moved to verse.

The lake embraces distant hills and devours the Yangzi, its mighty waves
    rolling endlessly.
From morning glow to evening light, the views change a thousand, ten
    thousand times.
On top of the tower the mind relaxes, the heart delights.
All honours and disgrace are forgotten.
What pleasure, what joy to sit here and drink in the breeze.

Fan Zhongyan (989–1052)

Said to have been constructed on the site of a reviewing platform for navy manoeuvres on the lake during the third century, the first tower was erected in 716. The present golden-tiled, square tower dates from 1985, but it has been rebuilt in the Song-dynasty style at great expense.

Legend has it that the tower was saved from collapse by the supernatural powers of Lu Dongbin, a Daoist (Taoist) Immortal, who also got drunk here three times. These occasions are remembered in the form of the Thrice Drunken Pavilion, which flanks the tower.

An excursion on to the lake can be made to Junshan Island, 15 kilometres away. Some 4,000 years ago, Emperor Shun, on an inspection tour, died at Mount Jiuyi on

(following pages) A fishing village along the lakefront of Honghu. Draining into the Yangzi, the lake can be used as a safety valve for flood control during the high-water season

the south bank of the lake. Two of his devoted concubines, hurrying to his side, became stranded on Junshan Island. The story goes that in their distress, their copious tears blotted the local bamboo, henceforth known as the Spotted Bamboo of Junshan. They drowned themselves in the lake, and their graves remain. In 219 BC, Emperor Qin Shihuangdi, also on a tour of Dongting Lake, was delayed at Junshan Island by a sudden storm. When he consulted his geomancer as to whether spirits were impeding his progress, he was told of the concubines' graves. In a fury he ordered the burning of the island and had five stone seals placed there, forbidding its name to be used or anyone to visit it.

On the 100-hectare (250-acre) island, Junshan Silver Needle Tea is grown, so highly prized that it was once presented as a tribute to the imperial court. The fine spindle tea leaves have the curious quality of sinking, floating, then sinking again in the brew.

Once China's largest freshwater lake, the Dongting now ranks second, due to sandbars and silt accumulation from the four rivers which feed it. As a result of flood prevention schemes—6,100 irrigation and drainage channels and 15,000 sluices—the surrounding land has become productive all year round and the lake acts as a reservoir for summer flood waters. The 3,000-square-kilometre lake abounds in fish.

Luxury goods from Guangzhou—from pearls to kingfisher feathers—reached the ancient capitals by way of the Xiang River, through Dongting Lake, down the Yangzi River to Yangzhou and then on up the Grand Canal.

THREE KINGDOMS' RED CLIFF

From the flat bank appears a sharp rock escarpment dotted with pavilions and paths. This is the site of the great Battle of the Red Cliff between the huge forces of Cao Cao of Wei and the combined, lesser armies of Shu and Wu in AD 208. Cao Cao had consolidated the power of the Kingdom of Wei in the north and sought to extend it to the Yangzi. His troops, all from the northern plains, were not accustomed to naval warfare. Nevertheless, he took his army of 200,000 men to launch his attack on the Kingdom of Shu, whose king, Liu Bei, called upon the King of Wu for assistance.

In urgent need of 100,000 arrows to repel the invaders, Zhuge Liang (adviser to Liu Bei) devised a brilliant stratagem. Twenty naval junks, beating war drums, but stacked high with only bundles of straw shrouded in black cloth, feigned an advance on the Wei encampment on a dark, foggy night. The Wei commanders responded by discharging their arrows into the indistinct hulks on the junks. By

(previous pages) Silhouetted against the waters of Honghu in Hubei Province, fishermen work their nets for an early catch

dawn, each junk bristled with thousands of arrows, more than enough for the army's requirements.

By another ruse, Cao Cao was persuaded by a spy in his camp to secure all his boats together for a forthcoming attack, so that his soldiers would feel as if they were on firm ground. The armies of Wu and Shu set fire to the boats in the midst of the battle and, with a favourable wind, the great conflagration brought about the defeat of Cao Cao, who fled northwards.

Red Cliff itself is said to have been forever scorched red by the flames of this day-long battle. In a victory celebration, General Zhou Yu of Wu, flourishing his writing brush, jubilantly inscribed the gigantic characters 'Red Cliff' (Chi Bi) on the cliff face, which can be seen to this day.

Pavilions on the hill commemorate specific incidents in the battle, and there is an exhibition of over 2,000 weapons, dating from the Three Kingdoms period, that were found in the area. The story of the battle is known to all Chinese, and this makes the site a very popular tourist spot, with river liners docking to visit the site and its museum displaying dioramas of the historic scenes.

HAN RIVER

The Han River, at 1,532 kilometres, the Yangzi's longest tributary, rises in the Qingling Mountains of Shaanxi Province. In 1488 it changed its course, separating the city of Hanyang from the fishing village of Hankou, as it then was. Though dykes line much of its lower course, this stretch has a history of frequent flooding. The British consular officer, August R Margary, who travelled all the way from Shanghai up the Yangzi and on to the Burmese border in 1876, only to be murdered by tribesmen as he crossed back into China, wrote of Hankou:

This year they have had no inundation, but it is of almost annual occurrence. Even at Hankow the foreign settlement is frequently submerged. The river rises six feet above the level of the fine stone bund they have made there, and quietly takes possession of all the lower rooms in the noble-looking mansions which the merchants occupy. All their dining-room furniture has to be removed above. Boats become the only means of loco-motion, and ladies can be seen canoeing in and out of their houses, and over the bund where they are wont to promenade at other times.

Flooding occurred 11 times from 1931 to 1949; in 1931 and 1935 boats sailed down the streets of Wuhan. Though much has been done in recent years to control the Han's waters, the danger of flooding is still very real.

A HANKOU FLOOD

*O*n the outskirts of Hankow, nearly all the so-called Chinese houses—
or, more correctly speaking, all the most miserable shanties, letting
in both wind and rain—on the bank of the river, are raised well up on
piles, thirty to forty feet above high-water mark; narrow wooden pathways running between the rows of houses, and small bridges connecting
these pathways where the houses are not continuous. In these wretched
dwellings live some hundreds of families, to all appearance without a
care, and in the greatest state of contentment. Their business, whatever it
may be, is mostly connected with boats and junks, for each house possesses either a sampan or a small, home-made, flat-bottomed boat, mostly rotten and leaky, which is continually bringing its occupants to grief,
and when not in use is moored to the lower end of the piles. The owners
ascend and descend by means of some iron spikes, driven in alternatively
on either side of one of the piles.

There is in times of flood the greatest distress among the riverside
population. When the water rises twenty-five, thirty, or more feet above
its ordinary level, many of these piles are swept away, down come the
houses, bringing their occupants with them, who are carried away in the
current. Whatever becomes of the remains of these unfortunates, no one
seems to know or to care; not one in twenty is recovered, or ever seen
again. Of course there is great lamentation among the survivors for the
next week; crackers are let off by the thousand, small floating fires are
set adrift on the stream to pacify the river god, gongs are beaten, and
altogether the priests have a busy time.

So little value do the Chinese set upon human life in disasters of this
description, which are of yearly occurrence in one part of the Empire or
another, that the whole thing is soon forgotten, a fresh crowd occupies the
places of the former crowd, piles are re-driven, shanties rebuilt, and so the
new lot live their careless, contented lives till, history repeating itself,
these people follow the lead of their predecessors.

In the early summer of 1887, the Bothwell Castle, a large ocean-
going steamer of three thousand tons, was lying at anchor opposite
Hankow, waiting for a cargo of tea. She had already been there two or
three weeks, and was likely to remain two or three more; the weather
being very bad, she made her holding secure with two anchors and a great

length of cable. Before receiving her full cargo, one of these sudden floods occurred, and a week or two later I received from Captain Tod the following account of the disaster. He said:

'One morning, shortly after breakfast, we heard a rumbling noise far away up the stream, and not long after an immense rush of water, like a large wave, came rolling down the river, carrying with it numbers of junks, boats, houses, trees, cattle, and I should be afraid to say how many human beings, all mixed up in the most inextricable confusion. We heard that the river Han had somewhere received an enormous and sudden flood of water, which, added to its already swollen state, had for many miles flooded the country, and was washing all before it into the Yangtze. Across our anchor-chains eight or ten junks had drifted, and were washed and piled up one over the other. It was impossible to reach them to set them adrift, and I was very much afraid the extra strain on the cables would be too much for them. Fortunately they held, thanks to the best of iron, without a flaw in any of the links.

Numbers of junks came sweeping down with the flood, all unmanageable, many coming broadside on across our bows, which went through them like a knife, the two parts of the junk floating past on either side of our ship. It was quite impossible to launch a boat, she would have been rolled over and swamped the moment she touched the water. With great difficulty and with much risk, we managed to save the lives of three or four dozen people; but, strange to say, some of them were very much displeased at being fished up out of the water. The Chinese said it was 'joss pidgeon', their fate, and as the river joss had taken away their all, he had much better take themselves also. Three or four afterwards tried to jump overboard. We put them ashore as soon as we could, and so relieved ourselves of any further responsibility.'

William Spencer Percival, The Land of the Dragon: My Boating and Shooting Excursions to the Gorges of the Upper Yangtse, 1889

THE HANKOU TEA RACES

The handsome, full-sailed tea clippers which plied the high seas between China and Britain from the 18th to the 19th century were initially confined to the coastal ports—first Canton, then Shanghai and eventually Fuzhou. As the British East India Company lost its monopoly and the tea trade gathered momentum, so did the competition between shipping companies, particularly as the quality of the tea could deteriorate on a long sea journey. The fastest ships charged the highest freight rates in this lucrative trade. This was the origin of the annual China Tea Races, first in elegant clippers and later in the early steamships.

Following the opening of the Yangzi River cities to foreign trade after the 1858 Treaty of Tientsin (Tianjin), the first tea clipper, the *Challenger*, reached Hankou in 1861.

The introduction of the steamship in the middle of the 19th century saw an end to these romantic sailing ships, and the opening of the Suez Canal in 1869 greatly reduced the sailing time. Nevertheless, the Hankow (Hankou) Tea Races continued. Each May, tea buyers, known as *chazi*, came to Hankou as the ships began to arrive from England, Russia and America. The Hankow (Hankou) Club sprang to life, with the Russian *chazi* drinking only champagne throughout the season. As many as 16 or 17 vessels would make up the British fleet, of which only two or three would be hot favourites and allowed to charge the highest freight rates.

Loaded with their cargo of black and green tea, the race began. The first leg from Hankou to the Red Buoy at Wusong (near Shanghai) could take as little as 36 hours if the ships did not run aground; then down the South China Sea to Singapore, where time was always lost in stockpiling coal for the last leg to London. In the 1877 race, two ships passed the Red Buoy together and reached Singapore with only 1 hour and 40 minutes between them. One ship lost six hours in port and arrived in London only 23 hours behind the winner after an exciting voyage of 31 days.

As the first ships were sighted in the English Channel, word was sent to the London brokers who would rush to the docks as the vessels berthed. In great excitement the tea chests were broken open for samples which were hurried off for inspection by the various buyers.

By the late 1880s India had moved into the lead of tea-exporting countries. The collapse of the China tea market brought about the end of a romantic era.

Picking tea leaves, gouache on pith paper, c.1870

Tea manufacture, gouache on pith paper, c.1870

WUHAN

At the centre of the Long River's course to the sea and on the main rail line between north and south China sprawls the tripartite city of Wuhan. Wuhan is set in the vast Jianghan Plain, a region that is more water than land. Levees protect the city from the seasonal ravages of the Yangzi. Wuhan serves as the capital of Hubei Province. It is comprised of three formerly separate cities—Wuchang, Hankou and Hanyang.

On the north bank lies Hankou, the commercial centre and port complex, now gleaming with a new skyline sprouting along its broad avenues. Hankou has always been the most developed of the three cities, ever since treaty port days. It is still the business and shopping heart of the city and contains the sites of former foreign concessions and the waterfront Bund. The passenger ship terminal in Hankou is shaped like a cartoon image of a ship, and it is from here that cruise ships bound for the Three Gorges and Chongqing depart.

The former British Customs House, with its clock tower now topped with a red star, remains on the waterfront street, Yanjiang Dadao. Its prominence is today eclipsed by mirrored nightclubs. New hotels line the waterfront where clipper ships once loaded tea. The jumbled old neighbourhoods and alleyways where foreign sailors once entered at their own risk have been torn down for grander shopping malls. Some of the graceful European-style buildings of the early century still exist, particularly in the area opposite the passenger terminal.

Across the Han River flowing from the north is Hanyang, known for the Turtle Hill (Gui Shan) overlooking the Wuhan Chang Jiang Da Qiao (Bridge), the Qing Chuan Pavilion with its superb river views and the Gui Yuan Si, an active Buddhist temple. Upriver in Hanyang are vast steel plants and factories.

On the south bank of the Yangzi are the administrative and educational campuses of Wuchang, the seat of the Hubei Provincial Government and Wuhan University. The Yellow Crane Tower (Huang He Lou), the famous symbol of Wuhan, rises above the Great River at Wuchang at the foot of the bridge. The Wuhan Chang Jiang Er Qiao (Bridge) links Hankou with Wuchang downriver. The calm reaches of Wuchang's East Lake (Dong Hu) with its bonsai gardens and excellent museums are the best antidote to the smoggy hubbub of the downtown districts.

Wuchang was the site of the 1911 uprising that led to the overthrow of the Qing dynasty. Mao Zedong enjoyed staying in this city and had his own villa on the shore of the Dong Hu.

The Tian He International Airport is just north of the city and directly connected to it by an expressway. As the city economy continues to grow, much of the old city

The Yellow Crane Tower (Huang He Lou), symbol of Wuhan and celebrated by Chinese poets throughout the ages. A climb to the top, at over 50 metres high, offers a superb view of the city

has been lost to redevelopment, and as in much of China, the new construction lacks the social web of the old neighbourhoods, though many of the traditional fragrances remain, especially by the riverside markets.

HISTORY OF WUHAN

The area on which Wuhan stands was settled in the first century; in the third century it was part of the Kingdom of Wu. Wuchang is the oldest of the three cities. By the Yuan dynasty (1279–1368) it was the capital of the region and was enclosed by a city wall until the end of the 19th century.

Hanyang was founded in the Sui dynasty (581–618) and remained a small walled city until a farsighted official of the Qing dynasty (1644–1911), Zhang Zhidong, established factories and an arsenal there in the 1890s.

Hankou was only a fishing village until the 19th century. It is, however, the city of Hankou which is best known to foreigners, for after it was declared a treaty port in 1861 it became a major centre of the tea trade and the focal point of the annual China Tea Races.

There were five Foreign Concessions—British, Russian, French, German and Japanese—situated side by side along the north embankment of the Yangzi. Ocean-going steamers from New York, Odessa and London anchored at their docks. Until the foreign import of opium ceased in the first decade of this century, opium-laden ships sailed up the river as far as Hankou.

Several historic buildings, dating from the time Wuhan was a treaty port, have been preserved along the riverside. Some, such as this one, are presently occupied by banks

(above and below) The old Customs House, with its distinctive clock tower, was designed and built by the British in the Renaissance style in 1924 as part of the foreign trading concessions in Wuhan, then known as Hankow. This historic building was renovated in 2000 as part of the Jianghan Lu pedestrianisation scheme

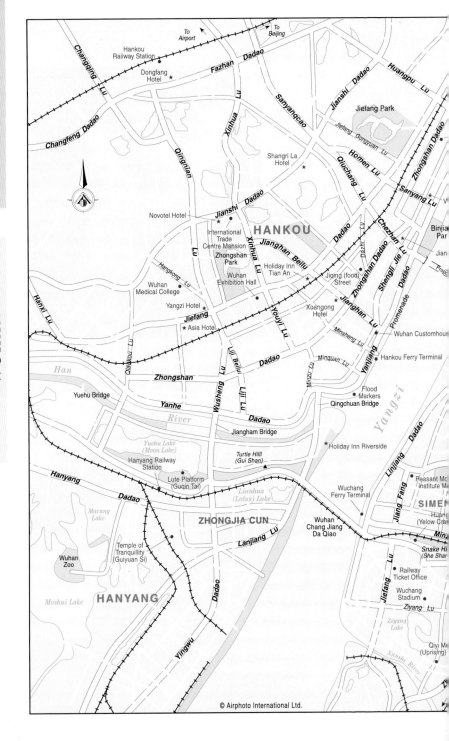

MIDDLE BASIN

WUHAN

© Airphoto International Ltd.

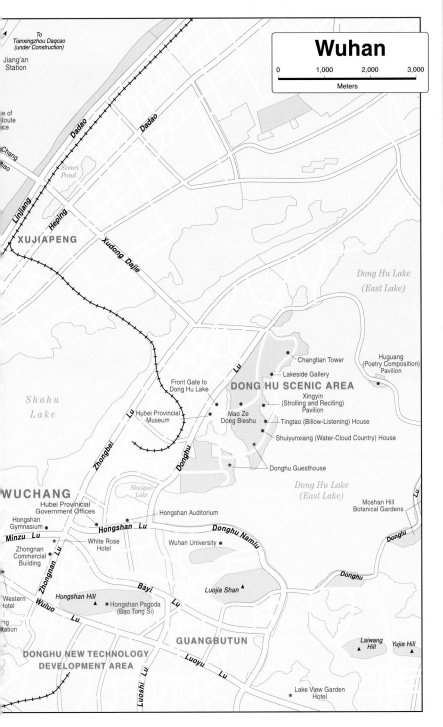

Wuhan

0   1,000   2,000   3,000

Meters

To
Tianxingzhou Daqcao
(under Construction)

Jiang'an
Station

e of
Route
ce

Chang

Dadao

Dadao

Simei
Pond

Linjiang

Heping

XUJIAPENG

Xudong Dalie

Dong Hu Lake
(East Lake)

Lu

Front Gate to
Dong Hu Lake

Changtian Tower

Lakeside Gallery

DONG HU SCENIC AREA

Huguang
(Poetry Composition)
Pavilion

Shahu
Lake

Hubei Provincial
Museum

Xingyin
(Strolling and Reciting)
Pavilion

Mao Ze
Dong Bieshu

Tingtao (Billow-Listening) House

Shuiyunxiang (Water-Cloud Country) House

Zhongbei

Donghu

Donghu Guesthouse

Shuiguo
Lake

WUCHANG

Dong Hu Lake
(East Lake)

Hubei Provincial
Government Offices

Hongshan Auditorium

Moshan Hill
Botanical Gardens

Lu

Hongshan
Gymnasium

Hongshan Lu

Donghu Namlu

Donglu

Minzu Lu

White Rose
Hotel

Wuhan University

Zhongnan
Commercial
Building

Zhongnan Lu

Donghu

Western
Hotel

Bayi

Hongshan Hill

Hongshan Pagoda
(Bao Tong Si)

Luojia Shan

ng
tation

Wuluo

Lu

Lu

GUANGBUTUN

DONGHU NEW TECHNOLOGY
DEVELOPMENT AREA

Luoshi Lu

Luoyu

Lu

Laiwang
Hill

Yujia Hill

Lake View Garden
Hotel

Jiqing Lu is popular for dining in the evenings. Restaurants serve local specialities while diners are entertained by licensed street musicians playing both modern and traditional instruments

Life in the foreign concessions was similar to that in Shanghai. Horse-racing was popular, with Hankou boasting two racecourses, one for Chinese and one for foreigners, on the sites of present-day Jiefang Park and Zhongshan Park. There was even a golf course, while the Recreation Club was considered by many to be the best in China at that time. There is now a new horse racecourse track open on the north side of the city en route to the airport.

In the 1911 Revolution, much of Hankou was burnt to the ground during clashes between revolutionaries and imperial troops.

After the fall of the then capital, Nanjing, to the Japanese in 1937, during the Sino-Japanese War, the Guomindang government made Wuhan its capital for a year, before moving to Chongqing. In the 1938 assault on Wuhan, casualty figures were in the tens of thousands.

The Communist Party was very active in Wuhan before 1949, organizing railway strikes and peasant training programmes. It was here that Chairman Mao, at the age of 73, took his famous 15-kilometre swim in the Yangzi during the Cultural Revolution days of 1966.

WHAT TO SEE IN WUHAN

When planning an itinerary, bear in mind that Wuhan is big. It requires plenty of time to get from place to place, more than one might imagine when initially looking at a map, especially with the increase in traffic that seems to blight all major cities in China today.

HANKOU

Hankou is the main commercial area of Wuhan. The old foreign concessions lined the embankment for three kilometres and this area is still interesting to stroll around. Many of the buildings display architecture from the colonial era and some bear plaques that detail their history. The old Customs House with its clock tower is a distinctive landmark. During the stifling summer months, the waterfront promenade is a popular place for locals to take an evening stroll in the hope of a cooling breeze off the river. When there is any kind of wind, kite flying is a favourite pastime in Wuhan.

The stretch of Jianghan Lu from behind the Customs House to Jinghan Dadao is the main shopping street. Much of it is pedestrianized and is lined with shops and boutiques bearing international brand names. Keep an eye open for the handful of beautiful slightly larger-than-life bronze sculptures along this street, particularly towards the embankment, that depict aspects of life in old Wuhan. A couple of men playing Chinese chess, for example, attract the attention of passers-by, who pause to discuss the various merits of the next moves.

In the evenings, nearby Jiqing Lu is transformed into a lively, brightly-lit outdoor food street. Restaurants fill the area with tables and chairs and serve local specialities to diners while they are entertained by licensed street musicians.

HANYANG

TEMPLE OF TRANQUILLITY (GUIYUAN SI)

This fine Zen Buddhist temple on Cuiwei Lu, where monks from the surrounding provinces gathered to study the scriptures, is 300 years old. The striking architectural complex includes Drum and Bell Towers, temple halls, the Luohan Hall and the Lotus Pond. The Luohan Hall contains 500 gold-painted wooden statues of Buddhist monk-saints; no two are the same. It is said the two sculptors employed on this task took nine years to complete it. The main hall has a statue of Sakyamuni Buddha which was carved from a single block of jade—a gift from Burma in 1935. The scripture collection includes the rare 7,000-volume Longcan Sutra. The temple runs a vegetarian restaurant for visitors.

QING CHUAN PAVILION (QING CHUAN GE)

The original pavilion was a 16th-century Ming-dynasty structure. The current pavilion is a 1983 reconstruction. The top floor of the pavilon offers a fine view of the Yangzi River and the Yellow Crane Tower, situated on the opposite bank.

LUTE PLATFORM (GUQIN TAI)

Opposite Turtle Hill (Gui Shan), which overlooks the Han River, is the Hanyang Workers' Cultural Palace Gardens, encompassing the charming Lute Platform, a small complex of courtyards, pavilions and gardens enclosed by a tiled wall. It was built in commemoration of two musicians, Yu Baiya and Zhong Ziqi, who lived 2,000 years ago. While visiting Hanyang, Yu played his lute but only Zhong understood and appreciated his performance. They became fast friends and arranged to meet again at the same time the following year. Yu returned only to find that his friend had died. At Zhong's grave, Yu played a farewell song and, vowing never again to use the instrument, broke it to pieces. This story has left an expression *zhi yin*, 'knows sound', meaning a very close friend who can hear your thoughts and emotions without needing to explain.

The Lute Platform is now a haven for Chinese opera lovers (mostly men) who gather on Sunday mornings to sip tea and listen to the performers. In the gardens, *wushu* and *taijiquan* (martial arts and exercise) classes are held. Paintings by local artists are on exhibition and for sale in the main hall. Nearby is a Qing memorial stone dedicated to the lute player.

WUCHANG

YELLOW CRANE TOWER (HUANG HE LOU)

On Snake Hill (She Shan) is the site of the ancient Yellow Crane Tower (Huang He Lou), widely celebrated by Chinese poets throughout the ages. Cranes are one of the traditional Chinese symbols of long life. The legend concerns a Daoist (Taoist) sage who flew away on a yellow crane to become an Immortal. The tower has been rebuilt many times. It has five levels covered with yellow tiles and supported by red columns. Being over 50 metres high, the top level offers a wonderful view of the entire Wuhan area. Beside the new Yellow Crane Tower (completed in 1986) is a white stupa that dates from the Yuan dynasty (1279–1368). A giant 'Peace Bell' ten meters high was added to the park behind the tower in 2000.

PROVINCIAL MUSEUM (HUBEI BOWUGUAN)

Off Donghu Lu, near East Lake, this excellent museum has a rich collection of artefacts excavated in the province and is highly recommended. Of special interest is a display of finds from the tomb of Marquis Yi of Zeng from the Warring States

Flood level marker from 1931, Wuhan

*Residents of Wuhan are ferried along the street outside the post office
by boat during the 1931 flood*

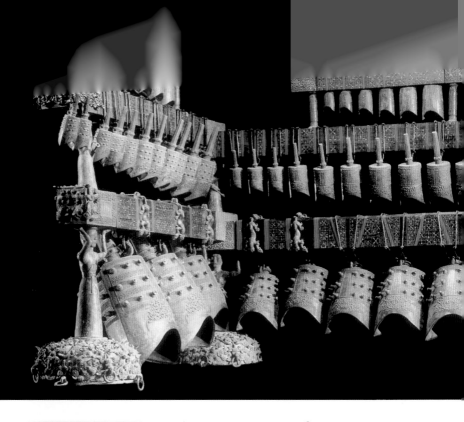

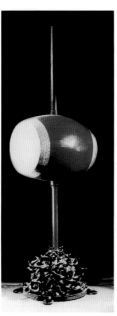

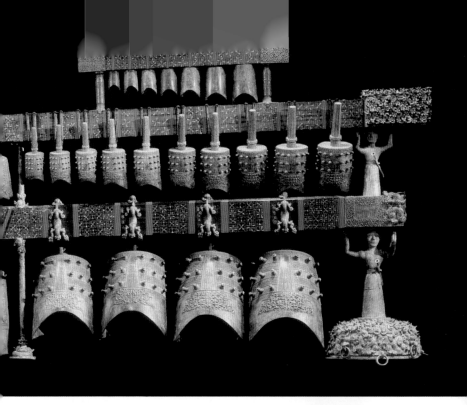

The highlight of the Hubei Provincial Museum is the collection of artefacts from the tomb of Zeng Hou Yi (Marquis Yi of Zeng) dating from the Warring States period (480–221 BC). The excavation took place in 1978 near Suizhou, a city in the north of Hubei Province, some 270 kilometres northwest of Wuhan. Over 15,000 relics were recovered from the tomb, including bronze ware, weapons, musical instruments, laquerware, gold vessels and jade objects.

The most significant discovery is the set of bronze chime bells, 65 in all, which hang in three tiers from a wooden and bronze stand (above). In the centre of the lower rack hangs the magnificent Bo bell (right). The 31 characters inscribed on its side explain its origin. When the king of the state of Chu heard of Zeng Hou Yi's death in 433 BC, he had the bell specially made for interment in the tomb. The intricately cast bronze stand (left) was designed to hold a 3.2-metre-tall wooden pillar which held the huge Jian drum, a reconstruction of which is shown (far left).

A pair of large bronze hu, or wine vessels, on a stand. A total of 117 well-preserved ritual bronze vessels were found in the tomb of Zeng Hou Yi, many of which are on display in the Hubei Provincial Museum, including the two excellent examples shown opposite.

A reproduction of a beautifully decorated horses helmet. The original, in lacquered leather, was preserved in perfect condition. The black lacquer was applied on both outside and inside. Several pieces of armour and thousands of weapons were unearthed from the tomb.

Exquisite bronze Zun (wine vessel) and Pan (plate). The Pan is 57.6 cm in diameter and 24 cm high. The Zun is 33.1 cm high. The vessel was made using a variety of techniques including whole founding, separate casting and welding. The hollowed-out ornaments are cast using the lost-wax method. One of the earliest examples of this technique discovered in China.

Bronze Jian and Fou (square inner container), decorated with hollowed-out or relief sculpture and dragons. The vessel, which is 63.3 centimetres high, acted as a wine cooler. Ice could be packed into the Jian which would cool the wine contained in the Fou.

period (480–221 BC). Among them is a set of 64 bronze chime bells. Replicas of these have been made and concerts of ancient music are given by a special chime-bells orchestra under the auspices of the Hubei Provincial Museum and Art Institute of Wuhan. The museum is open 8.30am–12.00 and 1.30–5pm.

HEADQUARTERS OF THE 1911 REVOLUTION (HONG LOU)

Known as the Red House, this building was the headquarters of the 1911 Revolution against the Manchu Qing dynasty, led by Dr Sun Yat-sen. Today, the building, in front of which stands a statue of Sun, is a museum to that revolution. It is located at the foot of She Shan on Wuluo Lu near the approach to the Yangzi River Bridge.

EAST LAKE (DONG HU)

A large scenic area, in the eastern suburbs of Wuchang, is centred on East Lake. Established in 1949, this enormous park covers 73 square kilometres of lake shore. The lake itself is six times the size of West Lake (Xi Hu) in Hangzhou. The park is full of natural beauty, containing over 372 plant varieties as well as more than 80 species of birds and fish. Around its shores are numerous pavilions, museums and halls, including a memorial to Qu Yuan, the third-century BC poet (see pages 355–7), and a monument (Jiu Nudun) to nine heroines who died fighting the Manchu troops during the Taiping Rebellion in the 19th century. A low causeway leads to Moshan Hill and its botanical gardens with views across the city and the beautiful countryside.

A cormorant fisherman with two of his birds greeting tourists in Wuhan

OLD MAN RIVER: CHAIRMAN MAO AND THE YANGZI

All his life Chairman Mao loved swimming and regarded it as the best of sports, the struggle of man against nature. The Yangzi had powerful associations for him. He grew up with the stories of the heroic battles of the Three Kingdoms period (AD 220–65) which took place along the Yangzi, and he often sailed the river. His luxurious boat, the *Kunlun*, later became a tourist vessel. A constant theme in his writings is the overcoming of natural and man-made obstacles through sheer determination and courage. As he once observed: 'The Yangzi is a big river, people say. It is big, but not frightening. Is imperialist America big? We challenged it; nothing happened. So, there are things in this world that are big but not frightening.'

Naturally the idea of taming the Yangzi greatly appealed to him. In his 1956 poem 'Swimming', written about the Yangzi, he dreams of a great bridge and a dam to reshape the river forever:

> *Great plans are afoot:*
> *A bridge will fly to span the north and south,*
> *Turning a deep chasm into a thoroughfare;*
> *Walls of stone will stand upstream to the west*
> *To hold back Wushan's clouds and rain*
> *Till a smooth lake rises in the narrow gorges.*
> *The mountain goddess if she is still there*
> *Will marvel at a world so changed.*

He was referring to the bridge at Wuhan linking Hanyang and Wuchang, whose opening he presided at a few months later in 1957, naming it 'Iron and Steel Rainbow'. Mao expected that the Three Gorges Dam would soon follow, but fierce controversy over the project delayed his dream until 1993, when work was finally begun.

In 1956, 1958 and again most famously in 1966, Mao made a series of highly publicized long swims across the Yangzi at Wuhan (the above poem was written after the first of these). These were all years when Mao felt that his position was threatened by rumours of bad health and by the machinations of his enemies. Swimming the Yangzi was his way of showing the world that he was still healthy and in command; that he could keep his head above water, so to speak.

The celebrated 1966 swim, when Mao was 73, was part of the launch of the Cultural Revolution and the cult of Mao as a superhuman figure. Power struggles had been going on behind the scenes. Mao's whereabouts were kept secret and he had appeared in public only once all year. There were rumours that he was gravely ill or even dead. Then came the 16 July swim. Accompanying 5,000 young swimmers in the annual race across the river at Wuhan, he is reported to have swum almost 15 kilometres (nine miles) in 65 minutes, swimming along with the currents. Pictures of Mao's head bobbing above the water, surrounded by swimmers carrying huge banners celebrating his achievement, were seen not only throughout China but around the world. The message was clear; even in his 70s, Mao was a force to be reckoned with.

The Wuhan steel mill, one of the country's largest, was constructed in 1957 and employs over 120,000 workers

河 清 有 日

Several times between mid-August and early September 1971 Mao visited major cities along the Yangzi River, including Wuhan, to meet local government officials with a mission to criticize Lin Biao, the deputy national chairman

BAOTONG SI
A Buddhist temple located on the slopes of Hong Shan. It features a Grand Hall, Meditation Hall and Abbots Hall. There are two gargantuan iron bells here, almost 900 years old, dating back to the Southern Song Dynasty. It is located inside Hongshan Park.

CHANG CHUN TAOIST TEMPLE (CHANG CHUN GUAN)
The largest and best-preserved Taoist temple in Wuhan. The temple consists of numerous corridors and stone staircases with grand eaves and arches. Decorating the halls are life-sized carvings and niches. Most of the religious relics were destroyed during the Cultural Revolution. Since restoration, the temple now displays a wide range of Taoist cultural relics. It is located in the Dadongmen area, near the intersection of Zhongshan Lu and Wuluo Lu.

WUHAN UNIVERSITY (WUHAN DAXUE)
Founded in 1913, it is still considered one of the best universities in the country. Its campus displays many examples of pre-1949 Chinese architecture. It is located at the foot of Luo Jia Shan near Dong Hu.

QIZHOU

About one hour's sailing east of Huangshi, the industrial and iron ore mining city below Wuhan, is the small town of Qizhou. Though it has a history of 1,000 years, it is famous as the home town of Li Shizhen (1518–93), a Ming-dynasty herbalist and physician. After practising Chinese medicine in his youth, Li spent 30 years rewriting and categorizing ancient Chinese medical books, travelling far and wide in search of specimens. His treatise formed 52 scrolls, with almost 2,000 entries. Sadly, he died before receiving recognition. However, his son presented a copy of Li's work to Emperor Wanli (1573–1620), a patron of scholarship. The emperor, much pleased with the work, ordered its wide distribution. Li Shizhen's classical works are the basis of traditional Chinese medical practice today and have been translated into a number of foreign languages.

The graves of Li Shizhen and his wife are situated at Rain Lake, north of the town, surrounded by gardens of medicinal herbs.

The local bamboo is used for making summer bed mats, and flutes made from this bamboo were widely praised as early as the Tang dynasty. Qizhou's White Flower Snake medicine is supposed to relieve rheumatic pains, while its Green Hairy-backed Turtles are used in medicines that allegedly cure tuberculosis and body fluid deficiencies.

About halfway between Qizhou and Jiujiang, the river leaves Hubei Province and thenceforth marks the provincial boundary between Hubei to the north and Jiangxi to the south as far as the mouth of Poyang Lake.

JIUJIANG

Though the capital of Jiangxi Province is Nanchang, Jiujiang is the main port for distributing products from Poyang Lake and the surrounding counties as well as much of the chinaware produced at the porcelain capital of Jingdezhen. It has the reputation of being the hottest port on the Yangzi, with extremely oppressive summers. Though once an important tea-buying centre in its own right, it was gradually superseded by Wuhan, and tea grown in Jiangxi was shipped either upstream to Wuhan or downstream to Shanghai. Today, cotton textiles form Jiujiang's main industry.

Jiujiang is the main access city to one of China's most famous mountain beauty spots, Lushan, lying only a short distance to the south, which attracts millions of tourists a year.

Reinforcing the banks of the Yangzi near Wuhan in 1983. Cities, towns, villages and farmland along the middle and lower reaches of the river have been under a constant threat of flooding for centuries. One of the main goals of the Three Gorges Dam is to eliminate this threat.

HISTORY OF JIUJIANG

In ancient times, nine rivers were said to have converged at this point, hence the name Jiujiang—'Nine Rivers'—though it was also called Jiangzhou and Xunyang. In its long history it has seen many upheavals; in the last century it was a Taiping stronghold from which the rebels held out against the imperial Qing armies for five years.

The area holds many memories for lovers of Chinese poetry. Tao Yuanming (365–429) lived at the foot of Lushan and was appointed magistrate of nearby Pengze County. This post was so poorly endowed that, rather than work 'for five pecks of grain to break one's back', he resigned after 83 days, preferring to eke out a living as a recluse in his home village. His essay *Peach Flower Garden* depicts his idea of a perfect society. Li Bai (701–62), implicated in the An Lushan Rebellion, was imprisoned briefly in Jiujiang in 757. Bai Juyi (772–846) also spent a period of official disgrace here as a middle-ranking official and is affectionately remembered. His poem *The Lute Song* tells of his sadness at his isolation in this small town. Su Dongpo was a frequent visitor to the area.

When Jiujiang was thrown open as a treaty port in 1862 it had suffered terribly as a consequence of the Taiping Rebellion (1850–64, see pages 456–7). A British member of Lord Elgin's mission noted in 1858:

We found it to the last degree deplorable. A single dilapidated street, composed only of a few mean shops, was all that existed of this once thriving and populous city: the remainder of the vast area, composed within walls five or six miles in circumference, contained nothing but ruins, weeds, and kitchen gardens.

Jiujiang was once one of the three centres of the tea trade in China, along with Hankou and Fuzhou. There were two Russian factories producing brick-tea, but these ceased to operate after 1917. The British concession in Jiujiang was given up in 1927 after looting by mutineering garrisons and mobs.

Economic recession set in by the 1880s with greater competition from tea producers in India and Ceylon. With the military advance downriver from Wuhan led by the Guomindang in 1927, the remaining foreign community fled on British and American warships to the safety of Shanghai, never to return. Jiujiang was surrendered officially by Britain in 1927.

WHAT TO SEE IN JIUJIANG

Sycamore trees line the streets of Jiujiang. The old downtown area is not large, sandwiched between Gantang Lake and the river bank. The old foreign concession area abuts the riversteamer dock and some old buildings remain—a church, the old French hospital and the Council House (now the Bank of China).

Crunchy, sweet Jiujiang tea biscuits made from tea oil, sesame and orange osmanthus flower date from the Song dynasty; so did the potent, strange-tasting local wine, Fenggang Jiu, made from glutinous rice and fermented in sealed vats for five years.

GAN TANG LAKE (GAN TANG HU) AND YANSHUI PAVILION (YAN SHUI TING)

Gantang Lake was divided into two by a dyke and bridge built in 821 during the Tang dynasty. Sixian Bridge, now enlarged, still stands on the causeway which one crosses to reach Yangyue Pavilion on the low hill overlooking the lake. It is well stocked with silver and grass carp, and seagulls skim its surface. It is said that in the Three Kingdoms period (220–265) the Eastern Wu general, Zhou Yu, inspected his warships from a reviewing platform on the lake, traces of which remain.

Linked to the shore by a zigzag bridge is the pretty Yanshui (Misty Water) Pavilion. A pavilion was first built here in the Tang dynasty (618–907) by the poet Bai Juyi during his unhappy posting in Jiujiang. It was named the Drenched Moon Pavilion after a line from one of his poems: 'Bidding farewell I saw the moon drenched by the river.'

In the Northern Song period (960–1127) a highly regarded Neo-Confucian philosopher, Zhou Dun, taught in Jiujiang and his son built a pavilion on the lake to his father's memory, calling it Yanshui Pavilion. The present island pavilion dates from the late Qing period (1644–1911). One small hall is dedicated to Bai Juyi, and other rooms display local archaeological discoveries. The city's antiques store is located here.

NENG REN TEMPLE (NENG REN SI)
The Qing halls here are the oldest buildings left in Jiujiang, although this Yuan-dynasty Buddhist temple was established earlier, in the sixth century. Three or four monks and several nuns tend the temple. The seven-storey Great Victory Pagoda, beside the temple, dates from the Song period (960–1279).

SUO JIANG PAGODA (SUO JIANG TA)
This hexagonal seven-storey pagoda, overlooking the Yangzi embankment to the north-east of the city, was built in 1585. Damage to the 35-metre high pagoda caused by shelling from Japanese gunboats in World War II is still visible.

WAVE WELL (LANG JING)
Near the waterfront is a small ancient well with a quaint history. Dug early in the Han dynasty (206 BC–AD 220), it connected with the Yangzi so that when a wind created waves on the river the surface of the well water would ripple too. The well became clogged and disused over the years until it was rediscovered in the third century, and the original inscription and date were uncovered. This was such a good omen that the well was renamed Auspicious Well. The poet Li Bai in the eighth century referred to it as the Wave Well in one of his poems, as did Su Dongpo.

DONG LIN TEMPLE (DONG LIN SI)
Twenty-two kilometres southwest of Jiujiang at the foot of Lushan is the Donglin (Eastern Forest) Temple, built in 386 for the monk Hui Yuan (334–416), founder of the Pure Land sect of Buddhism, whose overgrown grave is behind the temple. He spent many years translating Buddhist scriptures, and among his 123 disciples were an Indian and a Nepali. The temple reached its zenith in the Tang dynasty (618–907), with a vast library of scriptures and over 300 halls and residences. Seriously damaged during the Taiping Rebellion (1850–64), the temple was almost ruined in the Republican period (1911–49). Today there is a community of monks who hold daily services in the temple halls. Behind the temple in a bamboo grove is the Well of Intelligence—from which every visitor is anxious for a sip. The Luohan Pine trees in the courtyard are said to have been planted by Hui Yuan himself. Hui

Yuan is also said to have struck the ground with his staff, causing the Ancient Dragon Spring to gush forth, thus proving his right to establish himself here. Nearby is the Xi Lin Pagoda(Xi Lin Ta), all that remains of an earlier temple complex.

LUSHAN

Lushan, in the vicinity of Jiujiang, has always been appreciated by the Chinese as a mountain of great beauty and as a haven from the intense humid heat of the Yangzi valley summers. Its views eastwards to Poyang Lake and northward across the river are spectacular. Guesthouses and sanatoriums (over 1,000 of them) abound in the Guling valley.

April and May are the best times to visit, when the hills are covered with wild azalea and peach blossoms, and there are many waterfalls. In the enervating months of June, July and August, the average temperature on Lushan is a comfortable 23°C (73°F), and during this peak season 35,000 tourists visit each day. In autumn the numbers drop off markedly and one is able to enjoy the changing autumnal colours of the trees at leisure, though the waterfalls dry up.

The town of Guling was established at the end of the 19th century by foreign traders and missionaries as a summer retreat for their families from as far away as Shanghai. They built over 100 summer bungalows and an American hospital (now the Lushan Guesthouse). They would be carried by sedan chair along the narrow path up the mountainside. Today the town is almost perfectly preserved. Chiang Kai-shek's summer house—Meilu Villa—is still there near the lake, Lu Lin Hu, as is his library which now houses the Lushan Museum. Beside this is Lushan People's Theatre where in 1959 the Communist Party of China held its eighth plenary session, known later as the Lushan Conference, which resulted in the dismissal of the People's Liberation Army Commander-in-Chief, Peng Dehuai. In December 1926, the Guomindang held an important party conference at the same place to mediate between the rival Wuhan and Nanjing factions. Two more important party conferences were held there in 1959 and 1970. The Botanical Garden (Zhi Wu Yuan) was established in 1934; it has more than 4,000 kinds of flowers, trees and other plants.

Strange rock shapes, sheer peaks (the highest, Dahanyang is 1,543 metres), steep cliffs, overhangs and caves, as well as a wide variety of lovely trees, are some of the splendours of Lushan. Its mystery is captured by Su Dongpo, who wrote:

It's a ridge when looked at face to face,
It's a peak when looked at sidewise;
It's always not the same when looked at from afar or near, when looked at

from above or below.
You don't know what Lushan is really like,
Merely because you yourself are living in it.

Special Lushan dishes are the small Stone Fish from the Xilin River (best eaten in spring and autumn), Stone Ear (a black fungus), and Stone Chicken (a black-skinned frog found in the damp caves on Lushan, tasting rather like chicken and best eaten between June and September), as well as fish from Poyang Lake.

Lushan's Misty Cloud Green Tea (Yunwu Lu Cha), once sent as tribute to the emperors, should be sampled. The tea leaves are processed seven times to obtain their special fragrance.

Stone Bell Hill (Shizhong Shan)

After taking a small vehicular ferry across the mouth of Poyang Lake to Hukou, one may climb the small, 50-metre high Stone Bell Hill, to which visitors have been coming for centuries. The hill overlooks the lake and the Yangzi River, and the meeting of the waters is clearly defined by an abrupt colour change. Mystery surrounds the strange bell-like sound that can be heard at Stone Bell Hill. There are three theories: that the hill is shaped like a bell and is hollow inside; that the rock, when struck, rings like a bell; or that the water, lapping into the nooks and crannies around the base, causes a bell-like sound. Su Dongpo made three special trips to try to solve the mystery, and having eventually settled on the last explanation, wrote an essay on the subject.

The present buildings date from the mid-19th century when the Taiping rebel commander Shi Dakai, choosing the mouth of the lake as a defensive position, built a stronghold on the hill, occupying it between 1853 and 1857. The Qing armies, miscalculating their enemy's strength, entered the lake in their war-junks, where upon the Taipings stretched ropes across the lake mouth, dividing the Qing navy into two and routing them. The Qing general, Zeng Guofan, utterly humiliated, attempted to drown himself but was rescued by his retinue. The remains of the Taiping army stronghold can still be seen, and a pavilion on the hillside contains a stone tablet dedicated by Zeng Guofan to those who lost their lives in that battle (see pages 456–7).

Peng Yulin, also a Qing general, later built a wonderful villa here with winding balconies, small ponds, carved pavilions and exquisite gardens. The lovely two-storeyed Plum Flower Hall (Meihua Ting) was erected in memory of the cultivated young woman he loved but could not marry. She died of a broken heart and he painted 11,000 pictures of plum flowers with her in mind.

Bamboo raft on the middle reaches of the Yangzi River in Hubei Province. These huge rafts are disassembled and sold in markets on the lower reaches and used as construction scaffolding

This hill is also called the Lower Stone Bell Hill to distinguish it from the Upper Stone Bell Hill nearby. There is a delightful legend about the formation of these two small hills. The supreme Daoist (Taoist) deity, the Jade Emperor, instructed one of his officials to find two bells suitable for his palace. The official searched everywhere until he finally found two stone hills shaped like bells. He was delivering them to the palace when his carrying pole broke at the mouth of Poyang Lake; the stone hills fell to the ground and have remained there ever since.

DRAGON PALACE CAVE

Sixty-seven kilometres east of Jiujiang, this 1,700-metre long natural cave is in the scenic surroundings of Dark Dragon Hill (Wulong Shan), in Pengze County, Jiangxi Province. This natural beauty spot comprises eight adjoining caverns with interior limestone formations resembling palace lanterns, dragon thrones, boats and other objects. One section is called the East Sea Dragon Palace after the classic 16th-century Chinese novel *Pilgrimage to the West* (sometimes known as *The Monkey King*). Coloured lighting heightens the effect.

POYANG LAKE

The surface area of China's largest freshwater lake is around 5,000 square kilometres, increasing in size during the flood season and shrinking in winter. Five rivers flow into the lake and eight counties border it. The Yangzi, Poyang Lake and the Gan River form a link, via the Meiling Pass on the border between Jiangxi and Guangdong provinces, as far south as Guangzhou. Coupled with the Grand Canal, from Hangzhou north to Beijing, this formed the Imperial Way, a 3,500-kilometre trade and communications route that ran the length of the country. Vital to the survival of the empire, it was in use from the time of Kublai Khan and the beginning of the Yuan dynasty in 1279, until the appearance of the railways at the beginning of the 20th century.

From ancient times, this fertile region has been one of the 'rice-bowls' of China. The Poyang teems with fish, such as mandarin, anchovy and whitebait. It continues to fulfil its age-old function as a transport link for local produce—grain, tea, silk, bamboo, and particularly the porcelain from the kaolin (white clay) potteries of Jingdezhen, which have been producing since the second century BC, and supplying the imperial court from the fifth century on.

A 22,000-hectare (54,000-acre) nature reserve has been established in the vicinity of Wucheng on the western side of the lake. It hosts Asia's greatest bird spectacle in winter, when over 4,000 cranes, 40,000 swan geese and around a quarter of a million ducks flock here. Over 90 per cent of the world's population of the Siberian Crane winter at the reserve. Numbers have increased dramatically since the area became a protected reserve, with 1,700 Siberian cranes counted in 1988.

Owing to the lake's strategic importance, numerous naval encounters took place on its waters. Emperor Wudi (reigned 420–23) was embattled here. It was the site of a decisive battle in the overthrow of the Yuan dynasty in the 14th century. Another naval battle was fought between the Taiping rebels and the Qing imperial forces in 1855.

Local fairy tales connect a small island in the lake, Shoe Hill or Dagu Shan, with the stories of Xiaogu Shan (see below) further downstream. It seems that Xiaogu Niang Niang and her betrothed escaped from her Emei Shan prison with the help of a precious umbrella. The pursuing Immortal, confronting them at Poyang Lake, threw his flying sword at the precious umbrella and, in her confusion, Xiaogu Niang Niang lost one of her embroidered slippers, which fell into the lake and was transformed into a shoe-shaped island.

XIAOGU SHAN

About 35 kilometres below the mouth of the Poyang, the magical little island of Xiaogu Shan comes into view. It is situated by the north bank of the Yangzi in Anhui Province, while across the river is the county town of Pengze in Jiangxi.

The white walls and grey-tile roofs of Qisu Temple nestle into Xiaogu Shan's steep slope, and pavilions adorn its bamboo-groved peak. A handful of elderly monks inhabit the temple (first established in the Song dynasty, 907–1279), which is dedicated to Xiaogu Niang Niang, and visited by childless women offering incense to her.

As a result of silt accumulation, Xiaogu Shan now adjoins the riverbank. The characters 'First Pass of the Sea Gate' are painted on the rock face. Stairs lead up to the temple, but to reach the peak one must cling to chains fixed to the rock to negotiate the steep climb.

The island is named after the legendary Lin Xiaogu, later known as Xiaogu Niang Niang, who grew up in Fujian Province and became betrothed to a local village lad, Peng Liang. Unhappily, her parents died, and she was adopted by a Daoist (Taoist) Immortal at Mount Emei in Sichuan Province, where she studied Daoism for many years. One day, while gathering herbs on the mountain, she slipped and fell, and was saved by a wandering woodcutter who was none other than Peng Liang. Peng's mother, attending to the girl's injuries, noticed a small birthmark behind her ear and recognized her as the long-lost Lin Xiaogu. In renewing her betrothal to Peng Liang, Xiaogu broke her religious vows and was incarcerated by the Immortal.

With the help of a sympathetic monk she stole the Immortal's precious umbrella, and the lovers flew away. However, the pursuing Immortal cut off their escape at Poyang Lake with his flying sword, which tore the umbrella and caused Xiaogu to drop her slipper (see page 111). At Pengze the umbrella finally split in two. The lovers fell on different sides of the Yangzi, turning into two steep hills: Pengliang Ji on the south and Xiaogu Shan on the north. The temple on Pengliang Ji was destroyed in the Cultural Revolution (1966–76).

At the top of Xiaogu Shan is her 'Make-up and Dressing Terrace'. A stone tablet beside it describes her story, as well as a related anecdote concerning Zhu Yuanzhong, founder of the Ming dynasty in 1368, who was saved by the appearance of Xiaogu Niang Niang while retreating downstream one night after a naval defeat.

About 32 kilometres below Pengze the river enters Anhui and winds its way northeast across the province until, just below Ma'anshan, it enters the province of Jiangsu. Bulk carriers, strings of barges and fishing sampans—their nets attached to long bamboo poles extending forward and aft—frequent the stretch of river between here and Anqing, about three hours' sailing downriver. The south bank is hilly while the north bank is flat, broken only by trees and bamboo groves. A number of shallow lakes feed into the river.

ANQING

The city of Anqing, on the north bank, is situated in that area of Anhui Province called Huainan, meaning south of the Huai River. It is built along the Dalong Hills amidst pretty surroundings. Historical records refer to the appointment of an official to the town as early as the Spring and Autumn period (770–476 BC). During the Qing dynasty (1644–1911) and the Republican period (1911–49) the city was the capital of the province, though today the capital is Hefei, further north. Anqing's main function is to gather and distribute local produce; it also has a petrochemical industry.

The handsome octagonal Zhenfeng Pagoda, the major landmark, was built in 1570 amidst the remains of the Song-dynasty Welcoming the River Temple (Yingjiang Si). A fine view of the city can be enjoyed from its top storey.

The pagoda was built by a Daoist (Taoist) architect, Zhang Wencai, who was brought to Anqing specially from Baiyun Temple in Beijing. Stone balconies surround six of its seven storeys. Inside, over 600 Buddha images cover the brick walls.

Set into the lower half of the pagoda are images of the local prefect, Wang Erquan, who commissioned its construction, and other personages of the period.

The town was occupied by the Taiping rebels for six years, and one of its kings built a residence here. It seems that the imperial defences of Anqing left much to be desired, for when it fell to the rebels in 1853 Emperor Xianfeng wrote: 'Great has been my indignation on reading the memorial... how could that important provincial capital be captured by the bandits in one day?' The city, retaken in 1861, was ravaged. Travellers to the city 60 years later noted that large parts of it were still in ruins.

Riverboats stop at Guichi (at the mouth of the Qiupu River), which is the closest Yangzi port for those visiting the sacred Buddhist mountain of Jiuhua and the famous scenic area of Huangshan to the south. These can be reached by bus, although Wuhu, further downriver, offers more choice of transport.

WUHU

Wuhu, on the south bank of the river, is in southeastern Anhui Province at the confluence of the Qingyi and Yangzi Rivers. Its population is only 440,000, not large by Chinese standards. In the last century, Wuhu was one of the four great rice-marketing centres (the others being Wuxi, Jiujiang and Changsha), but it is now principally a producer of light-industrial goods, such as thermos flasks, machine tools, cotton textiles, kitschy mantlepiece clocks and cement. It is specially known for its scissors, its variety of local twig and leaf brooms and its wrought-iron pictures.

As a good transportation system links Wuhu with other parts of the province, the city is a transfer stop for visitors to the famous scenic spots of Huangshan and Jiuhua. However, this is the farthest up the Yangzi River valley you can travel by train from Shanghai and Nanjing. From here the train line travels north to Hefei.

HISTORY OF WUHU

In the Spring and Autumn period (770–476 BC) the city was known as Jiuzi. Its present name was adopted in the Han dynasty (206 BC–AD 220). By the Three Kingdoms period (220–65 AD, see page 42) it had become a strategically important town in the Kingdom of Eastern Wu. In a fierce battle between the Kingdoms of Eastern Wu and Shu, the Wu general Zhou Yu was killed. The King of Wu, Sun Quan, donned white mourning clothes and made a special journey to Wuhu to receive Zhou Yu's coffin.

In the Tang dynasty (618–907) the poet Du Fu's many visits were recollected in his poem, Thoughts on Staying Again at Wuhu. When Wuhu became a treaty port under the Chefoo (Yan Tai) Convention of 1876 a small foreign community resided here. Trading principally in rice, wood and tea, it had become a flourishing commercial port by the end of the 19th century. Trade dropped off severely in the 1920s and 1930s due to bandit activity in the area. When the city was captured by the Guomindang army in March 1927, anti-foreign riots broke out. The foreign community had to be evacuated by warships patrolling the Yangzi.

WHAT TO SEE IN WUHU

There is little of historical interest to be found in Wuhu, but a stroll along the east embankment of the Qingyi River is worthwhile. Here barges and small boats load and discharge vegetables, fruit, sand and everyday items; boat families and their pets add to the cacophony of noise. Bamboo rafts, at intervals along the river's edge, serve as platforms for the local women to do their washing. In the narrow streets parallel to the river, such as Zhongchang Jie and Shangchang Jie, shops sell fishing tackle and nets, baskets, firecrackers, bamboo steamers, and Chinese weights and measures. In the cobbled streets, bamboo chicken coops stand outside front doors that open into dark, high-ceilinged old houses. Xinwu Jie, running west off the main street, Zhongshan Jie, is busy with restaurants and food stalls serving crispy rice cakes, sweet dumpling soup and large dough fritters. Near the scruffy memorial to the 1949 revolution is Jiuhe Jie, which is now a market area. At No 26 a huge, fanciful, American-built Catholic Church, dating from the treaty port days, is open for worship on Sundays. At Jinghu Lake, in the town centre, people gather to play cards or chess and to sell their miniature potted plants.

ZHE HILL

The highest point in the city is only 86 metres, but the view from the pagoda at the top sweeps over the whole city and down the Yangzi. It seems that this five-storey Zheshan Pagoda and the Mid-River Pagoda (see below) were built at the same time, at the beginning of the Song dynasty (960–1279). A competition apparently developed between the two teams of builders. The two brothers engaged in the construction of Zheshan Pagoda, who were desperate to complete first and so avoid losing face, finished off the very top with a cooking wok turned upside down. A small zoo is to be found in the public park.

GUANGJI TEMPLE

Of the four main temples which existed in Wuhu, three were destroyed in the Sino-Japanese War and only the Guangji Temple, at the foot of Zhe Hill, remains. The main hall is hung with ten scrolls depicting the Buddhist Hell. The temple was established in the Tang dynasty (618–907) and Emperor Dezong (reigned 780–5) came here as a monk. When omens indicated that this was an unsafe place for him to reside, he went to live on the famous Buddhist mountain of Jiuhua, further south.

MID-RIVER PAGODA (ZHONG JIANG TA)

This six-storey pagoda stands at the point where the Qingyi River enters the Yangzi, a danger spot for navigation. A local fisherman named Huang suggested that this octagonal pagoda be built to serve as a lighthouse. Its name derives from its position—it is exactly in the middle of the lower reaches of the Yangzi.

WUHU ARTS AND CRAFTS FACTORY

The art of wrought-iron picture-making originated in Wuhu and this factory in Jiuhua Lu continues the tradition, besides producing pictures made of feathers or golden wheat stalks, poker-burned wooden decorations and copies of old paintings.

Iron picture-making is very laborious and amazingly intricate. This art form was started by an itinerant blacksmith, Tang Tianchi, during the reign of Emperor Kangxi (1662–1723). Tang used to sit and watch a local painter, whose work he much admired. The artist chided Tang: 'I paint my pictures, you beat your iron, but you will never make pictures by beating iron.' Tang promptly went away and produced an iron picture, 'using a hammer as a brush and iron as ink'.

A huge 'Welcoming Pine' iron picture by the artists of Wuhu adorns the Anhui Room in the Great Hall of the People in Beijing.

Wuhu, a city in Anhui Province along the lower Yangzi as it appeared in 1986. As one of the four major rice markets of China, the port is busy with boats and barges of all sizes. This stretch of the river is also home to the endangered Yangzi alligator.

STAGE IV

THE COASTAL DELTA REGION: MA'ANSHAN TO SHANGHAI

The deltaic plain of coastal Jiangsu—the most densely populated of China's provinces—is a veritable maze of natural waterways, man-made dykes and canals. Mulberry trees line their banks and humpbacked stone bridges link the picturesque towns and villages. These waterways serve as irrigation channels, drainage outlets and transport canals. Three staple grain crops—two of paddy rice and one of winter wheat—are harvested each year. Since earliest times, sericulture has been an important economic factor, and though cotton replaced silk in importance after the 1930s, silkworm breeding is still a major home industry and hard-cash earner for peasant families. Sericulture formed the basis on which the region's famous textile cities of Hangzhou, Suzhou, Wuxi, Nanjing and Shanghai were established.

Water conservation plans are underway to divert water from the Yangzi northwards, linking up with similar projects on the Huai River, which will eventually irrigate the large arid areas of north China.

Neolithic rice-growing cultures occupied this area as early as 5000 BC, domesticating pigs and dogs. By the fifth century BC much of the lower Yangzi formed one of nine huge provincial areas known as Yangzhou; its imperial tribute included silks, fruits and timber. During the Tang dynasty (618–907) the city of Yangzhou was the main port of call for Arabian traders.

The town of Jiangyin demarcates the estuary, and for the next 200 kilometres the Yangzi widens from 1,200 metres to 91 kilometres below the confluence with the Huangpu, the last of its tributaries. In ancient times the Yangzi was said to have had three mouths; down the centuries the river outlet was a source of much

The morning's fishing completed, a fisherman near Nanjing in Jiangsu Province wheels his small craft home. His trained cormorants perch obediently on the boat preening themselves. This fishing method is still practised in areas along the Yangzi River.

academic speculation in China, as silt deposits continually changed the shape and form of the river's mouth. Now its outlet to the Yellow Sea is divided into two by the intensely cultivated island of Chongming (1,083 square kilometres in area) and by several smaller islands, whose farming produce supplies the massive Shanghai area. In August 1983, when low-lying land in 30 Anhui counties that border the Yangzi was inundated by flood waters, nearly a million peasants battled to drain the land and sow autumn crops. Ninety people were reported dead and hundreds injured as the flood crest swept by. In Jiangsu, 500,000 civilians and soldiers reinforced dykes and stood watch as floods threatened Nanjing and other cities along the banks. Luckily no further serious damage occurred, although similar flooding claimed hundreds more lives in 1998.

MA'ANSHAN

Anhui's biggest industrial city, Ma'anshan mines much of the pig iron used in the Shanghai steel industry. It also has its own iron and steel works, limestone quarries, and chemical and cement factories. The city is linked to Wuhu and Nanjing by rail.

A touching story is told of the city's name, which means Horse Saddle Hill. When the Kingdoms of Chu and Shu were at war in the third century, General Xiang Yu of Chu was defeated by Liu Bei and attempted to retreat to Wujiang on the north bank of the Yangzi. Finding only a small boat, he had his precious mount ferried across first. At this moment Liu Bei's pursuing soldiers arrived and Xiang Yu, knowing he was trapped, cut his throat with his own sword. Seeing his master's courageous suicide, the horse leapt into the river and drowned. The boatman buried its saddle on the nearby hill.

Buildings on Coloured Stone Cliff (Caishi Ji), west of the city, commemorate the Tang poet, Li Bai (701–62). The three-storeyed Taibai Lou houses two Chinese boxwood statues of the poet, one depicting his immortal gesture of inviting the moon to join him in a cup of wine. Here too is the 'Tomb of Li Bai's Clothes and Official Hat'. According to the local legend, Li Bai's clothing was buried on Caishi Ji when he drowned after falling drunkenly from a boat one evening while attempting to embrace the moon's reflection in the river.

The Three Scholars Grotto (Sanyuan Dong) was allegedly built by three grateful gentlemen who, on their way to the capital to take the imperial examinations, found safety and shelter under the cliff when their boat was caught in a sudden and violent storm. After all three had gained first-class honours and promotions, they recalled their close shave and donated funds for the building of this grotto.

Nanjing

Nanjing—'Southern Capital'—along with Luoyang, Xi'an and Beijing, is one of the historical capitals of China, and the many imperial tombs and architectural remains in the city and its environs reflect its grandiose past. Today, the city is the capital of Jiangsu Province. Its industries include machine-building, automobile assembly, electronics, petroleum, iron and steel, textiles, shipbuilding and foodstuffs. A double-tiered road and rail bridge, completed in 1968, as well as a sleek road bridge, completed in 2001, span the Yangzi at Nanjing.

There is a visible military presence in Nanjing. Soldiers may approach you and gesture to not take photographs of that location. Many buildings and compounds in Nanjing are military areas and are not open to the public.

History Of Nanjing

With the Yangzi on one side, and surrounded on the other three sides by hills, Nanjing was thought to be auspicious as well as strategically important. First historical records date from the Spring and Autumn period (770–476 BC) when the area was divided between the Kingdoms of Wu, Yue and Chu. A walled town was built during the Eastern Han period (AD 25–220), known as 'Stone City'.

Between the third and 14th centuries, eight dynasties established their capitals in the city, some of them building magnificent palaces and forts. Though many of these minor dynasties had incompetent rulers and regimes weakened by intrigue and debauchery, Nanjing emerged as a cultural centre of painting, philosophy and Buddhism. In the sixth century, the Sui dynasty established its capital at Xi'an, and ordered the complete destruction of earlier dynastic buildings in Nanjing.

The city flourished again during the Tang dynasty (618–907), when the great poets Li Bai, Bai Juyi and Liu Yuxi lived here for a while. For a brief period, Nanjing (then called Jinling) became the capital of the Southern Song, but the dynastic base had to be moved to Hangzhou as the pursuing Nuzhen Tartar armies advanced. Marco Polo may have visited the city in 1275.

The founder of the Ming dynasty, Hongwu (Zhu Yuanzhang), captured Nanjing in 1356 and set up his capital here, building palaces, temples and pagodas. (The famous green- and white-glazed-tile Porcelain Pagoda of the Bao'en Temple, so often praised as one of the seven wonders of the world by earlier travellers, belonged to this period, though it was totally destroyed during the Taiping Rebellion (1850–64). Some of its tiles are on exhibition at the Nanjing City Museum.) He also enlarged the city wall to make it the longest in the world. Earlier Tang-dynasty poets had written lyrically of being entertained on 'singsong boats'—sort of floating bordellos—along the Qinhuai (a ten-kilometre, man-made river, said to have been dug during the second century BC, skirting the western and southern edges of Nanjing). A picture of more innocent pleasures is conjured up by a passage from The Scholars, an early 18th-century novel by Wu Ching-tzu:

After the middle of the fourth month in Nanking, the Chin-huai River becomes quite lovely. The barges from other tributaries of the Yangtze dismantle their cabins, set up awnings, and paddle into the river. Each vessel carries a small, square, gilt-lacquered table, set with an Yihsing stoneware pot, cups of the finest Cheng Hua or Hsuan Te porcelain, and the choicest tea brewed with rain water. Boating parties bring wine, dishes and sweetmeats with them to the canal, and even people travelling by boat order a few cents' worth of good tea to drink on board as they proceed slowly on their way. At dusk two bright horn lanterns on each vessel are reflected in the water as the barges ply to and fro, so that above and below are bright. Fluting and singing are heard all night and every night from Literary Virtue Bridge to Lucky Crossing Bridge and East Water Guardhouse. The pleasure-goers buy water-rat fireworks too, which project from the water and look like pear trees in blossom when let off. The fun goes on till the fourth watch each night.

Translated by Yang Hsien-yi and Gladys Yang

During the Ming dynasty (1368–1644), an imperial decree established a special government department to oversee brothels which catered to the 200,000 troops garrisoned in the city. The capital was moved to Beijing in 1420, but Nanjing remained a subsidiary capital and financial centre. In the Qing dynasty (1644–1911) troops were also garrisoned in the city.

The Treaty of Nanking (Nanjing) ending the Opium War of (1839–1842) was signed aboard HMS Cornwallis between the British and the Chinese. It ceded the territory of Hong Kong to Britain, opened five Chinese ports to foreign trade, and exacted a payment of 21 million Mexican dollars as indemnity from the Chinese. It was the first of what became known as the Unequal Treaties. The pseudo-Christian Taiping Rebellion made its headquarters in Nanjing in 1853 and occupied it for 11 years (see pages 456–7). Its leader, Hong Xiuquan, adopted the title 'Heavenly King' and appointed other leaders as Princes of the East, West, North and South'. The 'Heavenly King' built a large palace of which little now remains. The city was almost completely destroyed in the devastation and killings that followed the overthrow of this rebellion. Nanjing became a treaty port under the terms of the 1876 Chefoo (Yantai) Convention.

Following the revolution of 1911, Nanjing was declared the capital of the Republic of China in 1912. (Dr Sun Yat-sen, founder of the Nationalist Republic, was buried here in 1929.) The Nationalists regained control over Nanjing from the

*Every morning at seven o'clock people gather in this small park
in Nanjing to enjoy an hour of dancing before going to work*

local warlord in 1927, and it remained the capital until just before the Japanese occupation of the city in 1937, when an estimated 300,000 residents perished in what became known as the 'Rape of Nanjing'. In early 1949 the People's Liberation Army entered Nanjing, driving the Nationalist government, the Guomindang, before it, first to Guangzhou and then to Taiwan.

WHAT TO SEE IN NANJING

Nanjing's streets are lined with poplars and sycamore trees—some of which came from France—that provide some relief from the oppressive summer temperatures. Gardens and parks add grace and a sense of spaciousness to the city. Two lakes, Xuanwu Lake and Mochou Lake, are surrounded by parkland. Many of the historical relics—tombs, stelae and sculptures dating from the sixth century—are to be found in the hills and fields around Nanjing, the best known in the vicinity of Zijinshan (Purple and Gold Mountain).

Xuanwu Lake was originally a private retreat for the royal family. The 472-hectare park consists of a lake-shore path and five islands—Ling Zhou, Huan Zhou, Ying Zhou, Liang Zhou and Cui Zhou. Ling Zhou has an aviary. Ying Zhou sits inside Huan Zhou, separated by a lotus-filled moat. Huan Zhou has a man-made waterfall and a Tibetan Buddhist Temple built in 1937. The statues were installed in

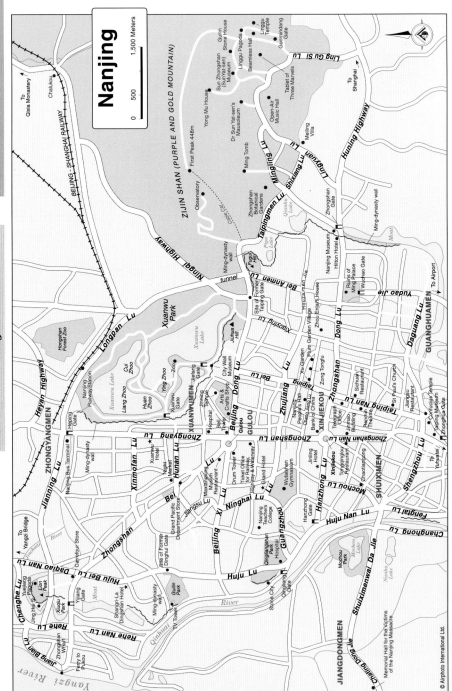

Nanjing

0 500 1,500 Meters

ZIJIN SHAN (PURPLE AND GOLD MOUNTAIN)

First Peak 448m

Linggu Temple
Linggu Pagoda
Guomindang Gate
Beamless Hall
Guilin Stone House
Sun Zhongshan (Sun Yat-sen) Museum
Yong Mu House
Tablet of Three Marvels
To Shanghai
Observatory
Dr Sun Yat-sen's Mausoleum
Open-Air Music Hall
Meiling Villa
Ming Tomb
Huning Highway
Zhongshan Botanical Gardens
Qianhu Lake
Ming-dynasty wall
Ming-dynasty wall
Moat
Wuchao Gate
Zhongshan Gate
Ningqi Highway
tunnel
Bei Anmen Lu
Taipingmen Lu
Mingling Lu
Shixiang Lu
Lingyuan Lu
Ling Gu Si Lu
To Airport
Nanjing Museum
Hilton Hotel
Ruins of Ming Palace
Yudao Jie
Daguang Lu
GUANGHUAMEN

Xuanwu Park
Hongshan Forest Zoo
Tongpan Lu
Xuanwu Lake
Cui Zhou
Liang Zhou
Huan Zhou
Ying Zhou
Nanjing Railway Station
Zoo
Jietang Gate
Xuanwu Gate
City Wall Museum
Jimiao Temple
Juhua Hall
Xiaoling Lu
Site of Former Taiping Gate
Houzai Men
Xu Garden
Plum Garden Village
Zong Tongfu
Zhou Enlai's House
Dong Lu
St Paul's Church
Jiangsu Restaurant

Heyan Highway
ZHONGYANGMEN
Heping Gate
Ming-dynasty wall
Jianning Lu
Xuanwu Hotel
Night Market
Hunan Lu
Zhongyang Lu
Hospital
Bjbu Tower
Arts & Crafts Shop
Beijing Dong Lu
GULOU
Zhujiang
Budiie
People's Hall
Bank of China
Zong Tongfu
Zhongshan Nan Lu
Taiping Lu
Gong's Hall
Sichuan Restaurant
Zhongshan Lu
Gulou
Telegraph Office
Jinhua Building
Peasant Theatre
Jiangsu Museum
Taiping Museum
Confucius Temple
Chaotiangong

Xinmofan Lu
Bei
Hunan Lu
Zhongyang Lu
XUANWUMEN
Hospital
Beijing Dong Lu
Xuanwu Gate
XINJIEKOU
Xinjiekou
Jinling Hotel
Zhongshan Nan Lu
Shengzhou Lu
Yuhuatai
To
Yuhuatai

Site of Former Dinghui Gate
Grand Pacific Department Store
Carrefour Store
Zhongshan
Jiangsu Lu
Maxtianging Muslim Restaurant
Drum Tower
Ticket Office for Railway, Highway & Waterway
Grand Hotel
Ninghai Lu
Nanjing Teachers' College
Wutaishan Gymnasium
Mochou Lu
Tongyingkou Restaurant
Chaoliangdong
SHUIXIMEN

To Yangzi Bridge
Huju Bei Lu
Dajiao Nan Lu
Chenghe Lu
Xuejiang Lu
Lion Peak
Jing Hai Si
Xudu Park
Yijiang Gate
Shangri-La Dingshan Hotel
Rehe Lu
Ming-dynasty wall
Gulin Park
TV Tower
Moat
Qinhuai
Beijing Xi Lu
Hanzhong Lu
Hanzhong Lu
Guangzhou
Xinfengou
Qingliangshan Hospital
Qingliangshan Park
Stone City
Qingjiang Gate
Huju Lu
River
Huju Nan Lu
Changhong Lu
Fengtai Lu
Mochou Lake
Mochou Park
Nanhu Lake
Nanhu Park

Qinhuai
Shuiximen
Zhongshan Wharf
Jiang Bian Lu
Ferry to Pukou
Yangzi River

JIANGDONGMEN
Shuiximenwai Da Jie
Jiang Dong Jie
Beijing Nan Lu
Memorial Hall for the Victims of the Nanjing Massacre

BEIJING – SHANGHAI RAILWAY

To Qixia Monastery
Chaliukou

© Airphoto International Ltd.

a 1993 restoration. Liang Zhou is the only island to feature some pre-republican artefacts—four Qing-dynasty pavilions. Cui Zhou has some new gardens.

Mochou Lake is graced by several Ming-Qing pavilions. One is located on the island and can be reached by hire boat. Local legend says that the Ming General, Xu Da, received the park as a gift from the emperor, when he beat him at chess. One pavilion is called Sheng Qi Ting (Winning at Chess Pavilion). Next to the Sheng Qi Pavilion is a walled garden containing a statue of the mythical heroine Mochou.

SIGHTS WITHIN THE CITY

MING DYNASTY CITY WALL (MINGGU CHENG QIANG)

Built by the first Ming emperor, Hongwu (Zhu Yuanzhang), this wall of clay bricks took 20 years to construct (1366–86), and included remains of an earlier Eastern Han city wall (Stone City). It encloses an area of 41 square kilometres, making it the longest city wall in the world. Its highest point is 18 metres and it varies in width from seven to 12 metres. Some 200,000 workers cemented the bricks—each stamped with details of the brickmaker and overseer—with a mortar mixture of glutinous rice, tung oil and lime.

Some long sections of the Ming city wall had no entry or exit points. There were no gates at all along the shore of Xuanwu Lake stretching from Taiping Men to Heping Men. Zhonghua Men was the only gate south of the city and there was one gate in the east between Taiping Men and Guanghua Men. The Republican government added gates after the 1911 revolution. By then there were 24 gates.

Still, in 1927 when the Guomindang attacked, the city wall was so impregnable that the resident foreign community became trapped inside the city. In order to escape they had to climb down the wall from Ding Shan using 'ropes' made from sheets. The wall was further extended in 1929 in order for the funeral procession of Sun Yat-sen to cross from west to east and in 1930, the Guomindang drafted a plan for the wall to become a ring road for traffic. From 1949 until the end of the Cultural Revolution, much of the city wall was destroyed. But original sections of the Ming wall are still so strong today that modern buildings have been constructed on top of them. In some places, people have made their homes in chambers inside the walls.

Since 1981 the Nanjing city government has taken steps to restore and reconstruct the city's ancient monuments. Work on restoring the wall is ongoing and numerous houses and factories around the wall have been demolished and replaced by green belts. Of note is a section along the Qinhuai River, in the Stone City area, that was converted to a park in 2002. In this park around Qingliang Men there are many strangely protruding sections of the wall dating back to 333 BC. They are laden with stones and shells as testimony to the fact that the Yangzi River was close by at that time. The wall is skilfully illuminated in the early evening.

Many areas of the city are still known by the Ming City gates which once stood there. Tai Ping Men is the local name for the neighbourhood but the gate is no longer standing. Recent accounts state that there are nine city gates still standing. Five gates are original Ming-dynasty gates and four gates date from the Republican era.

The five surviving Ming-dynasty gates are: **Wuchao Men** (Meridian gate)—located in the grounds of the old Ming Palace where Zhu Yuanzhang, or Taizu, lived in the 14th century. All the original palace buildings were destroyed between 1853–1864 during the Taiping Rebellion. **Zhonghua Men** (formerly Treasure Gate) is located in the middle of a traffic circle on Zhong Hua Lu, near the Qin Huai River. It served as a fortress housing 3,000 soldiers inside its 27 caves. This gate is the largest and was constructed at the site of the southern gate of the Tang city. Today it contains a bonsai garden and neighbouring sections of the wall are undergoing restoration.

Hanzhong Men sits in a park at the intersection of Huju Nan Lu, Huju Lu and Hanzhong Lu. This gate is disconnected from the city wall. It forms a long tunnel through the base of a fortress. **Qingliang Men**, built in 1368, sits beside Shitou Cheng Lu near Qing Liang Shan. **Heping Men** is located on top of a small promontory hill overlooking the northwest corner of Xuanwu Lake. It can only be viewed by appointment as it is within a military area. Taiping Men and Zhongyang Men are no longer standing but are the names of local areas. Some tour guides may claim that Zhongyang Men is still standing because they refer to Heping Men by this name.

The four surviving Republican era gates are: **Xuanwu Men**—built in the final year of the Qing dynasty just before the 1911 revolution. It provided access to five islands and the Xuanwu Lake park. This area was a private retreat for the imperial family. **Yijiang Men**, alongside Zhongshan Bei Lu, was built in 1921. There is a pavilion on top of the gate with a photographic exhibition of the Communist Party victory in 1949. From this spot, below you can see the wooded winding bends of the former city moat and to your west is Lion Peak. The second small hill seen to your right is Ding Shan where a community of foreigners from the treaty ports lived during the Guomindang occupation of Nanjing in 1927. **Zhongshan Men** was built in 1929 to facilitate the movement of Dr Sun Yat-sen's funeral procession towards Zijin Shan. It replaced the Ming-dynasty gate (Chaoyang Men). This gate is the main access to Ming Ling Lu, the road to the Ming Tomb. If you climb to the top of this gate, the view (on a clear day) of Zijin Shan and tree-lined Zhongshan Dong Lu is excellent. Facing west, to your right, you can see the remains of the old city moat, Yue Ya Hu Chen He. The Nanjing Museum is next to the gate; **Jiefang Men**, built in 1952, allows access to Xuanwu Lake Park.

Ge Ben-ling, a 55-year-old retired car mechanic, rises at 4.30 each morning before going to teach tai-chi at a playground near his home in Nanjing. This slow-motion form of exercise is said to have been developed by a monk who lived during the 13th or 14th century.

CITY WALL MUSEUM (CHENG QIANG BOWUGUAN)

The museum is to be found on top of the Jiefang Gate (No. 8 Gate) near the Rooster Crow Temple. It contains photographs of long-gone city gates, maps of the walled city, artistically inscribed bricks and a full-scale model of the city wall. Captions are in Chinese only.

THE DRUM TOWER (GU LOU) AND BELL PAVILION (DAZHONG TING)

The Drum Tower marks the centre of Nanjing. It was built in 1382, and was followed in 1388 by the Bell Pavilion, to the northeast. Both were used to sound out the two-hourly night watches over the city. The Drum Tower is a Qing-dynasty (1644–1911) reconstruction built over the 14th-century Ming foundations. A tearoom at the top offers a fine view of the city. The hexagonal Bell Pavilion, also originally erected in the Ming dynasty, houses a huge one-ton bronze bell and a memorial hall. The hall is dedicated to the two daughters of the artisan who was ordered by the emperor to cast the bell. Legend tells how, after the craftsman had made several unsuccessful attempts to produce a correct blend of metals for the bronze, the two girls threw themselves into the smelter, whereupon the composition of the alloy was miraculously perfected. As a result of this filial sacrifice, he was literally saved by the bell from certain execution, but the same story is told of two other bells in Beijing. The existing two-storey pavilion dates from 1889.

YANGZI RIVER BRIDGE (CHANGJIANG DAQIAO)

The bridge is an important symbol of modern China, spanning China's great east–west natural barrier and symbolizing the strength of the Chinese nation. The bridge is a source of great pride for many Chinese as subsequent to failed original surveys by some Western nations and the eventual reliance on Soviet expertise the bridge was finally designed and constructed by the Chinese themselves. The project started in 1960 and opened to traffic in 1968. Apart from the 5,000 technicians and regular workers, an army of volunteer students and others helped out in a labouring capacity. Official figures declare only a few people were killed during construction.

The bridge is of a double-tiered road and rail design. Before its construction it took a train over an hour and a half to cross the river by ferry. The total length of the upper highway deck is around 4,600 metres, whilst the railway section is about 6,800 metres long; approximately 1,580 metres of the bridge spans the Yangzi River itself. Visitors can ascend one of the 70-metre high southeastern gate towers for views and a walk on the road bridge itself. A large scale model of the bridge is to be found on the ground floor of the tower.

THE SECOND NANJING YANGZI RIVER BRIDGE (CHANGJIANG ER QIAO)

This sleekly designed bridge, which opened in 2001, is located 11 kilometres down-river from the old bridge and is in two sections, linking north and south via Bagua islet. An exhibition hall all about bridges, old and new, has opened on this small island.

NANJING MUSEUM (NANJING BOWUYUAN)

The original museum was founded by Cai Yuanpei, a respected scholar, in 1933 and constructed in the style of a traditional Chinese temple. The contents of the museum were moved to an adjacent new building in 1999 to commemorate the 50th anniversary of the opening of the museum. The displays are magnificent with many artefacts presented in cases that magically light up when approached and excellent English annotations. The old building now occasionally hosts temporary exhibitions. The museum is located between the Zhongshan city gate and the Hilton Hotel.

The 419,000 cultural relics here date from around the 11th century BC up to the founding of the People's Republic. Exhibits include jade, pottery and stone imple-ments from Jiangsu's prehistoric period; artefacts from the Longshan and associated cultures from 4000 to 2500 BC; and a wide range of porcelain, paintings and bronzes, as well as maps and displays of traditional handicrafts. The famous jade burial suit, exhibited abroad in the 1970s, belongs to this museum. It is thought to be 1,800 years old and is made of 2,600 rectangles of jade sewn together with silver thread. The jade suit was made to totally encapsulate the body with the object of preserving it, but when archaeologists dug it up in Xuzhou in 1970 all they discovered inside were bones.

One of the most fascinating exhibits is the large wooden copy of a statue of a man showing all the body's acupuncture points. The original bronze statue is believed to date from the Warring States period (480–221 BC). Another reminder of China's superiority in early medical pioneering is a portrait of Hua Tuo (141–203), who practised acupuncture and surgery and reputedly employed anaesthetics 1,000 years before they were discovered in the West. It is located at 321 East Zhongshan Lu.

RUINS OF THE MING IMPERIAL PALACE (MING GU GONG)

Nearby, on Yudao Jie near Wuchao Gate, is the site of the palace built by the first Ming emperor, Hongwu (reigned 1368–98). It was destroyed in 1645 and all that remains are some foundation stones, stone lions and the stone screen wall facing the former palace.

(following pages) The Yangzi River Bridge at Nanjing. Built in the 1960s with a span of more than one and a half kilometres, it is the longest double-deck road and rail bridge in China

TAIPING MUSEUM (TAIPING BOWUGUAN)

Housed in the remains of the former palace of the Eastern Prince of the Heavenly Kingdom is a detailed exhibition of maps, paintings, documents and other relics of the Taiping Rebellion (see pages 456–7). Many of the documents are copies, as the originals are held in Beijing. Linked to the museum is the charming Zhan Yuan, a traditional Chinese garden which originated in the early Ming dynasty and eventually became incorporated into the palace of the Eastern Prince, Yang Xiuqing, in the 19th century. Although this museum is located at 128 Zhan Yuan Lu, many of the Taiping exhibits and relics have been moved to Zong Tongfu at 292 Changjiang Lu. This includes military weapons, the imperial jade seal and the imperial robes of Hong Xiuquan.

NORTH POLE TOWER (BEI JI GE)

Built by the Guomindang in 1929 as a meteorological research institute, this site offers excellent views of Jiming Si and Xuan Wu Hu. A long winding road makes a steep climb to the top. The tower stands in a walled compound on the peak. Although it is not open to the public, staff may allow escorted visits.

CONFUCIUS TEMPLE AREA (FUZI MIAO)

A Confucius Temple has stood in this area since 1034. The last set of temple buildings, built in 1869, were destroyed by the Japanese in 1937. A new temple was built in 1984 as a centrepiece for a huge recreational and shopping area that has grown up along the banks of the Qinhuai River. Whilst all the buildings are new, there are four ancient stone tablets espousing the teachings of Confucius on the grounds. The temple itself is surrounded by numerous huge markets selling everything from arts and crafts to goldfish and clothing. The vast pedestrianized area also has a wide range of eateries offering local snacks, and is a hotspot for visitors in the evening when its recreated Qing-dynasty buildings are brightly illuminated.

In the Jiangnan Gongyuan area near the temple there is the site of an historic centre for official examinations. Provincial and national examinations were held here in the early years of the Ming dynasty (1368–1644) when Nanjing was the national capital, though it had been the seat for county exams since the tenth century. Even after the capital was moved to Beijing, candidates for high office still travelled to Nanjing from all over China. At that time Jiangsu, Jiangxi and Anhui provinces were one administrative unit. The Examination Hall comprised 20,644 tiny cubicles in which candidates were locked up and kept guarded during the lengthy examinations. They had to write essays to achieve official rank in the imperial bureaucracy. Food was passed in daily to sustain the candidates through the trying ordeal which often lasted one month.

Moat buildings were destroyed in the Qing dynasty and more recently by the Japanese in 1937. Some fragments of its highly decorated wall survive as do two large steles that describe the history and development of the hall in the Qing dynasty.

THE PRESIDENTIAL PALACE (ZONG TONGFU)

In many ways this magnificent complex of Renaissance, art deco and traditional Chinese style buildings accompanied by a classic Chinese garden can be viewed as the Forbidden City of Nanjing—both in terms of stature and disposition. Until the museum opened in 2000, the grounds were very much off-limits as they were occupied by the Jiangsu Provincial Communist Party.

The west of the complex, around the **Xu Garden**, is very much bound with the early Republican years and it was here that Dr Sun Yat-sen was inaugurated as provisional president of the new Republic in 1912. His modest brick and wood residence is to be found in the northeast of the garden, with an exhibition hall nearby. The centrepiece is a grandiose Renaissance-style building to the west of the garden. The **Xihua Ting** was built in 1910 and used as the Republican Party offices—it is where Dr Sun Yat-sen presided over the first cabinet meeting. However the history of the garden goes back much further to the early years of the Ming dynasty when it was Prince Han's residence. During the Qing dynasty it was the official residence of the Liangjiang Viceroy with jurisdiction over Jiangsu, Jiangxi and Anhui provinces. It was also the location of the palace of Hong Xiuquan, the Taiping leader and self-styled 'Heavenly King'. He lived here from 1853 until 1864, when his palace was burned down as Manchu troops recovered Nanjing.

The central axis of the complex is in the form of a long corridor leading to courtyards containing exhibitions, including one dedicated to the Taiping Rebellion and to the grand buildings of the Nationalist government that once housed all the government ministries between 1927 and 1937. The main Nationalist Government Building, the Zichao building, became the **Presidential Government Building** in 1948 when Chiang Kai-shek was inaugurated. His second floor office and the room of his inauguration on the third floor can be visited, alongside numerous other chambers that are tremendously well-preserved and steeped in history. One can even clamber down the steps of his personal air raid shelter to the east of the building.

PLUM GARDEN VILLAGE (MEIYUAN XINCUN)

At the end of the Sino-Japanese War, abortive peace talks took place between the Guomindang and the Communist Party of China. During this period—May 1946 to March 1947—the Communists made their headquarters at 17, 30 and 35 Meiyuan Xincun, a suburb close to the centre of Nanjing.

THE TAIPING REBELLION

There were many violent peasant uprisings between 1840–1911. But the Taiping Rebellion (1850–64) was more than just another revolt; it was the most devastating civil war the world has ever known. It affected nearly two-thirds of China, destroying entire cities and causing an estimated 20 to 30 million deaths, more people than China lost in the war against Japan (1937–45). A 1950s government census found that the population of provinces near the mouth of the Yangzi was still a total of 20 million lower than it had been in 1850.

The rebellions of the period were prompted by a series of interlinked misfortunes. The unpopular Manchurian Qing dynasty (1644–1911) was growing weaker and Western incursions more far-reaching. Thousands lost their jobs as traditional industries such as weaving were wiped out by Western imports. Corrupt officials taxed the peasants ever more extortionately in order to pay for these imports, the chief of which was opium. To make matters worse, untold numbers died in famine after terrible famine. These were caused by natural disasters, a huge population increase during the early Qing, and neglect of the irrigation systems.

The Taiping leader Hong Xiuquan was a poor schoolteacher from a village near Guangzhou (Canton) who had had some contact with missionaries and their teachings. After failing the imperial examinations several times, he suffered a nervous breakdown, during which he saw visions. These revealed to him that he was the son of God, the younger brother of Jesus Christ. His earthly mission was to expel the Manchu demons from China and to create a Heavenly Kingdom of Peace on earth (Taiping Tianguo), where all men and women would be equal.

The Taipings formally declared rebellion in 1851 and thousands of peasants and dispossessed workers rose up to join them. In 1852 they took to the water on a motley collection of boats and rafts, sweeping through the waterways of Guangxi, along the Grand Canal and up the Yangzi, sacking cities and amassing loot, boats and followers as they went. Their numbers grew to over a million people and they easily defeated the demoralized imperial troops in their path. In 1853 they reached Nanjing, where they set up their capital. From here they ruled over their Heavenly Kingdom for the next 11 years. At their peak, almost half of China was under their control.

After establishing their government, the Taipings sent an army to attack the Manchu capital of Beijing. But they were turned back by imperial forces organized by the big northern landlords. Returning to Nanjing, they consolidated their power, successfully repelling a Qing attack in 1860 and to many it seemed that they would become the next ruling dynasty.

Although it is hard to know how far the Taiping reforms extended throughout their territory, in Nanjing and its environs at least, land was divided equally between all men and women over 16, half-shares going to those under 16. Foot-binding, slavery and concubinage were abolished. Women served in their own battalions, which were commanded by female officers. Opium and infanticide were illegal.

Yet this supposedly egalitarian society was actually a totalitarian theocracy, run by the Heavenly King Hong Xiuquan himself and four assistant Kings. While ordinary Taipings were allowed only one wife and lived spartan, disciplined lives, the Kings lived in luxury surrounded by concubines. As time went on Hong became ever more paranoid and in 1856, suspecting the East King of treachery, he had him and about 20,000 of his followers killed in one bloody night. Later he also turned on the North King and had him assassinated.

Meanwhile after the defeat of 1860, the Manchus and Chinese gentry continued to fight the Taipings under the able leadership of Zeng Guofan. At first the Western powers remained neutral and many Westerners, particularly missionaries, were favourable towards the Taipings. But the devastation they wrought—some cities changed hands so many times in the fighting that there was little left to fight over—and a closer look at their version of Christianity, changed most people's minds. The final straw came when the Taipings closed in on Shanghai in 1862 and threatened the foreign community there. Thereafter the West supplied the Manchus with Western weapons and lent them commanders to train their forces. One such was 'Chinese Gordon', who took part in the burning of the Summer Palace and later died at Khartoum.

The end came with the long siege of Nanjing in 1864. As the siege wore on, Hong grew more and more out of touch with reality. After praying for Manna from Heaven, he told his starving citizens to gather ten loads each of grass and leaves and eat that. A few days before the imperial forces finally dynamited the city walls, Hong died of a lingering illness probably compounded by following the diet he had imposed on the others. Many committed suicide, chanting hymns as they did so, some by throwing themselves in the moat, others by torching their houses. Many of Hong's concubines hanged themselves in the Palace garden. Over 7,000 people were massacred in three days. Lord Elgin on visiting Nanjing soon afterwards, said that the desertion of the streets and the universal stillness reminded him of Pompeii.

The Communist delegation was led by Zhou Enlai and Dong Biwu. Zhou Enlai and his wife, Deng Yingchao, lived at No. 30, and the charming house and garden remain just as the couple left them, with jackets hanging from a hatstand and a battered leather briefcase on the chest of drawers in the spartan bedroom. A doorway knocked into the eastern garden wall connects No. 30 to No. 35, where Dong Biwu resided. This short cut enabled the Communists to evade constant surveillance by Guomindang secret agents posted in the streets outside. At No.17 is a small conference room where Zhou Enlai met the press during negotiations.

Visitors enter the house museums through a large modern exhibition hall containing many items of skulduggery. On the upper floor a large radio transmitter sits beside a compact version used for direct communication with Mao Zedong in Yan'an. Other exhibits include Zhou Enlai's pristine leather coat worn when he fled to Xi'an in December 1946, as well as the Communist party delegation's official camera. On the ground floor is the shiny-black Buick used by Zhou Enlai and Dong Biwu when they were engaged in peace talks with the Nationalists.

ROOSTER CROW TEMPLE (JIMING SI)

A temple was first built on this site over 1,700 years ago, although it was not known by its present name until it was rebuilt by the first Ming emperor Hongwu in 1387. All its buildings, including a nunnery that had been built in 1959, were destroyed by a fire in 1973. Reconstruction of the temple commenced in 1981 and in 1984 two large bronze statues of Buddha and Guanyin were donated from Thailand. The 45-metre high landmark Yaoshi pagoda was rebuilt in 1989 to complete the restoration.

QUIET SEA TEMPLE (JING HAI SI)

This temple was built in honour of Admiral Zheng He, during the reign of the Ming emperor Cheng Zu. Jing Hai means 'quiet sea', conveying the wish that Zheng He's fleet would have safe journeys. This temple, at the base of Lion Peak, was also the site of the 1842 Sino-British negotiations which resulted in the Treaty of Nanking ending the Opium War of 1839–42. The treaty was signed on board HMS Cornwallis anchored in the Yangzi River. The original temple was burned down by the Japanese in 1937 but rebuilt in 1987. On the site where the negotiations for the treaty took place there is now a museum, as well as an exhibition hall celebrating the return of Hong Kong, the last bastion of British imperialism, to China in 1997. A three-and-a-half ton copy of an ancient bronze bell was placed nearby in June 1997, as was as a commemorative stone tablet.

YUEJIANG PAGODA (YUEJIANG TA)

Affording great views across the city to the Yangzi River, a monolithic Ming-dynasty style structure on the top of Lion Peak was completed in 2001. Despite various proclamations to build such a structure since the time of the first Ming emperor, this is the first project that has actually come to fruition. The neighbouring complex houses various exhibition rooms and two stone lions that are reputed to be the largest in China.

RELIGIOUS ARCHITECTURE

Nanjing has a number of historic places of worship. Its long-established mosque on the corner of Taiping Nan Lu and Xiaohuowa Xiang was demolished in 2003, and a new one built. Nearby at 396 Taiping Nan Lu is St Paul's Church, a charming Protestant church built in 1922 that still holds regular weekend services. A Catholic church has recently been restored on Shipu Lu.

THE MEMORIAL HALL FOR THE VICTIMS OF THE NANJING MASSACRE

This is located at Jiangdong Men, the site of one of the many former execution grounds, where it is estimated that some 190,000 people were massacred, in addition to over 100,000 indiscriminate killings across the city. An excavated burial pit containing 280 skeletons, discovered in 1998, leads on to a sombre but enlightening memorial hall containing graphic photos and artefacts relating to the massacre that took place during December 1937 and January 1938. A copper pavement bearing the footprints of 222 survivors, who were witness to the events, was laid at the entrance in 2002 to mark the 65th anniversary of the massacre. The respectfully stark and desolate open area around the halls is littered with memorial stones to those who were killed at various sites around the city.

HEAVEN WORSHIPPING PALACE (CHAOTIAN GONG)

This site consists of four courtyards and three main buildings within a walled compound. Several of the buildings house exhibits of the Nanjing City Museum. The first two courtyards are free to enter, with a daily antique, curio and memorabilia bazaar in the second courtyard, where a statue of Confucius is also to be found. At weekends traders from all over China gather in the first courtyard around the Crescent Pool. Da Cheng Palace, in the third courtyard, is a museum of the Six Dynasties period in Nanjing's history. Costume performances of Ming court ceremonies are held in this courtyard. In the fourth courtyard, facing Chong Sheng Palace, is a new building housing relics from the Ming-dynasty era in Nanjing.

XIAO BAI LOU (LITTLE WHITE HOUSE)

This former British consulate is now a luxurious banquet facility. Built in 1919, it was the British Consulate where the British Consul was assassinated by Guomindang troops in 1927. His assassination triggered the exodus by the foreigners over the city wall. The building, located at 185 Huju Bei Lu, is kept in pristine condition. Visitors are welcome to look around inside. Brochures describing the building's history in English are available on request.

JIANG BIAN LU WATERFRONT
This waterfront avenue, just to the east of Lion's Peak, is dotted with small boat piers to the south of the Shanghai Port. It is a quiet and neglected part of town that is slowly being transformed into a commercial centre. The port itself, at the north end of the road, has been closed to river passenger traffic.

Going south one block brings you to the Da Ma Lu, a street of past importance that has some historic architecture, including the impressive former building of the Bank of Communications that was built in the 1930s. An old concrete embankment runs the length of the street obscuring views of the river. However the southern section, past the No. 2 pier, has a narrow raised pathway that can be reached by small steps. There are plans to build a new promenade in the future. At the intersection with Zhongshan Bei Lu is the Zhongshan Wharf from where you can take a ferry to Pukou on the northern bank of the river.

THE NANJING CHINESE MUSICAL INSTRUMENT ORCHESTRA
Nanjing is home to one of the finest orchestras of its kind, with professional musicians performing at a newly renovated small theatre. Even though the orchestra plays to tourists, its calibre is far higher than that of musicians generally engaged in staged tourist shows. The orchestra has travelled worldwide and has a repertoire ranging from mesmerizing classical folk melodies to provocative avant-garde concertos. Their private theatre is on the ground floor of the Minzu Yuetuan, at 101 Zhongshan Nan Lu. Performances are not staged regularly and you should contact the theatre on (025) 8454 7903 if you are interested.

SIGHTS OUTSIDE THE CITY CENTRE
YUHUATAI (TERRACE OF THE RAIN OF FLOWERS)
The main part of this huge verdant area, just to the south of Zhonghua Men, is concerned with memorials to the 100,000 Communist revolutionaries that were killed on this site—used by the Guomindang as an execution ground. In recent years a whole range of attractions has been added to the encompassing scenic area, including new gardens and restored historic buildings. The main focus of interest is the magnificent Martyrs Museum which was renovated in 1999. There are numerous artefacts on display, as well as photo biographies of many of those who perished, that are well annotated in English. Solemn music sets the scene and one

is struck by the young age at which many of them died. Just to the north of the museum is a tall memorial built in 1989 and inscribed with Deng Xiaoping's calligraphy. Near the north gate is the Statue of the Martyrs Execution that was built in 1979 using 179 pieces of granite.

According to legend it is said that Yun Guang, a Buddhist monk, lived and preached here in the sixth century. So eloquent was he that the heavens showered flowers upon him, and these turned into beautiful little agate stones. These rain-flower pebbles are sold to visitors in containers of water to enhance their colouration and a museum containing such stones can be found to the east of the area.

SIGHTS ON ZIJINSHAN (PURPLE AND GOLD MOUNTAIN)

The three peaks of Zijinshan (the highest is 448 metres) form this evergreen scenic area east of Nanjing. Some of the city's most famous sights are to be seen in this region.

MING EMPEROR'S TOMB (MING XIAOLING)

The first emperor of the Ming dynasty, Hongwu, was buried here in 1398, alongside his empress, Ma Hou, who died in 1382. The tomb, begun in 1381, is recorded as having taken 100,000 labourers 32 years to complete. Most of the buildings of the mausoleum have been destroyed; the Taiping rebels plundered the vicinity in the 1800s. The tomb is in poor condition compared with those of Hongwu's descendants, who were buried outside Beijing after the capital was moved there. The wall around the tomb is 22.5 kilometres long. The former approach to the tomb formed a long, winding S-shaped path. But now visitors miss much of the Sacred Way because Ming Ling Lu leads directly to the tomb. Along the **Sacred Way** are pairs of stone animals and, at the far end, statues of warriors and civil servants. The style of carving is typical of the early Ming period. The tomb was designated as a World Heritage Site in 2003.

The original Sacred Way started near the town of Weigang. The Xiama Men in the town is engraved with instructions 'get down from your horses'. At this point, all horse riders were to dismount, in respect for the emperor, and walk the rest of the distance to the tomb. The second gate, Dajing Men, is on Zhongshan Ling Lu. Opposite is Sifangcheng Pavilion which is near Shixiang Lu, the section of the Sacred Way with the 12 pairs of animal statues. A further section of the Sacred Way is found in the middle of a traffic strip on Weng Zhong Lu. Here there are stone statues of four civil officials and four generals.

Continuing on Weng Zhong Lu, you reach the Lingxing Men and the Jingshi Qiao (three parallel stone-arched bridges) at the entrance of the tomb. Following the brick avenue lined with cedar trees you reach Wengwu Men (the first outer wall

and the five gates). Passing through the Wengwu Men, you reach the Stele Pavilion (Bei Dian) containing five stone stele, including one engraved by Qing Emperor Kang Xi in 1699. You can also see a plaque posted on the outside of the building by the Qing government in 1909 commanding the preservation of the tomb.

Next comes the Xiaoling Dian (Sacrificial Hall). The original was constructed in 1383, but was destroyed during the Taiping Rebellion of 1850–1864. This Qing reconstruction was built in 1873, and is a much smaller one than the original. It sits on top of a raised rectangular flat platform with several tiers. The stone base of this platform and its tiers are decorated with the remains of protruding stone animal heads resembling alligators. In fact they represent a legendary animal, the lishou, which was a Ming symbol.

Continuing on up the long tree-lined avenue, you reach the Inner Wall, which is painted red and has a single gate. Passing through this inner Red Gate, the long tree-lined avenue continues until you cross a stone arched bridge (Da Shi Qiao) and reach the giant rectangular Ming tower. A tunnel cuts through the centre of the building at an inclined angle and emerges at the back, from where a flight of steps ascends to the top of the tower. Four walls are all that remain of a building that once stood there. From the top you have a view of the whole approach.

Behind the Ming tower sits the Bao Cheng, or treasure mound. Inside this circular mound are the unexcavated tombs of the first Ming emperor and his wife. To reach the Ming tombs either take Ming Ling Lu and Weng Zhong Lu from Zhongshan Men to the main gate of the mausoleum, or take Zhongshan Ling Yuan Lu from Ling Hang Gong Lu, near Weigang village, to see the whole Sacred Way from its starting point.

DR SUN YATSEN'S MAUSOLEUM (ZHONGSHAN LING)

Nanjing's most famous landmark is the elegant blue and white mausoleum of Dr Sun Yat-sen (1866–1925), father of the Chinese Republic. Dr Sun's body was kept at the Bai Yun Guan Temple in the Western Hills of Beijing until this mausoleum was completed in 1929. 'Universal Love' are the characters above the triple-arched centre gate, through which an avenue of tall trees leads to the main gate, with four Chinese characters inscribed saying 'All for the nation', 'Serving the public under heaven' and 'The world belongs to everyone'. A flight of 392 marble steps leads to the memorial hall in which is a gypsum statue of a seated Dr Sun (sculpted in France by a Polish friend, Landowski). Each step represents one article of the Nationalist Constitution. Dr Sun's remains are beneath a recumbent marble statue of him (executed by Japanese associates) in the circular crypt behind the hall. His wish had always been to be buried on Zijin Shan in Nanjing. The site for his tomb was selected by his wife, Song Qingling, on April 21, 1925. The mausoleum was

A stone camel, one of 12 pairs of animal statues along the Sacred Way at the Ming Emperor's Tomb in Nanjing, provides welcome shade for a group of children

designed by Lu Yanzhi and the colours are those of the Guomindang flag. The perimeter of the entire site was originally meant to take the shape of a giant bell, symbolic of Sun himself as the human alarm bell, but the growth of trees has now obscured this.

The full distance from the Gate of Universal Love to the Ceremonial Hall is 700 metres. There are a total of 14 flights of stone steps. Although the view from the top is spectacular in the daytime, a visit at night is worthwhile because the mausoleum is floodlit, the crowds are gone and admission is free.

After passing through the Mausoleum Gate, you ascend two more flights of steps and reach the second terrace with its Bei Ting (Tablet Pavilion), inside which is a stone stele engraved with the words, 'The Guomindang buried its prime minister Sun Zhongshan here on June 1, 1929.'

From the Tablet Pavilion you ascend eight more flights of steep steps to the third terrace and its Ji Tang (Ceremonial Hall), behind which is the tomb chamber itself. Above the three arched doorways of the Ceremonial Hall are engraved the characters for the Three People's Principles (San Min Zhuyi) of Nationalism (minzu), Democracy (minzhu) and People's Livelihood (minsheng), which were the core of Sun Yat-sen's ideology. Ascend the final short flight of steps leading into the Cermemonial Hall and you will see a white marble statue of a seated Sun Yat-sen. On the east and west walls of the hall is engraved the complete text of Sun Yat-sen's book, 'Outline of National Reconstruction' (Jianguo Dagang).

At the back of the room is a small doorway which leads into the Mu Shi Li Ceng (Tomb Chamber). This is a circular room with a dome over the top. In the centre of the room lies a white marble statue of Sun Yat-sen in a reclining position. Below this lies his coffin.

Exit the Ceremonial Hall and walk around the outside of the building to your right and you can visit the back of the domed Tomb Chamber which is known as the Mu Shi Wai Ceng (Tomb Fort). Here there is usually an outdoor display of photographs showing the construction of the tomb.

DR SUN YAT-SEN'S MUSEUM (SUN ZHONGSHAN JINIAN GUAN)

Located inside the Buddhist Scripture Hall (Cangjing Lou), with an interior reminiscent of his memorial hall in Guangzhou, this is an important museum dedicated to the father of modern China. The building was constructed in 1935–1936 and renovated in 1982. On the ground floor there is a collection of oil paintings depicting early Nationalist activities. On the upper three floors there are numerous photos chronicling his life, his death and the path to his final resting place.

(previous pages) Memorial arch at the Sun Yat-sen Mausoleum, Nanjing

YONG MU LOU

This is the house where Sun Ke, Sun's son, and Song Qingling stayed during their 1929 period of mourning immediately after Dr Sun Yat-sen's funeral. Sun Ke Lou and Yong Mu Lou can both be reached by a stone paved road from Linggu Temple, or by a steep stone-paved trail that ascends the hillside, starting from the road to Dr Sun Yat-sen's Museum, across the road from a small restaurant. The trail is unmarked. The house was rebuilt in the 1980s.

ZHENG QI TING

This is the site Chiang Kai-shek (Jiang Jie-shi) chose for his tomb in November 1946 before his flight to Taiwan. It sits at the end of a long, steep walking trail which climbs up from behind Zixia Lake in the Ming Tomb area. The pavilion is inscribed both by him and Sun Ke. A single Guomindang symbol adorns the centre of the ceiling.

ZIJINSHAN OBSERVATORY

Situated on one peak of Zijinshan, this third largest of China's observatories was built in 1934. There is a small but fascinating collection on display of magnificent Ming (1368–1644) reproductions of early astrological instruments: a celestial globe, an armillary sphere for detecting solar bodies, a gnomon (a sun and seasons dial) and an earthquake detector first made over 2,000 years ago. The last two instruments have had a disturbed history. In 1900, Germans absconded with the earthquake detector (which was then in the Beijing Observatory) but it was returned, along with the other instruments taken as spoils of war, in 1919. In the early 1930s the Japanese tried unsuccessfully to remove the gnomon; they even cut the base in half.

If you climb onto the platform of one of the observatory domes you will find yourself above the tree line, and, unfurling below you, a marvellous view of Nanjing and the Yangzi.

VALLEY OF THE SOUL'S RETREAT (LINGGU GONGYUAN)

The park, and the admission ticket for it, includes the Linggu Pagoda (Linggu Ta), the Linggu Temple (Linggu Si), the Beamless Hall (Wuliang Dian), the Baogong Stupa (San Juebei), the Zhigong Hall (Zhigong Dian) and the Guilin Stone house (Guilin Shiwu). A Ming-dynasty style archway, Red Mountain Gate (Hongshan Men) greets visitors to the area leading to the remarkably intact Guomindang Gate, embellished with blue and white Nationalist symbols over its five entrances to the cemetery area.

In order to build his grand mausoleum on an auspicious site, the Ming emperor Hongwu (reigned 1368–98) had first to remove an existing temple, the Linggu

Temple, to its present wooded peak. All that remains of that Ming temple is the 46-metre long Beamless Hall (Wuliang Dian).

The current **Linggu Temple** buildings are a Qing-dynasty reconstruction completed by Zeng Guofan in 1867. It has a special chapel devoted to the famous travelling Buddhist monk Xuan Zang (596–664) who went to India in the seventh century on a journey which lasted 16 years. In 645 he returned to the Tang-dynasty capital city of Chang An (Xi'an) bringing with him over 650 Buddhist manuscripts which he later translated into Chinese. This chapel devoted to him holds what is purported to be a piece of his skull, which is kept on public display in a clear wine glass sitting inside a small model pagoda. A community of monks live here.

Beamless Hall (Wuliang Dian) was originally a Buddhist temple which in 1933 was turned into a memorial to Guomindang military officers and soldiers who perished in the Northern Expedition of 1925–1927 and the anti-Japanese battle of 1937–1938. Around the hall there are three cemeteries containing over 1,000 bodies of military personnel. The names and ranks of 33,224 martyrs are listed on 110 black stone tablets inside the awesome Ming-dynasty structure. It was built in 1381 and is the only surviving Ming building in the park area. The structure itself is remarkable for having been built with no nails and no wooden beams. The ceiling is made of bricks forming a rounded vault over the walls. Today it contains an exhibit of mannequins acting out scenes from China's revolutions.

To the north of the Beamless Hall stands the nine-storeyed **Linggu Pagoda**, which was built by the Guomindang and completed in 1933. The walls are inscribed with the text of two speeches given by Dr Sun Yat-sen at the Whampoa Military Academy in Guangzhou. For the energetic, the long climb to the top of the circular staircase is rewarded with a fine view over wooded countryside. A short walk to the east of the pagoda brings one to the tomb of Tan Yankai, Chairman of the Nationalist Government, that includes some stone remnants from the Old Summer Palace in Beijing.

Zhigong Hall (Zhigong Dian) and Baogong Stupa (Baogong Ta) are both dedicated to the memory of the Liang-dynasty Buddhist monk Bao Zhi (436–514). Bao Zhi was originally buried on the site of Ming Xiaoling, but his grave was moved to near Linggu Temple in 1379, when the first Ming emperor's tomb was being built. The stupa was destroyed three different times, until finally the grave site itself was lost. The current stupa is a new construction dating from 1981. It no longer marks the actual grave site, which is now unknown. A few yards in front of the stupa sits Zhigong Hall, which was first built in 1934 and renovated in 1941. This hall contains stone tablets dated 1382 recording the moving of Bao Zhi's grave to the new site.

Guilin Stone House was the home of Lin Shen, chairman of the Guomindang during the 1930s. The house was built completely out of stone in 1932, and sits on top of a high promontory on the southern slope of Zijinshan. A steep, narrow,

The nine-storey Linggu Pagoda on Zijinshan (Purple and Gold Mountain)

stone-paved road approaches it from two directions, either Linggu Temple or Dr Sun Yat-sen's Museum. This site descends downward sharply in three directions and upward sharply in the fourth. The house was destroyed by the Japanese during their occupation, leaving behind the foundation and some ruined walls, including a staircase that now ascends into the air. The walls are still scarred black from the fire. The arduous climb is well rewarded as many stone statues and magnificent carvings embedded in the stonework of the house have survived. Many are copies borrowed from the Ming Tomb. Even though a notice at the base of the house claims that it was restored in 2000, thankfully this is not the case.

MEILING'S VILLA (MEILING GONG)
This three-storey house was built in 1931 by Chiang Kai-shek for his wife Song Meiling. It was often used by them as a weekend retreat. A voluminous room on the second floor and its attendant terrace is now a dining room that is available for group bookings and private parties. On the third floor there are four rooms containing original furnishings, maps and family photographs, including some of Dr Sun Yat-sen. Meiling's old black Buick is parked outside the house, at 9 Zhongshan Ling Lu. Song Meiling died in October 2003, in New York, at the age of 106.

AIR FORCE MEMORIAL (HANG KONG LIE SHI GONG MU)
Built by the Guomindang in 1932, it was badly damaged during the Japanese occupation. Restored and expanded in 1994, it now includes the names of both Chinese and foreign pilots who died in the air battles with Japan from 1932 to 1945. The memorial sits just off Jiangwangmiao Lu, on the north slope of Zijinshan.

ZIJINSHAN CABLE CAR (SHAN DING GONGYUAN)
A cable car takes passengers up to Shan Ding Gongyuan—the highest central peak of Zijinshan's three peaks. The top of this peak can also be reached via a stone paved road that begins from behind Linggu Pagoda and ascends the ridge, traversing the third peak and then ascending the second peak. This is a very long walk. You can also hire a taxi driver to take you there.

SIGHTS SOUTH OF NANJING
NIUSHOUSHAN
The tomb of famous Chinese Muslim Ming-dynasty admiral, Zheng He (1371–1435), whose ships sailed the seven seas in the 15th century (see page 97), is here. Take Zhongshan Nan Lu to Yuhua Xi Lu travelling out of the city heading south. When Yuhua Xi Lu forks, take the left fork onto Ningdan Lu and follow this across hills to Niushoushan.

The 12th-century fortifications of Yue Fei stretch from Hanfu Shan to Niushoushan, south of the city. Yue Fei (1103–1141) was a famous Southern Song general who wanted to recapture the north after the Song had been driven south to their new capital in Hangzhou. In 1129 he recaptured the Nanjing area and held a front line along the Yangzi. In 1136 he advanced to the Yellow River. By 1139–1140 he had raided Henan Province and the old Song capital at Kaifeng. However, at that point he was ordered to withdraw from north China by the Song emperor Qin Gui who preferred reaching a diplomatic solution with the Jin invaders. Yue Fei was recalled to the capital at Hangzhou and imprisoned, dying a mysterious death in 1141. A popular temple is devoted to him in Hangzhou on West Lake.

ZUTANGSHAN

Located on the southern slope of Zutangshan are the tombs (Nan Tang Er Ling) of two Southern Tang-dynasty emperors, Li Bian (Li Sheng) (937–943), and Li Jing (943–961). The two underground tombs are well lit and can be entered on foot without a guide. Located to the right of Li Jing's tomb, the tomb of Li Sheng is more impressive. Inside you will find three main rooms with domed ceilings, marble columns, detailed bas relief rock carvings of warrior guardians armed with swords, and other decorations such as dragons and stone tripod roof brackets just like those used on traditional wooden Chinese buildings today. Notice the ten side chambers where his wives and retainers were buried alive with him.

Near the entrance gate, there is a small museum displaying (with Chinese captions) some of the 640 artefacts discovered in the tombs when they were first opened in 1950. Over the wall behind the museum, you can see three stone statues overgrown with vines—two soldiers are facing each other and one scholar. This is the remains of the Sacred Way leading to these tombs.

SIGHTS EAST OF NANJING (QIXIA MOUNTAIN)

For visitors spending more than a few days in Nanjing, a visit to these sites on Qixia Hill are strongly recommended. Seventeen kilometres east of Nanjing, the drive to the Buddhist grottoes and temple of Qixia takes the visitor through an area rich in tomb sites of the nobility of the Liang dynasty (502–57). In particular there are stone figures from the tombs of three of Emperor Wudi's brothers, Xiao Dan, Xiao Hui and Xiao Xiu. Xiao Dan's tomb includes a well-preserved stele on the back of a stone tortoise and two large stone winged lions. Xiao Xiu's tomb figures include wonderfully carved winged lions, tortoises and columns.

QIXIA TEMPLE (QIXIA SI)

First built in the fifth century, this temple has repeatedly been destroyed and restored thereafter. The present temple buildings were erected in 1908. Serving as headquarters of the Jiangsu Branch of the Buddhist Association of China, the temple is an active centre of worship where the monks hold regular services. The temple also boasts an exceptional library of 7,200 volumes of Buddhist scriptures. Behind the temple is the Sheli Dagoba, one of the oldest stone dagobas south of the Yangzi River. This 15-metre high, five-tiered dagoba was built in 601, and is embellished with detailed carvings of Buddha's life.

QIXIA THOUSAND BUDDHA CLIFF (QIAN FO YAN)

There are 294 shrines and 515 rock carvings in niches and grottoes in the cliff-face near the temple. The earliest date from the fifth century, and they continued to be carved until the Ming dynasty (1368–1644). Many of their heads were defaced or lopped off during the Cultural Revolution (1966–76). One figure is a 13-metre high Buddha, said to have been carved by Zhongzhang, son of the magistrate-turned-hermit, Ming Sengshao, who donated his home as the original Qixia Temple.

ZHENJIANG

Zhenjiang, on the south bank, is situated in the middle of Jiangsu Province, at the junction of the Yangzi and the Grand Canal, 63 kilometres from Nanjing. It was the capital of the province during the Republican period (1911–49) when Nanjing was the national capital. Earlier Chinese travellers classified Zhenjiang's scenery as 'The Best Landscape under Heaven', and indeed the area known as the Southern Suburbs was often used as a theme in landscapes by famous Chinese painters. Marco Polo claimed to have visited the city in the 13th century, commenting: 'The people of Zhenjiang live by industry and commerce; they produce much silk and brocade and the rustic flavour of the place is suitable for the production of many things.'

The American Nobel Prize-winning writer, Pearl S Buck (1892–1973), author of *The Good Earth* and other novels about China, lived in Zhenjiang for 15 years before attending boarding school in Shanghai. Her missionary parents' house still stands in the northern part of the city, incorporated into a radio factory. Handicrafts include jade carvings, palace lanterns and screens of natural stone. Zhenjiang is also known for its black vinegar and pickled vegetables.

HISTORY OF ZHENJIANG

Zhenjiang, under various names, has existed for 2,500 years. In 213 BC, its importance as a ferry crossing led Emperor Qin Shihuangdi to conclude that Zhenjiang's fengshui (geomantic) powers were too strong. He ordered 3,000 prisoners to dig a tunnel through one of the hills to divert the influences.

During the convoluted politics of the Three Kingdoms period (220–265, see page 42), Sun Quan, ruler of the kingdom of Wu, made his capital here and Zhenjiang was the site of many 'mini-summits' on military strategy between the warring kingdoms. Thereafter the settlement grew steadily, benefiting greatly from the construction of the Grand Canal under the Sui dynasty (581–618). Its key location at the intersection of the Grand Canal and the Yangzi made it the hub of water transportation from the seventh century onwards.

Under the Song dynasty (960–1279) the city's development reached its height, producing fine silks, satins and silverware as tribute to the imperial court. Troops were stationed here to defend the river (Zhenjiang means 'guard the river')—a wise precaution, as it turned out, when they had to take on invading Jin troops in a naval battle near Jin Shan in 1130.

During the Opium War of 1842, Zhenjiang was bombarded by British men-of-war. Seven thousand British troops stormed the walled city, which was defended by only about 3,000 courageous Chinese soldiers. The governor of the city and his family committed suicide. On the British side, 105 soldiers were killed or wounded. This battle was a turning point, as it led to the signing of the Treaty of Nanking (Nanjing) only a month later. The treaty provided for the ceding of Hong Kong to Britain and for the payment of 21 million Mexican dollars by the Chinese as indemnity.

The city was again captured in 1853 by the Taiping rebels and held by them for four years, which left it crippled for some time. A small foreign concession area was established in 1861. A H Rasmussen, a Scandinavian trader who lived in Zhenjiang for many years, wrote:

Then I went into the silent street for a breath of fresh air and walked up and down the bund, three hundred paces one way and three hundred paces back. To get a little change I walked up and down the only cross street to the south gate of the Concession, two hundred paces one way and two hundred paces back.

Life was very restricted, and the hunting of wild boar in the surrounding hills became the main pastime for the resident foreigners.

Trade recovered, however. Customs house records show that in the first decade of the 20th century the value of goods transshipped in one year through Zhenjiang exceeded a staggering 35 million taels of silver (one tael is roughly 50 grammes or 1.8 ounces).

But the coming of the railway put an end to this spate of merchandise; by the 1920s, much of it was being conveyed by freight trains. Yet Zhenjiang is still a busy

(following pages) Golden Island (Jin Shan) with its temple situated on a bend in the Yangzi River at Zhenjiang. Sketched by William Alexander during Lord Macartney's embassy to China in 1793.

W. Alexander del.

VIEW of the TCHIN-SHAN, or GOLDEN ISLA

London P

Wilson sculp.t

YANG-TSE-KIANG, *or* GREAT RIVER *of* CHINA.

Nicol.

transportation hub. A new port at nearby Dagang has enhanced its importance and it is on the Shanghai–Nanjing railroad line. Industries include metallurgy, electronics and vehicle and ship construction.

WHAT TO SEE IN ZHENJIANG

With some 300 factories employing well over a third of its population, Zhenjiang is now indisputably industrial. Yet it still enjoys the appellation 'City of Forests and Hills', which was coined by the celebrated landscape painter Mi Fu (1051–1107) because it is flanked on three sides by tree-clad mountains.

The busiest area of the city is within the confines of Zhengdong Lu, Jiefang Lu and Renmin Lu. The old city is further west, near Boxian Park. The foreign concession was there; its British consulate is now the Zhenjiang Museum. On Boxian Lu an old American church still retains the stone plaque set into a wall which reads, though not clearly:

First Baptist Church
Organized
... D 1885
Rebuilt 1921

XIAO MATOU JIE (SMALL JETTY STREET)

Take this charming little cobbled street through the oldest part of town. The rows of Qing-dynasty (1644–1911) buildings are intersected by stone arches at regular intervals. One of these is the **Zhaoguan Stupa**—five metres high rising behind a stone archway—which dates from the Yuan dynasty (1279–1368). The names engraved on either side commemorate those who were officials of the prefecture when the stupa was restored in 1583.

The cobbled pathway was once lined with shops selling incense to devotees at Jin Shan Temple. West of the stupa is the **Western Ferry Crossing** (Xi Jindu Jie). Its stone steps once led straight down to the riverside, where there was a ferry service to Jin Shan and the other side of the Yangzi. Marco Polo is said to have come ashore at this place.

JIN SHAN (GOLDEN HILL)

The 44-metre Golden Hill, with its famous temple, was an island in the centre of the Yangzi until it merged with the river bank in the middle of the last century. Visitors used to take a ferry from the Western Ferry Crossing, and then rode mules to the top. Jin Shan Temple was first built over 1,500 years ago. In its heyday, the temple was looked after by 3,000 Buddhist monks.

Visitors may be shown the most interesting of the several sights and relics on Jin Shan. Jin Shan Pagoda was first built 1,400 years ago and rebuilt many times: in

Two hundred years ago Jinshan Temple stood on an island in the Yangzi River. Subsequent migration of the river channel to the north has abandoned the island as a low hill on the southern bank near Zhenjiang. The river can just be seen running along the horizon.

the Song dynasty as two pagodas, in the Ming as a single tower and three times in the Qing period. Fa Hai or Pei Gong Cave is identified by a statue of the monk Fa Hai, son of a Tang-dynasty prime minister. Fa Hai lived here when he came to the temple, having first studied at Lushan. It is said that when the monk discovered a pot of gold, he gave it to the local officials. The emperor ordered that the gold be returned to Fa Hai, to rebuild the temple, thereafter named Golden Hill Temple.

The extraordinary folk tale of the White Snake is connected to Fa Hai. The story tells of a 1,000-year old white snake, Bai Suzhen, who, longing for a life among mortals, changed herself into a beautiful maiden. She married a young herbalist, Xu Xian, whom she first met on the famous Broken Bridge on the West Lake in Hangzhou. The happy couple set up business dispensing medicines, but Suzhen's magical cures aroused the anger of the powerful Buddhist monk, Fa Hai. His machinations put the couple through many trials and tribulations, including imprisonment of Xu Xian, before he was eventually defeated. At one point Xu Xian escaped through the Bai Long Dong (White Dragon Cave) on Jin Shan, for though narrow it is said to lead to Hangzhou, where the herbalist and Suzhen were reunited.

In the temple, a bronze drum, presented in the Qing dynasty (1644–1911), is one of the treasures of the Four Precious Rooms (Sibao Shi). It is believed to have belonged to Zhuge Liang (181–234, see page 42) and to have doubled as a cooking pot when not being beaten in war. Another is Su Dongpo's official mandarin belt of 20 jade pieces. Su apparently had to forfeit his belt when he lost a debate on Buddhism with his friend, the monk Fo Yin.

Jinshan Temple in Zhenjiang has been an important Buddhist temple for centuries

The scroll-adorned Fo Dian (Buddha Hall), with its 18 luohan (disciples of Buddha) statues, is where the monks hold their services.

West of Jin Shan, along the road that runs beside an artificial lake, is Zhongling Spring, the 'Foremost Spring under Heaven'. It was graded by the Tang scholar, Lu Yu, whose Book of Teas listed and classified seven springs in China according to the water's compatibility with tea. Zhongling's water was judged the sweetest for brewing tea. The bubbling spring trickles into a small pool enclosed by bamboo groves, but today its water is anything but sweet.

BEIGU SHAN

Rising from the Yangzi the steep cliff face of the 53-metre high Beigu Shan was a natural fortification and was chosen by the King of Wu, Sun Quan, as the site of his capital, Tiewangcheng, in the third century. The Martyr's Monument now stands where the great Wu general, Zhou Yu, made his headquarters. The novel Romance of the Three Kingdoms (see pages 304–5) contains many stories concerning Beigu Shan.

The exquisite **Iron Pagoda** dates from the Song dynasty (960–1279) and has an extraordinary history of survival. Erected in the 11th century on the site of an earlier pagoda, it had nine tiers. In the Ming dynasty (1368–1644), a tidal wave destroyed seven tiers, which were later replaced. In the Qing (1644–1911), the upper tiers were again destroyed, this time by lightning. Several Ming tiers were discovered nearby during restoration in 1961 and replaced in position above the only two remaining original Tang tiers. Over 2,000 Tang (618–907) relics were also found at that time. The Ganlu (Sweet Dew) Temple buildings now house painting exhibits.

The Hen Stone was carved into the shape of a ram at the end of the last century. It is believed that the King of Wu sat on this stone when planning his strategy for the great Battle of the Red Cliff (see pages 402–3).

The pretty Duojing Lou (Tower of Many Views) is said to have been the dressing room of Liu Bei's wife, the sister of Sun Quan. Song-dynasty literati frequently held banquets in it.

Liu Bei's wife is said to have committed suicide from the Jijiang Ting (Sacrificing to the River Pavilion). She threw herself into the river upon hearing of the death of her husband at Baidi Cheng (see pages 42 and 54), after his defeat by her brother, the treacherous Sun Quan.

The two Shijian Shi (Sword Testing Stones), each split neatly in two, were reputedly cloven by the swords of Liu Bei and Sun Quan, who were at that time outwardly in alliance over regaining the city of Jiangling (present-day Jingzhou) but each secretly plotting to betray the other.

The three characters liu ma jian—'Hold back the horse from the cliff'—on the face below the hill, are associated with a story that also involves Liu and Sun. At a

COASTAL DELTA

banquet together, Liu, who being from the northwest was an expert cavalryman but was less adept at naval warfare, said to Sun, 'Now I know why southerners can row boats so well, and northerners manage their horses.' Sun took offence at what he considered a backhanded compliment, and challenged Liu to a race. In a drunken state they leapt on to their horses. As they reached the cliff edge Liu reined in his horse, but Sun could not and was saved from death only at the last moment by Liu.

JIAO SHAN

Four kilometres northeast of Zhenjiang, the tiny island of Jiao Shan can be reached by a local ferry. It was named after a hermit scholar-monk, Jiao Guang, of the Eastern Han period (25–220), who is said to have lived in what is known as the Three Summons Cave.

Thrice Jiao was invited by the emperor to take an official post, and thrice he refused. He lived to be 120 years old, treating and healing the local fisherfolk.

At the foot of the hill is **Dinghui Temple** (Temple of Stability and Wisdom), built on the site of an earlier temple in the Tang dynasty (618–907). It was burnt down and rebuilt in the Ming (1368–1644). Old ginkgo trees stand in front of the main hall which contains some fine bronze luohan (disciples of Buddha) statues, presented by temples at Wutai Shan in Shanxi Province.

The chief attraction of the **Jiao Shan Forest of Tablets** (Bei Lin), a collection of over 260 inscribed stones classified into literary, artistic and historic works, the earliest of which date from the Eastern Jin dynasty (317–420), is the White Crane Tablet cut with the calligraphy of Wang Yizhe (321–79). Wang was fond of white cranes (which symbolize longevity) and on seeing one on Jiao Shan asked if he could have it. The monk refused at first, but on learning Wang's identity agreed that he could collect the crane on his next visit.

Returning a year later, Wang discovered that the crane had died and had been buried, wrapped in yellow silk, on the hillside. His text of the sad story of the crane was preserved on a tablet on the hill. Later, during an earthquake, part of the inscription broke off and fell into the river. A thousand years later, in 1713, five pieces were recovered upstream, and were restored to their rightful place.

The Cannon Platform dates from the first Anglo-Chinese Opium War. (Another lies on Elephant Hill on the south bank of the Yangzi.) In the course of the war, British naval ships sailed up the river and, in a two-pronged attack, captured the stronghold, killing 500 Chinese troops. The walls, pockmarked with cannon shell, are made of rammed earth and sticky-rice water.

Near the top of the hill are viewing pavilions and the Bie Feng Yan cottage in which Zheng Banqiao (1693–1765), one of the Eight Eccentric Painters of the Yangzhou school, lived for five years.

The Iron Pagoda on Beigu Shan in Zhenjiang overlooks the Yangzi River and dates from the 11th century, during the Song dynasty

ZHENJIANG MUSEUM

A fascinating survivor of the foreign concession in Zhenjiang is the former British Consulate at the foot of a knoll overlooking the port. The compound consists of seven buildings, a couple of which now form the city's museum. They house a collection of ancient bronzeware, celadon, porcelain, fabrics and a cache of Tang-dynasty silverware (618–907) unearthed in the Danyang area in 1983. Outside in the overgrown garden lies the abandoned anchor of HMS Amethyst, trapped and nearly sunk by Communist shell-fire in 1949. Cannons brought back from Jiaoshan recall Zhenjiang's involvement in the first Opium War.

YANGZHOU

There is a little verse, much quoted in reference to Yangzhou, which goes something like this:

> *Brilliant moonlight, orioles, flowers and pavilions of jade,*
> *All attest to the past and present glories of Yangzhou.*

To these glories might also be added Yangzhou's tradition of producing beautiful women. Yangzhou was one of the most important cities on the Grand Canal and is a delightful place to visit, retaining to some degree the feeling of its rich cultural and historical traditions. A vehicular ferry from Zhenjiang crosses the Yangzi and from the north bank the drive to Yangzhou takes half an hour. Many traditional arts and crafts are still practised: lacquerware, paper-cuts, lanterns, embroidery, penjing (miniature gardens) and seal carving.

Yangzhou has one of the great cuisines of China and every foreigner knows—indirectly—about it, for Yangzhou is the home of the worldwide favourite Chinese dish of fried rice (Yangzhou chaofan).

HISTORY OF YANGZHOU

The city's history began over 2,400 years ago in the Spring and Autumn period (722–481 BC); one of the early nine provincial areas of China was called after it. The Sui emperor, Yangdi, initiated the construction of the Grand Canal here in 605, which eventually made Yangzhou the hub of land and water transportation. Emperor Yangdi visited the city three times in grand dragon-boats. He built a palace, retired and was buried here, after being assassinated in 618. Yangzhou was also a centre of classical learning and religion. Emperors, prime ministers and men of letters through the ages visited Yangzhou and many held official positions,

Smoke rises from the little tearoom on the Imperial Jetty, as breakfast is prepared. On his southern peregrinations this rather secret spot in Yangzhou was one of the favourite resting places of Qing dynasty emperor Qianlong.

including the great traveller Marco Polo, who was supposedly governor general of the city for three years, although no contemporary documents support this.

By the Tang dynasty (618–907) Yangzhou's trading links with Arab merchants were well established. A foreign community numbering about a thousand lived in the city. It was said that 'at night a thousand lanterns lit up the clouds'. The economy was based on the salt monopoly and on grain shipments to the capital.

Yangzhou, along with so many other middle and lower Yangzi cities, suffered badly during the Taiping Rebellion in the mid-19th century (see pages 456–7). In addition, the silting of the Yangzi and the flooding of the Grand Canal gradually undermined its entrepôt role, as grain shipments were increasingly transported by sea via Shanghai, rather than along the Grand Canal. Changes in the salt administration and the arrival of the railways were the coup de grâce in Yangzhou's decline.

During the late 18th century an individualistic school of painters sprang up, known as the Eight Eccentrics of Yangzhou, whose bold style has a strong following today.

What To See In Yangzhou

The streets of Yangzhou reveal much that is charming and interesting. Stroll down Guoqing Lu past craftsmen painting mirrors and making bamboo steamers and cloth shoes, then along Dujiang Lu where wooden-fronted shops, partitioned with

The elegant Five Pavilion Bridge (Wuting Qiao) dominates one end of Yangzhou's Slender West Lake

rattan matting, sell household goods, basketware and fireworks, and itinerant sugar cane vendors hawk their wares. The road eventually reaches the Grand Canal, where, from the bridge, boat life can be observed as it passes by. The courtyards of the small, grey-tiled houses are cluttered with pots of flowers and miniature *penjing* plants—a speciality of the region. Rows of white cabbage and strips of turnip hang out to dry. One may also walk along the small canals.

The **Imperial Jetty**, where the Qing emperors disembarked, is situated on the canal in front of the Xiyuan Hotel. Visit also Yechun Yuan, where a poetry club used to meet in the Qing dynasty (1644–1911). It is now a tea-house and specializes in Yellow Bridge Buns, which were first created to supply the troops during the Sino-Japanese War. Further on is the Luyang Cun, a garden filled with miniature plants, goldfish and birds.

SLENDER WEST LAKE (SHOUXI HU)

This is a beautiful man-made lake dating from the Tang dynasty (618–907) and surrounded by weeping willows and pavilions. The Fishing Platform at the end of the Dyke of Spring Willows was reputedly used by Emperor Qianlong (reigned 1736–96). Through its arches different views of the beautiful **Five Pavilion Bridge** (Wuting Qiao), built in 1757, are presented. The red pillars of the pavilions with their yellow-tiled roofs rest on 15 stone arches; extravagant claims are made about the splendid moonlit scene at the bridge at the Mid-autumn Festival—in a particularly auspicious year the moon is said to be reflected in the water under each arch. Near the bridge is a white stupa, whose origin is attributed to Emperor Qianlong. It seems that he remarked on a visit that though this scenic spot reminded him of Beihai Park in Beijing, it was a pity that there was no white stupa to complete the resemblance. The zealous local officials worked through the night to carve a full-sized stupa from salt. The emperor was duly impressed and, when he returned north, the permanent version that stands today was built. The Friendship Hall contains a stone tablet with a description of Marco Polo's three-year governorship in Yangzhou, and his portrait. The lovely Yu Garden was built in 1915 as the residence of the local warlord, Yu Baoshan.

WENFENG PAGODA

This seven-tiered wooden and brick pagoda stands beside a busy stretch of the Grand Canal south of the city, where boats load and unload goods—bamboo matting, soya beans, rice and cotton. Most of the boats are made of concrete; very few are of wood. Men beating gongs parade up and down with carts; they do the shopping for the boat-people who are too busy to go ashore and do their own. The pagoda offers a good overview of the town.

XIANHE MOSQUE (FAIRY CRANE MOSQUE)

This ancient mosque was first built in 1275 to serve the needs of the Arab traders and was rebuilt twice in the Ming dynasty (1368–1644). Its ancient pine and ginkgo trees are believed to be around 800 years old. The mosque is supposed to resemble a crane in shape: the main entrance is the head; the wells on either side, the eyes; the left-hand path, the neck; the prayer hall, the body; the north and south halls, the wings. Arabic scrolls executed in Chinese calligraphic style hang in one of the halls. There are some 3,600 Hui (Muslims) in Yangzhou.

TOMB OF PUHADDIN

Puhaddin was a 16th-generation descendant of the Prophet Mohammed, founder of Islam. He came to China in the second half of the 13th century and was in Yangzhou between 1265 and 1275, helping to build the Fairy Crane Mosque. He travelled to Shandong Province to spread the word of Islam, but became ill and died there. He was buried, according to his wish, in Yangzhou. A fine, carved white marble stairway leads to the cemetery. The majority of the 25 tombs here are those of Chinese Muslims but a few are the tombs of early Arab traders; the architectural style of the tombs is completely Arabian.

YANGZHOU MUSEUM

This building was originally erected in 1772 around the tomb of Shi Kefa (1601–45) who was in command of Yangzhou when the Qing armies moved south to consolidate their power. A supporter of the Ming dynasty, Shi and his 4,000 troops held out against the Qing army for ten days, five times refusing to surrender and fighting to the death. The museum's most prized possession is its collection of 18th-century paintings and calligraphy by the Eight Eccentrics of Yangzhou, whose rejection of the orthodox style of the day was a major breakthrough in Chinese painting.

GARDENS

The rich salt merchants of Yangzhou left a legacy of many exquisite gardens. The delightful Ge Garden north of Dongguan Jie was the home of a rich 19th-century salt merchant, Huang Yingtai. Its architecture, bamboo groves and landscaping are typical of the famous private gardens of Suzhou. The garden got its name from its bamboo leaves, shaped like the Chinese character for ge. On Xuningmen Jie is the popular He Garden, built by He Zhidao. It once belonged to the Qing Court's ambassador to France, and some Western architectural influences can be seen.

WENCHANG GE (PAVILION OF FLOURISHING CULTURE)

This 'mini' Temple of Heaven, dedicated to the god of literary success, is three

The seven-storeyed Wenfeng Pagoda standing beside the Grand Canal in the south of Yangzhou, as it appeared in 1983

storeys high and took ten years to build; just before completion it burnt down, only to be immediately rebuilt in 1585. Originally situated on a bridge across a canal, the area was transformed into a wide roadway, so Wenchang Ge now stands at the intersection of Wenhe Jie and Shita Jie. Nearby is the Stone Pagoda (Shi Ta), a highly valued Tang-dynasty relic. Its six sides are decorated with floral patterns.

TIANNING TEMPLE (TEMPLE OF HEAVENLY TRANQUILLITY)

The present buildings date from the Ming dynasty (1368–1644), though a temple existed here in the Song dynasty (960–1279). The Qing emperor, Qianlong, had a travel lodge built on one of his inspection tours. The temple is next to the Xiyuan Hotel.

DAMING TEMPLE

Daming Temple is part of a complex of buildings. The temple was built in the fifth century. Large incense burners with bells stand in front of the main hall in which services are held daily at 4pm.

The temple has strong ties with Japan. The Buddhist abbot, Jian Zhen (688–763), was invited to teach in Japan, and made five attempts to go there, but failed each time. It was on his sixth attempt, at the age of 66 and by then blind, that he succeeded in reaching the Japanese capital of Nara, where he set up a study centre at one of the temples. His contribution in bringing understanding of Chinese literature and arts, architecture, medicine and printing to Japan was commemorated in 1963, when a number of Chinese and Japanese Buddhists decided to build the Jian Zhen Memorial Hall. The walls are decorated with murals depicting his journeys. In 1980 the Japanese donated a wooden statue of Jian Zhen, a copy of the beautiful lacquer statue of the monk in the Nara Temple in Japan. In front of the wooden statue is an incense burner presented by Emperor Hirohito of Japan.

Pingshan Hall was built by the great Song-dynasty scholar, statesman and poet, Ouyang Xiu, in 1048 to entertain his guests when he was prefect of Yangzhou. A statue of him now stands in the hall. A student of his, Su Dongpo, also an official in Yangzhou, wrote a commemorative poem about Ouyang, which is engraved in stone on the walls.

In the gardens of the temple is another of the seven great springs of China, mentioned in the Tang-dynasty Book of Teas. This one is known as the 'Fifth Spring under Heaven'.

Parts of the Tang (618–907) city walls can be seen in the vicinity of Daming Temple and on Guanyin Hill, the site of the Sui Emperor Yangdi's palace.

NANTONG

Nantong is one of the 14 port cities opened to foreign investment projects under China's current policies of modernization. The city is an integral part of the Shanghai Economic Zone. The population of 7.4 million is engaged in industrial production, especially textiles. It is hoped that textile, precision machinery and communications industries will be established either as joint ventures or entirely foreign enterprises. Ten thousand-ton vessels berth at its deep-water harbour.

One of the city's heroes was Cao Gong, who in 1557 successfully defended the town against Japanese pirates roaming the coast of China. His heroic exploits earned him a high official position which he refused to accept. Cao was killed in another pirate raid shortly after. The Cao Gong Zhu Memorial Temple was built in his honour.

East of the city is Lang Shan (Wolf Hill), said to be haunted by the spirit of a white wolf. The temple on top is dedicated to a Song-dynasty Buddhist monk, whom legend endowed with magical powers over water demons. Boat people prayed to him for safe journeys. The main hall contains models of different types of river craft. At the base of Lang Shan is the Five Hills Park.

BAOSHAN

The giant Baoshan Steel Works on the south bank, near the mouth of the Huangpu River, is one of the largest in China. Japanese and West German technology and plant are being used. In the early stages the project ran into difficulties, not the least of which was the choice of site—marshy ground that caused subsidence. Moreover, the estuary was found to be too shallow to allow 100,000-ton freighters bearing imported iron ore to unload. The mill began operation in 1985.

HUANGPU RIVER

Just below Baoshan, boats pass by a large lighthouse and between buoys to turn south into the Huangpu River, on the last stage of the journey from Chongqing to Shanghai. On either side of the muddy river stretch wharf installations with facilities to handle ocean-going ships of 25,000 tons, and an annual shipping volume of about 100 million tons. This is China's largest port and its busiest. Apart from the hundreds of foreign and Chinese registered ships, the river is busy all day long with ferries, naval and police craft, lighters and dredgers.

The Huangpu is 114 kilometres in length, rising from Dianshan Lake southwest of Shanghai. Its banks were once simply mud flats. The river is subject to heavy silting from the Yangzi and requires constant dredging to keep the channels free.

ECONOMY of TIME and LABOR, exemplified in a CHINESE WATERMAN.

(top) Economy of Time and Labour, exemplified in a Chinese Waterman. *Copper engraving dated 1796 of an original sketch by William Alexander made during Lord Macartney's embassy to China in 1793. (bottom) Nineteenth century watercolour of a Chinese junk.*

*Nineteenth century paintings illustrating a fishmonger's shop (top)
and a poulterer's shop (bottom)*

Soon after entering the river, on the western bank is the area known as Wusong, where in 1842, during the Opium War, a fleet of British warships and support vessels opened fire on the ill-defended Chinese fort and its miles of earthworks. After a two-hour bombardment they forced their way up to Suzhou Creek and on to Shanghai. The fort was heroically defended but the Chinese were no match for the British fleet. Among the many Chinese casualties was a highly respected 76-year-old admiral who had been at sea for 50 years and who, it was said, wrapped himself in cotton wool before his battles to make himself invulnerable. This was a decisive battle, for it enabled the fleet to occupy Shanghai and move on up the Yangzi; later in the year, the Treaty of Nanking (Nanjing) was signed, opening many Chinese cities to foreign trade.

Before the opium trade was legitimized in 1860, opium clippers and steamers unloaded their cargo on to hulks permanently moored at Wusong, Shanghai's outer anchorage, before they were smuggled into the hinterland.

Gradually Shanghai's imposing skyline appears as boats sidle up to the berth alongside Zhongshan Lu, once known as the Bund, and lined with impressive European-style buildings from a bygone era.

This empty barge, passing through a lock on the Grand Canal in Jiangsu Province, is on its way to Xuzhou, in the north of the province, where it will be filled with over 3,000 tonnes of coal. The cargo is then shipped 150 kilometres south to fuel industries on the Yangzi River. Over 24 million tonnes of coal is transported in this way each year.

THE GRAND CANAL

The Grand Canal meanders some 2,500 kilometres through eastern China and remains the longest man-made waterway in the world. In ancient times it was crucial for the transportation of grain from the fertile Yangzi delta to the relatively barren north, and in developing communications across the vast territory that the waterway system served. From the Yellow River valley, from which Chinese civilization sprang, culture and learning spread southwards along the canal, until by the Tang dynasty (618–907) such cities as Yangzhou and Hangzhou had themselves become centres of art and philosophy.

The first link in this canal system was constructed in the fifth century BC by the King of the state of Wu. Called the Hong Gou (Wild Geese) Canal, it connected the Yangzi with the Huai River and was built to transport the king's troops and keep them supplied during the invasion of the neighbouring states of Song and Lu to the north.

The next major step in the overall construction of the Grand Canal came about during the Sui dynasty (581–618), when the emperor Yangdi came to power. Often portrayed as a vain and ambitious megalomaniac, he commissioned the building of a new capital at Luoyang. Constructed in 605, it involved hundreds of thousands of workers. With a new capital in place, Yangdi then had to ensure adequate communication with other parts of his empire. So his next and most impressive project was the digging of a canal to permanently join the northern and southern provinces.

It was a gigantic undertaking. Although it linked many smaller, existing but derelict canals, which had to be dredged, it nonetheless involved the construction of huge sections of new waterways. The emperor achieved this by press-ganging five-and-a-half million peasants into virtual slave labour. In some areas all males between the ages of 15 and 50 were forced to work, watched over by armed guards.

The result was a 2,500-kilometre canal, rising at one point to 42 metres above sea level, covering ten degrees of latitude. Stretching all the way from Beijing to Hangzhou with Luoyang at its centre, it connected China's five main rivers and linked the north to the fertile Yangzi river basin for the first time. It had taken just six years. During this time some two million workers were classified as *zhe*, a rather vague term meaning lost or missing.

This new canal meant barges could transport food and commodities virtually the whole length of the country, particularly grain from the lower

With most of his 65 years spent on the barges of the Grand Canal in Jiangsu Province, Huang Bing Zhang retired a few years ago. But bored with life on dry land he returned to work on the water once more, his barges carrying cargo destined for the industrial area along the Yangzi River.

Yangzi basin to the northern regions to feed the emperor's troops, who were pursuing the latest of Yangdi's despotic schemes—the invasion of Korea. However, it proved his 'bridge too far' and he suffered a defeat that contributed to his downfall and that of his dynasty—a brief but turbulent 29 years. Often accused of sheer extravagance in building the Grand Canal so that he could travel in luxury from his capital Luoyang to his holiday city of Hangzhou, he is seldom credited with the real economic benefit that it brought to China. The importance of his legacy of the Grand Canal cannot be understated and much of the prosperity of the following Tang dynasty (618–907) is attributable to it. During this time over 300,000 tons of grain were shipped northwards annually under the escort of 120,000 soldiers.

It is not until the 13th century and the Mongol Yuan dynasty (1279–1368) that we see any further significant addition to the Grand Canal. Kublai Khan became emperor of China in 1271, building his new capital on the site of present-day Beijing. Most of the previous emperors had built their capitals further south, to make it easier to defend themselves from the Mongols and to be closer to sources of food supply. However, Kublai Khan, with an empire extending well into Central Asia, decided to build his new city closer to his tribal homelands on the northern steppes.

Khanbaliq, as the new capital was called, was totally dependent on the Grand Canal for its survival. The emperor was aware of the need for a rapid supply of grain, unimpeded by pirates along the sea route and therefore set about transforming the canal system. By cutting a new section between the Yangzi and Yellow rivers, he shortened its length from 2,500 to 1,780 kilometres, significantly improving delivery time from the southern provinces.

A succession of imperial courts came to rely on the Canal not only for the supply of grain but commodities such as textiles, tea, sugar, salt, fruits, game, fish, meat, cooking oil, medicinal herbs, paper, writing brushes and inkstones, porcelain, lacquerware, pearls, jadeite, flowers; mineral ores—especially copper and lead for casting coins; building materials such as bamboo, reed, timber, bricks and stone—most materials for constructing the temples and palaces had to be transported along the Canal. In fact, the huge timber beams still seen in many of the imperial buildings today came from the forests of Sichuan, and were first floated down the Yangzi River as far as Yangzhou, before continuing up the Grand Canal.

The Jesuit priest Matteo Ricci, who lived and worked in China during the late 16th and early 17th centuries, wrote: 'Each year the southern provinces provide the [emperor] with everything needed or wanted to live well in the unfertile province of [Beijing]... all of which must arrive on a fixed day, otherwise those who are paid to transport them are subject to a heavy fine. The boats called cavaliers are commanded by palace eunuchs, and they always travel rapidly, in fleets of eight or ten. During the hot summer season much of the food stuffs would spoil before reaching [Beijing], so they are kept on ice to preserve them. The ice gradually melts, and so great stores of it are kept at certain stops, and the boats are liberally supplied with enough of it to keep their cargoes fresh until arrival.'

During the Qing dynasty (1644–1911) official corruption, flooding and silting caused the gradual decline of the Grand Canal. As we are told by the chronicler of Lord Elgin's 1857–9 journeys, sections 'of that once celebrated channel of internal commerce of the empire were destroyed by the flooding of the Yellow River; the consequence is, that the enormous Imperial Grain junks formerly employed now line the bank in rotting condition. They are singular specimens of natural architecture, of immense solidity, and capable of transporting from two to three hundred tons of rice each.'

Despite floods the canal around Suzhou, Wuxi and Yangzhou remained extremely busy. Laurence Oliphant, private secretary to Lord Elgin's 1857 embassy to China, recorded: 'There are as many different varieties of boats here as there are of vehicles in Fleet Street and the waterway was as inconveniently crowded as that celebrated thoroughfare usually is… Gentlemen's private carriages were here represented by gorgeous mandarin-junks, with a huge umbrella on the top and a gong at the entrance to the cabin, beaten at intervals by calfless flunkeys.' There is even a mention of the courtesan or flower boats: 'other junks there were, more gaudily painted even than these from whence issued shrill voices and sounds of noisy laughter and music.'

Today gone are the mandarin-junks, flower boats and regal precessions, but many of the craft now used are probably little different from those plying the waterway in previous centuries. During the Qing dynasty (1644–1911) official corruption, flooding and silting caused the gradual decline of the Grand Canal. Various attempts have been made since then to rejuvenate the Grand Canal along its entire length, but they invariably foundered due mainly to the age-old problem of water shortages in the arid north, and the waterway in this part of the country has been very much redundant for decades. However, in the south, throughout Jiangsu Province, the Canal is still a busy thoroughfare and forms part of a wider network of canals that remains the lifeblood this low-lying region.

The route of the Grand Canal also forms part of an ambitious scheme to channel water from the south of the country to the arid north, where increasingly heavy use of water, particularly for industry and agriculture, have meant that the traditional sources are drying up. (See the South to North Water Transfer Scheme (SNWTS) on pages 383–7.)

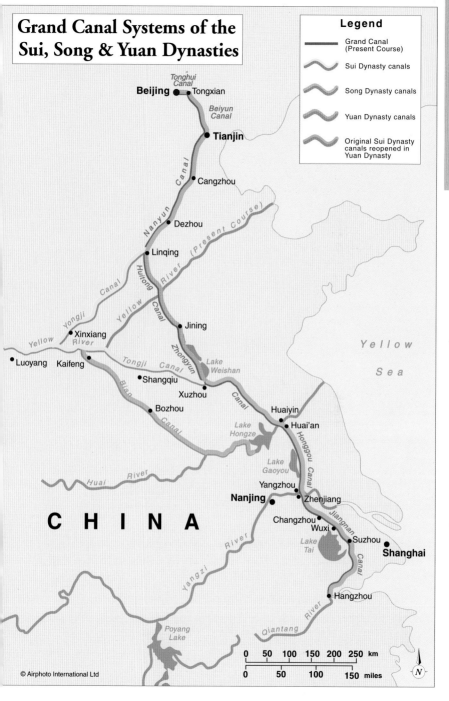

Grand Canal Systems of the Sui, Song & Yuan Dynasties

Legend

—	Grand Canal (Present Course)
～	Sui Dynasty canals
～	Song Dynasty canals
～	Yuan Dynasty canals
～	Original Sui Dynasty canals reopened in Yuan Dynasty

Tonghui Canal

Beijing • Tongxian

Beiyun Canal

Tianjin

• Cangzhou

Nanyun Canal

• Dezhou

River (Present Course)

• Linqing

Yongji Canal

Huitong Canal

Yellow Canal

• Xinxiang

Yellow River

• Jining

Zhongyun Canal

Lake Weishan

• Luoyang   Kaifeng

Tongji Canal

Bian Canal

• Shangqiu

• Xuzhou

• Bozhou

Canal

Huaiyin

• Huai'an

Lake Hongze

Hongou Canal

Huai River

Lake Gaoyou

Yangzhou •

Nanjing •

Zhenjiang

Changzhou •

Wuxi •

Jiangnan Canal

Lake Tai

Suzhou •

Shanghai

Yangzi River

Hangzhou •

Qiantang River

Poyang Lake

Y e l l o w   S e a

C H I N A

0	50	100	150	200	250	km
0		50		100	150	miles

N

© Airphoto International Ltd

A fleet of junks under full sail on the Huangpu River at Shanghai in 1983

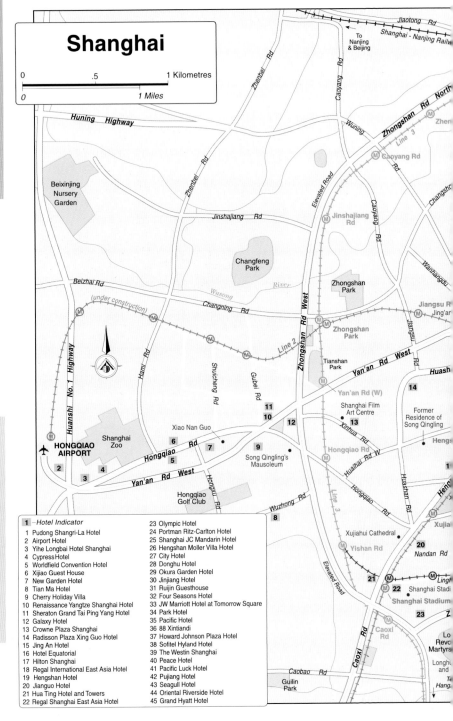

Shanghai

COASTAL DELTA

SHANGHAI

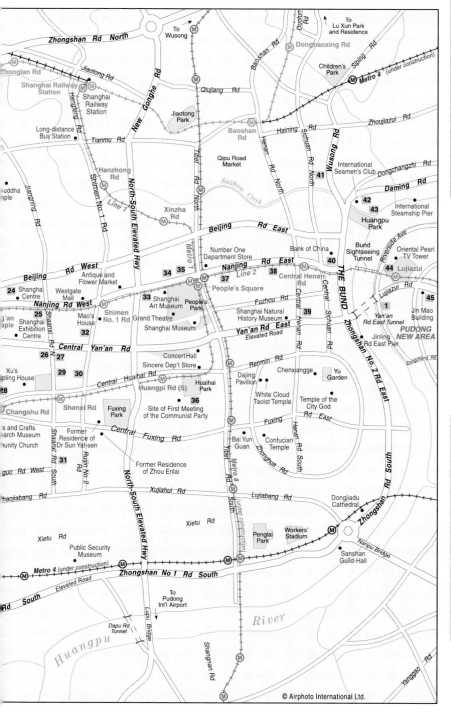

To Lu Xun Park
and Residence

To
Wusong

Zhongshan Rd North

Zhongtan Rd

Jiaotong Rd

Shanghai Railway
Station

Hengfeng Rd

Shanghai
Railway
Station

Long-distance
Bus Station

Tianmu Rd

Dongbaoxing Rd

Baoshan Rd

Siping Rd

Children's
Park

Metro 4 (under construction)

Qiujiang Rd

New Gonghe Rd

Jiaotong
Park

Baoshan
Rd

Haining Rd

Sichuan Rd North

Wusong Rd

Zhoujiazui Rd

Jiangning Rd

Buddha
Temple

Hanzhong
Rd

North-South Elevated Hwy

Shimen No.1 Rd

Line 1

Tiber Rd

Henan Rd North

Qipu Road
Market

Suzhou Creek

International
Seamen's Club

Dongchangzhi Rd

Daming Rd

41

Xinzha
Rd

Beijing Rd East

42

43

Huangpu
Park

International
Steamship Pier

Beijing Rd West

24 Shanghai
Centre

Shanxi Rd

Nanjing Rd West

25
Shanghai
Exhibition
Centre

Antique and
Flower Market

Westgate
Mall

Mao's
House

Shimen
No.1 Rd

33 Shanghai
Art Museum

Number One
Department Store

34 35

People's
Park

Grand Theatre

Shanghai Museum

Nanjing Rd East

37

People's Square

Metro 1

Metro 2

Bank of China

38

Central Henan
Rd

Bund
Sightseeing
Tunnel

40

THE BUND

Riverside Ave

Oriental Pearl
TV Tower

44 Lujiazui

Lujiazui Rd

45

Fuzhou Rd

Shanghai Natural
History Museum

39

Central Henan Rd

Sichuan Rd

Yan'an
Rd East Tunnel

Jin Mao
Building

1

Yan'an

Rd

Line 2

Jinling
Rd East Pier

PUDONG
NEW AREA

Dongchang Rd

32

Central Yan'an Rd

Yan'an Rd East
Elevated Road

Zhongshan No.2 Rd East

26

27

Xu's
Sampling House

29 30

Concert Hall

Sincere Dep't Store

Renmin Rd

Chenxiangge

Yu
Garden

Central Huaihai Rd

Huangpi Rd (S)

36

Huaihai
Park

Dajing
Pavilion

White Cloud
Taoist Temple

Temple of
the City God

Changshu Rd

Shanxi Rd

Fuxing
Park

Site of First Meeting
of the Communist Party

Fuxing Rd East

Henan Rd South

s and Crafts
earch Museum

munity Church

Former
Residence of
Dr Sun Yat-sen

Central Fuxing Rd

Bai Yun
Guan

Confucian
Temple

Shaanxi Rd South

31

Ruijin No.2 Rd

Former Residence
of Zhou Enlai

Zhonghua Rd

guo Rd West

haojiabang Rd

Xujiahui Rd

Metro 8 (under construction)

Tiber Rd South

Lujiabang Rd

Dongjiadu
Cathedral

Zhongshan Rd South

Xietu Rd

Xietu Rd

Penglai
Park

Workers'
Stadium

Nanpu Bridge

Sanshan
Guild-Hall

Public Security
Museum

Metro 4 (under construction)

Zhongshan No 1 Rd South

Rd South Elevated Road

North-South Elevated Hwy

To Pudong
Int'l Airport

Dapu Rd
Tunnel

Lupu Bridge

Shangnan Rd

River

Yanggao Rd

Huangpu

© Airphoto International Ltd.

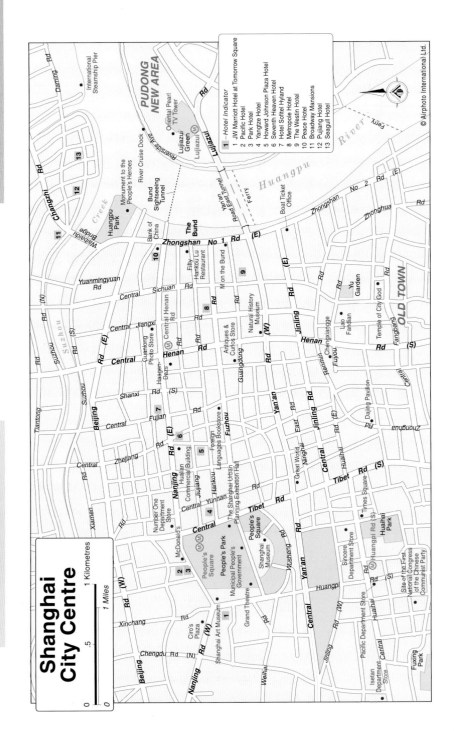

SHANGHAI

Shanghai City Centre

Hotel Indicator

1. JW Marriott Hotel at Tomorrow Square
2. Pacific Hotel
3. Park Hotel
4. Yangtze Hotel
5. Howard Johnson Plaza Hotel
6. Seventh Heaven Hotel
7. Hotel Sofitel Hyland
8. Metropole Hotel
9. The Westin Hotel
10. Peace Hotel
11. Broadway Mansions
12. Pujiang Hotel
13. Seagull Hotel

© Airphoto International Ltd.

PUDONG NEW AREA

International Steamship Pier

Oriental Pearl TV Tower

Lujiazui Green

Lujiazui

Huangpu River

Ferry

River Cruise Dock

Monument to the People's Heroes

Bund Sightseeing Tunnel

Huangpu Park

Waibaidu Bridge

Bank of China

The Bund

Boat Ticket Office

Yan'an Tunnel Road East

Zhongshan No 1 Rd (E)

Zhongshan No 1 Rd (E)

Fifty Hankou Lu Restaurant

M on the Bund

Natural History Museum

Yu Garden

OLD TOWN

Temple of City God

Liao Fandian

Antiques & Curios Store

Guangdong

Chenxiangge

Fuyou

Dajing Pavilion

Natural People's Heroes

Yuanmingyuan Rd

Suzhou Creek

Central (N)

Central (E)

Central Jiangxi

Sichuan

Central Henan

Henan

Jinling

Henan

Jinling Rd

Jinling Rd (E)

Guanming Photo Store

Haagen-Dazs

Shanxi Rd (S)

Fujian

Nanjing Rd (E)

Foreign Languages Bookstore

Fuzhou

Yan'an

Yan'an East

Central

Huaihai

Great World

Ninghai

Tibet Rd

Tibet Rd (S)

Times Square

Huaihai Park

Beijing

Central

Zhejiang

Hualian Commercial Building

The Shanghai Urban Planning Exhibition Hall

Number One Department Store

Central Yunnan

Jiujiang

McDonald's

People's Square

People's Park

Municipal People's Government

Shanghai Museum

Wusheng

Tibet Rd

Yan'an

Central

Huangpi

Sincere Department Store

Huangpi Rd (S)

Site of the First National Congress of the Chinese Communist Party

Shanghai Art Museum

Ciro's Plaza

Grand Theatre

Nanjing Rd (W)

Beijing Rd (W)

Xinchang

Chengdu Rd (N)

Weihai

Nanjing

Huaihai

Central

Jining

Pacific Department Store

Isetan Department Store

Fuxing Park

Daming Rd

Changzhi Rd

Shanghai

Shanghai, like Tianjin, Beijing and Chongqing, is a municipality that is directly administered by the central government. Shanghai is second to Chongqing in terms of population with a 2001 census putting the resident population at nearly 17 million. However it is estimated that at any time Shanghai has at least another three million 'floating population'. The city has historically been a major centre for trade and industry. Dulled by the Maoist years Shanghai is again aiming to restore its former status as Asia's leading centre for trade, finance and commerce. Shanghai is also establishing itself as a major convention and conference destination as well as a burgeoning centre for the arts and culture. It is also on the map for its sports activities that include international tennis events and Formula One motor racing at Anting in its suburbs.

Despite its modern appearance and aspirations, for many foreigners Shanghai conjures up past images and stories of adventure and intrigue. Many of these were probably no exaggeration, for Shanghai was a uniquely colourful, violent and unforgiving city. Even though huge areas of buildings dating back to the early part of the last century have been razed in recent years, many European style living quarters have survived—especially in the area of the former French Concession. Many landmark 1930s art deco apartments, clubs and commercial buildings have also survived, so that one can still clearly imagine the extraordinary life of pre-1949 Shanghai.

HISTORY OF SHANGHAI

The name Shanghai, which means 'on the sea', was first used in AD 960 when the settlement was a backward fishing village. In 1554, the town was surrounded by a seven-metre high crenellated city wall and a moat to protect it against the frequent incursions of Japanese pirates. By the 17th century there were signs of growing wealth, but when the British troops stormed its undefended walls in 1842, Shanghai was still only a county town of no great importance.

The first foreign settlement was established in 1843, when the newly-appointed British Consul arrived to negotiate for a 138-acre site north of the existing city. This site was joined with the American Settlement, founded in 1848 north of Suzhou Creek, to form the International Settlement in 1863. Subsequent negotiations with the Chinese increased the area of the International Settlement to more than 5,500 acres (about 22 square kilometres). The French Concession was established on 164 acres (about 0.6 square kilometres) in 1849 and was finally extended to about 2,500 acres (about ten square kilometres). The Japanese, also, had secured a concession by the end of the last century, which became a centre for cotton-spinning factories. These settlements were self-administered and were outside Chinese government jurisdiction.

The old Chinese City, occupied by one group of the Taiping rebels—the Small Sword Society—between 1853 and 1855, became the scene of lawlessness and fighting. The foreign community, concerned for its own safety, formed the Shanghai Volunteer Corps, recruited from local traders and diplomats. They were even prepared to take on the imperial troops: backed by British and American officers and men from visiting warships, the volunteers issued an ultimatum for the troops' removal, an action which precipitated the Battle of Muddy Flat in 1854. The imperial troops were duly driven away from their encampment, which was the site of the old racecourse, now the People's Park.

Shanghai was again threatened by the Taiping rebels in the 1860s, but they were quelled by the Ever Victorious Army made up of foreigners and Chinese, established for this very purpose. An American, Frederick Townsend Ward, a Frenchman, Henri A Burgevine, and a Briton, Charles George Gordon ('Chinese Gordon', later of Khartoum fame), took successive command and were all made officers of the Qing Imperial Army.

The nationwide upheavals in the 20th century—the 1900 Boxer Rebellion, the 1911 Revolution, the Sino-Japanese War—took their toll on Shanghai's millions. Hundreds of thousands of Chinese poured into the foreign settlements for protection and then stayed on. Nevertheless, Shanghai continued to flourish as an entrepôt with its staple exports of tea and silk, and imports of piece goods and opium. Banking played an important part in this great trading city, which had its own stock exchange.

The foreigners' lifestyle was grand and lavish for those who could afford to participate in clubs, race meetings, paper chases and nightclubs. The arrival in the 1930s of some 25,000 White Russian refugees enlivened the nightlife of cabarets and dance halls in 'Frenchtown', as the French Concession was called by the Anglo-Saxons. Chinese secret societies controlled the seamy side of Shanghai life, and the city was the Hollywood of China with a thriving movie industry.

But the Shanghai workers were subjected to appalling working conditions, overcrowding and exploitation, a situation leading inevitably to industrial unrest and revolutionary activity. The Communist Party of China was founded in Shanghai in 1921 at a secret meeting in the French Concession. The Party fomented strikes and uprisings—some of them actually planned by Zhou Enlai, later premier—but these activities were violently suppressed by the Nationalist government. This was a period of debate among Chinese intellectuals, who were influenced by the philosophies and experience of the more industrialized West. Many of these Chinese had studied abroad or at missionary institutions of higher learning in Shanghai.

SHANGHAI'S HISTORY THROUGH ITS NAMES

When the Chinese want to be literary, or brief, they call Shanghai 'Hu'. The name bespeaks Shanghai's origins as a fishing village, for *hu* is a bamboo fishing device, used in the third century by the people who lived around the Songjiang River (which was subsequently renamed Wusong River, and which forms the upper reaches of the Suzhou Creek). Shanghai is also sometimes known as Chunshen—or Shen for short—because in the third century BC, at the time of the Warring States (475–221 BC), the site on which the city now stands was a fief of the Lord Chunshen, prime minister to the King of the State of Chu. Another name with which Shanghai is associated is Huating. This was a county established in 751, over an area which covers part of present-day Shanghai.

Shanghai took its name from the Shanghai River, a tributary, long since gone, of the Songjiang. A township sprang into being on the west bank of the river, as, recognizing its natural advantages as a port, junks and ships came to berth there. This was Shanghai, which presently became the largest town in Huating County. In 1292, Shanghai and four other towns in Huating were brought together to form the County of Shanghai. It was at about this time that the Songjiang was renamed the Wusong River.

But today when most Chinese think of Shanghai, they think not so much of the Wusong as of the Huangpu River. Shanghai's qualifications as a deep water port were greatly improved when a canal—forming that part of the Huangpu downstream of Waibaidu Bridge—was dredged and widened in the fourteenth century. Ships crowded the wharves of Shanghai, and the port itself grew in size and importance, thriving off the trade in cotton and other goods between the coast and the inland provinces on the Yangzi River.

These were the foundations upon which the Western powers built when, with the opening of Shanghai as a Treaty Port, they came and carved out their enclaves there. The first of the foreign settlements, the British Concession, was bounded on the east along the Huangpu River by the Bund (today's Zhongshan No. 1 Road (E)), on the west by Yu Ya Ching Road (today's Central Tibet Road), and on the south by the Yangjingbang Creek (which, after it was filled, was named Avenue Edward VII and which is now called Yan'an Road (E)). The creek separated the British from the French

Concession; the latter started from a wedge between the British Concession and the old Chinese city, and then ballooned out to a large area to the southwest of the city. To the north of the Suzhou Creek, in the district known then and now as Hongkou, lay the American Concession. This was later merged with the British Concession to form the International Settlement.

In the British Concession, the streets spread out behind the Bund in a grid. The main thoroughfare, Nanking Road (Nanjing Road), ran westwards from the Bund. The streets parallel to it were named after China's other cities (such as Canton, Fuzhou and Ningpo), while those which ran perpendicular to it (ie north–south) were named after the provinces (such as Henan, Sichuan and Zhejiang). There was no mistaking the French Concession, because most of the streets there had French names: Rue Lafayette, Avenue Foch, to name but two. The smartest was Avenue Joffre (today's Central Huaihai Road), which was to the French Concession what Nanking Road was to the British. Needless to say, these were all renamed when the communists took over.

A view along the Bund in Shanghai during the 1920s, showing the Hong Kong Shanghai Bank building and the Peace Hotel

The beginning of the Sino-Japanese War saw bombing and fierce fighting in and around Shanghai, but the foreign concessions were not occupied by the Japanese until after the bombing of Pearl Harbour, when Allied nationals were interned. In 1943 extra-territoriality came to an end by common consent, but the Chinese only regained control of Shanghai after the defeat of the Japanese.

When a People's Republic was proclaimed in China at the end of the civil war, foreigners and Chinese industrialists, fleeing Communism, left Shanghai, many re-establishing themselves in Hong Kong.

SHANGHAI

(top) View of the Bund, Shanghai, published in the Illustrated London News, *Sept 1894*
(bottom) View of the waterfront from across the Huangpu River, Shanghai, in the 1920s,
when Pudong was still an area for shipbuilding and warehouses

Because of the city's long history of foreign capitalist exploitation and 'bourgeois attitudes', adherents of the Cultural Revolution in the 1960s and '70s were particularly vociferous in Shanghai, which became the headquarters of the so-called Gang of Four, the ultra-leftist elements of this chaotic period.

When China began to reform her economic system and opened her doors to the outside world, one imagined that there would be a resurgence of the entrepreneurial spirit in Shanghai. But it took some while for today's momentum to build. Until recently, Shanghai has been starved of investment, Beijing having siphoned off much of its huge earnings. As the population continued to grow, the problems of housing and traffic congestion grew ever more acute.

However, in 1988, Beijing and Shanghai entered a new revenue agreement. Instead of surrendering more than three-quarters of its annual revenues, Shanghai began contributing a fixed amount to the central government and keeping any surpluses for its own use. The revitalizing of Shanghai could scarcely be more ambitious: bridges; tunnels; an urban subway system; suburban housing; the technical upgrading and expansion of its textile industry; the building of a microelectronics industry in Caohejing, a would-be Silicon Valley; and the establishment of a new port and free trade and export processing zone in Pudong.

WHAT TO SEE IN SHANGHAI

While Shanghai's historical monuments may not compare with China's older cities, the city's appeal lies in its vitality, its 1930s European architecture in a medley of styles, and its bustling, tree-lined streets, crammed with shops. Above all, Shanghai still has a style and flair quite different from any other Chinese city.

THE BUND (WAITAN)

Walking along Zhongshan No. 1 Road (E), you can enjoy the faded grandeur of old Shanghai, for this was the Bund, where the great trading houses and banks had their headquarters. On one side is a line of imposing buildings constructed between 1897 and 1937, while on the other is the Huangpu River. The Bund has undergone a facelift, which included raising the level of the breakwater to prevent flooding. The raised pedestrian promenade gives a good view of the Huangpu River with the futuristic-looking buildings of the new Pudong New Area on the other side. As before, the improved riverside promenade of the Bund continually throngs with Shanghai residents, who stroll about in the hot summer evenings and in the mornings practise taijiquan and martial arts.

The **Bank of China** building at No. 23 and the **Customs House** at No. 13 are some of the few buildings that are still run by their original occupants. The former **Shanghai Club** at No. 2 was built in 1911 and was a great British bastion that denied membership to women and Chinese. Its famed Long Bar, which was 35.7 metres long, has long gone and the building has been empty since it was closed in 1998. Renovations are now underway for undisclosed new occupants. Next door at No. 3, in the former **Union Building**, a Chinese-American entrepreneur has opened a plethora of up-market shops and restaurants.

The most opulent building on the Bund can be found at No. 12. The former **Hong Kong and Shanghai Bank building**, with its two bronze lion guards, was built in 1923 and is now occupied by the Pudong Development Bank. Just inside the entrance are magnificent Italian mosaics of some of the world's greatest cities. The building also has a coffee shop where one can read, relax and absorb the atmosphere of the Bund. Nearby at the M on the Bund restaurant one can sit on an open terrace overlooking the river. The roof garden of the Peace Hotel is another great place to take a drink. The **Peace Hotel** at No. 20 was originally built in 1929 by Sir Victor Sassoon as his personal and company base. It was formerly the Cathay Hotel, within Sassoon House, and was the finest of its time. It was here that Noel Coward wrote his play Private Lives in the dying days of 1929. The south building of the Peace Hotel was originally the Palace Hotel, a British-run hotel that was completed in 1906.

Dancers practise their tango, one of the many early morning activities on Shanghai's famous Bund

An aerial view of Shanghai shows Suzhou Creek in the foreground and the Huangpu River looping around the new industrial area of Pudong in the distance

The Nanpu Bridge crosses the Huangpu River in the south of Shanghai

Tomorrow Plaza, just one of the many modern buildings to have sprung up in Shanghai in recent years. In the foreground, The China Power and Light Company Building overlooks the former racetrack and People's Park.

Ballroom dancing is a popular pastime among many Chinese in Shanghai

A brass band provides entertainment on Shanghai's Bund

The Chinese are insatiable snackers and streetside food can be found everywhere

Shanghai's streets are endlessly varied and a stroll among the backstreets can be rewarding

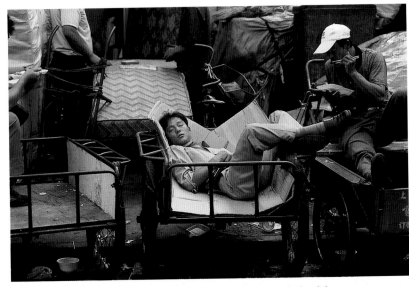

A bicycle porter grabs the chance of a nap during the lunch hour

At the end of the Bund, where Suzhou Creek meets the Huangpu River, the art deco **Broadway Mansions** and the old **Astor House Hotel**, dating from 1911 (now the Pujiang Hotel), have survived. Nearby **Huangpu Park** is infested with tour buses and includes large concrete spaces. It was originally laid out by the British and opened in 1868 as the Public Gardens, where British residents promenaded and enjoyed band concerts. Though the regulations of the International Settlement did indeed forbid Chinese (other than servants and nannies) as well as dogs from the gardens, the infamous sign 'No Dogs or Chinese Allowed' never actually existed. Chinese were allowed to enter after 1928. Municipal Council records stating this new regulation are to be found in a circular museum of photographs and artefacts found under the Monument to People's Heroes nearby. Another modest display of photographs of the Bund of yesteryear is on show at the other end of the Bund in the former **Signal Tower**. This tower was built in 1884 and was moved some 20 metres from its original site in 1995 as part of the new promenade scheme.

The visitor now has two options to cross the river from the Bund to the new promenade on the other side in Lujiazui. The more traditional and inexpensive way is to take the local ferry from Shiliupu Pier at the end of Jinling Road East. Another way is to go underground in the **Bund Tourist Tunnel** where modern pods glide through a sound and light show and cover the 650-metre journey in three minutes.

SOME POPULAR SHOPPING STREETS
HIGH STREET SHOPPING

On the face of it Shanghai's main shopping streets look just like their counterparts in any major Western city. In the Chinese mind Shanghai and shopping are synonymous. The millions that descend on Shanghai from all around China will find their way to **Nanjing Road**, China's number one shopping street. The main shopping section extends for over five kilometres from the Bund to Jing'an Temple. Shopping hours are generally from 10 am to 10 pm.

The road is divided into two sections: Nanjing Road (W), which used to be known as Bubbling Well Road and now houses some of China's classiest shopping malls and office towers; and the main part, Nanjing Road (E), which runs up from the waterfront and has largely been pedestrianized and public squares installed. Nanjing Road (E) is famous for its department stores, many of which have a long historic association with the street dating back to 1917.

Where Nanjing Road East crosses Central Tibet Road it becomes Nanjing Road (W). This part of the road has some of the most palatial shopping malls in the city. It passes People's Park and the Shanghai Art Museum, formerly the Municipal Library and before that the Shanghai Race Club. A little further up, opposite the Shanghai TV Station, is a large antique, bird, flower and pet market.

Another important shopping street is **Central Huaihai Road**, which was the former main street of the French Concession, then called Avenue Joffre. Apart from numerous international shopping malls it has a large fashion and accessory market at the junction with Xiangyang Road. Sichuan Road (N), in the Hongkou District, is also a good place to find ladies fashion shops and is popular with the locals.

For antiques, the **Dongtai Road** antiques market just to the east of the Tianqiaoping Garden parades a huge display of antiques, curios and artefacts. Many of the items can also be found in markets all over China—but this is a good place to hunt for fragments of Shanghai's past. The most well-known antique market, the **Fuyou Road market**, is heavily patronized by locals at the weekends and has hundreds of stall-holders on its four levels. The market has moved from Fuyou Road, but has kept its name and is now found at 457 Central Fangbang Road near the Yu Garden. It is really a weekend market, and starts early! Bookstores, antiquarian and modern, are a speciality of Fuzhou Road, as well as stationary and calligraphy accoutrements; though in earlier times it was a red light district. Another lesser known market is on Sinan Road very near the intersection with Taikang Road.

A word of caution: protect your wallet, and avoid all unsolicited offerings from street touts of either sex. They may approach you with offerings ranging from DVDs to copy watches and art gallery visits to ladies of the night.

THE ORIENTAL PEARL TV TOWER

The 468-metre TV tower, the third tallest in the world, symbolizes modern Shanghai—being the first perpendicular icon to rise in the Pudong New Area. It was completed in 1994 and includes two viewing decks, at 263 metres and 350 metres high respectively. In good visibility, which unfortunately Shanghai does not encounter too often, great views are afforded across the city and into the Yangzi River Delta.

SHANGHAI SCIENCE AND TECHNOLOGY MUSEUM

A stunning structure with equally stunning exhibits has made this museum a major attraction for all the family. Hundreds of interactive exhibits wait amongst the various zones one passes though—from the subterranean depths of the earth, to tropical rainforests and space-age technological environs. Allow a whole day for a visit and expect to queue for a while for those 'hands on' exhibits. The complex also houses an IMAX cinema and an IWERKS theatre.

THE OLD TOWN (JIUCHENG QU)

Renmin Lu and Zhonghua Lu form the perimeters of the old city wall (destroyed in 1912) that enclosed the Chinese City. Still within this area, which includes the famous Yu Garden, visitors jostle in the ever-crowded alleys of the bazaar, whose small shops, restaurants and teahouses provide local specialities of all descriptions. The narrow streets nearby reveal an intimate and fascinating picture of daily life. Take a walk up Dajing Road, with its lively local produce street market.

Should you get tired of walking around the Old Town you can always rest in the beautiful old **Huxinting** (mid-lake) **Teahouse**. This five-sided pavilion stands in the middle of a rectangular pool near the entrance to the Yu Garden, connected to land by the Bridge of Nine Turnings (zigzagged, it is said, because evil spirits cannot go round corners).

Nearby at 385 Central Fangbang Road is the **Old Shanghai Teahouse and Museum**. This teahouse has an admirable collection of genuine Shanghai historical artefacts such as old maps, a gramophone which plays records, copies of 'Shanghai Volunteers Corps' publications, and a wall poster of Sun Yat-sen. Although the food and drinks prices are high, the atmosphere is delightful.

DAJING PAVILION (DAJINGGE)

The Dajing Pavilion is the only surviving section of the Ming-dynasty wall that encircled Shanghai before 1911. The three-storey tower, which originally accommodated archers to repel Japanese pirates, later became the Guangong Temple and today houses an exhibition of the native city of Shanghai. A small model of the old

Aerial view from Pudong across the Huangpu River, with the entrance to Suzhou Creek beyond. In the foreground the Oriental TV Tower, a symbol of the technology and new prosperity of a city reinventing itself after decades of economic torpor.

town and a series of Chinese annotated visuals chronicling the area's history can be found on the second floor. The Pavilion is located at 269 Dajingge Road.

YU GARDEN (YU YUAN)

This Garden of Leisurely Repose on the northeast side of the old Chinese Town was first established in 1559 by a mandarin named Pan Yunduan. Laid out by a landscape artist, Zhang Nanyang, it has become one of the most renowned gardens in southern China. As the Pan family fortunes declined, the garden was neglected and overgrown until it was restored in 1760 by the local gentry. It became the headquarters of the Small Swords Society in 1853, during the early part of the Taiping Rebellion, and was badly damaged. Part of the garden became the bazaar and local guildhalls, but over 20,000 square metres (24,000 square yards) remain of tall rockeries, halls, ponds and pavilions linked by zigzag corridors. The Spring Hall, used by the Small Swords Society, houses exhibits of coins and weapons from that period. The five-ton porous Exquisite Jade Rock is one of the attractions: legend claims that when it was discovered some 900 years ago, it joined Emperor Huizong's collection of weird and grotesque rocks before finding a resting place in Yu Garden.

JADE BUDDHA TEMPLE (YUFO SI)

The yellow-walled temple buildings were constructed between 1911 and 1918. The two jade Buddhas (out of five brought back from Burma in 1882 by the priest Hui Gen) were first kept in a suburb of Shanghai. They are carved entirely from single blocks of jade and were a gift from Burma. Three halls make up the temple complex. In the Jade Buddha Hall is the tranquil two-metre high seated statue of Sakyamuni, while downstairs in the Reclining Buddha Hall is the white jade image of Sakyamuni in repose. Precious statues of the Northern Wei (386–534) and Tang (618–907) dynasties are on display in the temple's exhibition hall, along with hand-copied Tang-dynasty Buddhist scriptures and paintings. Services are held in the Grand Hall and visitors can pay to summon the monks and pray. Its role as a Buddhist College was expanded in 2003, with major renovations and the opening of the Jue Qun Hall, at the rear of the complex, to house a display of Buddhist heritage. The temple is best visited early or late and is located at 170 Anyuan Road.

SHANGHAI MUSEUM (SHANGHAI BOWUGUAN)

This spectacular world-class museum, costing around US$50 million, was opened in 1996. Designed by Shanghai architect, Xing Tonghe, the futuristic building with its circular roof with four decorative holders is, seen from a distance, said to resemble an ancient bronze. Six stone lions and two stone *bixie* (mythical beasts), guard the entrance to the museum and the granite walls of the building are decorated

The famous Huxingting Teahouse in the reflecting pool near the entrance to Yu Garden, in the old 'Chinese town' area of Shanghai

with designs found in ancient bronzeware. The museum has a fine collection of sculptures, furniture, paintings, calligraphy, coins, ceramics, ancient bronzes, jade-ware and minority handicrafts, all housed in state-of-the-art surroundings. The museum is in People's Square at 201 Renmin Avenue.

SHANGHAI ART MUSEUM (SHANGHAI MEISHUGUAN)

The museum is located in the former Shanghai Race Club at 325 Nanjing Road (W). It is immediately noticeable for its trademark clock tower. The building is marked with the insignia SRC, standing for Shanghai Race Club—the main staircase is deco-rated with iron railings in the shape of horse's heads. In the front stairwell on the third floor there is a European war monument devoted to the people of Shanghai who died in World War I, probably the only monument of its type still remaining. The one which stood on the Waitan was destroyed. It is possible to go up on the roof for an excellent view of the city. The museum regularly host exhibitions of major interna-tional artists and is the home of the Shanghai Biennale, the biannual arts festival.

SHANGHAI MUNICIPAL HISTORY MUSEUM
(SHANGHAI CHENGSHI BOWUGUAN)

An interesting museum dedicated to development of Shanghai is housed in the basement of the Oriental Pearl TV Tower. The focus is ostensibly on Shanghai after the foreigners arrived in the 1840s—though aspects of normal Chinese life, through a range of dioramas of shops and industries in the 19th and early 20th centuries, are portrayed alongside foreign life in the settlement areas. All aspects of life from Shanghai's famous cinema industry, to its curious form of criminal justice, its opium houses and its distinctive elements of architectural style are brought to life. One hall holds a collection of old trolley buses, trams, cycles and sedans. Another includes one of the precious lions that once stood outside the Hong Kong and Shanghai Bank on the Bund that is often rumoured to have been smelted down by the Japanese during the Second World War.

LONGHUA TEMPLE AND PAGODA (LONGHUA SI, LONGHUA TA)

The Longhua district in the south-western suburbs of Shanghai has been remod-elled as a major shopping and tourist area formed around its sites of historical inter-est, including the Longhua Temple and Longhua Pagoda. Situated in Shanghai's southwest area, the temple and pagoda were originally built between the 10th and the 13th centuries—historical records vary as to the exact dates. The temple belongs to the Chan (Zen) sect. The present seven-storeyed pagoda is just over 40 metres high and dates from the early Song dynasty, but was restored at the end of the Qing (1644–1911). The Longhua Temple nearby is a complex of five halls

The spectacular Shanghai Museum was designed by a local architect and opened in 1996 at a cost of US$ 50 million

flanked by bell and drum towers; the sound of the evening bell of Longhua was known as one of the old traditions of Shanghai. On New Year's Eve, this bell is rung 108 times at midnight. To hear this event is considered good luck. A flower terrace, overlooked from a tea-room, is also one of the attractions of the temple, for in its peony gardens there is a 100-year-old peony said to have been planted first in a Hangzhou temple during the reign of Emperor Xianfeng and later transplanted here. Engravings on a boundary stone indicate that the stone was placed at the southwest corner of this temple during the Five Dynasties period (907–960). The temple has recently undergone a comprehensive renovation and a vegetarian restaurant has been opened just inside its main gate.

JING'AN TEMPLE (JING'AN SI)

Though dating back over 800 years, remnants of the last round of building in the 1880s have been torn down and a new reinforced concrete complex is being built. The main hall should be complete by late 2004, but other building work is likely to continue until at least 2006. Throughout this period the evolving super-temple will remain open for visitors and worship.

TEMPLE OF THE CITY GOD (CHENGHUANG MIAO)

Located within the Yu Yuan Bazaar shopping complex, unlike the surrounding faux Ming-Qing style buildings constructed in 1994, this is an authentic temple first constructed during the reign of Ming Emperor Yong Le (1403–1424). It was renovated in 1926 and again in 1994. During the Cultural Revolution it was a factory, but reopened as a temple after the 1994 renovations of the Yu Yuan Bazaar. This Taoist temple is dedicated to the City God Qin Yu Bo, but also serves as a place of Taoist worship.

Despite Shanghai's modern façade, its population still lives in very overcrowded conditions

COASTAL DELTA

CHENXIANGGE NUNNERY (CHENXIANGGE SI)

With over 20 nuns in residence, this charming temple complex was first established as an estate by Pan Yunduan, the owner of the nearby Yu Garden, in the 16th century. It was rebuilt as a temple in the early 19th century and was ignobly converted into a factory workshop during the Cultural Revolution. Restoration began in 1989 and was completed in 1994 with the main structures—the Heavenly King, the Grand and the Guanyin halls—housing some fine Buddhist sculptures. A single master craftsman was employed to reproduce the statuary.

CI XIU AN MONASTERY

This small nunnery is in two sections. The new part faces Central Fangbang Road, west of Henan Lu, where the tourist part of the old town comes to a halt. The more interesting old part rests around the corner on a small and atmospheric lane (Zhenling Street). The richly-decorated small courtyard temple, built in 1870, has a prayer hall on one side with an eating area and dormitories on the other.

WHITE CLOUD TAOIST TEMPLE (BAIYUNGUAN)

This temple used to be hidden amongst the crowded lanes of old housing until they were demolished in 2003. Built in 1882, it covered an area much larger than the present site. It is now the only reminder left of the area's history—and a very fine one indeed. The highly ornate architecture, rich in stone and wood carvings, is complemented by the colourful and melodic daily rituals of its Quanzhen sect Taoist monks and worshippers. The temple possesses seven unique Ming-dynasty bronze statues, including two 'Heavenly Teachers'. It offers a serene and welcoming environment that does not see too many foreign visitors. The temple is also the centre for the Shanghai Taoist Association and Institute. Be sure not to miss the fine statuary on the upper floor, which also affords views of the temple's intricately carved roof ridges.

FA ZANG JIANG SI

Built in 1923, the huge main hall of this Buddhist Temple is on two levels. On the lower level, which is especially busy at weekends, worshippers join with the monks in prayer, whilst the upper hall houses giant Buddhist statues and fine bas-relief murals. Around 1,000 worshippers can be accommodated at any one time. Apart from the infectious atmosphere, what sets this temple apart from others is the interior and exterior design and decoration, which is a melange of Western art deco and traditional Chinese styles. The temple was restored and reopened to the public in 1999, after years of neglect and use as a factory. All the statuary contained within it is new. It is a fascinating place to visit and can be found at 271 Ji'an Road near Fuxing Road (E).

SHANGHAI

Shanghai's Bund at night

*Seen from the roof of Shanghai's famous Peace Hotel, the Oriental TV Tower
and skyscrapers of Pudong cast reflections in the Huangpu River*

XIAOTAOYUAN MOSQUE (XIAOTAOYUAN QINGZHI SI)

Tucked down a typical Shanghai alley off Fuzhou Road (E) this is the city's main mosque and serves as the headquarters for the Shanghai Islamic Association. The imposing protected building, completed in 1927, exhibits Western architectural characteristics with Chinese and Islamic adornments. The mosque was seriously damaged during the Cultural Revolution, but has now been restored to its former glory.

SHANGHAI BOTANICAL GARDENS (SHANGHAI ZHIWUYUAN)

South of the Longhua Pagoda at 111 Long Wu Lu, the gardens' greenhouses, bamboo groves and flower gardens cover some 67 hectares (165 acres) of land. Among the gardens' miniature penjing trees is a pomegranate over 240 years old.

GUILIN PARK (GUILIN GONGYUAN)

This traditional Chinese garden is full of wooden pavilions, lakes, trees, flowers, and a tea house. It was built in 1931 by a famous Shanghai gangster, Huang Jinrong, who dreamt of living the life of a Confucian mandarin. While sitting within its walls you can forget that you are in a city. The park is located at 128 Guilin Road.

SHANGHAI ZOO (SHANGHAI DONGWUYUAN)

Across 70 hectares, the zoo houses over 600 species of animals including giant pandas from Sichuan, golden-haired monkeys—which once frequented the Yangzi gorges—and rare Yangzi River alligators. It is situated at 2381 Hong Qiao Lu, near the airport.

REVOLUTIONARY SITES

Several buildings reflect the city's revolutionary history. In a two-storeyed building at 76 Xingye Lu, the Communist Party of China was founded in 1921; it is proudly shown to visitors as the site of the First National Congress of the Communist Party of China. The former residence of the late premier Zhou Enlai is situated at 73 Sinan Lu.

DR SUN YAT-SEN'S FORMER RESIDENCE (SUN ZHONGSHAN GU JU)

Dr Sun lived here with his wife, Soong Chingling, from 1919 to 1924. She adored the house and remained there, after her husbands death in 1925, until she was forced to move to Hong Kong in 1937. Situated in the former Rue Molière in the French Concession, the modest house with its simple furnishings was the scene for many historic meetings and in the 1930s Madame Sun hosted leading intellectual and political figures from around the globe, including George Bernard Shaw. It was also here that Madame Sun's sister, Meiling, was introduced to her future husband

Chiang Kai-shek. The house contains a fascinating library of over 2,700 titles, a Tang dynasty pottery horse, beautiful family photos and a feast of personal items.

FORMER RESIDENCE OF MADAME SOONG CHINGLING (SONG QINGLING GU JU)

Soong Chingling (Madame Sun Yat-sen) lived in this house on Central Huaihai Road for the latter part of her life, from 1948 to 1981. The residence was built in 1920 and has supposedly been kept the way it was during her lifetime. The sitting room and adjacent dining room, with French windows opening on to the huge lawn, contain a photographic record of Mao's visit to the house and a large selection of gifts received from foreign dignitaries. Outside, the garage houses two limousines, a Chinese 'Red Flag' monster and a Russian 'Jim' presented to her by Stalin in 1952. In front of the neighbouring exhibition hall is a gleaming marble statue of Song Chingling in repose—placed there in 2003 to commemorate the 110th anniversary of her birth. The hall contains an outstanding collection of artefacts ranging from books and family photos to personal correspondence and written exchanges with Nehru, Stalin, Mao and Zhou En-lai.

FORMER HOME OF CHIANG KAI-SHEK (JIANG JIESHI GU JU)

Chiang Kai-shek's former Shanghai residence is located at 9 Dong Ping Lu, and is part of the former Song family walled compound which included a home for each of the members of this most influential and wealthy family of pre-1949 China. The home of his brother-in-law, T V Song (Song Ziwen), is nearby on the corner of Hengshan Lu and Dongping Lu. Chiang began staying at this house during his short visits to Shanghai from the Guomindang capital in Nanjing after he married T V Song's sister, Song Meiling, in 1927. T V Song's house has become the fashionable Sasha's Bar and Restaurant.

LU XUN MUSEUM (LU XUN BOWUGUAN)

This museum is dedicated to China's great revolutionary writer, Lu Xun (1881–1936), who spent the last ten years of his life in Shanghai. It is located in the Honkou district inside Lu Xun Park. Lu is buried in Hongkou Park. He lived in a three-storeyed house at 9 Dalu New Village, Shanyin Lu, from 1933 until his death.

LONGHUA REVOLUTIONARY MARTYRS' CEMETERY (LONGHUA LIESHI LINGYUAN)

The area is also known as the Longhua Martyrs Memorial, as it has long been associated with those who gave their lives to free China from oppression. In the 1990s the cemetery and memorial hall were rebuilt and fabulously set in the

Longhua Park, next to Longhua Temple, to create one of the most peaceful and interesting green environments in Shanghai.

The vicinity had been a killing field during the days of the warlords, before the Nationalists asserted power in Shanghai in 1927 marking the period of 'White Terror'. The centrepiece is an impressive pyramidal Memorial Hall extolling the deeds of over 200 martyrs including student activists, leftist intellectuals, labour organizers and workers who gave their lives to free Shanghai from the shackles of foreign and native aggression. In another corner of the park are the buildings of the 1927 Guomindang headquarters, used at the end of the Northern Expedition from Guangzhou, that later became a detention camp.

EXCURSIONS FROM SHANGHAI
SUZHOU AND HANGZHOU
'In heaven there is paradise; on earth there are Suzhou and Hangzhou' is a proverb known to every Chinese. While today both of these earthly paradises have been invaded to some extent by industries and modern buildings, they still have considerable charm.

SUZHOU
Suzhou is the nearer of the two, being as little as 50 minutes by train or an hour by car from Shanghai. Known as the 'Venice of the East', the old part of town is still typified by small canals, small stone bridges and single-storied, white-washed houses. Above all Suzhou is noted for its gardens, of which only a handful are open to the public. The small, but ideal, **Master of Nets Garden** is regarded by many as the epitome of garden design and part of it has been replicated in the Metropolitan Museum of Art in New York. The Liu or **Lingering Garden** dates back to the 16th century and its beauty lies in its unique blend of moods and styles in four distinct sections. The **Humble Administrators Garden** is the largest garden with more than half its area covered by water.

Other historical areas include **Panmen**, the **North Temple Pagoda** (Beisi Ta) and the **Han Shan Temple**. Suzhou is proud to promote her heritage as the centre of the Chinese silk industry. Visits can be made to a silk-spinning factory and to the Suzhou Silk Museum and the Suzhou Silk Embroidery Research Institute.

HANGZHOU
Hangzhou's fabled **West Lake** was formerly perhaps China's best-known beauty spot. With its willow trees, lotus blossoms in July and arched stone bridges, it conforms to everyone's idea of what Chinese scenery should look like. Many Chinese come here for their honeymoon. The huge lake has four landscaped islands and the whole area is dotted with pavilions and temples.

Dating from the 15th century, Gongchen Bridge, in the north of Hangzhou, was the gateway to the city on the Grand Canal. It is one of the very few surviving classic three-arched bridges on the Grand Canal today.

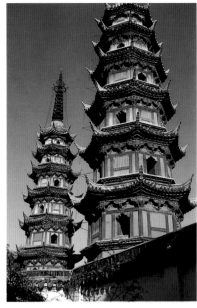

(left) The impressive 13-storeyed Pagoda of Six Harmonies (Liuhe Ta) stands overlooking the estuary of the Qiantang River just outside Hangzhou. (right) The Twin Pagodas (Shuang Ta) in Suzhou date from the Song dynasty.

Whitewashed canal-side cottages in Suzhou—the kind of scene that has been synonymous with the canal town and immortalised by local artists for centuries. During the last decade these cottages, along with many others, have been demolished to make way for modern housing.

Early morning taichi beside Suzhou's North Temple Pagoda (Beisi Ta). The original 11-storey pagoda was built more than 1,700 years ago in the Three Kingdoms period, but was destroyed by fire during the Song dynasty and later rebuilt with nine storeys in the Ming dynasty.

Just as modern motor vehicles now clog the many old narrow roads in historic Suzhou, the same is sometimes true for barge traffic

Dragon Well Spring, in the outskirts, is a natural wonder, as are the lush tea bushes of nearby Longjing (Dragon Well) Village. A Tea Museum gives an insight into the history and etiquette of tea drinking. Another popular destination is the 800-year-old **Lingyin Temple** set in woodlands next to the Feilai Feng, or 'Peak That Flew There'. According to legend this limestone outcrop was originally part of an Indian holy mountain which miraculously relocated itself in China. Hangzhou is as little as one hour 50 minutes from Shanghai by train.

WATER TOWNS

The Shanghai hinterland south of the Yangzi River (Jiang Nan) is dotted with small towns that are criss-crossed by canals and fringed with quaint vernacular architecture. As designated tourist hot spots, gondolas now ply the canals, museums have been created and markets and stores selling local products have sprung up. However they all still retain, to a greater or lesser degree, an ancient charm. **Zhouzhuang**, one of the larger towns, has been open the longest and still retains lots of charisma despite its hordes of visitors. Situated on a picturesque shore of Lake Dianshan, the original fishing village which forms its heart is in traditional Song-dynasty style. **Tongli** is a smaller town, crowded with ancient bridges and narrow alleys where

*The ancient canal town of Tongli, near Suzhou. The town also possesses an excellent example
of a classic Chinese garden. Completed in 1887 as part of a private residence,
it rivals the more famous gardens in Suzhou itself.*

500-year-old dwellings escape the view of most visitors. Never be afraid to explore
off the beaten track as one may stumble upon hidden gems, such as Tongli's classic
Chinese garden. Completed in 1887 as part of a private residence, it rivals any of
those of nearby Suzhou. Wuzhen is the most manicured town, with a large part
modelled as a living museum. Do not miss out on the rice wine distillery.

Shanghai's Outlying Districts

Those with more time who have seen Shanghai's major sights and visited Suzhou
and Hangzhou might be interested in visiting some of the outlying districts, which
are part of Shanghai Municipality.

SONGJIANG DISTRICT

The Songjiang District is interestingly diverse—its flat plains are interspersed with
numerous hills and its ancient treasures are to be found amidst the most modern
edifices. In town the most famous historical sights are to be found along the
Zhongshan Road, part of which has been recreated as 'Huating Old Street'. The Xi
Lin Temple and Pagoda was originally built between 1436 and 1449. The brickwork
of the seven-storey octagonal structure has survived, though the wooden eaves and

Shanghai Municipality and its Districts

JIANGSU PROVINCE

Yangzi River

CHONGMING COUNTY

BAOSHAN

JIADING

SHANGHAI URBAN AREA

PUDONG

Mouth of the Yangzi

QINGPU

Hongqiao Airport

Maglev

Pudong International Airport

SHANGHAI MUNICIPALITY

MINHANG

NANHUI

SONGJIANG

FENGXIAN

JINSHAN

ZHEJIANG PROVINCE

District Seats

© Airphoto International Ltd.

other features were replaced when it was last refurbished in 1994. Further along the street, the Songjiang Mosque was originally built in 1314, during the Yuan dynasty, making it the oldest in the region. Renovation work from 1985 has restored the character of this charming small enclave, with its mixture of Chinese and Islamic architecture, and it remains an important focus for the local Hui Muslim population. Nearby is one of the most important classical gardens in the Shanghai area. The renowned Zuibaichi Garden covers five hectares and was constructed in 1644. Therein the famed Ming-dynasty poet, Dong Qichang, spent many long hours drinking wine and writing verse.

The oldest surviving man-made structure in Shanghai, the Toroni Buddhist Sutra Stela, a 9.3-metre octagonal pillar covered with worn bas-relief and inscriptions dating back to 859, is also found here. The major attraction though is the

Square Pagoda Park created around Songjiang's best preserved pagoda. The Square Pagoda, built in the period 1068–1094, once stood in the central part of the Huating district in the Song dynasty. The nine-storey, 11th century pagoda was restored in the 1970s as the park was created, with much of its wooden structure still intact. It is accompanied by a large Screen Wall erected in 1370 and decorated with a massive brick bas-relief. Songjiang town is around 40 kilometres south-west of the city centre.

JIADING DISTRICT
Jiading is around 35 kilometres to the northwest of downtown Shanghai. The main sites in town are all within walking distance of each other.

The two main halls of the Confucius Temple hosted sacrifices to the great Sage as well as county and prefectural level examinations. The main Dacheng Hall now houses a new statue of Confucius and in its courtyard are small statues of his 72 worthy disciples. The neighbouring Minglun Hall, the former examination hall, is now a museum dedicated to the history of the imperial examination system. The attractive complex sits in a tranquil setting bounded by a large pond and is approached through an entrance containing three magnificent *pailou*. Next to the temple the Park of Dragons Meeting Pool (Hui Long Tan) was attractively laid out over 400 years ago and much still survives, but it is the nearby Qiuxiu Pu (Garden of Autumn Clouds) that steals the scenic prize. The garden was originally built in 1502 for Gong Hong, the head of the Ministry of Works. The original concept of creating a mountain forest in a city is still evident today, as seemingly expansive areas of water and hills come into view from a succession of vantage points from within the magnificent pavilions, their courtyards and corridors.

The Lao Jie (Old Street), with its recreated Ming-dynasty architecture as well as its small bridges and canals, is the nucleus of a new tourist area. However, some picturesque ancient houses have survived and at its core is the magnificently restored Fahua Pagoda (Fahua Ta). The structure was originally built between 1205 and 1207 and not in anyway restored until 1924, when the top of the tower was reinforced with iron. However, no major repair work was carried out to rectify the heavily tilting pagoda until 1994, when the expertise was sought of some of the team who had worked on the Leaning Tower of Pisa.

QINGPU COUNTY
With evidence of human existence going back 6,000 years Qingpu is presumed to have been the birthplace of Shanghai. The core of Qingpu town is pleasant and modern. However it is the splendidly laid out Qushui Yuan, or Garden of Meandering Streams, that is the main attraction. The garden was originally a small

temple yard when work started in 1745, but grew to be one of the finest gardens in Shanghai by the mid-nineteenth century. It is composed of 24 magnificent scenic areas.

The Qinglong Pagoda and Temple are to be found in the small town of Qinglong, some 15 kilometres northeast of Qingpu town. The impressive octagonal pagoda was built in the Northern Song dynasty (1041–48). Work on rebuilding the neighbouring temple, which was established in 743, started in 1993 and is still ongoing. Lake Dianshan (Dianshan Hu) is the main attraction for locals and a growing number of overseas tourists. A major attraction for day-trippers is the huge Grand View Garden (Da Guan Yuan). The garden, which took nine years to complete, is a modern recreation of a classical garden portrayed in The Dream of the Red Chamber, a popular Chinese novel. Fantastic views across the greenery of the garden and the neighbouring lake are afforded by climbing the recently built Song-dynasty style, 47.6-metre high Azure Cloud Pagoda (Lanyun Ta), just outside the entrance to the garden.

The nearby town of Zhujiajiao, with its whitewashed houses and small canals crossed by 36 ancient stone bridges, presents the visitor with an indelible reminder of another age. Most visitors take a Chinese gondola ride through the quaint town and gather on its most famous Ming-dynasty bridge, the Fangsheng or 'setting free' bridge, which is the largest five-arched bridge in eastern China. Among the visitor sites is a museum of postal history set in a magnificent Ming-dynasty building and a reconstructed traditional pharmacy. Zhujiajiao also has an elegant Temple of the Town God, which was built in 1763, and an active Christian church dating from the 19th century.

CHONGMING ISLAND

This is a delightful piece of rural countryside, incorporating several National Parks, situated in the middle of the Yangzi (Changjiang) River's mouth. It is a part of the Shanghai municipality although the environment is light years away from the urban centre. You can take a relaxing hour-long ferry boat ride from Wusong Port up the Huangpu and into the Changjiang to this island. Many former residents of the Three Gorges have been resettled on Chongming Island. It is also the place where the transatlantic telecommunications cable connects China with the USA. It is home to the Dongping National Forest Park (Dongping Guojia Senlin Gongyuan).

A vast new shipbuilding complex—the largest in the world—is being constructed along the south shore of Chongming Island, together with a new bridge over the broad Yangzi to Shanghai, which is destined to transform this quiet island forever.

Facts for the Traveller

VISAS

If you are travelling independently, either as a tourist or business visitor, you must obtain a visa before entry in to China. Applications should be made through Chinese embassies or consular offices in your country. If you are entering through Hong Kong, visas are easily obtained from various travel agencies, including CITS, CTS and the Foreign Ministry of the People's Republic of China. Visa applications can be processed on the same day in Hong Kong, though if you can wait two or three days the cost is considerably reduced. One to three month tourist visas (L visas) are readily available as well as business visas (F visas) which can be issued for up to one year, including multiple entries. Just one passport photograph and a completed application form are necessary. Generally business visas issued overseas will require an official letter from the official host organisation in China, whereas in Hong Kong this regulation can be waived. Tourist visas can normally be extended in Beijing or Shanghai for a maximum period of one month, on no more than two successive occasions.

Tourists entering China as part of a group may have a document listing members details on a single group visa prepared by their tour operator and handled by the tour leader or allotted group member. These are valid for the duration of the tour only and the whole group must enter and leave China together. However, some companies ask that you obtain your own visa to give greater flexibility to group participants who may add on optional tours to the beginning or end of standard tour itineraries. This also obviates any difficulties in amending the group visa that would result in a group member being unable to complete the tour.

Border formalities are generally painless and efficient. Those on individual visas receive entry and exit stamps and must complete entry and departure forms. Those on group visas do not receive passport stamps and are not required to complete entry or departure forms. Health declaration forms are issued on the journey to China and should be handed over on arrival. Your passport should be valid for at least six months after your departure from China.

CUSTOMS

The ordinary visitor is not required to complete a customs declaration form. There is no limit on the amount of foreign currency that can be taken into China. A litre and a half of alcohol over 12 per cent proof, 400 cigarettes (or 100 cigars), unlimited film and medicines for personal use may be taken in free of duty. The carriage of fresh food produce into China is prohibited by health and quarantine regulations. When buying antiques one must remember that only items made after the reign of the Jiaqing Emperor (1820) may legally be exported and all must bear a red wax seal affixed by the Bureau of Cultural Relics. Receipts for major purchases such as legitimate antiques and gold products should be kept in case inspection is required on departure.

AIR TICKETING AND TAXES

China's air ticket market is somewhat competitive, but is not fully subject to market conditions. Occasionally, government directives will decrease or increase the amount of discount that can be offered on tickets, and price wars break out quickly in times of relative deregulation. A 20 per cent discount off the listed fare is usually possible.

Tickets purchased in China are generally not subject to the restrictions of those bought outside the country. Although buying a ticket at the airport generally means paying full fare, airfares in China do not increase or decrease based upon advanced purchase. They are far more flexible than the non-refundable, non-changeable tickets that are now the norm of international air travel.

Safety on Chinese airlines has improved dramatically over the past 20 years. Once considered unsafe during the early 1980s, China's air fleet is one of the newest in the world. You are more likely to be on a new Airbus or Boeing aircraft when flying with a Chinese airline than with a US-based carrier. Although service still lags behind its Asian competitors, such as Singapore Airlines and Cathay Pacific Airways, Chinese airlines are often a low-cost alternative flying the same routes as their foreign counterparts. Air China should not be confused with China Airlines, a Taiwan-based carrier that has been involved with several serious accidents in recent years.

Departure taxes are payable on all flights from Chinese airports. Currently they are 90 yuan (around US$11) for international flights and 50 yuan (around US$6) for domestic flights. These must be paid in local currency. There is no charge for children under 12 years old.

GETTING THERE

The Three Gorges, which lie between Chongqing and Yichang, are the most popular destination for tourists.

Chongqing, one of the municipalities directly answerable to Beijing, is the normal starting point for downriver Yangzi cruises. Boat departures are normally early in the morning so it is usually necessary to spend the night in Chongqing. The journey through the Three Gorges to Yichang and on downstream to Wuhan takes three and a half days, while the upriver journey, from Wuhan to Chongqing, takes four and a half days. Following the completion of the San Xia Ba (Three Gorges Dam), and as a portion of the river becomes more lake-like up to 2009, upstream speeds are likely to increase, and downstream ones to slow slightly. Night navigation will become possible in formerly dangerous reaches, and may lead to the re-scheduling of boats other than those specifically for tourists. Cruise operators are usually careful to schedule their sailings to make sure you pass through the Three Gorges in daylight hours.

SCHEDULED SERVICES

WUHAN–YICHANG–CHONGQING–YICHANG–WUHAN

Going upstream from Wuhan, not only are there more ports of call, but the journey takes about 100 hours (four nights on board) compared with 57 hours (two nights on board) going downstream. Additional daily sailings make scheduled stops at towns not included in the regular downstream schedule.

Tickets may be bought through branches of China International Travel Service and China Travel Service in Chongqing and Wuhan or direct from Chaotianmen docks (opposite Wharf 2) in Chongqing and the Yangzi Passenger Terminal (80 Yanjiang Dadao) in Hankou, Wuhan. They are sold up to four days in advance of the sailing.

CRUISE BOATS

A more luxurious way of seeing the Three Gorges is to book on one of the many cruise ships catering mainly to foreign tour groups. Most sail the stretch between Chongqing and Yichang, or as far as Wuhan. Several de luxe cruise lines offer longer trips, some as long as nine nights, sailing from Shanghai to Chongqing, for instance. The boats operate from the beginning of April to October or November. Fitted out with private bathrooms for each cabin, air-conditioning, observation decks, gift shops and bars, these ships offer arranged excursions on shore and other entertainments during the cruise.

Many international travel companies run China tours which include a Yangzi River cruise on one of these de luxe ships, including Abercrombie and Kent, who have long been famous for de luxe cruises on the river (for addresses see pages 544–6). Bookings for all Yangzi cruises should be made well in advance, particularly for September and October, which is the peak tourist season. Although most people take these cruises as part of a group tour, it is also possible to buy individual tickets for the cruise only.

GETTING TO CHONGQING

BY AIR

Chongqing has an international airport. It is usually cheaper to fly from Shenzhen, Guangzhou or Zhuhai than to fly from Hong Kong directly. There are domestic flights from all major cities in China.

BY RAIL
The rapid expansion and modernization of the Chinese railway network has yet to make much difference to services to Chongqing. Trains south and west to Kunming, or south and east to Guangzhou pass on a single track line which is a miracle of engineering through spectacular mountain scenery and remote and impoverished areas. From Beijing's West Station it is a double overnight journey, and from Guangzhou about 11 hours.

BY ROAD
With China's rapidly expanding network of highways, travel by road must seriously be considered as an alternative to air and rail. In the past even relatively short road journeys could take many hours of uncomfortable travel, whereas they are more likely to take a fraction of that time in an excellent air-conditioned vehicle.

GETTING TO YICHANG
BY AIR
Yichang has air services an average of three times a week from major cities, including Beijing, Changsha, Chengdu, Chongqing, Guangzhou, Huangshan, Kunming, Nanjing, Qingdao, Shanghai, Shenzhen, Xi'an and Zhengzhou.

BY RAIL
There are direct trains from various cities, including Wuhan, Xi'an and Beijing, but many services require a change at the nearby junction of Yaqueling. From Wuhan long-distance buses and overnight sleeper buses may be more convenient.

GETTING TO WUHAN
BY AIR
There are scheduled services direct from Hong Kong, but there may be charter flights run by China Travel Air Service Hong Kong. There are domestic flights from all major cities in China. Air Macau has flights from Macau and China Southern Airlines flies three times a week from Fukuoka.

BY RAIL
Wuhan is on a fast north–south route between Kowloon and Beijing West Railway Station, with comfortable expresses leaving Hong Kong daily and arriving at Wuhan the next day. You may not use the Kowloon service when coming south from Beijing, but there are several other services each day, and there are direct trains to Wuhan from other major Chinese cities such as Chengdu, Xi'an, Tianjin, and Guilin.

CLIMATE

The three large cities along the Yangzi River—Chongqing, Wuhan and Nanjing—are known traditionally as the 'three furnaces of China'. Between April and September, the temperature in the Yangzi River valley reaches 36°C (97°F) and above. Spring and autumn are therefore the best seasons for making the river cruises. However, with the tall mountains and gorges through which the river threads its path, precipitation is very high and the peaks are often shrouded in cloud and mist. Summer rains are torrential. The winters are short, cold and crisp. Late-summer travel will coincide with the high-water periods, when the river rises swiftly, almost perceptibly.

CHONGQING
AVERAGE TEMPERATURES

	Jan	Feb	Mar	Apr	May	Jun	Jul	Aug	Sep	Oct	Nov	Dec
°C	7	10	14.5	19.5	23	25.5	29	30	25	19	14	10.5
°F	44.6	50	58.1	67.1	73.4	77.9	84.2	86	77	66.2	57.2	50.9

AVERAGE RAINFALL

	Jan	Feb	Mar	Apr	May	Jun	Jul	Aug	Sep	Oct	Nov	Dec
mm	15	20	38	99	142	180	142	122	150	112	48	20
in	0.6	0.8	1.5	3.9	5.6	7.1	5.6	4.8	5.9	4.4	1.9	0.8

WUHAN
AVERAGE TEMPERATURES

	Jan	Feb	Mar	Apr	May	Jun	Jul	Aug	Sep	Oct	Nov	Dec
°C	2.7	5.2	10	16.2	21.1	26.1	29.1	28.4	23.9	17.6	11.4	5.5
°F	36.8	41.3	50	61.1	69.9	79.8	84.3	83.1	75	63.6	52.5	41.9

AVERAGE RAINFALL

	Jan	Feb	Mar	Apr	May	Jun	Jul	Aug	Sep	Oct	Nov	Dec
mm	152	152	203	279	305	381	254	203	178	178	152	127
in	6	6	8	11	12	15	10	8	7	7	6	5

CLOTHING

Light summer clothing is all that is required between April and September, with a woollen cardigan or warm jacket for the cool evenings on board. To combat the summer mugginess, travellers should wear cotton rather than synthetic fibres.

The Yangzi River towns are very informal indeed; wear comfortable everyday clothes when you visit them. Steep steps from the jetties to the towns require walking shoes, and since the streets turn to mud within minutes of a heavy rainfall, you may need an extra pair. Umbrellas can be bought cheaply almost anywhere. On board the more de luxe ships, however, many like to dress a little more formally for the last night of the cruise; therefore women may want to bring a smart outfit and men a jacket and tie.

Warm clothes are essential for the river journeys during seasons other than summer. The boats can be draughty and the wind piercing. However, clothing is one of the best bargains in China, with excellent down or quilt jackets available in many of the big towns and cities. Bring a pair of light hiking boots as the terrain can be hilly, rocky and muddy.

MONEY
CHINESE CURRENCY
Chinese currency is called Renminbi (meaning 'people's currency') and this is abbreviated to Rmb. It is denominated in yuan, referred to as *kuai* in everyday speech. The yuan is divided into 10 jiao (colloquially called *mao*). Each jiao is divided into 10 fen. There are large notes for 100, 50, 5, 2 and 1 yuan, small notes for 5, 2, and 1 jiao, and coins and notes for 5, 2, 1 fen and 1 yuan.

FOREIGN CURRENCY, TRAVELLER'S CHEQUES AND CREDIT CARDS
There is no limit to the amount of foreign currency you can take into China. Traveller's cheques are changed at a slighter better rate than cash. All major European, American and Japanese traveller's cheques are accepted by the Bank of China. International credit cards may be used to draw cash at larger branches (1,200 yuan minimum, four per cent commission) and for payment in international hotels.

TIPPING
The accepted standard for tipping in the West is rapidly becoming the norm in modern China. While it is not normally practised in local establishments, tipping would certainly be expected by local guides, drivers and waiters in places frequented by foreigners.

BARGAINING
With the exception of stores with marked prices, always bargain in markets and shops. Even state-run stores will often give discounts on expensive items like carpets intended for tourists. Bargaining in China can be good-humoured or it can be infuriating; it is a game won by technique and strategy, not by anger or threats. Thus, it should be leisurely and friendly, and not be seen as a one-way process at all, since the Chinese enjoy it. Finally, it is bad manners to continue to bargain after a deal has been struck.

COMMUNICATIONS

China's post-office system is rather slow but reliable. Every post office counter has a pot of glue, as low-denomination stamps do not have glue on the back. International Direct Dialling is available everywhere, and even by satellite phone from the more luxurious cruise ships (although at huge expense). Long-distance calls within China are often clearer than local ones, and even fairly modest hotels have business centres with fax and (slow) Internet connections.

LOCAL TIME

Amazingly for a country measuring 3,220 kilometres from east to west, most of China operates from one time zone eight hours ahead of GMT and 13 hours ahead of EST. From Urumqi to Kashgar, local people work to a 'local time' which is two hours behind Beijing. This time difference is 'unofficial' but determines transport timetables and other services in the region.

PACKING CHECKLIST

As well as bringing along any prescription medicines you may need, it is a good idea to pack a supply of common cold and stomach trouble remedies. Taking a basic first-aid kit including antiseptic cream and plasters is a good idea. Outside the winter months you should pack insect repellent—though insect pests are not of great concern in the city centres. You should also pack anti-diarrhoeal tablets and painkillers—especially if you take aspirin as it is not widely available. It is wise to carry sun screen outside of the winter months. While it is not necessary to pack toilet paper these days, it is advisable to take some with you when going out sightseeing, as public toilets do not provide it. Bring plenty of film and batteries for your camera. Although film is widely available, you may not always be able to find the type you need. And besides, you have no idea how long it may have been sitting on the shelf in the hot sun. Comfortable, non-slip shoes are a must.

If you wear glasses bring along a spare pair as well as your prescription. Soft contact lens solutions are widely available, but RGP and hard lens solutions are difficult to come by.

A fairly comprehensive range of complimentary toiletries are to be found in all good hotels, including soap, shampoo, tooth paste, shower caps and often a lot more. Moisturizer is usually provided but you are advised to bring your own preferred brand. Wet wipes may come in useful as well.

HEALTH

For visits to China's major cities there are no mandatory vaccination requirements. In recent years the US Consulate in Hong Kong has recommended inoculations against hepatitis A and B, Japanese encephalitis, tetanus, polio, cholera and malaria for travellers to China. Still, you may be advised by your doctor to take certain precautions and you may wish to inquire about the desirability of taking a immuno-globulin shot before departure. Only if you are travelling on to more remote parts of China in the summer months should more consideration be given to protection.

It is highly advisable to pay attention to your daily water intake. Distilled and mineral water is widely available and provided in hotel rooms. Ice cubes and ice-creams are generally safe to consume—but caution should be exercised in the summer months and when eating outside the major hotels and restaurants. Mild stomach upsets are not uncommon. You should take some basic precautions—always peel fruit and avoid seafood in local restaurants during the summer months.

The discomforts caused by cigarette smoke have often been remarked on by foreign visitors. However the situation has seen a rapid improvement in recent years as the government has banned smoking in many public places—although a 'no smoking' sign does not ensure compliance. Smoking is not permitted on tour buses, Chinese international and domestic flights, or on most if not all parts of trains. Smoking is also prohibited at most major tourist sites.

The most common ailments contracted by visitors to China are respiratory tract infections and the common cold. Try and safeguard yourself as much as possible by reg-ulating your room temperature and maintaining your body temperature as best you can.

Of more concern in recent times has been the advent of SARS. On arrival you will notice that heat-seeking detectors will greet you at the airport to test your tem-perature—and many other strict safeguards have been put in place to protect the public. The past incidence of SARS should not obscure the fact that China is a very safe place to visit, but of course you should keep up with the latest health advice in general, just as you would when planning a trip to many other parts of the world. For the latest travel advice, not only on health but on visa and other matters, take a look at the UK Foreign Office site (www.fco.gov.uk/travel) or the site of the US State Department (http://travel.state.gov/china.html).

For the treatment of minor ailments many of the better hotels have a clinic or a doctor on call. For consultations and prescriptions payment is made on the spot and major credit cards are accepted. Of course it is essential for all visitors to have adequate insurance cover to meet with any eventuality.

View of the last turn in the Yangzi River in Xiling Gorge just before reaching Sandouping and the Three Gorges Dam upstream.

SPECIALIST TOUR OPERATORS

The following are a selection of the many companies which can arrange Yangzi Tours:

Abercrombie and Kent International, Inc
UK: Abercrombie & Kent Travel, Sloane Square House, Holbein Place, London SW1W 8NS. Tel (0207) 730-9600; fax (0207) 730-9376; www.abercrombiekent.com
Hong Kong: 19th Floor, Tesbury Centre, 28 Queen's Road East, Wanchai.
Tel (852) 2865-7818; fax (852) 2866-0556
USA: 1520 Kensington Road, Suite 212, Oak Brook, Chicago, Il 60523-2156.
Tel (630) 954-2944, toll-free (800) 554-7016; fax (630) 954-3324;
www.abercrombiekent.com

China Travel Service (CTS)
USA: 2/F 212 Sutter Street, San Francisco, CA 94108.
Tel (415) 398-6627, toll-free (800) 332-2831; fax (415) 398-6669
Los Angeles: Suite 303, US CTS Building, 119 S Atlantic Blvd, Monterery Park, CA 91754. Tel (626) 457-8668; fax (626) 457-8955
Hong Kong: (Main Office)
4/F CTS House, 78–83, Connaught Road Central. Tel 2853 3888; fax 2541 9777;
www.ctshk.com

Orient Royal Cruiser Ltd
China: (Head Office) 316 Xinhua Road, Suite E, Liang You Building, Hankou, Wuhan, 430012. Tel (027) 8576-9988, 8577-2220; fax (027) 8576-6688;
www.orientroyalcruise.com
USA: 43 Conforti Avenue, Unit 72, West Orange, New Jersey 07052.
Tel: (888) 543-8088, (888) 664-4888; fax (888) 287-8188; www.orientcruisetravel.com
Hong Kong: ORC (Asia) Ltd, Room 1318, Two Pacific Place, 88 Queensway.
Tel (852) 2824-9022; fax (852) 2824-9092

China Regal Cruises
Nantong Lihui International Shipping Co Ltd, 6/F Changhang Building, 133 Yan Jiang Avenue, Wuhan, 430014, China. Tel (027) 8276-3387; fax (027) 8284-9921;
www.regalchinacruises.net

Victoria Cruises Inc
USA: 57–08 39th Ave, Woodside, NY 11377. Tel (212) 818-1698; fax (212) 818-9889

China: 3/F, 3 Xin Hua Road, Chongqing, 400011. Tel (023) 6380 4512; fax (023) 6381 4474; www.victoriacruises.com

Viking River Cruises
USA: 21820 Burbank Boulevard, Woodland Hills, California, 91367. Tel: (818) 227-1234
Germany: Hohe Strasse 68–82, D-50667, Koln. Tel 0221-2586-100; fax 0221-2586-506; www.vikingrivercruises.com

Dragon Cruiser
Tel (023) 6903 0107, 6903 0170; fax (023) 690 30106, 6352 8814
www.dragoncruiser.com

Page & Moy Ltd
56 Burleys Way, Leicester, LE1 9GZ, England. Tel (0116) 250-7336; fax 0-8700-1062-11; Bookings: 0-8700-1062-12; www.go-nowtravel.com

Cox & Kings Travel Ltd
4/F, Gordon House, 10 Greencoat Place, London, SW1P 1PH, England. Tel (0207) 873-5000; fax (0207) 630-6038; www.coxandkings.co.uk

Explore Worldwide Ltd
1 Frederick Street, Aldershot, Hants, GU11 1LQ, England. Tel (0125) 276-0000; fax (0125) 276-0001; www.exploreworldwide.com

Peregrine Adventures
258 Lonsdale Street, Melbourne 3000, Australia. Tel (03) 9663-8611; fax (03) 9663-8618; www.peregrineadventures.com

Regent Holidays
15 John Street, Bristol, BS1 2HR, England. Tel (0117) 921-1711; fax (0117) 925-4866; www.regent-holidays.co.uk

Saga Holidays Ltd
The Saga Building, Enbrook Park, Sandgate, Folkestone, Kent CT20 3SE, England. Tel (0800) 504-555, from overseas (44) 01303 771-111; www.saga.co.uk

Sobek
1266 66th Street, Emeryville, CA 94608, USA. Tel 888-687-6235; fax 510-594-6001
www.mtsobek.com

Steppes East Ltd
51 Castle Street, Cirencester GL7 5ET, England. Tel 01285 651010; fax 01285
885888; www.steppeseast.co.uk

Sundowners
Suite 15, 600 Lonsdale Street, Melbourne 3000, Australia. Tel (03) 9670 5300;
fax.(03) 9672 5311; www.sundownerstravel.com

Travelsphere Ltd
Compass House, Rockingham Road, Market Harborough, Leicestershire, LE16
7QD, England. Tel 01858 468400; fax 01858 434323; www.travelsphere.co.uk

Voyages Jules Verne
21 Dorset Square, London NW1 6QG, England. Tel (0207) 616-1000; fax (0207)
723-8629; www.vjv.co.uk

HOTELS

KUNMING (Code: 871)
FIVE STAR
Bank Hotel, 399 Youth Road. Tel 3158-888; fax 3158-999
Dianchi Garden Hotel & Spa, Dianchi Road. Tel 433-2888; fax 433-2999; www.
spagardenhotel.com
Green Land Hotel, 80 Tuodong Road. Tel 318-9999; fax 310-3860; www.green-
landhotel.com.cn
Horizon Hotel, 432 Qingnian Road. Tel 318-6666; fax 318-6888
Kai Wah Plaza International Hotel (formerly known as Westin Kunming), 157
Beijing Road. Tel 356-2828; fax 356-1818
Kunming Harbour Plaza, 20 Hong Hua Qiao. Tel (0871) 538-6688, toll free (with-
in Mainland China only) 800-889 9988; fax (0871) 538-1189; www.harbour-
plaza.com/hpkm

FOUR STAR
Courtyard by Marriott, 300 Huan Cheng Xi Road, Tel: 4158-888; fax 4153-282
Golden Dragon Hotel, 575 Beijing Road. Tel 313-3015; fax 313-1082
Green Lake Hotel, 6 Cuihu Nan Road. Tel 515-8888; fax 515 7867
King World Hotel, 98 Beijing Road. Tel 313-8888; fax 313-1910
Kunming Hotel, 52 Dong Feng Dong Road. Tel 317 6842; fax 315 1921

Sakura Hotel (formerly Holiday Inn), 25 Dong Feng Dong Road. Tel 3165-888; fax 3135-189

DALI   (Code: 872)
FIVE STAR
Asian Star, South of Gucheng Gate, Old Dali City. Tel 267-9999; fax 267-1699

FOUR STAR
Manwan Hotel, Canglang Road. Tel 218-8188; fax 218-1739; www.cbw.com/hotel/manwan/index.html

LIJIANG   (Code: 888)
FIVE STAR
Guanfang Hotel Lijiang, Middle-snow Mountain Road. Tel 518-8888; fax 518-1999; www.gfhotel-lijiang.com.cn

FOUR STAR
Lijiang Jian Nan Chun Hotel, 8 Guanyi Street, Dayan Town. Tel 5102-222
Lijiang Jade Dragon Garden Hotel, 62 Jishang Alley, Xinyi Road, Dayan Town. Tel 518-2888

CHENGDU   (Code: 28)
FIVE STAR
Crowne Plaza Hotel, 31 Zong Fu Street. Tel 8678-6666; fax 8678-9789; www.ichotelsgroup.com
Jinjiang Hotel, 80, Section 2, Renmin Nan Avenue. Tel 8550-6666; fax 8558-1849
Sheraton Chengdu Lido Hotel, 15, Section 1, Renmin Zhong Road. Tel 8676-8999; fax 8676-8888

FOUR STAR
Amara Hotel, 2 Taisheng Bei Road. Tel 8692-2233; fax 8692-2323; www.amarahotels.com
California Garden Hotel, 258 Shawan Road. Tel 8764-9999; fax 8764-0123; www.ecccn.com
Chengdu Yinhe Dynasty Intercontinental Hotel, 99 Xia Xi Shun Cheng Street. Tel 8661-8888; fax 8674-8837
Tibet Hotel, 10 Renmin Bei Road. Tel 8313-3388; fax 8333-3526
Sichuan Huayang Garden City Hotel, 8 Daye Road. Tel 8666-3388; fax 8665-5672; www.scgardencity.com

Xinliang Hotel, 53 Shang Dong Avenue. Tel 8673-9999; fax 8673-9666

CHONGQING   (Code: 23)
FIVE STAR
Chongqing Marriott Hotel, 77 Qing Nian Lu, Yu Zhong District.
Tel 6388-8888; fax 6388-8777; www.marriott.com/property/propertypage/ckgon
Harbour Plaza Chongqing, Wuyi Road, Yu Zhong District.
Tel 6370-0888; fax 6370-0778; toll free (within China only) 800-889-9988;
www.harbour-plaza.com/hpcq
Hilton Chongqing, 139 Zhongshan San Road, Yuzhong District.
Tel 8903-9999; fax 8903-8600; www.hilton.com

FOUR STAR
Chongqing Guesthouse, 235 Minsheng Lu, Yuzhong District.
Tel 6384-5888; fax 6383-0643
Hoi Tak Hotel, 318 Nanping Road.
Tel 6283-8888; fax 6280-5747; www.hoitakhotel.com
Holiday Inn Yangtze Chongqing, 15 Nanping Bei Lu.
Tel 6280-3380, toll-free from US 1-800 HOLIDAY; fax 6280-0884;
www.holiday-inn.com
Huang Jia Grand Hotel, 85 Zhongshan Road, Qixinggang, Yuzhong District.
Tel 6352-8888; fax 6352-9999; www.yuangjiahotel.com
Kinglead Hotel, 9 Keyuan Er Road, Shiqiaopu.
Tel 6862-6666; www.kinglead.com
Wanyou Conifer Hotel, 77 Changjiang 2nd Road, Daping.
Tel 6871-8888; fax 6871-3333; www.wanyouhotel.com

YICHANG   (Code: 717)
FIVE STAR
Guobin Grand Hotel, 46 Shenzhen Road. Tel 620-6688

FOUR STAR
Peach Blossom Hotel (Tao Hua Ling Binguan), 29 Yunji Lu.
Tel 643-6666; fax 623-8888
Yichang International Hotel (Yichang Guo Ji Da Jiudian), 127 Yanjiang Dadao.
Tel 622-2888; fax 622-8186

WUHAN   (Code: 27)
FIVE STAR

Best Western Mayflowers Hotel, 385 Wuluo Road, Wuchang.
Tel: 6887-1588; www.bestwestern.com
Haiyi Jinjiang Hotel, 1 Hongshan Road, Wuchang. Tel 8712-6666
Holiday Inn Riverside, 88 Ximachang Street, Hanyang. Tel 8471-6688
www.china.basshotels.com
Oriental Hotel Wuhan, Hankou Railway Station Square, Hankou.
Tel 5888-668; fax 5888-558; www.orientaltravel.com
Shangri-la Hotel, 700 Jianshen Dadao Avenue, Hankou.
Tel 8580-6868; fax 8577-6868; www.shangri-la.com

NANJING (Code: 25)
FIVE STAR
Jinling Hotel, 2 Hanzhong Lu, Xinjiekou Sq. Tel 8471-1888; fax 8471-1666;
www.jinlinghotel.com
Hilton Hotel Nanjing, 319 Zhongshan Dong Lu East. Tel 6322-3855; fax 6360-0967
Mandarin Garden Hotel, 9 Zhuangyuanjing, Confucious Temple.
Tel 220-2555; fax 220-2988
Nanjing Grand Hotel, 208 Guangzhou Road. Tel 3311-999; fax 3315-385
Shangri-La Dingshan, Nanjing Hotel, 90 Cha Ha Er Road, Banjing.
Tel 8802-888; fax 8821-729
Sheraton Nanjing Kingsley Hotel and Towers, 169 Hanzhong Lu.
Tel 8666-8888; fax 8666-9999; www.starwood.com

ZHENJIANG (Code: 511)
FOUR STAR
Zhenjiang Hotel, 2 Zhongshan Xi Road. Tel 523-3888; fax 523-1055
Zhenjiang International Hotel, 218 Jiefang Road. Tel 502-1888

SHANGHAI (Code: 21)
FIVE STAR
Four Seasons Hotel, 500 Weihai Road. Tel 6256-8888; fax 6256-5678;
www.fourseasons.com
Hilton Shanghai, 250 Huashan Road. Tel 6248-0000; fax 6248-3848;
www.hilton.com
JW Marriott Hotel Shanghai At Tomorrow Square, 399 Nanjing Road (W).
Tel 5359-4959; fax 6375-5988; www.marriott.com
Okura Garden Hotel Shanghai, 58 Maoming Road (S). Tel 6415-1111; fax 6415-
8866; www.gardenhotelshanghai.com
Peace Hotel, 20 Nanjing Road (E). Tel 6329-0300; fax 6329-0300;

www.shanghaipeacehotel.com
The Portman Ritz-Carlton Hotel, Shanghai Centre, 1376 Nanjing Road (W). Tel 6279-8888; fax 6279-8800; www.ritzcarlton.com
The Westin Shanghai, 88 Central Henan Road. Tel 6335-1888; fax 6335-2888; www.westin.com/shanghai
Grand Hyatt Hotel Shanghai, Jin Mao Building, 88 Century Boulevard. Tel 5049-1234; fax 5049-1111; www.shanghai.hyatt.com
Pudong Shangri-La Shanghai, 33 Fucheng Lu. Tel 6882-8888; fax 6882-9998; www.shangri-la.com
The St Regis Shanghai, 889 Dongfang Road. Tel 5050-4567; fax 6875-6789; www.stregis.com/shanghai

SZECHUEN AND HOUPEH.

A CHRONOLOGY OF PERIODS IN CHINESE HISTORY

Neolithic	7000–2200 BC
Ha	2200–1800 BC
Shang	1766–1122 BC
Western Zhou	1122–771 BC
Eastern Zhou	771–256 BC
Spring and Autumn Annals	722–481 BC
Warring States	480–221 BC
Qin	221–206 BC
Western (Former) Han	206 BC–AD 8
Xin	9–24
Eastern (Later) Han	25–220
Three Kingdoms	220–265
Western Jin	265–317
Eastern Jin	317–420
Northern and Southern Dynasties	386–589
Sixteen Kingdoms	317–439
Former Zhao	304–329
Former Qin	351–383
Later Qin	384–417
Northern Wei	386–534
Western Wei	535–556
Northern Zhou	557–581
Sui	581–618
Tang	618–907
Five Dynasties	907–960
Liao	916–1125
Northern Song	960–1127
Southern Song	1127–1279
Jin (Jurchen)	1115–1234
Yuan (Mongol)	1279–1368
Ming	1368–1644
Qing (Manchu)	1644–1911
Republic of China	1911–1949
People's Republic of China	1949–

A GUIDE TO PRONOUNCING CHINESE WORDS

The official system of romanization used in China, which the visitor will find on maps, road signs and city shopfronts, is known as *pinyin*. It is now almost universally adopted by the western media.

Some visitors may initially encounter some difficulty in pronouncing romanized Chinese words. In fact many of the sounds correspond to the usual pronunciation of the letters in English. The exceptions are:

Initials
c   is like the *ts* in 'i*ts*'

q   is like the *ch* in '*cheese*'

x   has no English equivalent, and can best be described as a hissing consonant that lies somewhere between *sh* and *s*. The sound was rendered as *hs* under an earlier transcription system.

z   is like the *ds* in 'fa*ds*'

zh   is unaspirated, and sounds like the *j* in 'jug'

a   sounds like '*ah*'

e   is pronounced as the *o* in 'm*o*ther'

i   is pronounced as in 'ski' (written as *yi* when not preceded by an initial consonant). However, in *ci, chi, ri, shi, zi* and *zhi*, the sound represented by the *i* final is quite different and is similar to the *ir* in 'si*r*', but without much stressing of the *r* sound.

o   sounds like the *aw* in 'l*aw*'

u   sounds like the *oo* in '*oo*ze'

ü   is pronounced as the German *ü* (written as *yu* when not preceded by an initial consonant). The last two finals are usually written simply as *e* and *u*.

Finals in Combination
When two or more finals are combined, such as in *hao, jiao* and *liu*, each letter retain its sound value as indicated in the list above, but note the following:

ai   is like the *ie* in 'tie'

ei   is like the *ay* in 'bay'

ian is like the *ien* in 'Vi*en*na'

ie   similar to *ye* in 'yet'

ou   is like the *o* in 'c*o*de'

uai sounds like 'why'

uan is like the *uan* in 'ig*uan*a' (except when preceded by *j, q, x* and *y*; in these cases a *u* following any of these four consonants is in fact *ü* and *uan* is similar to *uen*).

ue   is like the *ue* in 'd*ue*t'

ui   sounds like 'way'

Examples

A few Chinese names are shown below with English phonetic spelling beside them:

Beijing	Bay-jing (*jing* sounds like *ging* in 'pa*ging*')
Cixi	Tsi-shee
Guilin	Gway-lin
Hangzhou	Hahng-jo
Kangxi	Kahng-shee
Qianlong	Chien-loong
Tiantai	Tien-tie
Xi'an	Shee-ahn

An apostrophe is used to separate syllables in certain compound-character words to preclude confusion. For example, *Changan* (which can be *chang-an* or *chan-gan*) is sometimes written as *Chang'an*.

Tones

A Chinese syllable consists of not only an initial and a final or finals, but also a tone or pitch of the voice when the words are spoken. In *pinyin* the four basic tones are marked ‾ ´ ˇ ` . These marks are almost never shown in printed form except in language-learning texts.

RIDING THE DRAGON'S BACK

*T*he raft slammed into the rolling white rampart, twisted, then kicked up on its side, hurling Sonny into the boiling currents. With split-second reactions Skip threw his body up against the overturning boat, and his momentum and weight seemed to arrest the flip. The raft hung as though flash-frozen for an eternal second, then flopped back right-side-up. Sonny, who grabbed a rope when going over, pulled himself in, and Skip grabbed the oars, regained control, and piloted the boat safely through the rest of the rapid.

It was an impressive show, and I had turned to express amazement to Jim Slade that the raft had not capsized, when Slade pointed to an over-turned raft entering the rapid's tail waves. It had to be John Yost's boat. We had been so intent on watching Skip's miracle run that we'd missed Yost's. He had failed to punch through the wall of water, and had capsized in a rolling wave above the abominable hole. The raft had fallen over on top of the two bow riders, and the upstream oar snapped like a chicken bone across Dick Moersch's head. Yost and his passengers were swept smack through the middle of the worst recirculating hole on this stretch of the Yangtze.

Both Yost and Moersch had been in capsizes before, Yost several times. Instinctively they swam for the left eddy, the closest and largest, reaching it four hundred yards below the capsize. Kramer was stationed in the shallows with a rescue line, which he succesfully tossed to Dick Moersch, pulling the doctor to safety. Yost swam to Skip's boat and was safely pulled in. John Ingleman, however, had never ben in a capsize. When the raft flipped over on top of him, he was sucked down deep, spun like laundry, then spat up below the hole, thirty feet downriver from the raft.

Instinctively he started swimming in the direction he was facing, towards the right, and he kicked and pumped his arms, but the powerful current kept carrying him further downstream. Then he was sucked into a second giant hole, and went under for what must have seemed like an eternity. Finally he popped up, obviously tired, but the river was showing no mercy, and dragged him on towards the distant bend.

Later, he remembered the thoughts that came to him as he struggled in the grip of the hostile current:

While down there I thought, "Please don't let this hole be a keeper, or I'm going to drown!" When I came out I was gasping for breath. I couldn't believe what I saw ahead: endless, giant rollers. How could I get through that and still be breathing? I trided to swim but was helpless, like a twig in a torrent. Down into a trough I slid grabbing for breathers, looking up at walls of water. I'd get buried in a wall, and wait for it to spit me out, to begin the process again. I was in serious trouble. I was helpless, gasping for breath, and my arms and legs were beginning to go.

Far away on the left bank I saw Kramer with the signal asking if I was okay. I signaled "No!" I knew there was no way a throw rope could ever reach me. My only hope was to get to the right bank which was so far away... I was totally exhausted and gave up swimming. I just tried to shove my jacket down so my mouth would be above water. I would never give up. I realized the river power might drown me regardless of my will. I thought of J. D., my son. Why did I do this? I can't breathe! Was I going to die?

Waves were rapidly sweeping me towards the cliffs on the right. I tried to get out of the main current. No use. I wondered if I would get dashed into the cliffs. Would I have the strength to get into an eddy? I tried feebly for two eddies. No way. I swooshed by the cliffs out into the middle again. I knew my only hope was a kayak rescue. I looked upstream and saw Sam two hundred yards away. I took heart, then felt despair when he was gone. I remember feeling rage, anger, at what I'm not sure. It may have been at myself, possibly the river, probably my absolute helplessness against the incredible power of the river. Because I was in such oxygen debt, I became dizzy. I was afraid of blacking out and drowning.

Sam Moore, in his C-1, did make it to Jon, and pulled him over to Skip's raft, where Jon—ashen, limp, barely conscious—was hoisted over the gunwale, crumpled into the boat, and retched.

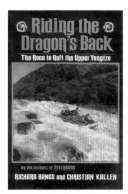

Richard Bangs & Christian Kallen,
Riding the Dragon's Back, *1989*

BIBLIOGRAPHY & RECOMMENDED READING

GENERAL BACKGROUND & HISTORY

Bergere, Marie-Claire, *Sun Yat-sen* (Stanford: Stanford University Press, 1998)

Crow, Carl, *Handbook for China* (Oxford University Press, Hong Kong 1984, facsimile of 4th edition, originally published by Kelly and Walsh Limited, Shanghai, 1933)

Earl, Lawrence, *Yangtse Incident: the Story of HMS Amethyst* (New York: Knopf, 1951)

Eastman, Lloyd E, et al, *The Nationalist Era in China, 1927–1949* (New York: Cambridge University Press, 1991)

Elder, Chris ed, *China's Treaty Ports* (Hong Kong: Oxford University Press, 1999)

Epstein, Israel, *Woman in World History: Soong Ching Ling (Madame Sun Yat-sen)* (Beijing: New World Press, 1995, Second Edition)

Han Zongshan ed, *Landslides and Rockfalls of Yangtze Gorges* (State Commission of Science and Technology, PRC & Ministry of Geology and Mineral Resources, PRC, 1988)

Johnston, Tess & Erh, Deke, *Frenchtown Shanghai: Western Architecture in Shanghai's Old French Concession* (Shanghai: Old China Hand Press, 2000)

Lan Peijin ed, *The Three Gorges of the Yangtze River* (Foreign Languages Press, Beijing, 1997)

Levathes, Louise, *When China Ruled the Seas...1405–1433* (New York: Oxford University Press, 1996)

Lou, Rongmin ed, *The Bund: History and Vicissitudes* (Shanghai: Shanghai Pictorial Publishing House, 1998)

Luo Zhewen & Shen Peng (compilers), *Through the Moon Gate: A Guide to China's Historic Monuments* (Oxford University Press, Hong Kong, 1986)

Murphy, Rhoades, *Treaty Ports and China's Modernization* (Ann Arbor: University of Michigan, 1970)

Perry, Hamilton Darby, *The Panay Incident: Prelude to Pearl Harbor* (New York: Macmillan, 1969)

Phillips, C E Lucas, *Escape of the Amethyst* (New York: Coward-McCann, 1958)

Rowe, William T, *Hankow: Commerce and Society in a Chinese City, 1796–1889* (Stanford: Stanford University Press, 1984)

Salisbury, Harrison E, *The Long March* (New York: Harper & Row, 1985)

Schiffrin, Harold Z, *Sun Yat-sen: Reluctant Revolutionary* (Boston: Little Brown, 1980)

Spence, Jonathan D, *God's Chinese Son* (New York & London: W W Norton & Co, 1996)

Stone, Albert H, & Reed, J Hammond, editors, *Historic Lushan, The Kuling Mountains* (Hankow: Arthington Press/Religious Tract Society, 1921)

Tretiakov, Sergiei M, *Chinese Testament: The Autobiography of Tan Shi-Hua As Told to S Tretiakov* (Westport CT, Hyperion Press, 1976)

Van Slyke, Lyman P, *Yangtse: Nature, History and the River* (Reading, Massachusetts: Addison-Wesley Publishing Company Inc, 1988)

White, Theodore H, & Jacoby, Annalee, *Thunder Out of China* (New York: W Sloane Associates, 1946; reprinted with new introduction by Harrison E Salisbury, Da Capo Press, 1980)

Wills, John E, *Mountain of Fame: Portraits in Chinese History* (Princeton: Princeton University Press, 1994)

Wu, Wo-yao, *Vignettes from the Late Chi'ing: Bizarre Happenings Eyewitnessed Over Two Decades* (Hong Kong: Chinese University of Hong Kong, 1975)

Xu, Silin, *Yue Fei: Glory and Tragedy of China's Greatest War Hero* (Singapore: Asiapac, 1995)

Yang Xin, *The Source of the Yangtze: A Photographic Account of the Landscape, Ecology and Humanity in the Headwaters of the Yangtze River* (Greenriver Book Series, WWF/Friends of the Earth (Hong Kong), 2000)

Zhao Songqiao, *Physical Geography of China* (Science Press, Beijing & John Wiley & Sons, 1986)

Travel and Exploration

Baber, Colborne E, *Travels and Researches in Western China* (London: John Murray, 1882; Taipei: Ch'eng Wen Publishing Co, 1971)

Baker, Barbara ed, *Shanghai: Electric and Lurid City* (Hong Kong: Oxford University Press, 1998, Anthology)

Bangs, Richard & Kallen, Christian, *Riding the Dragon's Back: The Race to Raft the Upper Yangtze* (New York: Atheneum, 1989)

Beaton, Cecil, *China Diary & Album* (London: Batsford, 1945; Hong Kong: Oxford University Press & John Nicholson Ltd, 1991)

Bell, Dick, *To the Source of the Yangtse* (London: Hodder & Stoughton, 1991)

Bird, Isabella, *The Yangtze Valley and Beyond* (London: John Murray, 1899; Virago Press, 1985)

Cooper, Thomas Thornville, *Travels of a Pioneer of Commerce in Pigtail and Petticoats: or, an Overland Journey from China towards India* (London: John Murray, 1871)

Cox E H M, *Plant-hunting in China* (London: William Collins Sons & Co Ltd, 1945; Reprinted with introduction by Oxford University Press, Hong Kong, 1986)

Farndale, Nigel, *Last Action Hero of the British Empire Cdr John Kerans 1915–1985* (Short Books, 2001)

Gill, William, *The River of Golden Sand: The Narrative of a Journey through China and Eastern Tibet to Burmah* (London: John Murray, 1880; Farnborough, UK: Gregg International Publishers Ltd, 1969)

Hayman, Richard Perry, *Three Gorges of the Yangzi: Grand Canyons of China* (Close-up Guides, Odyssey Publications, Hong Kong, 2000)

Hessler, Peter, *River Town: Two Years on the Yangtze* (HarperCollins, 2001)

Hobart, Alice Tisdale, *Within the Walls of Nanking* (New York: MacMillan Co, 1927)

Little, Archibald, *Through the Yangtse Gorges* (London: Sampson, Low, Marston & Co, 1898; Taipei: Ch'eng Wen Publishing Co, 1972)

McKenna, Richard, *The Sand Pebbles* (Annapolis: Naval Institute Press, 2000)

Meister, Cari, *The Yangtze* (Edina: Abdo, 2000)

Palmer, Martin, *Travel Through Sacred China: Guide to the Soul and Spiritual Heritage of China* (Royal House, 1996)

Pan, Lynn, *Old Shanghai, Gangsters in Paradise* (Reprinted by Cultured Lotus, Singapore, 2000)

Payne, Robert, *Chinese Diaries: 1941–1946* (New York, Weybright and Talley, 1970)

Percival, William, *The Land of the Dragon: My Boating and Shooting Excursions to the Gorges of the Upper Yangtse* (Hurst & Blackett Ltd, 1889)

Pollard, Michael, *The Yangtze* (New York: Benchmark, 1998)

Sergeant, Harriet, *Shanghai* (London: John Murray, 1991)

St John, Jeffrey, *Voices from the Yangtze: Recollections of America's Maritime Frontier in China* (Napa: Western Maritime Press, 1993)

Theroux, Paul, *Riding the Iron Rooster: By Train through China* (London: Hamish Hamilton, 1988)

Theroux, Paul, *Sailing Through China* (Boston: Houghton Mifflin Co, 1984)

Thubron, Colin, *Behind the Wall: A Journey through China* (London: Heinemann, 1987)

Till, Barry & Swart, Paula, *In Search of Old Nanking* (Hong Kong: H K S H Joint Publishing Company, 1982)

Wasserstein, Bernard, *Secret War in Shanghai* (London: Profile Books, 1998)

Wilson E H, *A Naturalist in Western China: With Vasculum, Camera and Gun* (London: Methuen & Co, 1913; Cadogan Books, 1986)

Winchester, Simon, *The River at the Centre of the World: A Journey Up the Yangtze and Back in Chinese Time* (London: Viking Press, 1997)

Wong, How Man, *Exploring the Yangtse, China's Longest River* (Hong Kong: Odyssey Productions Ltd, 1989)

Yatsko, **Pamela,** *New Shanghai: The Rocky Rebirth of China's Legendary City* (New York: John Wiley & Sons, 2001)

LITERATURE, AUTOBIOGRAPHY

Espey, **John J,** *Tales Out of School: More Delightful, Humorous Stories of a Boyhood in China* (New York: Knopf, 1947)

Han, **Suyin,** *Destination Chungking* (London: Jonathan Cape, 1942; Panther Books, 1973)

Hersey, **John,** *A Single Pebble* (New York: Alfred A Knopf Inc, 1956; Vintage Books Edition, Random House Inc, 1989)

Li **Po & Tu Fu,** Selected & translated with introduction and notes by Arthur Cooper (Harmondsworth: Penguin Books, 1973)

Luo, **Guangzhong,** *Romance of the Three Kingdoms* (Tokyo: Charles E Tuttle Co Inc, 1973). The classic 14th-century novel about the three Warring States along the Yangzi. *Excerpts from Three Classical Novels* (Panda Books, Beijing 1981) contains an excerpt from the novel entitled, *The Battle of the Red Cliff,* that vividly describes this event at a site just above Wuhan.

Lynn, **Madeleine,** *Yangzi River: The Wildest, Wickedest River on Earth* (Hong Kong: Oxford University Press, 1997). An anthology selection spanning 13 centuries, offers a literary history of China's longest river, including classical poetry and Victorian memoirs.

Waley, **Arthur,** *The Poetry and Career of Li Po* (George Allen & Unwin, 1989)

Wu, **Ching-tzu,** translated by Yang Hsien-yi and Gladys Yang, *The Scholars* (Beijing: Foreign Languages Press, 1973)

Xu, **Xuanzhong,** *100 Tang and Song Ci Poems* (Hong Kong: Commercial Press, 1986)

WEIGHTS AND MEASURES CONVERSIONS

LENGTH	MULTIPLY BY
Inches to centimetres	2.54
Centimetres to inches	0.39
Inches to millimetres	25.40
Millimetres to inches	0.04
Feet to metres	0.31
Metres to feet	3.28
Yards to metres	0.91
Metres to yards	1.09
Miles to kilometres	1.61
Kilometres to miles	0.62

AREA

Square inches to square centimetres	6.45
Square centimetres to square inches	0.15
Square feet to square metres	0.09
Square metres to square feet	10.76
Square yards to square metres	0.84
Square metres to square yards	1.20
Square miles to square kilometres	2.59
Square kilometres to square miles	0.39
Acres to hectares	0.40
Hectares to acres	2.47

VOLUME

Cubic inches to cubic centimetres	16.39
Cubic centimetres to cubic inches	0.06
Cubic feet to cubic metres	0.03
Cubic metres to cubic feet	35.32
Cubic yards to cubic metres	0.76
Cubic metres to cubic yards	1.31
Cubic inches to litres	0.02
Litres to cubic inches	61.03
Gallons to litres	4.55
Litres to gallons	0.22
US gallons to litres	3.79
Litres to US gallons	0.26
Fluid ounces to millilitres	30.77
Millilitres to fluid ounces	0.03

TEMPERATURE

°C	°F
-30	-22
-20	-4
-10	14
0	32
5	41
10	50
15	59
20	68
25	77
30	86
35	95
40	104
45	113
50	122
55	131
60	140
65	149
70	158
75	167
80	176
85	185
90	194
95	203
100	212

WEIGHT

Ounces to grams	28.35
Grams to ounces	0.04
Pounds to kilograms	0.45
Kilograms to pounds	2.21
Long tons to metric tons	1.02
Metric tons to long tons	0.98
Short tons to metric tons	0.91
Metric tons to short tons	1.10

Index

Page number in **bold** indicates photograph

Page number in **bold** indicates photograph

Page number in **bold** indicates photograph

Page number in **bold** indicates photograph

Page number in **bold** indicates photograph

Page number in **bold** indicates photograph

PHOTOGRAPHY CREDITS

Front cover photography: Richard Hayman; back cover: Wong How Man
Photography by How Man Wong, with additional photography/illustrations courtesy of Anthony Anderton 74–5, 88, 183 (both), 240 (all), 260 (top); Magnus Bartlett 1, 78, 95 (top), 100–1, 106–7, 108, 119 (both), 125, 131, 132–3, 144, 146, 151, 161, 162; Kevin Bishop 263, 266, 269, 270 (both), 272 (all), 351, 352 (all), 353 (all), 354 (both), 355, 387, 392, 393, 394 (both), 409, 410, 411 (both), 414, 440, 445, 448, 474–5, 476, 478, 492, 494, 509, 528 (all), 529 (both), 530, 531; Bill Bleisch 14, 173 (both), 174 (both), 176; Anthony Cassidy 464–5, 512 (both), 513 (all), 514, 519, 522; Cecil Beaton Collection, Imperial War Museum 195, 196, 251; Bobby Chan, sketches 289; Elizabeth Childs-Johnson 284; China Yangtze Three Gorges Project Development Corporation 371, 374, 375, 376, 380-1; John Colling 271; Caroline Courtauld 323 (top), 462, 483, 484; GEOPIC™ images © Earth Satellite Corporation 52–3, 60–1; GEOCARTO™ image © 2001 Geocarto/Airphoto International Ltd. 54–5; La Grande Artère de La Chine: Le Yangtseu, Joseph Dautremer 4, 364; HSBC 490-1; Richard Hayman 21, 163 (both), 164, 256, 311, 326 (top), 330, 332, 342, 343, 344, 345, 366, 394 (top); Hong Kong China Tourism Photo Library 338, 356; Hubei Provincial Museum, Wuhan 418–9, 420–1; Bill Hurst 225; Illustrated London News 507 (top); William Lindesay 308 (bottom); Ingrid Morejohn 208, 214, 228, 234, 249, 277 (both), 278 (all); Pat Morrow 16, 252; Tom Nebbia 111, 314, 358–9, 422, 427, 452–3, 486, 543; Joseph F Rock, © National Geographic Society 186; Kim Roseberry 124, 127, 137, 138 (all), 170 (both), 206–7; Malcolm Rosholt 87; Shanghai Fine Arts Publishing Company, Chen Zongliang 510 (top), 510 (bottom), Pu Xingxing 511; Raynor Shaw 116, 159, 178; Teresa Coleman Fine Arts Ltd 407 (both); Audrey Topping 290–1, 303 (top); R Wada 313; John Warner 417 (bottom), 506, 507 (bottom); Wattis Fine Art 77, 316-7; Sydney Wong 280.

CSGB/16/08

Make the most of your journey with ODYSSEY books, guides and maps

"...The Odyssey guide is a good read, full of historical background; the one to read before you go..."
—*The Times*

"...for coverage of Chongqing and the Gorges, and of the more placid and historically notable sites below Yichang and downriver to Shanghai, it is unrivalled..."
—*Simon Winchester*

"It is one of those rare travel guides that is a joy to read whether or not you are planning a trip..."
—*New York Times*

"...His panoramic shots of mountain valleys are dizzying and lovely; so too are his photographs of religious ceremonies, with the villagers dressed in their finery..."
—*New York Times*

"...Essential traveling equipment for anyone planning a journey of this kind..."
—*Asian Wall Street Journal*

"...It's a superb book, superbly produced, that makes me long to go back to China..."
—*John Julius Norwich*